READING THE SHAPE OF THE WORLD

POLITICS & CULTURE

Avery Gordon and Michael Ryan, *editors*

Politics and Culture is a serial publication that publishes material from a diverse number of disciplinary perspectives, from literature to law, from anthropology to political science, from cultural studies to sociology. The serial is concerned with the political significance of cultural forms and practices as well as with the cultural character of social institutions and political formations.

Reading the Shape of the World: Toward an International Cultural Studies,
edited by Henry Schwarz and Richard Dienst

Prosthetic Territories: Politics and Hypertechnologies,
edited by Gabriel Brahm Jr. and Mark Driscoll

After Political Correctness: The Humanities and Society in the 1990s,
edited by Christopher Newfield and Ronald Strickland

Body Politics: Disease, Desire, and the Family,
edited by Michael Ryan and Avery Gordon

4

POLITICS AND CULTURE

READING THE SHAPE OF THE WORLD

Toward an International Cultural Studies

edited by

HENRY SCHWARZ &
RICHARD DIENST

WestviewPress
A Division of HarperCollins*Publishers*

Politics and Culture 4

Published in 1996 in the United States of America by Westview Press, Inc., 5500 Central Avenue, Boulder, Colorado 80301-2877, and in the United Kingdom by Westview Press, 12 Hid's Copse Road, Cumnor Hill, Oxford OX2 9JJ

Reading the shape of the world : toward an international cultural
studies / [edited by] Henry Schwarz and Richard Dienst.
p. cm. — (Politics and culture ; 4)
Includes index.
ISBN 0-8133-2876-4. — ISBN 0-8133-2877-2 (pbk.)
1. Civilization, Modern—1950– 2. Criticism. 3. Politics and literature. 4. Literature, Modern—20th century—History and criticism. 5. Culture. I. Schwarz, Henry. II. Dienst, Richard, 1962– . III. Series.
CB430.R36 1996
909.82'5—dc20 96-10242
CIP

The paper used in this publication meets the requirements of the American National Standard for Permanence of Paper for Printed Library Materials Z39.48-1984.

10 9 8 7 6 5 4 3 2 1

Contents

PART THREE
NARRATION AND THE SENSE OF PLACE

PART FOUR
THE DYNAMICS OF RECOGNITION

Credits

Samir Amin, "Culture and Ideology in the Contemporary Arab World" was previously published as "Cultural Nationalism in the Arab World," *Rethinking Marxism* 6, 3 (1993):9–27. Reprinted by permission of The Guilford Press.

Svetlana Boym, "The Archaeology of Banality: The Soviet Home," *Public Culture* 6, 2 (1994):263–293. Reprinted by permission of The University of Chicago Press.

Neil Larsen, "Brazilian Critical Theory and the Question of 'Cultural Studies,'" was previously published as "La teoría crítica basileña y la cuestión de los 'cultural studies,'" *Revísta de Crítica Literaria Latinoamericana* 19, 39 (1994). A translated version appeared in Neil Larsen, *Reading North by South: On Latin American Literature, Culture, and Politics* (Minneapolis: University of Minnesota Press, 1995). Reprinted by permission of *Revísta de Crítica Literaria Latinoamericana* and the University of Minnesota Press, respectively.

Supriya Nair, "'Invented' Histories: Cultural Production in George Lamming's *Season of Adventure*" will appear in Supriya Nair's forthcoming volume *Caliban's Curse: George Lamming's Revisioning of History* (Ann Arbor: University of Michigan Press, 1996). Reprinted by permission.

Doris Sommer, "About Face: The Talker Turns," *boundary 2*, 23, 1 (Spring 1996):91–133. Copyright © Duke University Press. Reprinted by permission.

1

Introduction: Warning! Cautious Readers!

HENRY SCHWARZ AND RICHARD DIENST

ABOUT A DOZEN YEARS AGO, Wlad Godzich introduced a collection of Paul de Man's essays with the provocative title, "Caution! Reader at Work!" Godzich's cautionary gesture was in part directed toward those readers of de Man's criticism who felt overwhelmed by the sheer virtuosity of the master's performances, an intimidation amply registered in the many critiques of his authoritative style. Cautioned, but with an entirely different sense of the dangers involved, the reader is invited into this collection of contemporary cultural criticism. He or she will no doubt find an impressive dexterity here, too. But now the critics themselves have become more cautious, and older performances of critical mastery have given way to careful explorations of cultural mystery. The intimidating gesture is no longer the critic's to perform; and indeed in several of these chapters we find critics brave enough to admit that meaning slips their grasp. This admission of strict interpretive limits, however, is by no means complacent and in no way lets the reader off the hook. If anything, this new tentativeness in the field of critique imposes demands on the reader as high as any exacted by reading de Man. As a changing world has compelled literary critics to engage with the multiple forces that shape their own positions, the stakes of criticism remain as high as ever. But its objects have become much more complex as readers have learned to engage worldly problems with an interpretive caution equal to their prudence before texts. These projects of criticism today rest on a single basic claim: The practice of reading remains our best model for engaging with, and accepting responsibility toward, the shape of the world.

The hardest lessons left over from two decades of the "theory wars" still stand: We have to become more attentive to the dangers and difficulties of language and to the pitfalls of mastery before meaning. But this new modesty toward the critical enterprise has not brought about a return to simple formulations or a consensus around basic verities. Critical work has become more difficult as practitioners have come to understand what de Man phrased our "constitutive blindness" toward the critical act itself, the struggle for insight that is always crucially dependent on the blindness it cannot hope to dispel. This difficulty is magnified as U.S. academic cultural criticism looks elsewhere for its understanding, away from the terrors of the word toward its various constituencies, its potential audiences, and its many entanglements in the current structures of power. It is not enough merely to "read" the world like a text; the comfort of that metaphor would be denied by the readers gathered here, each of whom confronts issues of power and position, mastery, and interpretability that are dizzyingly unstable. It is essential when reading the world to realize that one is always already misreading and to comprehend the dead end of "getting it right." But in doing so, these readers make a strategic gambit: to read the shape of the world as if the world can be shaped by reading, as if the world can be put in better shape when people become attentive to, cautious about, and answerable for the shaping force of words and images. We use "reading" here as shorthand for a complicated set of political and ethical commitments reaching far beyond institutional requirements or individual skills. The chapters continue to refine this account of reading in ways we consider urgent in the present situation. We must relearn circumspection, they seem to say, when all around us the fascination with "otherness" blooms; the collection as a whole seems as skeptical of the institutionalization of other cultures as it does of its own hermeneutical mastery. Yet it is skeptical, if it can be put this way, in the most positive sense, for each chapter resolutely addresses the risks and responsibilities of opening academic criticism to the immense heterogeneity of the world. At this time, without such a strategic risk, reading would become unimportant. We have tried here to put reading to work wherever we can and thereby to demonstrate the ways in which criticism can evade the threats of next-big-thing marketing and boxed-in professionalization. With these provisos, then, we welcome you. Let the reader beware: Cautious critics are at work!

Our survey of resistant and emergent images of the world is marked by the texture and contours of cultural study in the Euro-American academy (with some significant exceptions, of which more further on) and is drawn particularly from that effort by which the academy has attempted to represent its "outside"—the increasing tendency to describe and analyze cultural production from places previously ignored (or worse, worked over)—by the fixed canons of Western academic research. In this institutional moment, all the writers see danger and promise. Although the dangers are manifest to anyone who cares to look, the promises advanced here are equally guarded and suspicious. We would argue that that is exactly as it should be: Reading the world is risky business. At worst, an act of reading can destroy a part of the future by slashing and burning its way to textual dominion. At best, however, the practice of reading can, through continual interruption and reassemblage, participate in the remaking of priorities and practices. In offering this set of readings, we have, of course, tried neither to represent the progressive academy as a whole nor to summarize the potential for committed intellectual work in this emerging field. In imperfectly attempting to capture (or imagine) the new shapes of an emerging world through the unpredictable processes of solicitation and editing, this collection suggests some directions, however fragmentary or not yet fully articulated, for future research and action.

What is the role of academic cultural study in the contemporary global situation? The need to criticize grandiose New World Orderly pronouncements is registered as an urgent project by all, and none of these chapters have shied away from countering such bold images in projecting their own discrete interpretations of worldly knowledge. If any agreement is reached in these pages, it is that History has not reached its end, the neoliberal market system is not the last word in social organization, and corporate conglomerates are not the best custodians of creative expression. At the same time, the contributors recognize that Fukuyama's prophecy is seeming truer every day in places we would never have expected, and an image of the world as stably UN-ified is taking hold in locations that have diligently resisted it. In attempting to introduce and analyze these contemporary problems, we have brought forward various maps and methodologies, all of which have produced usable representations of worldly knowledge in the past. One thing the present collection makes clear, however, is the very nonsystematicity of current academic forays into mapping the world today. Far from pointing us toward the Next Big Paradigm, this volume brings together multiple and unsteady states of theory and practice that run the gamut from what some might regard as high totalization (as with the persistence of grand historical categories in Samir Amin and Michael Sprinker) to the dramatic refusal of closure enacted in the scrupulous silences of Azade Seyhan and Doris Sommer. Although in their subject matter all of the contributions make similar imaginary migrations—across nations, cultures, languages, and disciplines, producing, in the process, a very complicated image of the world indeed—they do so in a wide variety of ideological and methodological styles, including but not limited to such familiar axes as Marxism, feminism, deconstruction, and semiotics, as well as some less-comfortable protocols of reading: schizo-analysis, strategic essentialisms, the poetics of unintelligibility. That challenging multiplicity itself is reason enough to proceed carefully.

In reading the shape of the world, we all participate in confirming or contesting dominant images, whether in words or pictures, concepts or sound bites. One thing seems certain today when we ask what "shape" the world is in: The repertoire of images offered by dominant discourse offers only a few rudimentary possibilities, in which the map always precedes the territory. Every day on television, it is possible to watch an ideological match game played with childlike simplicity as each event is shaped to slot into one of the acceptable holes until the world is once again sewn up as a patchwork of the expected images. Previous ideological topographies of the world registered a yawning gap (or, depending on one's perspective, a towering mountain range, an iron curtain—or for some, perhaps, a Christo wrapping job) between socialist East and capitalist West—the division of global political economy known as bipolarism. But the image of that divide has softened significantly since 1989, its high peaks eroding, its valleys silting up with the effluvia of wrecked political structures. Similarly, the world could once have been imagined as a three-way duel between the underdeveloped southern tier, or third world, and both of the feuding industrialized blocs of the North. Apparently the collapse of the former USSR and the international outbreak of neoliberalism (with its Pacific Rim heartland) have also rendered that tripolar image obsolete. As walls come crashing down everywhere and capitalist democracy breaks out like fever (so the image goes), a new world image has announced itself. It is no less ideological, subjective, biased, or incomplete than any other imaginary description. Yet this image, for the first time in history, belongs to an economic system deploying extensive media and military apparatuses, so this particular picture is practically guaranteed to gain vast currency. It is a promise from nowhere, and it comes free with every transaction. According to the rules of total market warfare, everybody must be mobilized, everything can seek its fullest value elsewhere, and every message (whether good or bad) bears proof that there is no turning back. And so the word gets around: among the black-market vendors in Moscow, in the industrial boomtowns of southern China, in the crackdown South American regimes implementing IMF discipline, throughout the splintering kleptocracies and abandoned client states of sub-Saharan Africa. And so on.

When we daily confront the scattered traces of this vaunted "world" in our universities and newspapers, at bus stops, and of course on TV, it becomes especially crucial to respond to it in the sphere of public culture. For we all know that the happy faces on TV munching their way toward the McDonaldization of the globe really represent an image of exclusion. It is necessary to offer a profusion of other images in return without feeding into the same televisual collage. Yet it is difficult to project counterworlds that will accommodate and enable an effective intellectual practice. We feel that such an effort must be part of any criticism that refuses to justify itself in terms of institutional expertise or scholasticism. In an atmosphere of authoritative certainty, criticism waits too long on the vine, wilting under the inexhaustible self-absorption of those who claim to seek only the truth. But spontaneity has its own weaknesses. If, on one hand, one jumps too quickly toward a counterimage where antagonistic positions can be charted and strategies mapped out for action, criticism may be doomed to follow the empiricist script of the opponent. If, on the other hand, the need to resist this premature totalization is then countered by a desire to explode all systematicity, criticism limits itself to ironizing attacks on the organic metaphors and rhetorical symbols of such totalizing narratives. It offers epistemological hygiene but no real plan for change. Coyness and cleverness, like absolute truth-claims, have to be unstitched along their hidden seams through a productive reading that can cut and paste. Where a third option might lead us in imagining what's to come is not at all certain; in fact, many of the chapters opt for a synthesis that is preeminently unsure, caught somewhere within the tension between imagination and reason, between the scrutiny of understanding and the serendipity of new invention. It is not entirely inappropriate to describe this move as an aesthetic one so long as we realize that no art can be innocent any longer. The long-separated faculties, if not healed per se, have been reassembled and rearticulated so that all forms of reason and ethics bleed into the aesthetic dimension, and art reemerges as a guiding concept for the work of cobbling together the discourses that hold our world in view.

To hazard yet again a periodizing move: If 1980s deconstruction reevaluated aesthetics in a way that forcefully denied the autonomy or disinterestedness of that category, among the projects of the late 1990s will be to reclaim that reevaluation and even more firmly align the discourses of art and culture with those of social power and position. All around us, social struggle is being turned into cynical forms of "art" that are seemingly freed from the conditions of production. But once the aesthetic has been dislodged from the ontologies of the subjects and groups that produce it, it becomes a realm of "hauntology" (as Derrida has recently put it), peopled with spectral identifications and forceful abstractions masquerading as inevitable laws. Thus the most basic institutions of public knowedge are being "haunted" in this way, recast in terms formerly reserved for disinterested contemplation: Wars are spectator events, social welfare is reduced to black and white, and education becomes a process of attraction and repulsion. In response, recent cultural criticism has come a long way in surpassing the slogans of textuality to reconsider the supremacy of reading. Our readings of texts are now more securely lodged in the modalities of the senses, not in order to reconstruct the individual subject but rather to reconnect cultural production more directly and vibrantly to the social bodies that always need and use it. All these connections and bodies can be called images—no matter what form they take, how long they last, or how they are transmitted—and such images certainly generate and punctuate whatever passes for knowledge. The insistent questions in contemporary criticism about voices, tonalities, and visibilities are not, as they used to say, mere metaphors; this is the terrain where the varied operations of social power can be recognized and grasped. In some ways, then, are the debates of the 1990s driven to revisit earlier debates on culture and politics from the 1930s (not to mention the 1840s and the 1790s)? Is it time for the realization of Walter Benjamin's prophetic theories about politicizing art? If so, is that because we have only now begun to attain the conditions, long-dreamt-of but-never-like-this, for reclaiming the unplotted dynamism of History in the present tense? Perhaps the term "culture" in the 1990s will cease reminding us of our debts to tradition and instead show us how historical processes still provide us the means for our own revolutions. But how will we recognize that chance when it appears? What if it shows up *all the time?*

That is why questions of criticism still revolve around the place of imagination, especially the place of images in a world where the connective and collective capacities of visual knowledge are squandered constantly. Blissfully unknowing, television makes plain what Spinoza demonstrated long ago: There can be as many worlds as there are modes of constructing and constellating images. But the buzzing of knowledge, no matter how well organized and nailed down to "facts," does not add up to a finished perspective. For the world is always just an image or two away—and it never gets any closer. Every attempt to grasp a global situation must stake its claims of truthfulness on some well-chosen set of images, metaphors, and framings. (Derrida has been elaborating this lesson for years.) The dislocating process of visuality operates as much in the official discourses of history and economics as it does in the thriving literature of experience and hope. In every text images hold the place of the world, marking in the moment of seeing—which is also a kind of reading—the effort with which we attempt to compose ourselves within the horizon of our actions and to join that horizon with those of others. If "reading" remains the best practical model of worldly knowledge, visuality remains the grounding and binding metaphor for its practice. Years after the most thoroughgoing critiques of representation (which the name of Paul de Man has already signaled), after the lengthy inventories of the crafty frames of mimesis, beyond diagrams of the cunning mastery of the gaze, and in spite of the melancholy diagnoses of the blindness of Reason, critics still face the task of reading beyond the agency of the letter and seeing beyond the channels of objective knowledge. These chapters provide ways of reading that can describe the intransigence of the world beyond our analytic powers to break it down.

Such motifs are now being developed by various strands of leftist cultural criticism as it moves past the Marx-Freud axis toward what we might call, paradoxically, an imaginary materialism. But how does this multivalent tendency, which is so attentive to phantasmatic slippages and discursive solidities, approach the most phantasmic and most solid object of all, the world? Is this a thing that must be left to the experts, those whose images of it have hardened into data banks, policy procedures, and development plans? Or is it possible for us to pursue a pedagogy of images that encourages recombinations, superimpositions, cuttings and switchings—thus creating other kinds of knowledge? Cultural critics, who know how to do things with images, ought to be the first ones to claim such resources to outflank the epistemologically secure and politically deadening accounts of the world put forth by the mass media and the established disciplinary formations. It is precisely here, in the various mobilizations of a global imaginary, that academic intellectuals can recognize that they are cultural workers who now have as much to learn (methodologically as well as politically) from filmmakers, artists, playwrights, and novelists as they do from economists, political scientists, and sociologists. (Scientists of all stripes are beginning to make this move already, and this is surely one of the most promising signs of a new intellectual politics.) To pursue our program, it will be necessary to recast "theory" as the construction of images, both abstract and concrete, that are capable of making connections, multiplying "identifications," and registering distinctions. Whatever we call it—and "theory" will still serve as long as it is heard as an indefinite plural—this work can and will become the art of drawing prospects out of problems, of finding threads of community in the midst of discontinuities, and of making risky disturbances in the settled order of the present.

The speculative project of eighties "theory" has enabled, as its academic and pedagogical counterpart, a practice of reading capable of locating the markers of historicity and worldliness built into every text, especially that one we still call "lived experience." Epochal frames (befores and afters, not yets and henceforths) and worldly landmarks (heres and theres, everywheres and elsewheres) inhabit every kind of discourse, even the most forbiddingly abstract or the most playfully abstruse. These frames and markers can be distinguished from the specific stories and maps they make possible, so that one can analyze how each textual structure inevitably opens onto other streams of images otherwise invisible up to that point. That dynamic, and its relationship to the so-called real world (or, if you like, the Real) would be another topic for another time. Here we want to reiterate that practices of reading become creative only when a diffraction of perspective takes place, allowing other histories and worlds to materialize in the midst of the old ones: In seeing anew, we must make new images. That lesson sounds familiar in the context of literary and cultural interpretation, but it becomes a daunting task when carried out against the official discourses that claim to monitor and control reality itself.

Even among those in the field of cultural studies, there is no generally accepted imaginary atlas, no landmarks visible from everywhere. (Perhaps this "weak" epistemology is constitutive of the field and is somehow the inverse of the strong axiological force that holds other disciplinary groups together.) Gone is the centrality of any one magisterial figure on the current map of theory; gone too are the heavy methodological armaments, the theory-weapons that enabled legendary readings as powerful as pitched assaults on the ramparts of the logocentric tradition. This kind of theoretical authority has been replaced not so much by imprecision or cloudiness as by a new vocabulary of tentativeness and experimentation, even an innovative trepidation, as by a literary and cultural criticism that has increasingly demanded a density of worldly knowledge with all the risks that entails. Whereas it seems fair to say that most of the chapters assembled here begin from the standpoint of literary and cultural theory and that many select their exorbitant subjects as illustrations of conceptual ensembles familiar from one or another of the great critical movements of the recent past (structuralism, semiotics, deconstruction, hermeneutics, feminism, ideology critique), all are complicated by the irreducible differences of specific cultures and the necessity of grappling with the imaginary dimension of localized "common sense."

This is not to say that our contributors have rejected outright the possibilities for a "science" of criticism but rather that they hold that nominalized category in deepest suspicion. Science in its Western, Enlightenment form seems to presuppose some kind of objectivity or neutrality, a universalist key by which the secrets of locality can be definitively unlocked and demystified in the name of some overarching and worldly Reason. In its historical course, however, the guiding genius of Reason has proved to be irreducibly partial, its projects and agendas inextricably tied up with the Western mission of global domination: "Science" in the non-Western world presents itself not so much as a universalizing and panhumanist pact but as a proud conspiracy of the only true humans, the Europeans, to impose their local order over every far-flung region of the globe. By contrast, another type of objectivity is tenuously advanced in these pages, one that disavows the pretended neutrality of Western science and yet clings to some kind of common ground. It is an objectivity defined by a refusal to give up the immense terrain claimed by the march of Western Thought and by a commitment to make knowledge a struggle that can be fought over every last letter. To attempt finally to name this project is perhaps premature; it could be an "image" not yet legible on our current maps of the world. Just as the discourse of New Worldism attempts to articulate, for oppressive ends, a structure that has not yet attained fully functional existence, this new commonality would define itself by means of shared symptoms rather than some ultimate cause. Preemptive decisions about the shape of the world today often mistake the complexity and flux of our present condition for a repetition of some prior malady that can be cured by the application of tested medicines. "This time we'll get it right" is the slogan of parties in every corner of the arena, yet in the current conjuncture all those remedies can grow tired and lose their potency overnight.

Against this mood of weariness we would like to suggest that the tools for explaining the contemporary crisis are already before us, written in the actions of those who step forward to block catastrophe wherever it threatens. The shape of the world becomes legible when domination meets resistance. To decide that the world order still under construction has put itself beyond knowability would be both politically disastrous and theoretically debilitating. This order is imposed by a mass of transmissions—financial, military, institutional—in which the imaginary forces of national and transnational interest become absolutely material. In response people send back a different kind of message, drawn from diverse imaginary resources and engaged with another kind of materiality, in order to interrupt the circuits of control. These countertransmissions deserve to be called "culture" in the emergent sense of that word: "culture" as inevitably cross-cultural, crisscrossing borders and traditions in an effort to gather strength for its tasks ahead. By mobilizing a sense of cultural imagination, critics can use their specific knowledges and positions to pass along new images of the world.

The pieces gathered here are, of course, broadcasts of necessarily mixed signals. The difficult approach to the global is matched by an equally problematic engagement with the local. Wide-ranging cultural concerns are generally brought into focus by an acute sense of literary practices and possibilities. We have arranged the chapters in four sections, divided according to the centers of gravity pulling on the fields in which these works participate. Yet all our boundaries necessarily overlap, methods are mingled, and the sense of scale is constantly shifting.

The opening set of chapters addresses the possibilities of "reordering the world" through new theoretical paradigms. Azade Seyhan takes up the concepts of "minor literature" and "border culture" that have grown out of literary studies since the early 1970s or so. As she shows, these notions not only disturb the stability of canons and upset historical periodizations but also insist upon the necessity of dialogue in the sharing and reworking of cultural identities. Yet it is striking that these issues are here drawn against the inheritances of Enlightenment and modernist thinking; put in this trajectory, the current debates appear to be both resurrections of old projects and fitful attempts to escape old dead ends.

Far from evading the narrative obligations of historical thinking, postmodern and postcolonial theorists have had to propose alternate periodizing schemes. As Richard Dienst argues, there remains a historical layer generally ignored in the culture wars: the elusive but decisive movements of the global economy. In surveying recent accounts of global economics, he suggests ways this other Other of the contemporary world might be understood in the categories of cultural analysis.

In a complementary vein, Joel Reed situates current theories of nationalism in the geopolitical and geoeconomic spheres. Moving between the frameworks of world-systems history and deconstructive reading, Reed shows how the recent work of Wallerstein, Balibar, Derrida, and Jameson together proposes new coordinates in which to recognize the variants of nationalist ideology. If it is no longer possible to presuppose a transparently global frame in which nationalisms can be read as either autochthonous or strictly interdependent, it might nevertheless be possible to recognize various "nonsynchronous" global referents built into each nationalist formation, serving as an allegorical anchor and a deconstructive hook at the same time. Reed provides a model for detecting such referents, thereby enlisting Derrida and Jameson in the same theoretical task.

Written as both a report on and a response to a collective work in progress, George Yúdice's chapter brings forth a series of important questions about the relationship of cultural analysis to the reconception of an effective public sphere. Through an interrogation of the concept of "civil society," Yúdice discusses a number of options (some widely acknowledged, others not) facing intellectuals and cultural workers throughout the Americas. What comes across most strongly, he suggests, is the need for "transnational public spheres"—a need brought into view by cultural studies even if the larger political promise of the idea has remained unfulfilled.

The second section, "Old Empires and Contested Zones," contains reflections on a series of key sites in the current realignment of global power. Each of the four areas treated here might belong to the contemporary "periphery," if that term can still be used to designate such different situations. Samir Amin's sweeping account of the route of capitalist modernization in the Arab world not only investigates the pattern of traditionalist revival in the current conjuncture; he restates principles of a Marxist theory of global systems, and he draws comparisons between the Middle East and other zones in the world economy to remark upon striking consistencies in the patterns of response to European hegemony. Amin does not attempt to locate the alternatives to the new world system in one particular country or in some new theoretical configuration. In calling for an extension of Marxism to the problems of local cultures and ideologies, he upholds his long commitment to internationalist perspectives.

Like Amin, Neil Larsen emphasizes the decisive importance of worldwide imperialism in the cultural formation of these contradictory zones. Here, in an argument that moves between the inherited European forms of cultural studies and recent currents in Brazilian critical theory, he insists that the transnational operations of class remain unacknowledged in much criticism even though such an analysis would bring forth not only better political analysis but a clearer sense of the politics of theory itself.

Svetlana Boym's tour of Soviet and post-Soviet domestic space shows how the mundane details of everyday life speak of historic struggles over the definition of private and public culture. The richness of her account serves to underscore the importance of a kind of close reading: The objects of ordinary life can be revealed as highly charged compromises over needs, desires, and unformulated demands. In this particular contested zone (the new households as much as the territory of the former Soviet Union itself) there seem to be no decisive political victories or finalized cultural hierarchies, only traces of practices that remain ideological and aesthetic responses to a situation that eludes comprehensive understanding.

Such a perspective insists that the operations of nationalism, like imperialism, can always be read in the images of daily life, in the most familiar settings and on the surfaces of the body. Grant Farred's chapter works this kind of analysis in another scene, following the vicissitudes of South African black nationalism through its prominent cultural practices. Farred explores the tremendous organizing and articulating power of each new image even while assessing the limits of the black nationalist agenda in the new South Africa. Yet in a dialectic spirit shared by others in this book, Farred suggests that cultural activism strikes its limits because it is engaged in an unavoidable struggle with circumstances: Reading the contours of a dead end is the precondition to the next attempt to move onward.

"Narration and the Sense of Place" groups together four chapters that rethink some fundamental cultural texts from the perspectives of nation, gender, empire, and diaspora. Sangeeta Ray investigates the contradictory discourses of national belonging in two very different novels of the South Asia diaspora. Critically applying Homi Bhabha's theories on hybridity to both, Ray argues that the celebration of the migrant and the uneasy but liberatory habitation of interstitial spaces "erases the other side of migrant experience that is conformist, regular, unexceptional, and ordinary." In this critique she restores some sense of the "enduring legacy of a linear logic that imbues most narrative acts" and engages with the densities of specific cultures that can variably determine the experience of migrancy.

Supriya Nair turns to the invention of a usable past in the production of "national" histories of the African diaspora. George Lamming's novel reveals Vodoun to be an enactment of the fragmentation and elusiveness of a submerged diasporic history. The emphasis on imagination in Caribbean discourses of the nation "explodes the totalizing boundaries of the existing nation, allowing it to travel across the rigidities of geopolitical mappings." In an important rereading of Fanon, Nair explains how magic and superstition illustrate the crucial role of the fetish in the creation of national identifications, which must always proceed through the imaginary rather than essentialized "natural" affiliations.

Michael Sprinker rereads the solutions devised by Rabindranath Tagore to the conundrum of nationalism in colonial South Asia, framing them within an explanation of the expansionist tendencies of global capitalism. In a richly historical account detailing the clashing ideologies of nation in the 1910s, Sprinker's Tagore offers continuing relevance for the politics and ideology of contemporary India and more generally for the postcolonial nationalisms around the world.

Henry Schwarz reexamines a long stretch of Indian colonial history in order to trace the persistence of English cultural codes in the vernacular literature of Bengal. Combining generic analysis with social history, Schwarz applies an interdisciplinary methodology to the reading of canonical texts of the Bengal Renaissance. Formal markers in these texts indicate the tenacity of English cultural standards despite their overt attempts to break free of them; marks of gender emerge as possible sites where subversions of colonial logic are enacted.

Part 4, "The Dynamics of Recognition," includes three sensitive probes into the possibilities of cross-cultural knowledge in the contemporary world. Ipshita Chanda confronts the theoretical extention of Western feminism to foreign locations, proposing that in this migration post-Enlightenment European theory often remains rooted in the epistemological grounds it seeks to refute. Uncritical claims for internationalism can imply a dangerous "lack in us identified by the other which must be filled by the domestication of our oppositional impulses." She critically examines the "willing mental diaspora" of postcolonial peoples all too eager to sign on to cosmopolitan programs, tracing these themes through the "similarities within difference" that characterize the ideologies of gender manufactured in two radically dissimilar sites of British colonial activity.

Alicia Borinsky's humorous account of the "domain of misencounters, capricious pronouncements, and false attributions" that make any sense of self possible offers a rejoinder to the more anguished descriptions of dislocation and hybridity encountered today. Borinsky offers a refreshing and humane treatment of the indeterminacy of essentialized identities such as gender and place, interweaving these determinations into a floating poetics of translation. "A humble but decisive form of knowledge about humanity emerges from the arbitrariness with which individuals are tossed in different directions by history." As in her novels and poetry, Borinsky relentlessly celebrates new meanings.

Doris Sommer's chapter closes the volume by virtue of its very openness. We felt it provided a strikingly clear sense of one way to move in a world that seems overwhelmingly large yet too small for certain cultures to coexist. Her answer, produced through the very act of reading, cannot be summarized, only performed. It is a crucial intervention into the politics of cultural cooperation in Latin America, which by way of Emmanuel Levinas's ethics, Enrique Dussel's philosophy, and Mario Vargas Llosa's novel *The Storyteller,* takes its reader to the central question of worldly understanding: What do we do with each other?

How can we ever answer that question? We look, we relate, we read, we think, and we hope to act accordingly.

Caveat lector!

ACKNOWLEDGMENTS

We would like to thank Eric Hayot for his editorial assistance at the earliest stage of this project, Melanie Stafford of Westview Press for her assistance in the final stages, and Michael Ryan for making everything alright.

PART ONE

REORDERING THE WORLD

2

From Minor Literature, Across Border Culture, to Hyphenated Criticisms

AZADE SEYHAN

IN THEIR WIDELY quoted book *Kafka: Toward a Minor Literature*, Gilles Deleuze and Félix Guattari have charted the conceptual domain of what they call minor literature. The term denotes the use of a "major," or high-status, language by a community whose members are outsiders in the realm of this language. In the voices of outsiders, minorities, or marginal collectivities, the major language is accented by an alienation process whereby the certainties of its enunciations are questioned, lost, or subverted from within. The authors apply this concept of minor literature to Franz Kafka's work, which can be construed as a regulative metaphor for linguistic and cultural estrangement of a Czech-speaking Jewish writer in Prague writing in German. In other words, Kafka's work constitutes a textual island colonized by German where German rules as a stranger estranged from itself. The minor literature in practice is delimited, assumes a considerable critical distance from the major language, and challenges the inviolability of the latter's identity. Deleuze and Guattari maintain that the concept of minor literature, as they define it, leads to an understanding of the conditions and limits of our own intellectual heritage and its relation to other cultural traditions:

> We might as well say that minor no longer designates specific literatures but the revolutionary conditions for every literature within the heart of what is called great (or established) literature. . . . There has been much discussion of the questions "What is a marginal literature?" and "What is a popular literature, a proletarian literature?" The criteria are obviously difficult to establish if one doesn't start with a more objective concept—that of minor literature. Only the possibility of setting up a minor

> practice of major language from within allows one to define popular literature, marginal literature, and so on.[1]

In proposing the model of minor literature as a blueprint for reading a wide range of noncanonical literary works, Deleuze and Guattari have provided readers eager to foray into fields of unfamiliar literatures with a conceptually flexible framework. Indeed, the defining categories of minor literature are often cited in studies of so-called minority or ethnic literatures produced in such major languages as English, French, and German. Deleuze and Guattari present a persuasive case for the wide-ranging use of their model:

> How many people today live in a language that is not their own? Or no longer, or not yet, even know their own and know poorly the major language that they are forced to serve? This is the problem of immigrants, and especially of their children, the problem of minorities, the problem of a minor literature, but also a problem for all of us: how to tear a minor literature away from its own language, allowing it to challenge the language and making it follow a sober revolutionary path? How to become a nomad and an immigrant and a gypsy in one's own language? Kafka answers: steal the baby from its crib, walk the tightrope.[2]

What Deleuze and Guattari sketch in their model of minor literature is a politically informed critical program whereby otherness or marginalization can be experienced in and through a self-reflexive use of one's own language. However, the liberal structures of the model can be conveniently imposed on token samples of minority literatures by traditional scholars who, in an attempt to "update" their methods, often obfuscate the heterogeneity of these literatures. Although I find the concept of minor literature, as a whole, a critically productive field of investigation, I would like to point to the theoretical and practical constraints on its applicability and investigate the possibilities of its transportation across newer critical borders and its transformation into a more differentiated mode of cultural inquiry. Our studies of others should be read and understood in both their diachronic and synchronic contexts, that is, in their historical and conceptual transfigurations and not merely in terms of singular models or additions to reading lists of a few titles such as Maxine Hong Kingston's *The Woman Warrior* or Chinua Achebe's *Things Fall Apart.* As it is, we are exposed to a very small volume of the world's cultural production, and sanitizing what we have garnered in isolated chambers of conceptual models negates the possibility of a genuine multicultural sensibility. How can we move from the concept of minor literature to something like hyphenated criticisms that are characterized by sites of transition and transformation at the shifting borders of history, politics, and cultures? It would be useful at this point to summarize the three markers of minor literature in order to examine and expand their conceptual potential in a self-reflexive praxis of cultural studies.

What are the defining markers of minor literature? Deleuze and Guattari offer a triadic schema that charts the path of minor literature from deterritorialization to political engagement and collective articulation. The concept of a deterritorialized major language as a vehicle of self-expression for a community coincides with the use of German by the Jews of pre–World War I Prague. They no longer have access to their "primitive Czech territoriality"[3] and, therefore, appropriate a major language—German—that, though cut off from its original territory, serves them in the capacity of a "'paper language,'"[4] just as the English of the Indian subcontinent is the language of formal education, of national newspapers and trade and scholarly publications, and of bureaucracy. This first feature of minor literature is certainly characteristic of modern postcolonial literatures written almost exclusively in English and French in India, Pakistan, the Philippines, and the former British and French colonies in Africa, and it is also relevant, for example, to literature written in Russian by Uzbek, Kirghiz, Azeri, or Armenian writers. However, it cannot be applied across the board to minority or ethnic literatures. Obviously, deterritorialization does not characterize the status of English, French, and German works written by a multiplicity of immigrant groups living in the United States, England, Canada, and Australia; by Arabs and Africans in France; and by Turks, Greeks, Arabs, Italians, or Portuguese in Germany. They do not use a deterritorialized major-status language but one that still occupies its natural territory and has, furthermore, annexed the minor literary territory of the nonnative writer who contributes to the literary history of the host country in the currency of its native major language. Thus, when Deleuze and Guattari compare black English to Prague German,[5] they ignore the initial precision of their own definition, for although black English, Spanglish, or Nuyorican may be subversions of standard American English, they are firmly rooted in their locales of origin and expand the existing variations of the standard language rather than exporting it somewhere else.

The second feature of minor literature, its strongly politicized orientation, is not readily discernible in terms of Kafka's own work. Kafka's political agenda unfolds in a highly ritualized performance of writing where allegory as the regulative trope can portray the political only nonmimetically. Nevertheless, drawing on Kafka's diaries, Deleuze and Guattari conclude that the individual and psychological dimensions of minor literature expand to penetrate a political space and articulate themselves in terms of a "political program."[6] The term political is used here in its broadest sense. It is not an act of social intervention. Nor is it a confrontational critique of political oppression. Rather, it implies that individual concerns are inextricably linked with the intensity and immediacy of sociopolitical contexts and restraints. The "cramped space" of minor literature "forces each individual intrigue to connect immediately to politics. The individual concern thus becomes all the more necessary, indispensable, magnified, because a whole other story is vibrating within it. In this way, the family triangle connects to other triangles—commercial, economic, bureaucratic, juridical—that determine its values."[7] Although the specter of a network of oppressive familial, commercial, and bureaucratic systems is always evident in Kafka's parables and stories, the highly allegorized nature of his writing blunts the provocative edge of his political views. This is perhaps why Georg Lukács read Kafka's work as a portrayal of the fragmented subjectivity of the modern individual, a condition that rendered an effective formation of politicized collectivities impossible. Although "[t]he diabolical character of the world of modern capitalism, and man's impotence in the face of it, is the real subject matter of Kafka's writings,"[8] writes Lukács, the "basically allegorical character"[9] of his work transforms the world into an atemporal abstraction of a transcendent loss, "an allegory of transcendent Nothingness."[10] The political effectiveness of Kafka's writing may be contested. It is when Deleuze and Guattari casually oppose major and minor literatures in terms of individual and social interests that they engage in unjustified generalization in order to overstate the political case for minor literature: "In major literatures, . . . the individual concern (familial, marital, and so on) joins with other no less individual concerns, the social milieu serving as a mere environment or a background."[11] Any overview of contemporary minority or postcolonial literatures readily reveals that political critique is a requisite condition of their formation. However, it does not follow that a "major" literature is, by definition, depoliticized. Every rhetorically gifted writer presents language in its contestatory and revolutionary stations and transitions.

Closely linked to the political disposition of minor literature is its practice of collective articulation. Since this form of writing originates in communities marked by a loss or erasure of national consciousness or collective identity, memories and other fragments of historical and cultural repositories need to be pooled. Here "literature finds itself positively charged with the role and function of collective, and even revolutionary, enunciation."[12] Immigrant and exiled writers often endeavor to reclaim and preserve cultural legacies destroyed and erased in their own countries by oppressive regimes. Intellectual goods are smuggled across borders and transplanted in foreign soil. However, their reinscription often takes on the form of a negotiation between the contesting and conflicting ideologies of national and ethnic minority groups in exile that are all heirs to the same intellectual legacy. Thus, any minor literature is inescapably the expression of a collectivity in all its agreements and conflicts. It is easy to see how the spatially and temporally negotiable model of minor literature developed here can be quite attractive for scholars who are eager to add works representing cultural diversity to their reading lists. However, in the face of the growing introduction of underrepresented, lesser known, and emergent literary discourses into our curricula, Deleuze and Guattari's model suffers from an inadequacy of explanatory options. Oddly enough, despite its strong emphasis on the political orientation of minor literature, it understands politics in a highly sanitized way, as the natural and inevitable extension or habitat of individual life. None of these shortcomings would indicate a major problem for their model if they did not suggest its use as a general system for understanding all forms of minor, minority, exile, immigrant, oppositional, or marginal literatures. In its well-delineated way, it does contribute considerably to a broader understanding of Kafka's work. Although in the final analysis, Deleuze and Guattari call for a critical examination of the uses of one's own language, the need for self-reflexivity in language, their argument does not address the question of understanding the semiotics of another cultural model. Therefore, the hermeneutic proposal of making self-understanding the condition of understanding the other does not really work. Of course, in all fairness, any model that is explanatory in terms of a narrowly defined field of cultural production—be it the writing of the Prague Jews in German during the beginning of this century, American slave narratives, the Chicano border ballad, or contemporary Nuyorican poetry recited in New York cafés—would fail if expected to travel far and wide to account for other traditions of writing.

The questions of the possibility of transplanting Western theories in outlandish locations, of locating or recovering so-called indigenous theories, or of theoretical negotiations between multicultural sites cramped in a narrow curricular space retain their currency and urgency. I do not propose any final answers here. However, I am interested in unobstrusive theoretical gains made in areas of cultural study that have not been granted much curricular space. One of the most promising conceptual metaphors of recent developments in cultural studies is that of border or borderlands culture, represented in a wealth of historical contexts in the work of many Chicano/a writers and critics. Although these representations are never self-consciously theoretical, the metaphor of border culture generates a field where idea and action in the form of change, exchange, import, export, clash, reconciliation, and dialogue are interlinked. A better understanding of the dynamics of borderland cultures can be an invaluable tool in our future training in border crossings.

The critically mature stage of minority or ethnic literatures attained in the work of such writers as Maxine Hong Kingston, Bharati Mukherjee, Salman Rushdie, Sandra Cisneros, Ana Castillo, and Gloria Anzaldúa is a far cry from earlier examples of immigrant writing that constituted more or less autobiographical accounts of ethnic passages or linear narratives recounting personal, familial, or community histories. Various formal strategies of blocking transparencies are in operation, such as code switching, use of culturally encoded metaphor, literal translations into a foreign idiom, and subtle or overt bilingualisms. "I think that incorporating the Spanish, for me, allows me to create new expressions in English," states Cisneros in an interview, "to say things in English that have never been said before. And I get to do that by translating literally. I love calling stories by Spanish expressions. . . . All of a sudden something is added to the English . . . a new spice is added."[13] Similarly, across the Atlantic in Germany, another woman writer, this time a Turk, Emine Sevgi Özdamar, literally translates Turkish proverbs, metaphors, and jokes into German, creating a field of fantastic visuality and play that transforms the analytic weight of German into the impossible lightness of Scheherazade's magical language. Seen by critics as a testimony to the power of storytelling reminiscent of an age when stories were told, not written, Özdamar's work was awarded the highly coveted Ingeborg Bachmann Prize for literature in 1991. The writers of the so-called Third World have created an aesthetic zone often only accessible to forms of critical reading schooled in the semiotic intricacies of other cultures.

Though written in highly stylistic and readable English, the works of a Rushdie or Kingston defy facile understanding, for they create a semiotic domain where unfamiliar forms of signification challenge the reader to undertake a certain amount of serious investigation in another cultural discourse. Here the literary language parts company with conventionally prescribed meanings and becomes what Roland Barthes has called a "second-order semiological system," or a "metalanguage."[14] It is in this second language, which Barthes calls myth—the total sum of language, painting, images, rituals—that one talks about the first. Thus, our reading of Chinese, Chicano, Native American, or other ethnic literatures in English has to take into account a language codified in a certain mythologized way. The reader has to decode a linguistic system intricately linked to a cultural mythology. This requires several turns of translation. Like the Latino salsa, this writing is a "crossover combination of many musical forms, expresses multiculturalism and crossing borders, moments of alliance, convergence and clash among distinct social groups and sectors."[15] In a similar vein, Deleuze and Guattari locate this crossing of the borders in the revolutionary narratives of minor literature in the "polylingualism of one's own language" and the "linguistic Third World zones by which . . . an assemblage comes into play." This configuration takes the form of "pop—pop music, pop philosophy, pop writing, Worterflucht."[16]

A concrete poetics of these crossover zones is enunciated in the concept of border culture. Although the topos of border originated in an actual topography, at a geographical border, it has since traveled to sites where borders mark passages not necessarily in space but rather in time, in history and memory. Though not intended as a theoretical blueprint, Gloria Anzaldúa's *Borderlands/La Frontera: The New Mestiza* presents a poetic performance of its own critical message. A crossover of various genres, it presents its story in a collection of poems, reminiscences, personal and collective histories, and critical combat. The concept of border culture that is developed in this account is far more politically astute than that of minor literature. It is also more generative of radically new paradigms of understanding and signification. Like the characters that populate its pages, *La Frontera* consistently resists generic limitations that may be geographical, historical, or cultural. It expands in translation. The space of writing designates a position of questioning, challenging, and struggle: "The U.S.-Mexican border es *una herida habierta* where the Third World grates against the first and bleeds. And before a scab forms it hemorrhages again, the lifeblood of two worlds merging to form a third country—a border culture. Borders are set up to define the places that are safe and unsafe, to distinguish *us* from *them.* A border is a dividing line, a narrow strip along a steep edge. A borderland is a vague and undetermined place created by the emotional residue of an unnatural boundary. It is in a constant state of transition."[17]

The border sites constitute zones of perpetual motion and translation, confrontation of languages and cultures. As the concept of border shifts, so does that of identity. The *mestiza* is "caught between *los intersticios,* the spaces between the different worlds she inhabits."[18] The concepts of home and border become transportable, carried around in the form of political commitment and critical vision: "In leaving home, I did not lose touch with my origins. . . . I am a turtle, wherever I go, I carry 'home' on my back."[19] As a lesbian of color, Anzaldúa lives on the margins, moves perpetually into new borderlands. In one of the last poems of the book, "To Live in the Borderlands Means You," she observes, "To survive the Borderlands / you must live *sin fronteras* / be a crossroads."[20] Once she establishes a definition of the concept of Borderlands, she subjects it to a critique whereby she forcefully questions the male-controlled domain of her culture. However, Anzaldúa's account is not an expression of political confrontation; neither is it yet another postmodern self-reflexive analysis. Border culture is an open-ended dialogic encounter. It provides a critical space not only for political contestation and cultural clashes but ultimately for a new progressive exchange of languages and discourses. "I am participating in the creation of yet another culture," writes Anzaldúa, "a new story to explain the world and our participation in it, a new value system with images and symbols that connect us to each other and the planet."[21]

In a similar vein, Chicana writer Sandra Cisneros experiences the border culture in Chicago, a place far away from the U.S.-Mexican geographical border. Her cycle of stories *The House on Mango Street* relates the coming of age of a Chicana in Chicago. Esperenza, the protagonist, lives in a multicultural space, at the crossroads of many languages and histories. Her point of departure was never literally a primordial home or a homeland, and the house of her dreams never arrives. Although Esperenza is removed from the geographical space of her native culture, the physical distance to Mexico intensifies the bonds of memory. She is empowered by the plurality of experience in her relocated Borderlands, where Anglos, blacks, and various groups of immigrants enter an ongoing dialogue. In this new alternative space, stronger identities for the displaced subject are forged. The space of this writing is not simply the playing field of a postmodern, indeterminate aesthetic but one of cultural border crossings, transformation, and translation. The notion of border cultures is pluralistic and emphasizes the specificity of different cultural histories and their internal dynamics as opposed to the homogenizing critical categories implied in labels like minority, ethnic, or non-Western literatures.

Border culture with its valorization of many languages, dialogues, and sites of translation incorporates and expands theoretical insights developed elsewhere, most notably in Bakhtinian notions of dialogism and in heteroglossia. The dialogic mode prevents monologism. Every speech interacts with another and is subject to infinite conditioning and transformation in this interaction. The dialogic imagination governs the generation of knowledge in the sphere of heteroglossia."[22] In turn, heteroglossia designates a certain configuration of physical, social, and historical forces that lend speech its unique meaning, which cannot be replicated at a different juncture in time and space. The concepts dialogism and heteroglossia highlight and validate the dynamic flow of change, crisis, and transformation that informs human language and discourse at all cultural levels. Bakhtin argues, for example, that the simultaneous use of various genres in the novel (diary, letter, confession, aphorism) relativizes "linguistic consciousness in the perception of language borders—borders created by history and society, and even the most fundamental borders (i.e. those between languages as such)—and permits expression of a feeling for the materiality of language that defines such a relativized consciousness."[23] The imagined conversation between languages and voices at the heteroglot site takes on concrete form in the Borderlands, where languages and cultures clash and harmonize and traffic in social-speech forms of varying currency. Borderlands house every variant of unofficial, hybrid, carnivalesque forms of speech, languages for which there are no official dictionaries and that move "from English to Castillian Spanish to the North Mexican dialect to Tex-Mex to a sprinkling of Nahuatl to a mixture of all these."[24]

In spite of this wide playfield of ideas that characterize the Borderlands paradigm, most Chicano critics do not think that their critical insights have been properly conceptualized. Angie Chabram, for example, argues that new passages in Chicano writing need to be "reviewed in light of new conceptual frameworks that assess and evaluate the altered nature of Chicano critical discourse, its linkages with other emergent discourses, its appropriation of contemporary literary theory, and its relationship to greater critical traditions."[25] Forging interlinkages between existing and emerging discourses, between cultural borders and literary and linguistic traditions, is necessary if we are to preserve the dynamic of genuinely diverse modes of cultural criticism. "Populating critical histories with the intention of the newly discovered sensibilities and expressive modes of national minorities, women, and working-class sectors," writes Chabram, "involves more than just refurbishing linkages obfuscated under the weight of deliberate cultural suppression and/or benign neglect."[26] This is a shrewd assessment of the many misguided curricular innovations being undertaken in various literature departments in this country. In his recent *Beyond the Culture Wars,* Gerald Graff argues that "however admirable the intention, adding courses in non-Western culture to existing general education requirements (as is now being done or contemplated at many schools and colleges) will only once more postpone the debate that has always been avoided in the past. It is not that non-Western courses are inherently separatist, as so many charge, but that the *established curriculum* is *separatist,* with each subject and course being an island with little regular connection to other subjects and courses."[27]

This absence of dialogic encounters in the curriculum is evident in most literature programs. In his essay in a special issue of the *German Quarterly* devoted to the question of interdisciplinarity in German studies, Steven Taubeneck argues that many German departments in the United States have carefully protected the sacred borders of *Germanistik* (a more traditionally conceived study of Germanic languages and literatures), which have remained stubbornly impervious to the demands of noncanonical traditions. These departments, claims Taubeneck, "tend to recycle the old reading lists, to polish up the old questions, and generally to conduct 'business as usual.' *Germanistik* remains largely entrenched in idealist, masculinist, and universalist assumptions that prevent students from approaching concerns of contemporary everyday life."[28]

Since this pronouncement, several special sessions at the Modern Language Association (MLA) and German Studies Association meetings, special issues such as "Minorities in German Culture" of the *New German Critique* (1989), DAAD (German Academic Exchange) proceedings on the conference "German Studies in the USA: A Critique of 'Germanistik'?" (January 19–22, 1989, Scottsdale, Arizona), and occasional essays and anthologies have investigated the possibilities of transforming the discipline of *Germanistik* into the interdisciplinary or transdisciplinary area of German studies. Many programs in German are now listed as German studies majors in college or university catalogs. Recent MLA job-information lists mostly advertise for applicants who have specialized in cultural, feminist, or film studies, preferably all of the above. Understandably, job seekers eagerly add to their CVs the names of a few women and ethnic writers and film texts under those flexible categories "teaching and research interests" or "work in progress."

The results of these efforts, however, have not so far produced a new curricular paradigm that enables a genuine and reflexive knowledge of sociocultural traditions in German. The net effect of the flurry of this activity has not been a change in the curriculum but often mere additions to reading lists. Taubeneck's observation about recycled reading lists and repolished ideas still maintains its currency. Why does a genuine reform in literary study effectively elude the discipline? The reasons are many and complex, but for the purposes of my argument I would like to briefly focus on two areas that, I believe, present obstacles in the conception and implementation of curricular innovation. One is the assumption that we are working against a so-called canon that has deliberately excluded the work of "low status" languages and writers. The cannon directed against the specter of this canon would be a countercanon exclusively representing the lost, erased, forgotten, and newly reclaimed texts of an occluded literary history. The mere inclusion of these texts in departmental reading lists does not imply a critical engagement with them. This requires very serious work that is not often undertaken. Another well-intentioned but problematic strategy is to marginalize in our teaching historically overrepresented works by retaining them in the syllabi but refraining from redefining their place. Our focus has recently been on the new, the most current, the most "in" topics such as "From the Berlin Wall to the Berlin Mall." Although the development of such courses is informed by an innovative spirit, problems arise when curriculum design is motivated by professional expediency—a strike-while-the iron-is-hot mentality—and topics are not invested with universal critical appeal. When the Berlin wall came down, three of my colleagues, in political science, history, and German, respectively, got together and offered a course on the wall for which almost 200 students signed up. A mere two years after the fall of the wall, a new colleague offered a course on the implications of its fall and lectured to only two students for the whole semester. In other words, the introduction of current topics and issues does not guarantee enduring interest if these issues are treated in a time-specific, narrowly defined fashion devoid of frameworks of contiguity that link them to larger social and cultural histories.

Supplementing reading lists with works that belong to socially defined minorities such as women and foreigners or Muslims does not really constitute for these works an entry into the canon, for the canon is not a reading list but an abstract construct determined by a complex constellation of social, political, publication, and reception histories; literacy patterns; cultural habits; and institutional practices. The question, then, is not one of challenging the abstract notion of an exclusionary canon but, following Walter Benjamin, of recontextualizing our reading histories in such a way as to locate in them responses to questions necessitated by our current sociocultural concerns. We definitely need to supplement our reading lists or syllabi with works of underrepresented classes and groups, but this is not enough. Adding the name of a woman or person of color to the reading list in itself does not inaugurate a practice of critical reading. What we consider a canonical tradition usually reflects the biases of our present concerns rather than an imagined collection of works retroactively so organized. In "The Mirror and the Vamp," an exemplary essay that resituates feminist criticisms in their larger literary history of formation, Sandra M. Gilbert and Susan Gubar state that "in order to foster . . . a cultural metamorphosis, we must understand its historical roots; since the future can only be reinvented if we reinterpret the past. That feminist criticism can be defined through metaphors similar to, if different from, those which govern other forms of critical discourse means that we can enter into precisely the dialogues that will allow us to see in a new light an image of the shifting cultural heritage we are continually seeking to change."[29]

In this spirit, it would be more inspiring to locate junctures of crisis and reconfiguration in our own cultural histories, where our present concerns can be linked with critically productive points of investigation. What were the paradigm shifts that have gradually ushered in the necessity for those areas of inquiry that we nowadays call cultural studies? Which periods of critical innovation anticipate our own? A very brief look at these junctures may help put some of our present questions in perspective.

The seventeenth century witnessed the beginning of an ongoing debate in European intellectual history about what constitutes modern consciousness. The so-called *querelle des anciens et des modernes,* the famous confrontation between the proponents of classical art and the advocates of aesthetic modernity, was instrumental in the formation of a radical sense of the modern and its cultural constructs. More recently, literary criticism and critical theory have been engaged in the equally daunting task of investigating the conditions of the transition from modernity to postmodernity. In *Irony and the Discourse of Modernity,* Ernst Behler has convincingly argued that the definitive transition to modernity was fully realized only when the arts were granted the possibility of "infinite progression."[30] Until then, only philosophy and the sciences were seen as reflecting the infinity of truth and nature, whereas poetry and the arts were circumscribed by well-established criteria of excellence beyond which they could not go.

At the end of the eighteenth century, in the discourse of early German romanticism, which bore the literary fruits of Kant and Fichte's critical philosophy, literature and the arts were informed not only by their propensity for progression but also by a praxis of self-critique. As a new discipline, literary criticism assumed the task of investigating the conditions and limits of epistemological, ethical, and aesthetic systems and values. The demands imposed on literary criticism gradually shifted the grounds of its function from the aesthetic to the sociocultural. This move, in turn, necessitated the establishment of new critical categories such as the position of the knowing subject, which requires the understanding of otherness, the perception of the world of experience as a network of signifying systems, and the reading of works of art as allegories of their larger historical context.

Although the argument about whether postmodernity represents a radical break from modernity or an expanded version of it will never be satisfactorily answered, it is probably safe to assume that both movements resulted in a progressive erasure of the boundaries that separated the arts and literature from other modes of knowledge and practices of everyday life. Until the theory debates, it seemed that the paradigm of literary study was informed by a dichotomy between the works of the canon and those of popular culture. With the advent of poststructuralist theories of discourse and representation, which demonstrated the socially and ideologically conditioned nature of all linguistic constructs, the opposition between canonical and noncanonical texts became untenable. The practice of literary criticism expanded to include the investigation of all manifestations of material culture from comic strips and hard rock lyrics to videos and highway billboards. In other words, the boundaries of the literary work dissolved, and it was subsumed by the larger cultural context, where literature would be one system among several signifying systems. At this point, all written productions from diaries to political flyers and e-mail messages could constitute an area of critical investigation, and the time is ripe for the study of texts that were once deemed products of low or marginal cultures.

Furthermore, poststructuralist debates have created a heightened awareness of the representational status of so-called truths, of knowledge, of ideologies, and of the power relations between nations, races, and sexes. This insight has had far-reaching ramifications in our educational and cultural life. It has revitalized our thinking about intellectual history and refashioned our practice of criticism and, more specifically, literary criticism as a form of cultural critique. I believe that a certain critical archaeology of literary traditions can facilitate dialogues between our present concerns and their earlier manifestations and enable curricular negotiation and innovation. A more fruitful approach than adding new but separate courses to the curriculum would be to investigate the points in the past when questions of cultural change and representations of otherness were raised in different yet comparable contexts. What were the conditions for the necessity of raising these questions? To what extent were they answered? What kinds of ideological biases determined their formulation? In this way, cultural transitions can be seen not as isolated instances but in a certain dialectic in the original sense of the term, that is, in a dialogue with the present.

Let us briefly consider the critical implications for cultural studies of an eighteenth-century genre—the German *Bildungsroman.* Like Bakhtin's definition of the novel and postmodern immigrant texts, this romantic genre is a mixed one, often an amalgam of confession, diary, songs, poetry, conversation, fragment. If we consider our confrontation with "others" as *Bildung* (in its broadest sense as learning another language, discourse, practice), we can reclaim from literary history insights that can guide our efforts to introduce new structures of knowledge in curricular reform. In the romantic *Bildungsroman,* the process of *Bildung* is depicted "in its broadest sense as formation, education, and diversification, that is, as the move from a unified subjectivity to the multiplicity of experience."[31] *Bildung* is always a formation through which individuals, collectivities, and their languages and cultures form their own image, *Bild,* in the mirror of the others. The stations of the protagonist's *Bildungsreise* (journey of education) often take on the form of encounters with exotic persons and locales. Here, exotic designates distance in time or space or both. Thus, characters from classical Greece or the ancient Orient as well as contemporary characters from distant lands and historical and modern sites coexist in the narrative space of these novels.

In *The Experience of the Foreign,* Antoine Berman writes that "*Bildung* is always a movement toward a form, *one's own form* ."[32] This movement as voyage "is also the experience of the *alterity of the world:* in order to have access to that which, in the guise of a becoming-other, is in truth a becoming-itself, the same must experience *that which is not itself,* or at least what *appears* as such."[33] The hero of the romantic novel or novella attempts to fulfill the pedagogical imperative by learning other forms of discourse and understanding other histories and geographies. The process of knowledge in romantic idealism progresses through the successive stages of encounter with alterity, translation, interpretation, and understanding. For Novalis, one of the most prominent poet-theorists of early German romanticism, self-understanding can only be the product of understanding the foreign. This understanding, invention (or formation), and expansion of one's own culture through other cultures led the romantics to the study and translation of works in classical, European, and Oriental languages. These translations, which Berman calls German romanticism's "experience of the foreign," may have constituted a genuine attempt to understand the foreign and let it speak for itself. However, having been alerted to the ideological implications of textual activity by modern critical debates, we can question whether the romantic desire for translation was a desire for appropriation and appropriative representation. At this point I may speculate that the valorization of the appropriative aspect of translation by the romantics points to the problem in their understanding of other cultures. Like anthropology (as it is critiqued in the work of Johannes Fabian and Bernard McGrane, among others[34]), the romantic text may have aspired to recognize the other as its own projection and was likely to be deceived by this projection. McGrane calls anthropology "the modern West's monologue about 'alien cultures.' Anthropology never *listened* to the voices of 'alien cultures,'" he claims indignantly. "It never *learned* from them, rather it studied them; in fact studying them, making sense out of them, making a 'science' about them, has been the modern *method* of *not* listening, of avoiding listening, to them."[35]

What I am trying to illustrate by these brief glances into the pages of modern literary history is that the inclusion of texts by the so-called others in our reading lists and syllabi needs to be more than a token gesture. In my discipline, German, for example, a great deal of energy goes into putting together reading lists representing the minority literatures of Germany, especially the literary production of a significant number of successful Turkish writers. Recently, there has been an inflation of conference papers and journal articles on this minor literature of the Turks in Germany. None has a clue about the contexts that have shaped the writing of this group: no knowledge of Turkish politics, form of government, art, literature, myths, rituals, ideas, and educational systems except hearsay. Most reiterate clichés about military culture, machismo politics, Islamic fundamentalism and terrorism, or, on a more positive note, the fabled storytelling gifts of Middle Eastern cultures, a throwback to the stories of *A Thousand and One Nights.* It makes a lot more sense to read the products of this minor or border culture in the nexus of the history of German Orientalism, earlier travel literature and ethnographies, shifts in the representations of Turks, Arabs, and Asians brought about by changing political relations and practices of everyday life, and in comparative studies of immigrant writing. A critical engagement with another culture has to be performed in the spirit of a dialogue. The ideal dialogue requires the learning of another language, culture, history, and geography—literally; there are no shortcuts. Otherwise, paradigms of multiculturalism and diversity cannot be immune to appropriative strategies and avoid complicity in deliberate misunderstandings and misrepresentations of Third World or non-Western peoples.

We need to be careful about adopting uncritical anthropological methods in our readings of other cultures. If we are merely practicing a self-critique (of not understanding the other) and are not willing to invest a great deal of time and energy in learning another language and culture, if we are unwilling to translate this culture in a nonappropriative manner, then it makes no sense to list token texts. "Anthropological 'scientific method,'" observes McGrane, "*is* the decay of dialogue, the sustained, cultivated, and epistemologically enforced atrophy of dialogue."[36] In order to activate a genuine sense of dialogue with other cultures, we could expand the ideas developed in the notion of borderlands culture to create a field of hyphenated criticisms. A border culture is by definition a hyphenated one. It is Mexican-American, Russian-Turkish, Italian-Austrian. A hyphen both separates and connects; in an extended sense, it both contests and agrees. It creates new dialect(ic)s, such as Chicano-Spanish, Algerian-French, Turkish-German. The concept or model of borderlands culture is effectively movable; it has already been stripped from a strictly physical condition to be transformed into a contingent structure of history and geography. In this way, traditions separated in time can be hypenated in a new conversation. Likewise, traditions separated in space, such as Western and non-Western, can assume hyphenated and carefully differentiated identities that will help them retain their particular histories but encourage partnership and participation in new syntheses. We need to tease out the critical implications of cultural differences, strip them from their temporally and spatially fixed contexts, and reformulate their questions in the contexts of shifting borders and demographics. Then and only then can we maintain a dialogue between our past and present critical concerns and gain an understanding of the translatability of others in a way that does not silence them.

NOTES

1. Gilles Deleuze and Félix Guattari, *Kafka: Toward a Minor Literature,* trans. Dana Polan (Minneapolis: University of Minnesota Press, 1986), 18.
2. Ibid., 19.
3. Ibid., 16.
4. Ibid.
5. Ibid., 17.
6. Ibid.
7. Ibid.
8. Georg Lukács, *Realism in Our Time: Literature and the Class Struggle,* trans. John Mander and Necke Mander (New York: Harper and Row, 1971), 77.
9. Ibid., 78.
10. Ibid., 53.
11. Deleuze and Guattari, *Kafka,* 17.
12. Ibid., 17.

13. Sandra Cisneros, *Interviews with Writers of the Postcolonial World,* ed. Feroza Jussawalla and Reed Way Dasenbrock (Jackson and London: University Press of Mississippi, 1992), 289.

14. Roland Barthes, *Mythologies,* trans. Annette Lavers (New York: Hill and Wang), 114–115.

15. Marc Zimmerman, *U.S. Latino Literature: An Essay and Annotated Bibliography* (Chicago: MARCH/Abrazo Press, 1992), 43.

16. Deleuze and Guattari, *Kafka,* 26–27.

17. Gloria Anzaldúa, *Borderlands/La Frontera: The New Mestiza* (San Francisco: Aunt Lute Books, 1987), 3.

18. Ibid., 20.

19. Ibid., 21.

20. Ibid., 195.

21. Ibid., 81.

22. M. M. Bakhtin, *The Dialogic Imagination,* trans. Caryl Emerson and Michael Holquist (Austin: University of Texas Press, 1981), 426.

23. Ibid., 324.

24. Anzaldúa, *La Frontera,* preface, n.p.

25. Angie Chabram, "Conceptualizing Chicano Critical Discourse," in *Criticism in the Borderlands: Studies in Chicano Literature, Culture, and Ideology,* ed. Héctor Calderón and Josć David Saldívar (Durham and London: Dukc Univcrsity Prcss, 1991), 127–148, 136.

26. Ibid., 145.

27. Gerald Graff, *Beyond the Culture Wars: How Teaching the Conflicts Can Revitalize American Education* (New York and London: W. W. Morton, 1992), 13.

28. Steven Taubeneck, "Voices in the Debate: German Studies and *Germanistik,*" special issue of *German Quarterly,* "*Germanistik* as German Studies: Interdisciplinary Theories and Methods" 62 (1989), 220–226, 220–221.

29. Sandra M. Gilbert and Susan Gubar, "The Mirror and the Vamp: Reflections on Feminist Criticism," in *The Future of Literary History,* ed. Ralph Cohen (New York and London: Routledge, 1989), 144–166, 166.

30. Ernst Behler, *Irony and the Discourse of Modernity* (Seattle and London: University of Washington Press, 1990), 50.

31. Azade Seyhan, *Representation and Its Discontents: The Critical Legacy of German Romanticism* (Berkeley/Los Angeles/Oxford: University of California Press, 1992), 19.

32. Antoine Berman, *The Experience of the Foreign: Culture and Translation in Romantic Germany,* trans. S. Heyvaert (Albany: State University of New York Press, 1992), 44.

33. Ibid., 45.

34. See Johannes Fabian, *Time and the Other: How Anthropology Makes Its Object* (New York: Columbia University Press, 1983); and Bernard McGrane, *Beyond Anthropology: Society and the Other* (New York: Columbia University Press, 1989).

35. McGrane, *Beyond Anthropology,* 127.

36. Ibid.

3

Nationalisms in a Global Economy

JOEL REED

I APPROACH INTERNATIONAL cultural studies through the contradiction that nationalism is one of the strongest forces defining the international scene. Daily we are inundated with news about nationalism in each of the "three worlds," and the fact that this news is brought to us through global media with corporate circuits that literally encircle the planet highlights its paradoxical nature. And yet the disdain with which these nationalist movements are reported demonstrates that multinational capital finds in them its politico-economic antagonist; not surprisingly, supranationalist movements of a quite different character, such as pan-Africanism, pan-Arabism, or international socialism itself, are even more vehemently disparaged (if their names are ever uttered). The general media avoids explicit references to its corporate affiliations, but the specialized business press teems with warnings of the dangers nationalism poses to corporate finance. *Economist*, for example, cautions that nationalism will hamper "free trade" in Asia and that nationalism poses an even greater threat to the expansion of the "global firm" than temporary shortages of capital.[1] *Management Review* reports its fears of a "cold peace" in which nationalism and worldwide economic integration meet in global space with disastrous results, though an author in *International Management* is confident that despite economic cooling trends, commercial values, not national ones, will triumph in the end; *Marketing News* finds reason for similar optimism.[2] Other authors ponder the effects of nationalism on multinational petroleum corporations in the Middle East, banking in Africa, chances for including Latin America in corporate "global strategy," and the expansion of both electronics production and communication networks in "developing countries."[3]

The business press recognizes in nationalist movements multiple sites of resistance to a flow of multinational capital that increasingly moves along the same lines of communication as the electronic media themselves. Viewed against the perspective of the capitalist world system, nationalism has been called by Immanuel Wallerstein, Giovanni Arrighi, and Terence K. Hopkins an "antisystemic movement," one that has perhaps run its course as an anticapital locus, and yet it remains or "survives" on the international scene.[4] As the rubric of the "antisystemic movement" illustrates, nationalism survives not only in political practice but also *in theory;* mirroring the fundamental paradox of international nationalism is the international proliferation of its theories. At last count over a dozen recent books and journal special issues have been published in the United States on various historical and geographical national formations.[5] The best of these differ from their predecessors in focusing less on positivistic features of nationalism, such as common language, culture, and "psychology" within a demarcated territory and economy.[6] Instead, these studies are concerned with the fluid relationships between these features and between nationals and nonnationals, rather than with specific reified characteristics, and with the very subjective, rather than positivistic, processes of creating national identity. The most interesting of the contemporary studies contest nationalism while also contributing to a critical understanding of newer forms of multinational geopolitical organization. Even more than the business press, these authors see in nationalism ideologies that block the development of global socioeconomic formations—not "multinational capital" but internationalism—while also recognizing the strategic importance some nationalisms have had in combatting Western political, cultural, and economic colonization.

In this chapter I develop a sense of nationalism's new forms by considering some of these theoretical investigations. Reading this body of theory demonstrates that what Fredric Jameson calls the "cognitive mapping" of the present situation demands the ability to cross borders of academic study previously as clearly drawn as those of nation-states themselves. I first turn to recent work by Wallerstein in two collaborative projects that explicate the political economics of present nationalism through its theoretical contradictions: *Antisystemic Movements,* written with Arrighi and Hopkins, and *Race, Nation, Class: Ambiguous Identities,* his dialogue with Etienne Balibar. Reading these works next to that of Jacques Derrida demonstrates, however, that a critique of the political economics of nationalism in the world system leaves out the philosophical history whose echoes continue to call from within present formations. In *The Other Heading: Reflections on Today's Europe,* Derrida uses Paul Valéry's "quasi-political" writings as a springboard into the philosophical and ethical issues surrounding national and transnational identities.[7] After discussing *The Other Heading,* I will consider the third panel of this critical triptych, Fredric Jameson's *The Geopolitical Aesthetic: Cinema and Space in the World System.*[8] Here, Jameson reads contemporary films from around the world as allegorical attempts to map the spatial dilemmas of late capitalism that are no longer fully comprehensible within national confines. At first glance these texts would seem to have little to do with each other, grounded as they are in such distinct fields. Yet if, as Jameson has argued, one defining feature of postmodernism is the complete commodification of the aesthetic, then for historical reasons we might expect connections among these critiques of political economy, philosophy, and film.[9]

All of these texts work between the borders of international culture, theorizing nationalism in a global era through discussions of a range of economic, political, and cultural formations, commonly calling for—and developing—forms of analysis that are grounded in the new global configurations we currently face. They all recognize that late capitalism (in conjunction with its "cultural logic," postmodernism) has produced cultural forms that defeat older methods of critique. Pointing to one such example, Arrighi, Hopkins, and Wallerstein write that "one direction of electronification, as world-historical process, bears integrally on the central class-forming process by integrating the technical divisions of labor, . . . the other . . . bears integrally on popular consciousness of conditions of existence"; however, "we collectively lack as yet the theoretical ideas to gauge the directional impetus that this ongoing development will give to popular struggles" (*AM*, 75–76). As both condition and effect of the present conjuncture of nationalism and multinationalism, the media, and electronic culture at large, figure as a particular topos through which a set of more fundamental paradoxes can be seen. The relationships of core to periphery, centralization to decentralization, and the universal to the particular will focus my discussion of all these texts.

This set of oppositions is featured in these works, and my discussion of them, for their presence in both the empirical and subjective fields of nationalism. But this further dichotomy of "material" and "ideal" too has a place in my consideration, and I suggest that Louis Althusser's intervention in this topic through his discussion of overdetermination is especially important to understanding contemporary nationalism.[10] As he first formulated it, the overdetermined contradiction between labor and capital "is specified by the forms of the *superstructure* . . . by *the internal and external historical situation* which determines it on the one hand as a function of the *national past* . . . and on the other as functions of the existing *world context*. . . ."[11] Far from being only a structural theory of synchronic multiple causality, overdetermination can also help explain the temporal contradictions of contemporary nationalism, which by all accounts looks anachronistic in a global economy. Althusser too noted this anachronism when he included nationalism among his list of ideological "survivals," concluding that these survivals can be explained through overdetermination.[12] Overdetermination, then, is a strategy for specifying both the presence of a deferral—or nonsynchronism, as Ernst Bloch has called it—between subjective and material social features and for understanding the *apparent* indeterminacy of social causality.[13] Through attention to this deferral, we can see that nationalism shocks the business writers I previously cited because it asserts a sense of identity—and (most importantly) concomitant trade and industrial policy—that fits into a more properly modernist economy rather than a postmodern one.[14] In this sense contemporary nationalism develops a residual (modern) subjectivity within a dominant (postmodern) mode of production.[15] Althusser's "overdetermination" and Bloch's "nonsynchronous contradiction" remain important tools for understanding the odd anachronisms of nationalism in the era of multinational capital, for they read subjective structures through material ones without sacrificing attention to the slippages of deferral.[16]

Reading the antinomies of contemporary nationalism through their nonsynchronicity is the ultimate advantage these new theoretical texts have over their predecessors, but our attention to these texts should not stop there. I also suggest that the theoretical relationships between these authors are themselves important for understanding their work about international nationalism, for these texts too are representations of international culture. Nationalism is not only an "object" in the world to discover and investigate but is in some ways constituted—both negatively (or critically) and affirmatively (by its proponents)—in theory. In fact, one of the shifts marked in the most recent investigations of nationalism is the recognition that it both *has* theories and that it must be theorized, not only documented.[17] In this way, as Althusser argued in the 1960s, "theory" itself can be understood as a site of political struggle, a situation that—like that of present nationalism—is as much a result of postmodern culture as it is its "antisystem," and grasping the conceptual affiliations among these works on nationalism themselves contributes to that "cognitive mapping" I earlier invoked.

Wallerstein and his collaborators are very clear in their intentions to develop a global structuralist theory that reveals patterns in economic history unavailable to a more narrowly focused, local history. They "are in search of the system-wide structural processes that have produced" movements that are also "antisystemic," or working against the structure that produced them (*AM*, 1). As explained in Wallerstein's earlier works, capitalism has been developing as a world system throughout its five-hundred-year history as the nation-states that accumulate capital (or the "core" areas) do so by drawing it from the rest of the world (which, from the point of view of the core, becomes the "periphery"). As a feature of the global system, nationalism carries within it the dialectics of system and antisystem, for it is systemic when it provides the ideological support for underdevelopment by core regions and antisystemic when it becomes the vehicle for resistance in the peripheries to colonization either by Western nations (in an earlier stage of capitalism) or by the globalization of markets (in late capitalism). These themes, also developed in Wallerstein and Balibar's *Race, Nation, Class,* demonstrate the interconnections of class and nationality as antisystemic bases, or the ways the struggle against capital is overdetermined by both class and nation. Both class-based social movements and national ones contest the state apparatus; accordingly, although socialism is in theory an international movement, in practice it is local or national in character because it strategically employs a nationally bound civil society in its attempts to capture the state.

However, in a signal toward these works' divergence from classical Marxist studies, much of both *Antisystemic Movements* and *Race, Nation, Class* is premised on the understanding that the present world situation is fundamentally shaped by the development of late capitalism and that an "old left" class analysis on its own fails to map either present social dynamics or a future course of action against that world system. On this map, "the lines between social movements and national movements have become increasingly difficult to disentangle" (*AM*, 25). In addition to social movements based on race, both Wallerstein and Balibar are particularly interested in gender. Balibar slightly modifies Althusser's view that the family-school diad is the privileged site of capitalist education, the place we learn the racist and nationalist ideologies that preempt class analysis (*RNC*, 102–103). Wallerstein finds that the family has an even more directly economic function as a place where surplus value can be extracted at no cost, for housework is still not considered labor despite its necessity and centrality in reproducing the means of production. "The way we induce women—and the young and aged—to work to create surplus-value for the owners of capital, who do not even pay them a little bit, is by proclaiming that their work is really non-work. We invent the 'housewife' and assert she is not 'working,' merely 'keeping house'" (*RNC*, 35). His discussions of household structures ground the call for wages for housework in the structure of capitalism, not just within the patriarchal family. The universalism proclaimed by capitalism's global slogan that the market's benefits are equally free to all tensely co-exists with the structural exclusion of 53 percent of the world's population. At the same time, the family is the site of a "tense link" between universalism and exclusion, for it can either perpetuate chauvinist attitudes or be turned into a school for traditions of resistance (*RNC*, 111–112).[18]

Just as the household perpetuates nationalism and racism while providing the basis for its opposition, nationalism is both antisystemic and ideologically subservient to the needs of the capitalist world system. We can presently witness in the United States, France, and Germany that the economic crises of late capitalism demand increasing austerity within the First World; these crises lead both to the "denationalization" of labor in increased immigration and to increased racist nationalism when the First World subject, having experienced the *embourgoisement* enabled by the world system, faces the loss of social services it had come to count on and turns its anger on the foreigner (see *AM*, 91–93). In turn, these events, overdetermined as they are by the politico-economic spaces of the core and periphery, the center and the perimeter, enable the production of new political and social relationships across national borders. At the grassroots level we can see these relationships in the global movements of women, indigenous peoples, and environmentalists, though even intrastate cultural and economic treaties could help establish internationalism as they erase national administrative borders.

Without a doubt, the blurring of the boundaries between national and social movements strengthens their antisystemic effects: "'National-liberation movements' [claim] the double legitimacy of nationalist anti-imperialism and proletarian anti-capitalism" (*AM,* 27), and it is in recognition of these effects that Jameson pointed in 1981 to the need for the "Left [to] grasp the immense Utopian appeal of nationalism."[19] But the trick with utopian impulses is that they reveal the desire to "escape" ideology while remaining mired within ideological antinomies. Thus, nationalism itself operates through homologous sets of binary oppositions: inside/outside, self/other, exemplary/particular, or universal/exclusive. For example, nationalisms make universal claims as vehicles for freedom within nations and for equality with other nations—thus attempting to unite class differences—while also excluding and persecuting the nonnational or foreigner.

Etienne Balibar demonstrates that these antinomies are themselves inseparable from the connections of national identity with those of race and from the nation's position within the world system. Balibar's exploration of these forms of contradiction and the ways they multiply to a plurality of racism*s* and nationalism*s* (see *RNC,* 38–39, 49–50) demonstrates his own approach to a "new theory" of nationalism, one freed from the simple contradiction against which Althusser also argued. Balibar points out that "the notion of nationalism is constantly dividing" (*RNC,* 47) and that this "notion" or theory itself must be interrogated for its responsibility in constituting the object of its inquiry (*RNC,* 55).

In his concern with these multiplicities Balibar is equally close to a "poststructural" theory of nationalism as a neo-Marxist one, revealing affiliations with both deconstruction and the Althusserian group. The plurality of nationalisms, overdetermined by racism, is inaccessible through "classical schemas of causality, whether mechanistic (the one as the cause of the other, 'producing' the other according to the rule of the proportionality of the effects to the cause) or spiritualistic (the one 'expressing' the other, or giving it its meaning or revealing its hidden essence)" (*RNC,* 50). Readers of Althusser and Balibar's work will recognize here Althusser's earlier dismissal of mechanical and expressive causalities in favor of structural causality, itself tied to the earlier notion of overdetermination.[20] By importing these concepts into a theory of nationalism, Balibar brings back the earlier rejection of economism while also avoiding the essentialist logic that is a large part of nationalist ideology itself.

Through these avoidances, Balibar confirms the deconstructive potential of overdetermination and (paradoxically) structural causality. His concern is with the "fluctuating gap" between "the representations and practices of nationalism and racism," a gap best understood if racism is viewed as "*a supplement of nationalism* or more precisely a *supplement internal to nationalism,* always in excess of it, but always indispensable to its constitution and yet always still insufficient to achieve its project, just as nationalism is both indispensable and always insufficient to achieve the formation of the *nation*" (*RNC,* 54). Whereas the mutually supportive ideologies of race and nationality are clearly visible within countless nationalist formations and have been discussed by theorists of nationalism at least as far back as Ernest Renan[21] (farther even: In the eighteenth century "race" and "nation" were nearly synonymous terms), Balibar provides a theory that deconstructs the antinomy of particularism and universality underlying the race-nationality pairing: "The excess [racism] represents in relation to nationalism, and therefore the supplement it brings to it, tends both to universalize it, to correct its lack of universality, and to particularize it, to correct its lack of specificity. In other words, racism actually adds to the ambiguous nature of nationalism" (*RNC,* 54).

For Balibar, the supplementary relationship between the privileged term (universality) and the term its logic demands be excluded (particularism) demonstrates that "the concept [of nationalism] never functions alone, but is always part of a chain in which it is both the central and the weak link" (*RNC,* 46). Because nationalism is part of a signifying chain, Balibar, like Benedict Anderson, insists on the "imagined" or fictive features of nationalism, its reliance on *fictive* ethnicity or, as Wallerstein puts it, on the "construction of peoplehood."[22] With this fictional aspect, these critiques of the political economic contradictions of "late nationalism" bring us back to the study of rhetoric, discourse, and aesthetics in Derrida and Jameson's works.

Those familiar with Wallerstein's previous works would expect to find that these books' concerns with the fictional constructions of nationalism merge with a focus on the relationships of core and periphery. But it is surprising that when his theories of capitalism as a world system are articulated with the recent work of Balibar, they point to a theorist who would seem to have staked his career on arguing against world-system-building perspectives: Jacques Derrida. Wallerstein and Balibar's recent work demonstrates that late capitalism constantly veers between centralizing and decentralizing tendencies—a spatial dynamic Derrida investigated in "Structure, Sign, and Play in the Discourse of the Human Sciences."[23] In *The Other Heading* Derrida takes up the forms of this spatial instability not on a global scale but in a particular site of global intrastate reconfigurations with the political and economic reshaping of Europe.

The "heading" of Derrida's title is a translation of the French *cap,* a prefix that leads Derrida to numerous word plays, but two forms of "capital" focus his investigation: the capital city or center and economic capital. As Derrida explores the ways nationalism and Eurocentrism demand a focal point, a center for the concentration of political and economic power, he recognizes that today there also exists a drive toward decentralization or globalization through multiple centers. Yet if we extend the "global" rhetoric further to one of *universalization,* we can see how this term functions as what Freud called a "switch-word," providing the hinge between the ideology of decentralization and its opposite. For just as Wallerstein discusses the ways capitalism must necessarily "assert and carry out a universalist ideology as an essential element in the endless pursuit of the accumulation of capital," reducing "everything to a homogeneous form denoted by a single measure of money" (*RNC,* 31), Derrida discusses the ways capital, more than ever after the fall of the Soviet bloc, is recentering all of Europe into a homogeneous economic system under the rhetorical banner of the so-called free market (*OH,* 99).

"Free-market" rhetoric is couched in official state proclamations about a unified Europe and disseminated through the media, which is itself expanding into previously closed markets. Derrida repeatedly argues against the media's accumulation of *cultural* capital, through which it "would control and standardize [across the lines of the nation-state], subjecting artistic discourses and practices to a grid of intelligibility, to philosophical or aesthetic norms, to channels of immediate and efficient communication, to the pursuit of ratings and commercial profitability" (*OH,* 39). But lest we think that this is a purely contemporary phenomenon, Derrida traces today's attempts to centralize cultural authority and capital back to Paul Valéry, who in *The Freedom of the Spirit* (1939) writes: "If the material of culture is to become capital, there must also be men who need and know how to use it. . . . I say that our cultural capital is in peril" (*OH,* 67–68). Valéry centers capital—in both economic and cultural senses—in Europe and Europeans, with Paris at *its* center, imperiled by "*the rise of exotic peoples to civilized life* [which] *threatens what used to distinguish the spirit of Paris.* We have known it as the capital of quality and the capital of criticism. We have every reason to fear for these glories" (*OH,* 121–122). Through Valéry's anxiety about the already-merging core and periphery, Derrida leads us to find historical precedents of the logic of nationalism that Wallerstein and Balibar examined. Valéry writes that "our special quality . . . is to believe and to feel that we are universal—by which I mean, *men of universality.* . . . Notice the paradox: to specialize in the name of the universal" (*OH,* 74).

The Other Heading reveals the interlinked logics that connect the antinomies of universal and particular and of the centered and decentered with nationalism, supranationalism, the media, and capital itself, as expressed within the rhetoric of philosophy and popular discourse. Derrida's previous focus on rhetorical or discursive (rather than "material") forms has led to his dismissal by those on both the academic left and right, but his consideration of these rhetorics and their histories is crucial to understanding how these antinomies work today. As his discussions of economic, cultural, and "spatial" capital demonstrate, the *word* "'capital'. . . compounds interests" (*OH,* 65), and this focus on the word is not misplaced if we recall the importance of language to national interests and to "materialism" itself. (Even) Valéry writes, "There is no market, no exchange without language; the first instrument of all trade is language" (*OH,* 125). National languages accumulate cultural value and are tools for the accumulation of economic capital; analogously, philosophy itself, the tool Valéry finds necessary for the accumulation of a national-Eurocentric spirit, is "marked" by the "national trait": "Nothing seems to define a certain race or nation better than the philosophy it has produced" (*OH,* 128). Valéry demonstrates how nationalism is a "philosopheme," something that, as Derrida writes, "*presents itself,* claims itself . . . in the name of a privilege in responsibility and in the memory of the universal and, thus, of the transnational—indeed of the trans-European—and finally of the transcendental" (*OH,* 47). Balibar approaches a similar problematic when he labels racism "a philosophy of history, or, more accurately, a *historiosophy*" that provides nationalism with a theory of historical regress and degeneracy (*RNC,* 55). Meanwhile, Jameson's *Geopolitical Aesthetic* is devoted to investigating the "ideologemes" that enable the cognitive mapping of the world system, those units of ideology that can "tak[e] on the finished appearance of a philosophical system on the one hand, or that of a cultural text on the other" (*PU,* 87).[24] Each of these formulations reveals nationalism's theoretical and discursive bases and forms. These cultures of nationalism are as important to consider as its material conditions—especially in the postmodern age, in which culture and market merge and the "pluralization of consumption" is transmitted through video images available to anyone with access to a TV.

The theories or philosophies of nationalism these writers critically examine are also enmeshed in the utopian dichotomy, as is their own discourse, through, as Derrida might argue (and as we have seen in Valéry), the "promise" of philosophy as a universal language. Derrida's own spirit of hope is expressed superficially in the title *L'autre cap,* which speaks not of capital's centralization or of nationalism's dispersals or of Europe's self-proclaimed missions but of something in another time and space: "outside Europe, but not to close off in advance a border to the future, to the to-come of the *event,* to that which *comes* . . . from a completely other shore" (*OH,* 69). He is thinking through "something that remains to be thought . . . that must have the structure of a promise—*and thus the memory of that which carries the future, the to-come, here and now*" (*OH,* 78). Elsewhere Derrida conveys this utopian temporality through the future perfect tense, the "will have been" that frames a memory in the future of a past event, which I would relate to Althusser's "determination in the last instance by the economic." For in an often neglected passage, Althusser writes that "[f]rom the first moment to the last, the lonely hour of the 'last instance' never comes," thereby promising access to an event—the ultimate determination by/of the economic, the access to the real of History that would signal the end of capital, and of the nation-state itself—seemingly endlessly deferred, but toward which we nonetheless strive.[25]

Pulling back somewhat from the final instance of this utopian fantasy, we know from Jameson's *Geopolitical Aesthetic* that the nation-state, despite international culture and "neotraditional images," continues its nonsynchronous existence, the paradoxes of which account for the appearance of endless deferral, the idea of multinational capital being too large for us to grasp without recourse to older spatial categories. This unknowable globalization lends the nation the cloak of having always already been here; hence the imagination of something other than it seems than necessity infinitely postponed. Jameson argues that with the apparent erasure of class differences within postmodern culture, geographic ones seem more workable: hence the viability of the nation long after the stake of multinational capital has been driven through its heart. As Derrida's *Other Heading* looks at Europe as a single example of intranational organization, Jameson takes us back to Wallerstein's theories of the world system, globe-trotting through world films to examine their nonsynchronous expressions of cultural and economic configurations.

The nonsynchronous is built into Jameson's definition of postmodernism, which is not some completely new stage but rather one marked by the approaching completion on a global scale of the earlier period, with modernism therefore looking like the cultural logic of globally incomplete modernization.[26] Economically, this nonsynchronism surfaces in what has been called uneven development, which is finally now evening out through the full proletarianization of national workforces. As wage labor has spread throughout the world, we would say that modernization has too (shifting back to Jameson's periodizing terms), though not at the same rate everywhere.

Cultural developments also proceed unevenly, though despite the teleological implications of "development," Jameson grants no special privileges or aesthetic priority to the First World. In aesthetic production Jameson finds "cognitive maps" of the world situation; films from different parts of the world are symptomatically slanted from their respective positions. By combining the perspectives from a range of the world's cultures, he achieves a larger sense of the totality of the world system than would otherwise be available. In "Third-World Literature in the Era of Multinational Capitalism," an essay that forms an important foundation to the readings of *The Geopolitical Aesthetic,* he points to one reason for this form of relational study: "A study of third-world culture necessarily entails a new view of ourselves, from the outside, insofar as we ourselves are (perhaps without fully knowing it) constitutive forces powerfully at work in our general world capitalist system."[27] Lying beneath the surface of this assertion is the connection of the world system with "ourselves," presumably First World intellectuals, whereas other worlds reveal avenues of thought otherwise blocked due to our position within the global system. Jameson's own utopian strain resides here in the sense that if there is a priority implied in uneven or nonsynchronous development, radical Second and Third World texts (and not all films from the Second or Third World merit this label, as the discussions in *The Geopolitical Aesthetic* of Andrei Tarkovsky and Zhou Xiaowen demonstrate) not only best map the present situation but also point to the way out. Here then, a faith can be felt that from Derrida's perspective seems "transcendental," yet for one who feels the pressures of (Sartrean) engaged criticism more directly, is all the more necessary.

Where Derrida searches for programs beyond "*Eurocentrism* and *anti-Eurocentrism*" (*OH*, 12–13), Jameson reveals strains of, if not Third Worldism, then anti–First Worldism.

Jameson avoids, however, a nostalgia for a lost past projected onto the space of the Third World by recognizing the permutations that late capitalism brings to the antinomy of universal and particular: "In the postmodern, the relations between the universal and the particular, if they persist at all, must be conceived in an utterly different way from those that obtained in previous social formations" (*GA*, 155). In a sense, then, the opposition between these two terms is deconstructed *not* through an analytical method but by the development of capitalism into a world system through which the "particular" or the "local" (in spatial terms) is not "traditionally" local but is already overdetermined by the world system, in which "even the center is marginalized" (*GA*, 155). As First World intellectuals have not yet gained a sense of their own global marginality, Third World artists and critics can demonstrate from the other side the permutations of the universal/particular antinomy. Whereas the cognitive maps of First World films are instructive in telling us where we have been, in other worlds we find lessons about where to go.[28]

However, the maps Jameson finds within these world texts are not directly accessible from *any* perspective. "[T]he world system is a being of such enormous complexity that it can only be mapped and modelled indirectly, by way of a simpler object that stands as its allegorical interpretant" (*GA*, 169). The temporal gap of the nonsynchronous leads to a formal one: the distance between the allegory and its meanings, through which the essentially literary quality of Jameson's readings comes through. This allegorical method brings us back to the relational problems of nation and world, nationalism and multinationalism, through a "kind of scanning that, moving back and forth across the text, readjusts its terms in constant modification." We should remember, though, that this modification is not distinct from the films' temporal features, for nonsynchronicity itself is often the subject of these films' allegories.[29]

In his reading of American films Jameson focuses on a few allegorical systems (or ideologemes): detective genres, war movies, and conspiracy films. Technology has a special place within all of these: "Information technology will become virtually the representational solution as well as the representational problem of this world system's cognitive mapping" (*GA*, 10). If "print" was the medium—according to Benedict Anderson—through which the nation "imagined" itself in the eighteenth century, then computers, video, and satellites are the technomedium of multinationalism, something perhaps even clearer in Wim Wenders's *Until the End of the World* (1991) than in the films Jameson discusses.[30] Wenders's film puts into aesthetic practice an apparently theoretical knowledge of the present world system (while projecting its story into the "near-future"[31]), whereas the films of the 1970s and 1980s that Jameson considers seem still to struggle with the shift from modernism to postmodernism; these struggles point directly to the conceptual difficulties of representing the capitalist world system and are manifest in the nonsynchronism of their allegories. For example, Jameson discusses the repeated use in Alan Pakula's *All the President's Men* of typewriters and telephones rather than the computer technology that had already transformed news production, arguing that these outdated technologies signify the just barely comprehended shifts in geopolitical space that accompany late capitalism.

Although the "national question" figures into Jameson's discussion of First World films, it does so as a lost referent, a collectivity whose absence is felt within the presence of something larger than itself can be intimated only through the conspiracy plot that heralds "the tendential end of 'civil society' in late capitalism" (*GA*, 48). Conspiracies are a "new kind of political narrative . . . which is more consistent with the dynamics of the world system than an older anthropomorphic or 'humanist' kind" (56). Pointing to the late 1970s–early 1980s "gang films" as representations of civil war, Jameson proposes an extension and modification of this thesis (which, however, he acknowledges omitting).[32] More contemporary films like Spike Lee's *Malcolm X* (1992) and, more pertinently and dramatically, John Singleton's *Boyz N the Hood* (1991) and the Hughes brothers' *Menace II Society* (1993), both set in Los Angeles (the United States' most Third World city), reveal from the other side the formation of new communities from within the complete breakdown of an American "civil society." These LA films demonstrate the desperate efforts to maintain a community whose overdetermined self-destruction was exponentially exacerbated during the twelve-year Reagan-Bush regime. A quite different reaction could be mapped in films about racist communities, such as Costa-Gavras's KKK love story *Betrayed* (1988) or Geoffrey Wright's *Romper Stomper* (1993), about Australian skinheads. These more recent films demonstrate the survival of certain forms of nationalism (the Nation of Islam, the revolutionary violence whose other side Sartre called "colonial neurosis,"[33] and national-front racism) within the cultures of postmodernism's most advanced stages, showing that the uneven development of this cultural dominant does not match the borders on conventional maps.

It is these kinds of "exceptions" that brought criticism to Jameson's theory of "national allegory"; nonetheless, I think his extensions here of that concept demonstrate its continued importance.[34] For, despite the accusations that his work erases the differences of various cultures by making a claim for a single interpretive framework, the readings of the second part of *The Geopolitical Aesthetic* demonstrate the range of aesthetic responses to the overdetermination of nationalism by the world system, and the ways the specificity of national culture establishes the parameters within which this world system is felt, thought, and thus represented. Jameson explores the conjunction of temporal, cultural, and national differences between the ways the First and the Second World would draw a "cognitive map" in his discussion of Soviet film—especially Alexander Sokurov's *Days of Eclipse* (1988), based on the Strugatsky brothers' novel *A Billion Years to the End of the World* (1976). In what might otherwise be dismissed as individual "style,"

Jameson finds formal indications of these differences: The use of black-and-white film mediated through colored filters indicates technological and economic nonsynchronicity as well as "a significant formal response to the image culture of postmodernism itself, in a situation in which the return to black-and-white photography is the impossible Utopia of the lost object of desire," that is, in part, the aesthetics of high modernism (*GA*, 97). Jameson argues that formal solutions such as this use of color attempt to resolve a number of conflicts produced by the uneven development of postmodernism, such as the technological ones between Soviet and heavily capitalized Hollywood productions, or those produced by "minor" national ethnic struggles against a hegemonic Russian nation-state. When formal problems confront those of narrative content, such as the protagonist's failure to achieve his goals, new layers of allegorical interpretation become possible, which themselves shift in reference to either the 1976 novel or the 1988 film. Where the novel allegorizes the Brezhnev bureaucracy's impedance of socialism, the film translation of a decade later faces a different (though more powerful) Other to socialism: the market capitalism that during the late 1980s was already transforming the cultural, political, and economic composition of the Soviet Union. For their ability to imagine the national situation from within socialism—even if this is an impeded or deferred socialism—films such as this one draw cognitive maps one couldn't find in the United States. Yet the sense throughout Jameson's chapter on Soviet film is that the hopefulness of this world situation is on the wane and that as the antisystem of the Second World has been reabsorbed by late capitalism, one must still look elsewhere, set a course for another heading, as Derrida might say, to reach a future project.

It is on this search, then, that Jameson turns to two very different Third World models of cognitive mapping, one from Taiwan and the other from the Philippines, nations that occupy very different spaces of the world system. Taiwan could be characterized as "a post-Third-World country that never really joins the First World (in the sense of capital export and of becoming a new center of the world system)" (*GA*, 145), a nebulous status the Philippines has not yet achieved. Edward Yang's *Terrorizer* (1986), then, can be read as "national allegory" in a number of ways. For example, Jameson finds that its protagonist, Li Li-chung, figures Taiwan's position within the world system; as petty bourgeois bureaucrat, living a kind of joyless, though not exactly uncomfortable, dependency on a "system," he represents "the new face of a dependency most often dramatized in terms of tendential impoverishment and the 'development of underdevelopment'" (*GA*, 146). This process works, Jameson argues, because the petty bourgeois are "emblematic of the fate of the nation . . . at least in the popular imagination." Once again, in a pattern familiar to Marxist cultural critics and historians, we see that the bourgeoisie, a *particular* class, generalizes, or *universalizes,* its interests and aspirations through the space of all classes of the national imagination, thus reproducing a model of ideological imperialism I previously considered in the connection of the First World nation to the rest of the world.

But if Yang's film critically allegorizes late capitalism's reconfigurations of global space (and also social class), Kidlat Tahimik's *The Perfumed Nightmare* is an affirmative project of cultural politics. If the Third World contains the last vestiges of some alternative to late capitalism, it can also demonstrate some radically other means of social organization—unless, Jameson notes, the West has wiped out any alternative besides "sterile" nationalism and fundamentalism, which themselves necessarily take postmodern form.[35] However, rather than seeing Kildat's film as some postmodern form of exoticism that glorifies in a fantasized total otherness, Jameson finds in it an alternative to capitalism *and* its conventional (and now defunct) antisystemic other. In this Third World film he finds a "third way" of cognitive mapping, an evocation of a space of human production that "does not know the structural oppression of the assembly line or Taylorization, which is permanently provisional, thereby liberating its subjects from the tyrannies of form and of the pre-programmed. In it aesthetics and production are again at one" (*GA*, 210). The "again" of this formulation *does* reveal a latent nostalgic rhetoric of a "return" to something before late capitalism, a nostalgia that could indeed merge with the Third Worldism Jameson rejects when he is more conscientious. But this "again" should also return us to our starting assumption that one feature of postmodernism is the complete commodification of culture. Jameson finds in *The Perfumed Nightmare* a very contemporary merger of these polarities (commodity/culture, aesthetics/production), but one that moves beyond those "pre-programmed" markets that have territorialized the world. With this movement beyond comes another return to the particularity or difference of antisystemic nationalism, a "cultural nationalism" that attempts to work not through the logics of exclusion and rejection but with those of strategic incorporation of up-to-date Western technology and culture in order to arrive at something indigenous. Jameson describes this "cultural-nationalist alternative" as "a politics which draws on indigenous cultural traditions in order to summon the force and will to dislodge the invader . . . here inscribed as an impulse rather than a program, as an aesthetics of revolt rather than its concrete politics . . . a message transmitted by the quality of the image, rather than its structural implications" (*GA*, 208). With this focus Jameson summons a vision of a specifically postmodern praxis, a melding of theory and practice based in media-politics, that works as a simulacrum of antisystemic nationalism in which the message is its medium, not the practice of nationalist exclusion. This praxis differs from "sterile" nationalism by targeting not a human Other, a scapegoat on whom the evils of completed modernization and globalization of culture are blamed, but instead late capitalism itself with its universalizing tendencies and homogenizing impulses.

If this sounds like "cultural politics" severed from its "material" forms, that's because still, despite ourselves, we think through the dichotomy of the ideal and the material that postmodernism itself has deconstructed. Jameson's argument that "cultural politics . . . must now—at least in the First World—be the primary space of struggle" (*GA*, 212) or that "cognitive mapping is the supreme remaining form of praxis" (*GA*, 58), is based in our present situation, in which reification itself, "new left" social movements, and class unite on the terrains of new antisystemic movements. This struggle in theory, this use of theory as a form of resistance, has an honorable history of its own, documented in Terry Eagleton's discussion of the ways radical theory develops during times when direct action is forestalled.[36] When the "new left" has not yet achieved social movements that keep up with the globalization of capital, then theoretical antisystemic movements that can at least cognitively map directions for knowledge and action are all the more important. Although not, perhaps, emphasizing the world-changing power of theoretical interpretation as much as Jameson, Derrida reminds us that in what is popularly called the age of information, the production of information will have effects: "Paradoxically, what is called theoretical discourse has, I would say, no more 'influence,' but is more directly in contact with decision-making instances—it is both more permeable and more penetrating. It communicates along new, more diversified, more overdetermined trajectories with the 'general' discourse of society."[37]

These debates over the politics of theory, culture, and the "aesthetics of revolt" are grounded in postmodernity, though we should remember that not all postmodernism is alike. Far from signaling the end of metanarrative, postmodernism brings us a multiplicity of world, or global, stories whose medium of the image and the TV has still more centralizing power than print, even as it draws from information bureaus in numerous world capitals.[38] This debate over the presence of meta- and micronarratives is itself somewhat outmoded for its reliance—like that of the new texts on nationalism—on analytical methods that are recognizably literary or textually based. Though this is less the case with Wallerstein, we saw the connection between his constructed peoplehood and Balibar's fictive ethnicity. With Derrida's readings of the texts of philosophy and the state, and with Jameson's allegorical cartography, however, we are firmly on literary grounds. The presence of these textual methodologies exemplifies the ways recent theories of nationalism are less positivistic than their predecessors, though they also hint at the ways nationalism's new ambiguities are themselves produced by the conceptual strategies that describe them. So here again we see evidence of the postmodern, in a blurring of the lines between aesthetic acts and political ones but also in a nonsynchronism within these theories, which employ methods of analysis grounded in the texts of print culture to discuss phenomena whose globalization is enabled by the electronification and image-culture that present those very problems of space and social form that nationalism today attempts to resolve. In light of this dilemma, Derrida's call for a "telemetatheoretical" analysis (*OH*, 109) is more than just neologistic word play. Caught in their own nonsynchronicity, these new theories revise the grand nineteenth-century narratives of capitalism and nationalism by introducing new characters or historical agents. As is the individual character of realistic narrative, nationalism is already "outmoded," yet these categories of nation and character (or agency) "still exist" (*GA*, 176), as does capital itself, though as all these texts make clear, in mutated and still mutating forms. Yet these analyses also show that the capitalist world economy is approaching that point at which "a slight push can lead to a very large deviation" (*RNC*, 231). The need to imagine new world systems, or the necessity for "thinking differently or thinking at last what is announced here in the enigmatic form of the 'possible'" (*OH*, 46), is now all the more important.

NOTES

I am grateful to Katie Hauser for our many discussions about "late nationalism" and for her comments on earlier drafts of this chapter.

1. See "Fortress Asia?" *Economist* 325 (October 24, 1992):35–36; and "The Global Firm: R.I.P.," *Economist* 326 (February 6, 1993):69. On the economic "threats" of nationalism in Asia also see Robert A. Scalapino, "The United States and Asia: Future Prospects," *Foreign Affairs* 70 (1991–1992):19–40.

2. Larry Reynolds, "The Future of International Economic Policy," *Management Review* 82 (March 1993):30–32; Lynn Stongin Dodds, "Merger in a Cold Climate," *International Management* 47 (May 1992):62–65; Cyndee Miller, "Nationalism Endangers Smooth Transition to Unified EC Market," *Marketing News* 26 (February 17, 1992):1, 10.

3. Constantine S. Nicandros, "The World Oil Industry: Challenges of the New Century," *Executive Speeches* 6 (April 1992):14–19, and *Executive Speeches* 7 (October/November 1992):18–22; Edward L. Morse, "The Coming Oil Revolution," *Foreign Affairs* 69 (Winter 1990/1991):35–56; James Alexander, "Africa: Still Getting There Slowly," *Banker* 141 (December 1991):54–56, 58–63, and "Latin America: The Key to a Successful Global Strategy," *Executive Briefing* (February 1989):5, 8–9; Bruce C.P. Rayner, "A New Global Economic Order to Come of Age in the '90s," *Electronic Business* 15 (December 11, 1989):16–19; Khalil F. Matta and Naji E. Boutros, "Barriers to Electronic Mail Systems in Developing Countries," *Information Society* 6 (1989): 59–68.

4. Immanuel Wallerstein, Giovanni Arrighi, and Terence K. Hopkins, *Antisystemic Movements* (London: Verso, 1989). Further text citations are given with the abbreviation *AM*.

5. Recent books on nationalism from American and British presses (though their authors are more "international") include Aijaz Ahmad, *In Theory: Classes, Nations, Literatures* (London: Verso, 1992); Etienne Balibar and Immanuel Wallerstein, *Race, Nation, Class: Ambiguous Identities* (London: Verso, 1991) (further text citations are given with the abbreviation *RNC*); Homi K. Bhabha, ed., *Nation and Narration* (London: Routledge, 1990); Liah Greenfeld, *Nationalism: Five Roads to Modernity* (Cambridge: Harvard University Press, 1992); Harry Goulbourne, *Ethnicity and Nationalism in Post-Imperial Britain* (Cambridge: Cambridge University Press, 1991); E. J. Hobsbawm, *Nations and Nationalism Since 1780* (Cambridge: Cambridge University Press, 1990); James Mayall, *Nationalism and International Society* (Cambridge: Cambridge University Press, 1990); Dawa Norbu, *Culture and the Politics of Third World Nationalism* (London: Routledge, 1992); Andrew Parker, Mary Russo, Doris Sommer, and Patricia Yaeger, eds., *Nationalisms and Sexualities* (New York: Routledge, 1992); Louis L. Snyder, *Contemporary Nationalisms: Persistence in Case Studies* (Malabar, Fla.: Krieger, 1992); Michael Watson, ed., *Contemporary Minority*

Nationalism (London: Routledge, 1990). Including recent studies more specifically on literature and nationalism would extend this list significantly. Two somewhat less recent but still influential books are Benedict Anderson, *Imagined Communities: Reflections on the Origin and Spread of Nationalism* (London: Verso, 1983, 1991); and Partha Chatterjee, *Nationalist Thought and the Colonial World: A Derivative Discourse* (London: Zed Books, 1986, and New Delhi: Oxford University Press, 1986).

Recent journal special issues on nationalism include "Theorizing Nationality, Sexuality and Race," *Genders* 10 (1991); "Britishness and Europeanness: Who Are the British Anyway?" *Journal of British Studies* 31, 4 (1992); "History, the Nation and the Schools," *History Workshop* 29–30 (1990); *Journal of Contemporary History* 26, 3–4 (1991); and *Feminist Review* 44 (1993).

6. These features are drawn from Stalin's famous definition of nationalism. See Joseph Stalin, *Marxism and the National Question* (Moscow: Foreign Languages Publishing, 1954).

7. Jacques Derrida, *The Other Heading: Reflections on Today's Europe,* trans. Pascale-Anne Brault and Michael B. Naas (Bloomington: Indiana University Press, 1992). Further text citations are given with the abbreviation *OH.*

8. Fredric Jameson, *The Geopolitical Aesthetic: Cinema and Space in the World System* (Bloomington: Indiana University Press, and London: British Film Institute, 1992). Further text citations are given with the abbreviation *GA.*

9. There are also less "world historical" connections among these authors: Jacques Derrida marks his growing closeness to "Balibar's discourse" in "Politics and Friendship: An Interview with Jacques Derrida," in *The Althusserian Legacy,* ed. E. Ann Kaplan and Michael Sprinker (London: Verso, 1993), 204. Though Wallerstein is not mentioned in *The Geopolitical Aesthetic,* the book's long title demonstrates its debt to the author of *The Modern World System* and *Geopolitics and Geoculture;* in an earlier essay Jameson discusses Wallerstein's theory of "antisystemic movements"; see "Conversations on the New World Order," in *After the Fall: The Failure of Communism and the Future of Socialism,* ed. Robin Blackburn (London: Verso, 1991), 255–268.

10. Louis Althusser, "Contradiction and Overdetermination," in *For Marx,* trans. Ben Brewster (London: Verso, 1969, 1990), 87–128.

11. Ibid., 106.

12. "What is a '*survival*'? What is its theoretical status? Is it essentially social or 'psychological'? Can it be reduced to the survival of certain economic *structures. . .* ? Or does it refer as much to *other structures,* political, ideological, structures, etc.: *customs, habits,* even '*traditions*' such as the '*national tradition*' with its specific traits? . . . How, then, are we *to think these survivals?. . .* Surely with *the overdetermination of any contradiction and of any constitutive element of a society. . .* " (ibid., 114–115).

13. As Balibar notes, overdetermination and indeterminacy are not interchangeable terms; see Balibar and Wallerstein, *Race, Nation, Class,* 181. Bloch discusses nonsynchronism, or "unsurmounted remnants of older economic being and consciousness," in "Nonsynchronism and the Obligation to Its Dialectics," *New German Critique* 11 (1977):22–38.

14. Here, Ernest Gellner's connection of the rise of nationalism to that of modernism, by which he means industrialization, rings true. See Gellner, *Nations and Nationalism* (Oxford: Basil Blackwell, 1983). On the connections between the rise of nationalism and the development of capitalism through both its mercantile and industrial stages, see Samir Amin, *Class and Nation: Historically and in the Current Crisis,* trans. Susan Kaplow (New

York: Monthly Review Press, 1980), 1–35; Wallerstein touches on this history in *Historical Capitalism* (London: Verso, 1983), 51.

15. Raymond Williams's ideas of heterogeneous temporality in his discussion of residual, dominant, and emerging cultures provide a different angle on this process of cultural deferral. Williams's concept of periodization allows room for exceptional cultural elements at any given moment; a dominant or hegemonic culture contains traces of that culture's history as well as newly incorporated social practices. See Raymond Williams, "Base and Superstructure in Marxist Cultural Theory," *New Left Review* 82 (1973):3–16. Homi K. Bhabha's "DissemiNation: Time, Narrative, and the Margins of the Modern Nation," in *Nation and Narration,* 291–322, discusses Williams's ideas in a similar context, though he leaves to the side the fact that Williams articulates this model within his essay on the base/superstructure model, where he directly addresses the relationships between "economic" and "cultural" formations. The ways the nation seems to point backward in time has economic, as well as cultural and ideological, implications.

16. Though less directly concerned with its economic codeterminations, Slavoj Žižek has recently provided an original psychoanalytic theory of nationalism that adds a great deal to an understanding of its "subjective" features. See especially "Eastern Europe's Republics of Gilead," *New Left Review* 183 (1990):50–62; and "Formal Democracy and Its Discontents," *American Imago* 48 (1991):181–198. At the same time, specific case studies have demonstrated the persistence of these economic determinations. Two recent discussions of nationalism in the former Yugoslavia bear out my point. Mary Kaldor writes in "Yugoslavia and the New Nationalism," *New Left Review* 197 (1993), that "new nationalism is not just a grab for power. It is also a grab for wealth. . . . Control of territory means the takeover of property, the capture of hostages who can be exchanged for food, weapons, money and other hostages, access, by force, to other sources of income" (110). In "Beat the Devil," *The Nation* 256 (May 31, 1993), Alexander Cockburn points to other factors: "The great accelerator of the breakup of Yugoslavia and the erosion of civil relations was the shock therapy prescribed by the I.M.F. In 1986 the dinar was worth $22. By 1989 it had been devalued 200 times, to 11 cents. No social fabric can take such a beating" (727).

17. In *Imagined Communities* (1983) Benedict Anderson commented on nationalism's "philosophical poverty and even incoherence" (5). Balibar directly addresses this observation in Balibar and Wallerstein, *Race, Nation, Class,* 65 n. 24.

18. The essays collected in E. P. Thompson's *Customs in Common* (New York: New Press, 1992) lend historical weight to this theoretical claim about the radical side of "tradition."

19. Fredric Jameson, *The Political Unconscious: Narrative as a Socially Symbolic Act* (Ithaca: Cornell University Press, 1981), 298. Further text citations are given with the abbreviation *PU.*

20. See Louis Althusser and Etienne Balibar, *Reading Capital,* trans. Ben Brewster (London: Verso, 1970, 1979), 186–187.

21. See Ernest Renan, "What Is a nation?" (1882), trans. Martin Thom, in Bhabha, *Nation and Narration,* 8–22.

22. This fictive quality of ethnicity or peoplehood is a recurrent theme of Balibar and Wallerstein's *Race, Nation, Class.* For Balibar's discussions, see, for example, 49, 93–100; Wallerstein explores it most fully in his essay "The Construction of Peoplehood: Racism, Nationalism, Ethnicity," 71–85. Eric Hobsbawm's notion of "invented tradition" has much in common with this feature of "peoplehood." See Hobsbawm and Terence Ranger, eds.,

The Invention of Tradition (Cambridge: Cambridge University Press, 1983). Jameson's term "neoethnicity" is related to this fiction of identity; see Fredric Jameson, *Postmodernism or the Cultural Logic of Late Capitalism,* (Durham: Duke University Press, 1991)341–342, 346–347; and Jameson, *The Geopolitical Aesthetic,* 117.

23. Jacques Derrida, "Structure, Sign, and Play in the Discourse of the Human Sciences," in *Writing and Difference,* trans. Alan Bass (Chicago: University of Chicago Press, 1978): 278–293.

24. Jameson, following Greimas's discussion of the "seme" as the smallest unit of semantic meaning, defines "ideologeme" as "the smallest intelligible unit of the essentially antagonistic collective discourses of social classes" (*The Political Unconscious,* 76). This formation can "manifest itself either as a pseudoidea—a conceptual or belief system, an abstract value, an opinion or prejudice—or as a protonarrative, a kind of ultimate class fantasy about the 'collective characters' which are the classes in opposition" (87). "Ideologemes" are invoked by name only once in his *Geopolitical Aesthetic* (22), though the concept could be read back through all of the analyses the book accomplishes.

25. Althusser, "Contradiction and Overdetermination," 113.

26. See *Postmodernism,* 307–310, 366.

27. Fredric Jameson, "Third-World Literature in the Era of Multinational Capitalism," *Social Text* 15 (1986), 68.

28. Jameson's focus on these "lessons" draws from discussions of the importance of the much-maligned didactic or pedagogic function of art; see *Postmodernism,* 50; and *The Geopolitical Aesthetic,* 188, 193.

29. Jameson discusses postmodern allegorical reading in *Postmodernism,* 167–168.

30. *Until the End of the World*'s characters effortlessly cross national borders that are just as easily permeated by multinational information systems and electronic capital; the technology that makes these transfers possible becomes itself a "star" of the film and is fetishized both through the glossy beauty of the movie itself (partly enabled by, as the closing credits advertise, SONY's cutting-edge videotape and monitors) and in the ways technology makes possible new intersubjective networks for the transfer of vision from one perception system to another (this transfer is not just of images but of the ways images are perceived by the brain). This technology is the target of a double-chase, by both a vague U.S. federal intelligence–corporate conspiracy and a bounty-hunting Raymond Chandleresque detective. The vision-recorder also inspires in its users an addiction to the images of their own dreams that can be overcome only through a nonsynchronous return to print culture in the form of a novel apparently based on the movie itself. This mixture of genres, or mediums, is foreshadowed in earlier scenes when David Byrne's lively singing head provides a music-video contrast to the crashed party to which it is broadcast and when a tape identified as the singing of Pygmy children lulls the female protagonist to sleep. Jameson's frequently cited "Hansen-Bordwell hypothesis" would argue that the inclusion of these other mediums within film can only reverify the cinema's formal superiority (see 62, 76, 140). However, in addition to this formal issue, the latter of these scenes indicates the global system in another way, by introducing the Third World that will later figure more importantly through the Aborigines whose "wisdom" and "mystical affinity with nature" stand in stark contrast to the technology that has completely seduced the film's First Worlders. *Until the End of the World* employs each *analogon* Jameson discusses as symptomatic of First World attempts to map late capitalism. It also includes some of the latest antisystemic movements, for its open-

ing frame of nuclear panic and its closing one of a space station that monitors oceanic pollution evoke two distinctly intranational political tendencies—the nuclear and environmental movements—though their co-optation within the film demonstrates the dialectical relationship of system and antisystem. All of these features, in addition to its multinational producers and international cast, mark the film as a distinctly global production as a text constructed within the "geopolitical aesthetic."

31. And here, just as he is with Tahimik Kidlat's *The Perfumed Nightmare,* Jameson could be pleased at finding his theory of cognitive mapping "validated by conscious artistic production," though I suspect Wenders is glorifying in the present "geotopical cartographies" rather than "inventing" new ones (see *GA,* 189).

32. See *GA,* 83 n. 15.

33. See Jean-Paul Sartre, preface to Frantz Fanon's *The Wretched of the Earth* (1961), trans. Constance Farrington (New York: Grove Weidenfeld, 1991).

34. For these criticisms, see Aijaz Ahmad, "Jameson's Rhetoric of Otherness and the 'National Allegory,'" *Social Text* 17 (1987):3–25, reprinted in Ahmad, *In Theory: Classes, Nations, Literatures* (London and New York: Verso, 1992); Jean Franco, "The Nation as Imagined Community," in *The New Historicism.* ed. H. Aram Veeser (New York and London: Routledge, 1989), 204–212. See Fredric Jameson, "A Brief Response," *Social Text* 17, 26–27. For a different response, see Henry Schwarz, "Provocations Toward a Theory of Third World Literature," *Mississippi Review* 49–50 (1989):177–201.

35. On "sterile passions of nationalism and religious fundamentalism" see Jameson, *The Geopolitical Aesthetic,* 188. See also the same volume, 116–117, for related discussion and (as Jameson notes) *Postmodernism,* 386–391.

36. Terry Eagleton, *Walter Benjamin, or, Towards a Revolutionary Criticism* (London: Verso, 1981), 81–100.

37. Derrida, "Politics and Friendship," 229–230.

38. The argument that postmodernism signals the end of explanatory metanarratives is Jean-François Lyotard's, first articulated in *The Postmodern Condition: A Report on Knowledge,* trans. Geoff Bennington and Brian Massumi (Minneapolis: University of Minnesota Press, 1984) and more recently explicitly linked to an anti-Marxist criticism in "The Wall, the Gulf, and the Sun: A Fable," in *Politics, Theory, and Contemporary Culture,* ed. Mark Poster (New York: Columbia University Press, 1993), 261–275. In his introduction, 1–13, Poster accepts and echoes this "post-Marxist" argument. But in Derrida's recent writings, too, we find these permutations; *The Other Heading* weaves its analysis between a critique of the anti-Marxism now prevalent in Europe and one of Marxism; "Politics and Friendship" similarly attempts to negotiate these two positions, though Derrida responds to an attempt to reimagine history with the statement that "I'm still too Marxist to think that" (229) In support of this last statement, see Jacques Derrida, *Spectres of Marx: The State of the Debt, the Work of Mourning, and the New International,* trans. Peggy Kamuf (New York: Routledge, 1994); this text appeared too late for me to consider it here..

4

Cultural Studies and Civil Society

GEORGE YÚDICE

If there is any hope that modernization will prevail over decadence and that States will be reformed to promote the public interest, we'll find that hope in civil society. The little that has been accomplished recently in the prioritary task of mitigating the fatal effects of the neoliberal program and of questioning the absolutism of the market, has come from civil society. But, who can say what should be understood by civil society today?[1]

WHO CAN SAY what should be understood by civil society today? This question was addressed tacitly and explicitly by the participants in the First Meeting of the Inter-American Cultural Studies Network in Mexico in May 1993. Officially founded at this meeting, the network gathered over sixty representatives from a dozen countries in the Americas with the purpose of promoting comparative and collaborative research. Participants were particularly interested in offering alternative perspectives to the emerging transdiscipline of cultural studies, which to date has been dominated by British and U.S. scholars.[2] Despite the diversity of topics discussed at this meeting, the focus of interest and debate turned on the problems confronting projects to strengthen civil society, particularly in the wake of the epochal changes that took place in the 1980s and early 1990s: the consolidation of a neoliberal political economy, the withdrawal of the state from the public sector, the rise of new group politics based on identity, and the permeation of the entirety of public space by the mass media.

Cultural studies must deal with this challenge to (re)construct civil society, in particular the contending public spheres in which cultural practices are channeled and evaluated. Civil society is, following Gramsci, the ensemble of symbolic practices by means of which a discursive consensus is struck among the diverse sectors that constitute the socius and through which an image of the totality of that socius is projected. If civil society, however, entails such a totality, how can it be conceived today when all societies are undergoing powerful deterritorialization processes? Since the 1970s this understanding of culture—and the social image that emerges from it—has been undergoing a crisis not only in those countries coming apart after the demise of communism, as in Eastern Europe, but all around the world, as much in the economic "center" as in the "peripheries." Whether these disarticulation (and rearticulation?) processes are characterized as "fragmentation" (Beatriz Sarlo) or "democratization of differences" (Nelly Richard), they correspond, among other things, to new globalizing forces of post-Fordist "flexible accumulation" (David Harvey) or "disorganized capital" (Scott Lash and John Urry) with their attendant delegitimation of the metaphysics of work on which both capitalism and Marxism are based;[3] the dissemination of mass media and their leveling effect on morally and aesthetically sanctioned values and authority; back and forth migrations that produce transformation and often hybridization of (national, political, and group) identities; new technologies of symbolic production that prioritize information over knowledge and the consumption of images over critical thinking. All of these factors result in a "disingenuous reception of signs" that, according to Nelly Richard, "certifies the value" that also rests on (metropolitan) power.[4]

The very fact of the emergence of cultural studies is implicated in this new conjuncture. Cultural studies pretends to account for this process of disarticulation and rearticulation (the "decentering of the centers," in Richard's words) from every possible perspective and according to an omnivalorizing transdisciplinarity, nevertheless remaining as the privileged site of deterritorialization. Cultural studies, of course, takes interest in the crises of national identities unleashed by globalization processes throughout the world and according to new paths of influence between West and East, North and South, but the asymmetry of what traditionally has been characterized as imperialism continues to inflect these new but still unequal paths of influence between "center" and "periphery." Cultural studies, as it has been institutionalized, may have been born in England under the impulse to valorize and legitimize popular culture (e.g., in the work of Richard Hoggart, E. P. Thompson, and Raymond Williams), but political solidarity with the working class has been displaced, especially in the United States, as the focus of interest has shifted to the mass media, consumer capitalism, and identity politics. Today this latter image of cultural studies is quickly disseminating itself around the world like the Cocacolization ("Americanization" in Ben Wattenberg's enthusiastic endorsement) of yesteryear. The only difference is that cultural studies is extending its global reach according to a "marginocentric" logic, that is, extracting academic value from all that can be taken to be "marginal" (hence the fad of making use of such labels and phrases as "marginality," "in the margins," "crossing borders," and so on in the titles of many books and essays in cultural studies).

Intellectuals from Latin America and other "peripheral" societies have become suspicious of a center that seeks to decenter itself only to relegitimize itself in a globalizing context that focuses on alterity, marginality, subalternity. But this decentering is, of course, effected in the center's own knowledge-producing institutions and with the participation of postcolonial intellectuals, who are critical but amenable to wearing the mantle of marginality. In other words, metropolitan cultural studies demonstrates a will to peripherality precisely when it yields cultural and institutional capital. In the best of cases, it appropriates perspectives from the South, but only to maintain its own position in the intellectual vanguard. According to Richard,

> The much invoked "nomadism" of a dispersed and ramified (delocalized) power does not mean that the marks of inequality have been erased from the surface of the postcolonial map. . . . The international circuit of control and influence administers the "symbolic capital" of metropolitan theory, valorizing those discourses that enjoy the academic and institutional accreditation that comes with an *authorized* link to the chain of "universities, journals, institutes, exhibitions, book series" that provides the staying power and meaning of current debates, giving them greater density and influence.[5]

The critique of the co-optative potential of metropolitan cultural studies has to do fundamentally with the problem of civil society, accentuating the imperative that students of national public spheres recognize the fact that today all public discourse is traversed by transnational messages and transactions and forms of local reception that resignify, if not resist, those messages. I leave the discussion of the dangers of colonization by discourses of diversity built into metropolitan cultural studies (e.g., multiculturalism as it is constructed in the United States) for the conclusion.

In her commentary on the papers by Jesús Martín-Barbero and Rosa María Alfaro on the role of the media in the crisis of civil society in Colombia and Peru, Jean Franco proposed examining public spaces rather than the dominant, public spheres, which is the traditional approach. According to her, the notion of public space does not have the idealizing drawback of the public sphere because, unlike the latter,[6] its existence and operationality do not depend upon autonomy from the state and the economy. Consequently, as is discussed further on, social negotiations in public take on a more tactical character than the rational debate attributed to the ideal bourgeois public sphere. This sphere has been defined, from Kant to Habermas, as the forum in which civil society (i.e., the institutionalized terrain of the lifeworld) submits ideas and opinions to critical discussion for the conduct of social life.[7] The concept of public space does not presuppose this autonomy, which has proved to be illusory not only in "peripheral" or "developing" countries but also in the "developed" democracies of the "center."

Perhaps the best example of this lack of autonomy (and concomitant lack of critique) is found in the mass media, discussed by many of the participants at our meeting. The media, most argued, are traversed—perhaps irremediably—by the logic of the market and by political interests. For Jean Franco, however, this lack of autonomy does not invalidate the examination of public spaces in order to detect zones of action that offer possibilites of unanticipated participation by subordinated groups. On the contrary, the mode of imbrication of public space with these interests offers a perspective for understanding how claims and demands are negotiated by diverse groups or social sectors (women, ethnic and racial minorities, youth, etc.) that use or move though this space. It is in the appropriation of public spaces, for example, that it becomes possible for these groups to satisfy needs and demands that were not foreseen in the construction of these spaces. One of Franco's examples is that of shopping malls that serve more than just the interests of shopkeepers; they are also used as meeting places by youths for unprogrammed activities.

Franco does not, however, offer this case as an example of a space of critical discussion, as in the public sphere idealized by Habermas. For Franco there are no uncompromised or disinterested public spaces that might serve the general good of the collectivity. All spaces are traversed by interests, and their political potential resides in the ways in which they are open to use or are forced to open up to practices that were not programmed. There are resonances in this notion of the appropriative *perruque* that Michel de Certeau attributes to subordinated individuals and groups who destabilize imposed systems of conduct through their subversive and nomadic reception.[8] There is no guarantee, however, that the "subversion of the system" as a strategy or tactic will open civil society toward greater democracy. It is just as probable that a space can be "poached" by narcotraffickers or reactionary vigilantes as by subaltern youths who seek to satisfy their erotic drives and their will to style.[9] What is important about these spaces is that in them, as in the coffee house discussions cited by Habermas, are laid the bases for constituting the identities of social groups. It is incumbent on intellectuals and critics, then, to come to understand how these phenomena are produced and not disdain them because they do not conform to an idealized critical discourse thought to be necessary for the conduct of society.

This is the task that Jesús Martín-Barbero takes on in the realm of the media, particularly in relation to urban youth cultures. Martín-Barbero's paper touched on many important issues, but for the purposes of this chapter I would like to limit discussion to what it contributes to the debates on civil society and public spheres. In the first place, Martín-Barbero advocates going beyond the limiting ideological and theoretical positions that presented "the relations and conflicts between culture industries and popular cultures as external to each other or simply as a question of resistance."[10] If we can get beyond this Manichean dichotomy, it becomes possible to "rethink the relations between culture and politics, . . . to connect cultural politics to the transformations in political culture, particularly in relation to the latter's communicational implications, that is, to the weave of interrelations that social actors constitute" and thus to think of mass communications not as a "mere problem of markets and consumption" but rather as the "decisive space in which it is possible to redefine the *public* and to construct democracy."[11] It is precisely in this endeavor that "Cultural Studies and media studies speak to each other."

Situating his media analysis in the context of postmodernity and transnationalization, Martín-Barbero emphasizes two results—one "positive" and the other "negative"—of the fragmentations, decenterings, heterogenizations, and hybridizations brought about by them. On the one hand, insofar as the "traditional spaces of collective gathering are disarticulated, [which] de-urbanizes everyday life and makes the city less likely to be used," the audiovisual media, especially television, become "the means to return the city to us, to relocate us in it," in its "imaginary territories."[12] On the other hand, this public space can have a "phantasmatic" character, to use Walter Lippmann's phrase,[13] since "the technological space of communication has become decisive in the design and reorganization of societies [here Martín-Barbero is referring to the integration of Latin American countries on the basis of market rather than cultural relations] from which the State withdraws, leaving without foundation and without meaning what until a few years ago we understood as public space and public service."[14] The irony is that the integration of Latin America is being achieved through the creation of "phantom" or "neutral publics."

The reconfiguration of civil society in today's era of electronic reproduction is like a double-edged blade; it cuts two ways. On the one hand, it opens up space, but on the other, it produces phantasmatic knowledge. The task of cultural studies should be to help think through how to endow these spaces with a truly democratic character. Perhaps due to a lack of presentations dealing with the new social movements, few proposals for rebuilding civil society were optimistic. At best there was the appropriative perspective offered by Martín-Barbero. There were many criticisms of the penetration of public space by the media, echoing Adorno's position on mass culture. Beatriz Sarlo, for example, without going so far as to reject the possibility that certain culture industries (particularly cinema) can still offer a culture of critique, nevertheless opined that the new electronic technologies (especially video games) do not provide the necessary distance for developing critical thinking, particularly when these technologies and practices are subordinate to a market rationality. In contrast to the literary text (she gave the example of the epic ballad *Martín Fierro*), which produces this distancing by means of its literary autonomy, or "its own laws of speed [of reading] and semanticity," the video game produces, in the best of cases, skills of "velocity and contact with surfaces."[15] For Sarlo, the "acquisition of elementary skills in non-mass-mediated discourses poses the requirement of a *slower* temporality and consequently a more continuous attention to messages that do not tend to repetition but to difference. Read with the skills produced by audiovisual culture, these discourses appear semantically impoverished because the information that they yield requires more time to be read and digested."[16]

But even if audiovisual culture could provide critical skills (as some of the other participants who were in disagreement with Sarlo argued), she points to other problems that have to do with limits to participation and access to these technologies. On the one hand, there is no possibility in Latin America for a widespread skilling in audiovisual culture because there is an enormous lack of resources. It would be nearly impossible to equip schools with computers. And even if this were not impossible, there would still be the "need for a strong symbolic intervention, one which is not based on spontaneity." On the other hand, audiovisual culture is characterized by a gender asymmetry, since electronic equipment, video games for example, are used mostly by boys and men. (This observation was also refuted by technophile Alejandro Piscitelli of the Latin American Council of Social Science [Consejo Latinoamericano de Ciencias Sociales, or CLACSO][17] and several other participants.) Consequently, skilling in these practices does not have a universal applicability and does not advance the democratization of society. In sum, there is no justification for a "communcational optimism," as far as Sarlo is concerned, particuarly nowadays when the state is withdrawing from public life, leaving the production and circulation of audiovisual culture to market forces. Thus, the true organizers of public space appear to be the "managers of the privatized culture industry" and not public institutions; hence the need to support politically the intervention of the state in the construction of a public sphere. One possible criticism of Sarlo's position is that she has substituted a political for a communicational optimism, entrusting to the state (which to all appearances continues to be as corrupt as ever in countries such as Argentina, Brazil, and Mexico, to mention just the largest ones) the unlikely outcome of a disinterested and critical culture.

Sarlo was not alone in her skepticism toward "communicational optimism"; Teixeira Coelho went further and expressed an overwhelming pessimism about the possibilities of constructing civil society. He took as his motto a widespread attitude in contemporary Brazilian culture that does not augur well for mitigating the corruptness of politicians and the market-driven rationality of the media: "I'm not here to explain but to confuse."[18] Modernity, says Teixeira Coelho, has not brought enlightenment of any kind. On the contrary, modern politics and the culture industries have produced something worse than a phantasmatic public sphere: a "culture against the people." The cultural field has not offered any effective forms of resistance, especially if we focus on literary works that say nothing to illiterate or barely literate masses or television programs aimed at markets and not people. "In this context . . . encouraging research that seeks to detect what the cultural imaginary has to offer is a sheer waste of time and funds." Instead, Teixeira Coelho recommends that cultural studies contribute to the transformation of the cultural field: "More urgent [than research] are frequent and intense meetings with groups of intellectuals and activists inside and outside the university to turn the question [of cultural resistance] on its head, into a program to fight the inertia [of institutional structures] and to motivate the search for viable cultural options for the social moment in which we are living."[19]

Without necessarily endorsing a "communicational optimism," some of the participants rejected Teixeira Coelho's position, for it was not evident where the inspiration and energy to transform the cultural field would come from, particularly if, as Teixeira Coelho alleged, it was permeated by cynicism and a lack of interest in the majorities. Others defended the good intentions of most Brazilian (and, by extension, Latin American) intellectuals and academics, holding weak institutional supports accountable for their relative ineffectiveness. Still others preferred to shift the ground of discussion to the "organic" intellectuals and activists of the grassroots movements, including alternative media projects. Agustín Lao, in his critique of Jesús Martín-Barbero's and Rosa María Alfaro's presentations, asked why such alternative projects, particularly those of indigenous communities, were not mentioned. For Lao these movements constitute contestatory public spheres that require recognition and validation by society if they are to be effective. It is up to intellectuals and academics, then, to collaborate in their legitimation. Without dismissing the importance of these efforts in alternative media, Alfaro attempted to explain the complexity involved in putting them into operation. She illustrated this complexity with an example from her own participation in an alternative media project within her own institution, the Asociación de Comunicadores Sociales "Calandria." Researchers from "Calandria" showed an antifeminist film to a women's group in a poor neighborhood in Lima. The film told the story of a nun who was raped, the nun's pursuit of the rapist, his repentance, and the resolution of the conflict in the "happy ending" of their marriage. To the surprise of the researchers, who expected a critique of the film by the women's consciousness-raising group, most of the women liked the story. Alfaro's conclusion is that alternative media projects that seek to "emancipate" popular groups from colonization by the media have to deal with a complex situation in which tastes, for example, are already informed, at least in part, by the media. In this particular case, it became evident that political demands do not line up in any strict fashion with the affective constitution of a public. Any interpellation of a group must work through a complex stratification—on the one hand, of desires and pleasures inscribed by traditional narratives (especially as they are taken up by the new media) that reproduce unequal relations of power and, on the other, of political demands that presuppose an ideological break with those affective structures. Even in the case of an "optimistic" alternative media project, then, there are obstacles to the formation of effective counterhegemonic strategies.

The foregoing critique of one alternative media project does not mean, of course, that it is impossible for cultural studies to work more effectively toward a "culture on behalf of the people." It must recognize, to this end, that the "people" are traversed by various and often contradictory concerns. Taking as a point of departure the premise that "the media are cultural and political mediations not only in the discursive field but also in the realm of knowledges and kinds of dialogue and interaction among social actors," Alfaro mentioned various institutions of civil society that do not simply accommodate to the "construction of consensus and solicitation of support for political interests."[20] Institutions such as "Calandria," in which Alfaro works, analyze the ways in which the media disseminate "disorienting signs," particularly the news programs and those that involve the "participation of the people" (or "publics," in their consumerist definition). They seek to understand "the conducts, strategies and use of the media on the part of politicians, focusing on the success and failure of these strategies." The objective is to contribute to the critical examination of the media in the context of civil society, to "reform university curricula and forums of discussion in a way that the academy can engage the media and politicians, to contribute to the development of our countries and their troubled democratic processes."[21]

We might respond with Teixeira Coelho's warning about the effectivity of research and ask if there might not be another kind of intervention, something more in line with what the Mexican anthropologist Guillermo Bonfil Batalla proposed in his last essays: to redefine the researcher as a collaborator in the projects of subaltern communities. Bonfil proposed this collaboration as a needed retooling for social scientists who were seeing their traditional functions disappear not only because of the paradigm crisis in the social sciences but also because of recent political and economic transformations (e.g., neoliberalism and privatization). These changes displaced the anthropologist from his or her function as a facilitator of national integration in the pact that had been struck between the state and civil society in the postrevolutionary period under Cárdenas.[22] At the time of our meeting, when it seemed that the integration of Mexico was oriented more to the North American Free Trade Agreement, the Cárdenista project no longer seemed to make sense. And certainly, if a social scientist or intellectual subscribes to a progressive vision for Mexican civil society, his or her efforts cannot be made on behalf of integration within the laissez-faire model being promoted by Salinas de Gortari and, subsequently, Zedillo. Rather than an administration of communities, the intellectual's and the academic's agenda must be, as Bonfil put it, to "side with society" and to work, as Jorge Castañeda argues in a recent book, to "establish an authentic Latin American welfare state that extends its protection to the majority of the population."[23]

Participants at our meeting suggested various ways in which academics could work for the expansion of democracy in civil society. Mary Louise Pratt, for example, made a defense of the "politics of identity" of women and ethnic, racial, and sexual "minorities" in the United States. An important component of identity politics has been the challenge to the criteria for the production of knowledge and participation in social institutions. The opening of these institutions to other ways of thinking rooted in the cultural ethos of different and subaltern groups can serve as a platform for the restructuring of civil society. Norma Alarcón and other participants gave the example of feminism as the social movement that had produced the greatest openings in the United States. They also expressed disappointment at the lack of a gender analysis in most of the presentations at the meeting. They argued that not only women should take gender and sexuality into account and that not only women's issues are subject to gender analysis. These recommendations were worked into the agenda of the second meeting of the network, which took place in December 1994.

I argued that the transformation of civil society cannot be achieved on the basis of identity politics alone. On the one hand, "identity goups" do not remain fixed in time and throughout social change; on the other, there are no guarantees that the successes of identity politics in a given social formation (say, the United States) can be reproduced in others (say, Peru or Argentina). The difference in the political potential of identity politics has to be examined in the specific terrain of state institutions, the judiciary, the economy, consumer markets, mass culture, and the political apparatuses of the societies in question. These are the "media," so to speak, through which identities are contested and negotiated. It is not the case that identity groups form independently of this conjuncture; their emergence owes just as much to the possibilities opened up in these media, co-optative as they may be, as to their own struggles to overcome discrimination and hardship. Since these factors are not the same in different social formations (particularly the welfare state, consumerism, and a working judiciary), it is not likely that the identity politics of one formation will work in another.

While it is true that identity politics and its dominant ideology—multiculturalism—have achieved a relative democratization of some institutions (some school systems and universities, museums and exhibition spaces, certain foundations, and even certain business settings, as demonstrated by the adoption of "corporate multiculturalism"), the fact is that these openings have not had the slightest impact upon the conduct of the macropolitics of the economy, foreign relations, the armed forces, scientific research, and so on. Such an impact is made even more difficult by the weak linkages among "identity groups." There are, for example, regions where there is pronounced conflict between African Americans and U.S. Latinos, particularly where the latter, as in Miami, are perceived to take the lion's share of jobs in times of economic crisis and job flight. The intersection of identity politics, as inflected by race, gender, and sexuality, is too complex, in my estimation, to be reduced to the simplicity of an "evil" normativity (Anglo or Eurocentric) on the one hand and a "good" multicultural pluralization on the other. Even multiculturalism (which in reality is a discursive terrain contested by several different tendencies, not all of which are easily teased apart) evinces its own globalizing and colonizing inclination when it represents itself as somehow isomorphic with the world, thus creating an image of the United States as the only legitimate society in which *every* difference is included.[24] From the many affirmations of this representativity and globality, let me quote one that comes from what Lucy Lippard has characterized as the most progressive of art journals, *High Performance:*

> The U.S. stands on the edge of a new frontier—a world both home and abroad, that is in flux and out of balance. . . . The new frontier is a complex global society that will demand the power of the imagination and the forces of regeneration to meet its challenges.
>
> For America's artists and cultural institutions this is a time of great opportunity. We can offer more than a colorful banner and a theme song in support of this quest. We bring our untapped capacities as bridge builders, translators and problem solvers. We bring the language and technology of transformation. . . .

> America, the lone remaining "superpower," must now learn to operate in an environment of shifting, toppling, and even flattening hierarchies—a world where information technology, multinational finance, world famine, ethnic conflict and ozone depletion are but a few of the interconnecting threads in the emerging global fabric. . . .
>
> While we were watching the transformation of the world on CNN, the U.S. has undergone a metamorphosis as well. The dramatic shift in population from north/east to south/west, the move from an industrial to a service- and information-based economy, the ongoing deterioration of our human services, education and public works infrastructures, our widespread political disaffection, and our emergence as the globe's first truly multicultural society, are but a few indications of the monumental changes taking place.[25]

This euphoric multicultural manifesto is not very different—in its attention to the contribution of diversity to a competitive advantage in "bridge building" in a global (cultural) economy—from corporate multiculturalism's project to diversify the workforce in recognition that in the near future it will be composed of a majority of workers of "color." This corporate multiculturalism, which has developed side by side with social and aesthetic multiculturalism, sees diversification as a necessity in order for the United States to compete in the global economy. According to one manual of "diversity management," "To prosper in the future we must value, understand, and better utilize our diversity in business, education, government, as well as society in general."[26] Rhetorically the text makes the claim that workers of "color" and women must be represented among middle and upper management; there is the not-unfounded suspicion, however, that this practice will attempt to integrate in a nonconflictive manner a largely black and Latino and female working class into a nonunionized job market with fewer benefits, in keeping with the tendency of corporate capitalism to maximize its profits by expending less on labor.

Diversity, however, is a discourse that cuts many ways, seemingly empowering "minorities" by a rhetorical appeal to inclusion that, contradictorily, can work against these groups. That is why there is increasing opposition to Latin American immigrants in the United States, including opposition from some "minority" sectors that oppose immigration for fear of loss of jobs. This opposition is even evident among academics and artists who would like to draw a clear line between U.S. Latinos and Latin Americans, particularly when it comes to a redefinition of what constitutes "American" art and culture. Referring to the 1993 Whitney Biennial, one Chicano art critic objected to the museum's plans to broaden the definition of American art to include Latin Americans, fearing that the latter, most of whom come from a middle- and upper-middle-class background, will preempt U.S. minority artists: "[T]here is a . . . danger in using non-American artists to challenge the notion of a homogeneous national culture. One does not have to cross borders to find artistic practices that—whether through their outright difference, or through their critical engagement of dominant aesthetics—upset, expand, subvert, and undo the category of 'American' art. . . . At the very moment when the Whitney Museum should identify and proclaim racial and sexual minorities as part of a new American patrimony, the curatorial agenda is redirected to the international sphere, instead."[27]

This critic puts his finger on the use of multiculturalism against the very groups that the rhetoric says it seeks to empower. The other side of the coin is, of course, the stereotyping of the culture of Latin Americans and other Third World subjects, who are sought out by curators to demonstrate that "American" culture can be "inclusive." By appealing to the "difference" of these widely varying groups, multiculturalism ironically ends up homogenizing them. Consequently, U.S. multiculturalism has been looked upon with much caution by Latin American intellectuals, artists, and activists, to the point that they discern in it a family resemblance to cultural imperialism. This is, perhaps, the reason many Latin American participants at our meeting did not espouse the call for "all of us in the Americas" to join in a common purpose to combat "high" European theory (Derrida, Foucault, Lacan, Bourdieu, etc.). On the one hand, they argued, what difference does it make where one gets one's insights? On the other, they were suspicious about a project defined and already established in the North. That is, the diverse Latin American approaches to questions of difference and Eurocentrism are not necessarily compatible with those of U.S. intellectuals, who, as is evident in some of the rhetoric reproduced in my discussion of multiculturalism, often display a "We are the world" syndrome.

This caution with respect to U.S. identity politics and multiculturalism requires a careful analysis, particularly now that Latin American national cultures are undergoing pronounced transformation. José Manuel Valenzuela Arce addressed this topic in his study of the fragmentation of youth culture in Mexico under the current shift to neoliberalism and official integration via NAFTA into the North American economy. The "lost decade" of the 1980s produced "a severe lack of opportunities for Latin American youth, many of whom lost their idea of a future along with the downfall of any notion of progress. . . . There appeared in Mexico a large number of poor youths organized by barrio, gang and cliques. They have had an enormous impact on the cultural expression of *cholos,* punks, rockers and *chavos banda,* and they have produced important cultural recreations on which rest their strong identity group formation."[28] Valenzuela compares these groups to African American and Latino youths, but one would have to question whether their practices can have an expansive effect on Mexican public spheres (phantasmatic or not) comparable to that of U.S. identity groups, particularly as their imaginary is projected through the media and the consumer market and a clientele role is constructed for them in the welfare state apparatuses. Paul Gilroy and Greg Tate, for example, have observed that hip-hop culture would not have been projected throughout the nation and throughout the world without the medium of mass culture and consumerism.[29] We might surmise that rather than strike such a relation to consumerism and the media, these Mexican youths will most likely recycle the images and sounds that are marketed from the United States. Furthermore, they have a different insertion into the (weaker) welfare state and the workforce, and their country has a more subordinate standing in the world economy. Therefore, their "difference" is not needed to legitimize a global, multicultural character to which the country makes no claims.

There are other experiences that distinguish Latin American from U.S. youth. For example, in the conclusion to his presentation, Antônio Arantes explained that it is difficult to examine urban space in São Paulo over any extended period due to the short life span of the poor youths (many of them not making it past twenty-one years of age) with whom he has worked. In her response to Arantes's paper, Teresa Caldeira observed that in São Paulo nearly 900 youths had been killed in 1991, most of them at the hands of vigilantes or the military police (who often wear civilian dress and constitute a sizable portion of the vigilantes). In the same period, twenty-three youths were killed under similar circumstances in New York. Of course, many more youths die in the United States due to urban violence, most often involving firearms wielded by other youths.[30] The difference, however, is that in the United States most of the violent deaths are not *directly* carried out by state apparatuses and by some business constituencies but fostered by an uncaring national atmosphere in which youth, especially youth of "color," are devalued and have few economic, social, and educational resources.[31] This, of course, is also the case in Brazil, except that there even fewer resources are available. Street children, who are routinely killed, have out of desperation and for survival organized a new social movement. But even with the attention they gained after their first international meeting in 1992 in Brasília, with over 1,000 representatives from throughout Brazil and other countries, several of the leaders were killed by the military police.[32] The point is not so much that in São Paulo the police kill thirty-eight times as many youth as in New York (although that in itself is a telling statistic) but rather that the method of dealing with unemployment, lack of educational opportunity, hunger, and racism is death to the poor. During the mammoth environment summit—Eco 92—in June 1992, the military police combed the Zona Sul and downtown areas, removing poor youth (most of them black and mulatto) in order to make the streets safe for the visiting dignitaries. Teresa Caldeira's research on urban violence has confirmed that youths from the slums are detested as polluting elements by the righteous middle classes.[33] In the United States, despite the deep frustrations that the LA riots made evident, identity politics does have a role to play in engineering some kind of symbolic retribution for subaltern groups. In Brazil, however, not only would such a maneuver be repudiated by dominant groups who control the media and who do not perceive poor youth as a targeted market worth their attention, it would likely make even less of a difference than in the United States as a means to revalorize the status of poor youth.

The debates on civil society in our meeting eventually came around to discussion of the role of the state. Fredric Jameson argued that the relation of civil society and the state was necessarily different in the United States and in Latin

America. In the North, he suggested, where there is a civil society but a weak social link to the state, consequently, the strategy should be to recuperate the state. In the South, the state has traditionally brokered social demands, most often in a populist and paternalistic, when not authoritarian, fashion. The challenge there, as García Canclini had already argued, is to construct a viable civil society as an informing instance over the state. The problem in Latin America, however, is that the already weak welfare state is being debilitated even more by the adoption of neoliberal economic policies. The construction of civil society in Latin America cannot neglect the role of the economic.

It is this economic necessity that raises the question of international economic relations, as Manuel Castells and Roberto Laserna explain:

> The forces that struggle for social change in Latin America have oscillated for decades between the blind alley of populism and the artificial paradise of dogmatic marxism. When, in the 1980s, democracy was painfully and partially reestablished in the majority of countries, there were a series of attempts to put into practice a pragmatic reform that would pave the way for a slow but solid reconstruction of the social fabric, which is a necessary condition for development. But the difficulties imposed by the wider process of international restructuring, together with the traditional evils of Latin American politics (including the armed forces, so frequently antagonistic to popular demands), have obstructed and made more difficult the majority of these reformist efforts, putting democratization at risk and opening the way to the old pendular swings between demagogy and repression. Nevertheless, beyond the limitations of most of the current leaders and political parties, the perspective of a cautious but deep social reform, that permeates not only the economy and technology but also politics and institutional and even cultural life, seems to be the only way out within the framework of the dramatic transformation of the world system. The challenge for Latin America is . . . the invention of a politics capable of articulating processes of social reform and technological modernization within the purview of democratization and competitive participation in the global economy.[34]

At our meeting there were more critiques of the obstacles to the formation of democratic civil societies than concrete proposals for constructing them. Perhaps the "lost decade" in the Latin American economies has extended its sense of loss to the hopes for renewing civil society in the 1990s. In the conclusion of his presentation, Néstor García Canclini expressed his doubts that the "atomized groups" that constitute Latin America's predominantly urban landscape could be articulated in a viable civil society that might also serve as the foundation for reconstructing national economies. "A common denominator of these atomized 'communities,'" he added, is that they "form around symbolic consumption rather than productive processes. It is therefore difficult to imagine how they might contribute to reviving the economy."[35] García Canclini went on to add that "since we are not politicians we are not obliged to calculatingly oversee the limits of governability or the realism of politics." In the Latin American context it is indeed a judicious policy to eschew a politics of "calculation" and of reproducing the "politicized intellectuals" of yesteryear. However, the challenge is to invent new ways of participating in politics instead of just giving them up. Cultural studies, particularly those trends that are not limited to a "politics of representation," does have something to offer. In contrast to traditional academic disciplines that defended the autonomy of their knowledges, it provides a project for inventing new intellectual and institutional intersections that may have the effect of expanding civil society. To stay within the autonomous sphere of the production and analysis of *culture per se* ("proper cultural enterprises," as García Canclini says) is not desirable, since culture is *not* independent of politics and the market. The challenge, then, is to imagine a cultural studies project that can transform institutions, taking its model, perhaps, from feminism and other social movements that effect change by realigning knowledges, practices, and laws in ways that render illegitimate the boundaries on which institutions have relied to reproduce a status quo.

This is easy enough to state. How can it be done? I have already mentioned two proposals, one from a Latin American perspective, the other from a United States perspective. Beatriz Sarlo argued insistently against a politics of representation and for the recuperation of party politics and its linkage to the state. Mary Louise Pratt and others argued just as insistently on behalf of an identity politics that might begin at the less macropolitical level of transforming institutions toward a democratic ethos of inclusion. I have also reviewed some of the drawbacks raised in regard to these proposals, namely that formal politics is increasingly ineffective and that in the Latin American context identity politics cannot, for infrastructural reasons, produce the same results as in the United States. However, the kind of discussions held at our meeting marked the beginnings of a new strategy on behalf of reconstructing civil society on a transnational basis. If the economy and the mass media have been extending their reach ever more globally, why shouldn't a democratically oriented cultural studies movement attempt something analogous? After all, many of the issues raised, such as urban violence, withdrawal of the state from the public sector, and discrimination against "minorities" and the poor, traverse the entire hemisphere. Cultural studies can contribute to the formation of transnational public spheres that address these problems. This is, indeed, the raison d'être of the Inter-American Cultural Studies Network.

There are, of course, drawbacks to this proposal too. In the first place, the transnationalization of public spheres—what I call "cultural brokering"—is achieved largely through a politics of representation and does not necessarily have impact upon much-needed infrastructural inequities. In the second place, such a transnationalization also leaves unanswered a fundamental question: How are the participants in these spheres of mediation to be selected? It seems to me that if the decision were left up to the discretion of U.S. intellectuals, particularly those in cultural studies who sympathize with multiculturalism, the selection of Latin Americans might be carried out according to a U.S. dynamic, as I have previously argued. But if the decision is left solely to Latin Americans, it is not unlikely that these intellectuals will tend to reproduce their own class and intellectual privilege. (As the U.S. organizers of this meeting sought out Latin American counterparts, they often were asked to invite the "best," meaning by this the Jamesons, Lyotards, and Habermases. Some clearly showed a disinclination to meeting with African American and Latino intellectuals and academics.) This difference of perspectives, however, is quite valuable and can be helpful in elaborating critiques of our own best intentions, both in the North and in the South. A transnational public sphere such as the one we are trying to build should be able to contribute to the conduct and critique of more effective civil societies.

NOTES

This chapter is, in part, a report on the First Meeting of the Inter-American Cultural Studies Network at the Universidad Autónoma Metropolitana–Iztapalapa, Mexico, May 3–5, 1993. The biases toward certain cultural studies tendencies are my own, although shared by some—certainly not all—of the participants at this meeting. More information is available at http://www.wideopen.igc.org/IACSN-Cultural-Studies/index.htm.

1. Néstor García Canclini, "Una modernidad que se atrasa: La cultura bajo la regresión neoconservadora" [A modernization that lags behind: Culture under the neoconservative backlash], paper presented at the First Meeting of the Inter-American Cultural Studies Network, Iztapalapa, Mexico, May 3–5, 1993.

2. Other projects of the network are the publication of a semiannual bulletin and a book series in Spanish, Portuguese, and English to be circulated widely throughout the hemisphere; the establishment of a system of list services (particularly bibliographic and other databases) and electronic conferences so that members can stay in touch and conduct collaborative work; a program for the exchange of materials; the sponsorship of symposia, conferences, and workshops. Interested parties may write to Center for Cultural Studies, Inter-American Cultural Studies Network, 33 W. 42 St., Rm. 801, New York, NY 10036, or send faxes to (212) 982–1066 and e-mail to gayhc@cunyvm.cuny.edu.

3. David Harvey, *The Condition of Postmodernity* (Cambridge: Basil Blackwell, 1989); S. Lash and J. Urry, *The End of Organized Capitalism* (Madison: University of Wisconsin Press, 1987). See also María Milagros López, "Post-Work Selves and Entitlement 'Attitudes' in Peripheral Post-Industrial Puerto Rico," paper presented at the First Meeting of the Inter-American Cultural Studies Network, Iztapalapa, Mexico, May 3–5, 1993.

4. Nelly Richard, "Los delineamientos del saber académico: Líneas de fuerza y puntos de fuga" [The delineations of academic knowledge: Lines of force and points of escape], paper presented at the First Meeting of the Inter-American Cultural Studies Network, Iztapalapa, Mexico, May 3–5, 1993.

5. Ibid., p. 12.

6. According to Jürgen Habermas, the bourgeois public sphere of eighteenth-century England developed as "the genuine domain of private autonomy [in] oppos[ition] to the state." It was a domain of debate, criticism, and opinion formation subordinate neither to the state and its apparatuses (state institutions) nor to market-oriented media. In this latter case, "the public sphere assumes advertising functions. The more it can be deployed as

a vehicle for political and economic propaganda, the more it becomes unpolitical as a whole and pseudo-privatized." By this reasoning, the welfare state and consumer capitalism have rendered the (idealized) public sphere phantasmatic, to use Walter Lippmann's characterization. See Jürgen Habermas, *The Structural Transformation of the Public Sphere: An Inquiry into a Category of Bourgeois Society,* trans. Thomas Burger (Cambridge: MIT Press, 1989), pp. 12, 175. The date of publication of the first German edition is 1962.

7. See Jean L. Cohen and Andrew Arato, *Civil Society and Political Theory* (Cambridge: MIT Press, 1992), p. ix.

8. Michel de Certeau, *The Practice of Everyday Life,* trans. Steven F. Rendall (Berkeley: University of California Press, 1984), p. 25. This perspective has also been theorized and worked out in detail by Jesús Martín-Barbero in *De los medios a las mediaciones: Comunicación, cultura y hegemonía* (Barcelona: Gustavo Gili, 1987). See also Henry Jenkins's elaboration of the *perruque* in *Textual Poachers: Television Fans and Participatory Culture* (New York: Routledge, 1992).

9. For such a critique of the *perruque,* see George Yúdice, "Marginality and the Ethics of Survival," in *Universal Abandon? The Politics of Postmodernism,* ed. Andrew Ross (Minneapolis: University of Minnesota Press, 1988), pp. 214–236.

10. Jesús Martín-Barbero, "La comunicación en las transformaciones del campo cultural" [The role of communications in the field of culture], paper presented at the First Meeting of the Inter-American Cultural Studies Network, Iztapalapa, Mexico, May 3–5, 1993.

11. Ibid.

12. Ibid., p. 14.

13. Walter Lippmann, *The Phantom Public* (New York: Macmillan, 1927).

14. Ibid., p. 15.

15. Beatriz Sarlo, "Modernidad y después: La cultura en situación de hegemonía massmediática" [Modernity and afterwards: Culture in a context of mass mediated hegemony], paper presented at the First Meeting of the Inter-American Cultural Studies Network, Iztapalapa, Mexico, May 3–5, 1993.

16. Ibid., p. 10.

17. Piscitelli is vice-executive secretary of the CLASCO, which is based in Buenos Aires.

18. José Teixeira Coelho Netto, "Uma cultura contra o povo" [A culture against the people], paper presented at the First Meeting of the Inter-American Cultural Studies Network, Iztapalapa, Mexico, May 3–5, 1993.

19. Ibid., p. 21.

20. Ibid., pp. 17–18.

21. Ibid., p. 20.

22. Guillermo Bonfil Batalla, "Desafíos a la antropología en la sociedad contemporánea" [Challenges to anthropology in contemporary society], *Iztapalapa* 11, 24 (1991):18–19.

23. Jorge Castañeda, *Utopia Unarmed: The Latin American Left After the Cold War* (New York: Knopf, 1993), p. 451.

24. See my "We Are NOT the World," *Social Text* 31/32 (1992).

25. William Cleveland, "Bridges, Translations and Change: The Arts as Infrastructure in 21st Century America," *High Performance* (Fall 1992):84–85.

26. *Workforce America! Managing Employee Diversity as a Vital Resource,* quoted in L. A. Kauffman, "The Diversity Game: Corporate America Toys with Identity Politics," *Village Voice* (August 31, 1993):30.

27. Personal communication.

28. José Manuel Valenzuela Arce, "Las identidades culturales frente a la globalización" [Cultural identities in the face of globalization], paper presented at the First Meeting of the Inter-American Cultural Studies Network, Iztapalapa, Mexico, May 3–5, 1993.

29. See Paul Gilroy, "It's a Family Affair," *Black Popular Culture,* a project by Michele Wallace, ed. Gina Dent (Seattle: Bay Press, 1992), p. 309; and column by Greg Tate, *Vibe* (September 1992):15.

30. See James Brooke, "Big Outcry Doesn't Slow Killing of Youths in Rio," *New York Times,* January 3, 1994, p. A9.

31. This concern has become so pronounced that black intellectuals and politicians are organizing to find new solutions to crime by blacks against blacks rather than the traditional solution of "stiffer prison sentences and more jail cells." Steven A. Holmes, "Prominent Blacks Meet to Search for an Answer to Mounting Crime," *New York Times,* January 8, 1994, pp. 1, 8.

32. Gilberto Nascimento, "Jovens dizem ter sido torturados por policiais" [Youths report having been tortured by the police], *Folha de São Paulo,* November 19, 1992, pp. 3–5; Edna Dantas, "Meninos superlotam celas em Brasília" [Children are overloaded in cells in Brasília], *Folha de São Paulo,* November 18, 1992, pp. 3–3; Antônio José Mendes, "Populaçao rejeita casas de apoio a menor" [Population rejects shelters for minors], *Jornal do Brasil,* January 17, 1993, p. 25; "Encontro reúne 1.000 meninos de rua" [Meeting gathers 1,000 street youths], *Jornal do Brasil,* November 19, 1992, p. 8.

A recent widely publicized incident was the massacre of eight street children in Rio by a death squad composed of military police in plain clothes. See Human Rights Coordinator [hrcoord in igc:hr.child], "Brazil: Child Murders Shroud Rio," newsdesk@igc.apc.org in igc:ips.english (July 27, 1993).

33. See Teresa Pires do Rio Caldeira, "Crime and Individual Rights: Reframing the Question of Violence in Latin America," paper presented at the seminar "Derechos Humanos, Jusiticia y Sociedad," *CEDES,* Buenos Aires, October 22–24, 1993, p. 2.

34. Manuel Castells and Roberto Laserna, "La nueva dependencia: Cambio tecnológico y reestructuración socioeconómica en Latinoamérica" [The new dependency: Technological change and socioeconomic restructuring in Latin America], *David y Goliath* 18, 55 (July 1989):16.

35. García Canclini, "Una modernización que se atrasa" [A modernization that lags behind], p. 14.

5

The Futures Market: Global Economics and Cultural Studies

RICHARD DIENST

Who Knows?

Not long ago Meaghan Morris gave me a theoretical riddle disguised as a casual remark. She said, "I have the feeling we are going to spend the nineties trying to figure out what happened in the eighties." Of course I agreed at once, so quickly that I failed to ask what she meant. Is this a prediction, a program of study, or an expression of plain bewilderment? Do we know what "the eighties" were, or what "the nineties" will be? How will we figure it out, and what is the point of trying? And the most obvious, most often asked question of all: Do we know who "we" are?

At first thought, this "we" may have been no more than the two of us talking on the phone. With a little contextual pushing, this "we" would also include all those people who do cultural criticism or theoretical inquiry of various kinds, whether in the United States or in Australia or in both or elsewhere. For that small but diverse group, Morris's remark carries a moody imperative: It will be necessary to understand what has happened to all of us. But if "the eighties" signifies an epochal event—an event that appears to be already over, leaving behind a mysterious legacy and an undeniable obligation—this "we" cannot be limited to scholars or writers. Who, then, needs to figure out the eighties? Again, who is this "we"?

Without a doubt, as George Yúdice has suggested,[1] "we" are not the world: The very temptation to speak for a global subject of history must be cut short, and the all-too-easy rhetoric of universality must be rendered unusable. Those among us who are employed by corporations, private institutions, and governments must refuse the professional privilege of speaking in a prefabricated collective voice. But even if this grand "we" cannot be spoken on behalf of everybody, perhaps this "we" cannot leave anybody out, either—or rather, this "we" that we want to be is still waiting to appear, guiding the very course of our analyses, which must now be pursued everywhere precisely because its zones are not already fixed in the maps of present understanding. "Making it up as we go along" has never before seemed such an attractive and necessary procedure. And alongside this rather hopeful project, in which Morris is joined by many other contemporary thinkers, isn't there also a note of exasperation? It is as if the moment when "we" can figure out what has happened always comes too late or, what amounts to the same thing, that the moment when we can say "we" always comes too soon.

The riddle has already become quite tangled, but it seems that much more urgent. Clearly, the eighties names a problem in the representation of global history in which personal memories and immense abstractions already come into play. But this representational difficulty cuts in several directions at once. It cannot be wrapped up simply by finding some discursive common ground, whether that would mean compiling an exhaustive statistical digest, sketching out a sufficiently sinuous narrative, or outbidding the old theoretical positions. To do justice to the complexity of the matter, several tasks must be kept in sight at once. First, in keeping with the spirit of that telephone call, I want to suggest that those of us engaged in "cultural studies"—whoever that may be—have a lot of work to do if we want to catch the drift of global events, especially if we hope to contribute to the creation of alternate and multiple kinds of knowledge. We have to be "worldly," as Edward Said put it, which means that our work requires the invention of new means of worldliness. There have been a number of remarkable probes in this direction, especially the rich and varied material hastily grouped under the name of "postcolonial theory," which is centrally concerned with challenging the conventional epistemologies of history, anthropology, geography, and cultural aesthetics.[2] The operation I will sketch here addresses the specific capacity of our writings to cut across institutional and media knowledges by making "theoretical images" that can serve as radically mobile instruments of thinking.[3]

Second, this more general emphasis on the intersection between the fabrication of images and the fabulating function of historical thinking serves as a way to revisit Fredric Jameson's persistent calls for new tools of global representation in light of the devaluation of schemes drawn from nineteenth-century philosophy, science, and art.[4] To "figure out" the contemporary situation without resorting either to the tropes of sublimity or to the schematic shorthand of economics, theoretical work will have to cultivate its own powers of imagination and transmission. Everything that comes to hand can enter the mix, and every mixture can be handed along for reshaping. In this way, theory may yet avoid the confines of institutionalized disciplines and rigidifying groups. Finally, in belated response to Morris, I will compile several versions of the eighties. Although these accounts never quite add up, each one is somehow plausible and useful on its own terms, allowing us to ask overlapping questions about the techniques of historical representation, the crucial mechanisms of capitalist accumulation, and the possibilities of envisioning the world in some other way. As a guiding thread, I will outline just one theoretical image—"debt"—to tie these questions together in an exorbitant way. I hope that this outline will give us some ideas about what to do (and where to go) next.

What Happened?

There is only one place to mark the opening of history: with the sensation that something has happened. Perhaps something seems to have burst before our very eyes, unforgettable and incomprehensible all at once; or perhaps the disquiet of morning has insistently reminded us that there was a disturbance in the night. One way or another, the moment of the event has to be reconstructed, somehow fixed, drawn out of the buzz of lived time, and drawn up for reinspection. But there is no way to draw an image of an event without setting up interference patterns in all directions: Every act of historical speculation sets out its own rhythms, blackouts, intensifications, and perimeters of surprise.

At first, "the eighties" can be only a loose set of images, hastily but spontaneously collected from diverse strata, shot through with the bolts of simultaneity that align personal lives with public histories. But the rearrangement of calendar time is merely a way to get the order straight, and inasmuch as every historical narrative needs a plot, its telling will turn into a search for presages and aftershocks. What is not often recognized, however, is that periodization is a kind of metageneric device, practically demanding that each period have its own kind of story, its own organizing logic, its own resurrected pasts and unrealized futures. Periodizing, in other words, does not arrange units of the same kind: Rather, it classifies and arranges its elements according to traits that are liable to change with each scheme. That is why historical writing always seems ready to burn up upon reentry into the atmosphere of the present moment: It takes form only by preserving, within the terms of its particular narrative, the legible proof of its own "relative" incoherence, instability, and transitoriness. In being marked off, each period must bear the insignia of its limits and the marks of its special doom, and in that sense every period we frame for analysis will somehow seem either suffocatingly restricted or stupidly out of control. A period necessarily "begins" in one register and "ends" in another, as its various plans come unhinged, its projects are fulfilled or given up for hopeless, and its social mechanisms mutate in order to overcome the limits of old dispositions. But we can hardly recognize the aleatory uncertainty of historical periods from our vantage point: On the contrary, to draw up a periodization scheme, we trace back a narrative arc describing a trail of images like drops of blood so that when the montage is shown in forward motion, in its "proper" sequence, it cannot help but appear both fitful and inevitable. Thus the exercise or habit of periodization must be grasped as something more than a retrospective organizing heuristic: It is a way of modeling our own contemporary desires for significance, whether fleeting or abiding, which try to make visible the other desires that we hope will animate history or life. Benjamin expressed this dimension of materiality, even corporality, in one of his crystalline notes: "Writing history means: to give the count of years its physiognomy."[5] Periodization is an experiment of competing orchestrations and syncopations played out in the atmosphere of public discourse—it sets its images and arrangements of time against both the appearances of permanence and the forgetful attractions of the present moment.

But rather than attempting to account for all the abstract possibilities of historical thinking, we should return to that specific sensation with which we began: The eighties happened, and now they're over. It is a great game to choose the defining features, the starting and ending points, and the sudden outbreaks that give the images of a period its distinct tangibility. The search for reference points has to begin somewhere, even with an arbitrary stab, and here we are, speaking about the possibilities for a global cultural studies. For a far-flung band of intellectuals, the eighties will be remembered as the time when the postmodernism debate became an inescapable frame of reference for discussions of history, the importance of places and placements, and the tasks of intellectual work. The slogan of postmodernism was itself a globalizing invocation both because the term was supposed to designate a worldwide phenomenon and because it was quickly taken up as a genuinely international topic of discussion. Somewhere between those two functions of the word—descriptive and polemical—postmodernism has served to direct intellectual inquiry into new tracks. Even if there turned out to be no widespread agreement about the content or parameters of postmodernism (let alone its very existence as a legitimate category or periodizing term), it can still be understood as a remarkable episode in the internationalization and telecommunication of questions and lexicons originating in artistic and academic circles, and thus it can serve as the first item in our inventory of the eighties.

The strongest accounts of postmodernism were concerned to establish its validity as a grand-scale epochal term despite a widespread reluctance to employ older kinds of historical and global categories. The very term only makes sense when both ends of the dilemma are kept intact, and for this reason I would suggest that if postmodernism is *not* positioned in the oscillation described by Jameson—in which it already exists *everywhere* as a condition and possibility but only *here* and *there* as a project—then we should scrap the whole effort and reinvent the problem from scratch. As is well known, Jameson attaches his conception of postmodernism onto Mandel's long-cycle theory of capitalism. There the post–1940s era appears in two segments: a boom lasting into the late 1960s or early 1970s (exactly the moment when Mandel writes his book *Late Capitalism,* published in 1972), and then a downturn lasting into the prolonged ellipsis of the present moment. It is equally well known that Mandel's account stresses the way in which capitalism has pursued both the commodification of all production and the development of world market mechanisms that allow capitalists to take advantage of "underdeveloped" productivity and "unequal" exchange relationships wherever they may appear in international trade. Mandel predicts trouble for the growth-sector transnational corporations that led the sixties boom: "The more the monopolies think they have withdrawn from the law of value nationally, the more they become subject to it internationally."[6]

What is striking, from the historiographic angle that interests us here, is that Mandel was inclined to mark a historical high-water mark of the internationalization of capital around 1972: After that date, and precisely because corporations and states were beginning to abandon the old geoeconomic division of territory (with its patterns of locally distributed value), capitalists could henceforth expect several decades of hard chasing after profits. Far from projecting a teleological fulfillment or structural completion of some capitalist grand plan *in the present*, then, Mandel's story pauses at the moment when the dynamic phase has overcome its most immediate barriers only to find stagnation of profits, a slowdown in technological innovation, unproductive accumulation, inflationary danger, and political chaos. This moment of reversal announces the punctual reappearance of a dialectical deficit between actual historical developments and the abstract "laws of motion" of capital: The capitalist mode of production can neither fulfill the promises that carry it onward nor efficiently discharge the energies it builds up in the process. From the perch of Mandel's theory, capitalism operates according to the geometry of the clinamen and the asymptote, cresting ever farther toward total revolution only to swoop ever farther toward utter breakdown. These boundary limits remain equally unthinkable within the domain of history as we know it—except as visions of the as-yet-unfulfilled totalization of a world finally delivered from the constraints of capitalism.

Something of the pessimism and hesitation of this very specific historical perspective can be glimpsed in Jameson's 1984 essays on postmodernism and "Periodizing the 60s." The first piece is the famous anatomy of a now-triumphant cultural logic; the second is a celebration of the disruptive cultural energies released during the bygone global boom. The sixties, in this account, do not run from 1960 to 1969 but start in 1959 with Castro in the Sierra Maestra and end later with a marvelous concurrence of worldwide political disasters in 1973.[7] Jameson offers a summary of the era by treating its key economic features as general traits: "The Sixties were . . . an immense and inflationary issuing of superstructural credit; a universal abandonment of the referential gold standard; an extraordinary printing up of ever more devalued signifiers." That these phrasings do not preserve a safe metaphorical distance between finance and culture can be inferred from the forecast he goes on to offer: "[The] Eighties will be characterized by an effort, on a world scale, to proletarianize all those unbound social forces."[8] The dialectical rhythm is clear: Once the liberating and utopian sixties boom ends in 1973, the constraining and vengeful bust must begin there as well. With this bit of dramatic chronology, what we have been calling the eighties regroups everything since 1973 under the sign of ruling-class resentment and long-term retrenchment: It specifies a series of motifs (crisis, inflation, universal abandon, etc.), a plane of analysis (capitalism understood in terms of its overall geographical organization and its technological drive), and a narrative built around an inverted and antagonistic relationship to the sixties (which will be played out in terms of immediate generational identifications, the tempo of nostalgia and forgetfulness, and the attrition of long-term ideological and institutional struggle[9]). The problem of historical description here hinges on the way material processes may be said to carry out such a conflict between imaginary passions—an exuberant revolutionary creativity on one hand and a reactionary discipline of productivity on the other—which can be identified in all of the available social texts, including everything from the creation of cultural documents and spatial-geographical practices to legal realignment and wholesale politico-economic restructuring.

Few historical works have the ambition to trace such a scramble of connections: It is hard enough to locate the crucial events and to sketch a few rudimentary lines of determination. But throughout other accounts of recent economic history, Marxist or not, there is wide agreement that the concatenation of "shocks" to the world economy in the period 1971–1973 signals the appearance of a systemic crisis and the beginning of a realignment. For mainstream economists hankering after the semblance of monetary stability and trade equilibrium, these years spell the Fall into disorder, epitomized by what was seen as the self-alienation of the dollar. (These patient souls, always waiting for history to right itself, perhaps felt that the settlement of the 1986–1994 Uruguay GATT and the founding of the World Trade Organization signal a step back on track.) For others, this period not only establishes unprecedented economic structures—namely, the world market in capital itself—but necessitates the invention of new techniques of explanation. Let us examine the economic history of these years in more detail.

In a series of sophisticated analyses, Alain Lipietz, Michel Aglietta, Mike Davis, and others associated with Regulation School economics have argued that this restructuring is something besides a cyclical adjustment to hard times: It marks the breakdown of the complex socioeconomic system called Fordism, a breakdown accompanied by the first moves toward the construction of a replacement arrangement that will not necessarily be a "system" in the same way. According to Lipietz, Fordism was more than a philosophy of production and management: It was an interdependent "regime of accumulation" in which all aspects of economic activity, controlled by various kinds of social procedures, had fallen into a productive alignment and mutual reinforcement.[10] Fordism names a configuration of (1) production techniques (factories arranged in assembly lines and tasks designed for individualized efficiency), (2) consumption patterns (mass production of consumer goods as a primary motor of growth), and (3) a set of characteristic political forms (especially bourgeois democracy, union-management cooperation, and Keynesian fiscal policy) that prevailed in the industrialized countries of the West. (The manifold character of the concept itself testifies to its roots in the Althusserian school and its attempts to define the coordinates of "overdetermined conjunctures" in the history of capitalism.) By the early 1970s, Fordism was said to be falling apart in its original homelands, requiring a renegotiation of its assumptions and linkages there ("post-Fordism"), whereas components of its model have been exported to certain newly industrialized countries (especially in Southeast Asia) in time for their takeoffs in the 1980s ("peripheral Fordism").

Perhaps such an epochal shift cannot be pinned down to a definitive chronology, but Lipietz points to two major events as the immediate conditions of possibility for the disintegration of the Fordist regime. First comes the December 1971 Smithsonian agreement, effectively ending the 1944 Bretton Woods monetary system that had stabilized currency exchanges among the industrialized countries on the basis of the exchangeability of dollars for gold. By halting gold convertibility, the U.S. government shifted the basis of its monetary sovereignty from the universal acceptability of its gold reserves to the regulative capacity of the Federal Reserve. The somewhat devalued and more volatile dollar could henceforth retain most of its own privileges without having to guarantee, directly, any other currencies. But what looked like a unilateral move toward currency independence was rather a strategic shifting of responsibility into multilateral codependence. When the system of fixed exchange rates among the major industrial countries was dismantled over the next few years, the U.S. government was free to satisfy its borrowing appetites on the world credit markets with no more advance collateral than its good name. That reputation, of course, rested on the proven willingness of the U.S. government to intervene in every possible way to create and maintain markets, as well as on its limited but specific methods of channeling domestic production priorities to aid the balance of trade. While the dollar was being redefined to enhance the interests of U.S.-based transnational industrial and financial sectors—which remain loyal to the national interest as long as the hegemonic currency works in their favor—some responsibility for the fiduciary stability of international trade was shifted to SDRs (special drawing rights), the international reserve currency operated through the International Monetary Fund. In the splintering division of labor among financial institutions, it fell to the IMF and its partner, the World Bank (and, more recently, the Bank of International Settlements), to become the chief enforcers of monetary hygiene around the world, a task they would later execute with zeal.[11] But more important, the displacement of gold meant that the management of foreign reserves—stockpiles of other governments' money—would paradoxically become the crucial form in which a government would try to guarantee its own financial sovereignty. Dollars, of course, would be the first reserve currency of choice well into the eighties, losing some ground by the middle of the decade to the deutsche mark, the ECU (European currency unit), and the yen. With this series of moves, the United States had applied superpower strategy—a kind of financial brinksmanship—to the world economic system.

If these monetary maneuvers have been treated as the cynical and canny exercise of high-level policy, the next event—the 1973–1974 oil crisis—has been mythologized as a veritable eruption of the Outside and a return of the non-

Western repressed. The OPEC price hike, which can be understood as a *result* as much as a *cause* of changes in the monetary order (especially dollar devaluation), and the ensuing interstate jockeying (in which U.S. political hegemony was visibly weakening) thus necessitated a relatively greater outflow of dollars and other currencies into economies that would not tie up very much of the money in their own long-term capital investment projects. Instead of being drawn into the adventure of long-term national modernization, dollars would be circulated back into the capital and equity markets. This first oil shock, transmitted and magnified by the necessity for everybody to play the currency game once exchange rates began to float, soon brought vastly greater volume and liquidity to global monetary circulation. For the period between 1973 and 1979, dollars (in the form of "petrodollars," "Eurodollars," or as Lipietz calls them, "xenodollars") tumbled through the world banking system, building up as deposits to be lent out again, fueling an inflationary round of investments and a tremendous flightiness in currency values.[12] For the Third World countries hoping to start their own peripheral Fordism, debts began to pile up, increasingly granted by commercial banks at inflation-sensitive rates. (Of the four Asian "tigers," only South Korea had begun heavy borrowing while enjoying special strategic protection from the United States.[13]) Meanwhile, private capital found itself less subject to the governance or policy posture of central banks, which would nevertheless continue to serve as protectors of national interests and lenders of last resort.[14] Thus the honeycomb of "sovereign" nations remained the operative structure of the international division (and disintegration) of labor even as the thick tides of money slipped into another sphere where capital would be concentrated and filtered through international mechanisms. This is not to say that money was freed from all legal rule but rather that it has begun to create its own zone of jurisdiction, its own charmed circularity, in which national laws can be escaped by submitting the so-called grounded laws of value to the circulatory laws of teletransmission. It is only through a certain powerful *recourse to the imaginary* that capital has moved past its former limits. (I will return to this point later; it marks the difference between economic history and theoretical description.)

The next blow arrives promptly, heralded by another oil price hike. If monetary proliferation was somehow a "solution" to the crisis of the Fordist development model, the imposition of British and American monetarism in 1979–1981 was an attempt to destroy the model directly by abolishing the obligations of currency to support national trade and social welfare and by choking off all those economic agents (at home or abroad) who were insufficiently buoyed by cash flow. In a word, the state would no longer mediate the process of social reproduction. As Lipietz puts it, "Monetarism was no longer prepared to wager the cost of investment against the anticipated value of the product in the making. . . . It ripped open the safety-nets of monopolist regulation, assailing the powerful Welfare State institutions that stabilized social demand, and breaking the thread of pseudo-validated values in process. It cast into the abyss a world which, being still enchanted with the dream of credit-based expansion, was still actually moving forward."[15] In order to free the phantasm of money from its social "responsibilities," the whole postwar weave of political arrangements, ranging from households to the highly contested system of national sovereignty and regional autonomy, would be uprooted and exposed directly to vicissitudes of the capital markets.[16] In Britain and the United States, the election of conservative governments was accompanied by immediate deregulation of financial markets coupled with central bank austerity and the stoking of highly sectoral internal demand through military spending. (Mike Davis has persuasively argued that the monetarist turn had already started in the United States with Carter and the California "tax revolt" of 1978.[17]) The financial authorities of Germany, France, and Japan (home to most of the other major banks) had all fallen into this course by the early 1980s. Deregulation seemed to follow a trial-and-error course with some central banks proceeding through a series of little jumps (as in Japan, still wedded to state-guided investment) and others building up to big leaps (as with Britain's "big bang" of 1986). In a climate of such uncertainty about the long-term rules of the game, it was only a matter of time until the capital flows began to dry up in some quarters, making the rollover of borrowing on its previous scale much harder, and soon bankruptcies rippled through the banking world.

In summer 1982, a string of international bank collapses was topped by the announcement by Mexico that it would suspend payments on its immense debt. The specter of Third World defaults rattled the once-voracious private lenders, and the circuits of foreign investment seized up. Of course, the action by Mexico (accompanied by rumblings from Brazil and Venezuela, and soon others) became inevitable only because so much of its earnings were already being reabsorbed by private banks, government lenders, the IMF, and the World Bank. The gross inflows of capital to Latin America, in fact, had turned negative in 1982, and debt service costs would continue to mount. To cover the immediate crisis, the Federal Reserve and the IMF stepped in with more money, choosing to endorse, or "pseudovalidate," the debts (i.e., they extended more credit to aid the repayment of loans) rather than face the consequences if major banks began to default. (Citicorp, Chase Manhattan, Hanover, and Bank of America were all exposed to Latin American debt far beyond their assets.)[18]

For Antonio Negri, the Mexican crisis of 1982 brought an end to the development cycle begun in 1971 with Nixon's opening salvo of financial deregulation. In his ongoing investigations of the antagonisms running though the history of capitalism, Negri always emphasizes the constitutive power of working populations in their resistance to capitalist mobilization. In this period scheme, 1968 was the peak of worker resistance to prevailing industrial organization, which was met with an essentially defensive answer over the following years: "From the 70s on, we have had the bad luck to live in the most cruel and stupid period of restructuration and repression." In this running battle, the Mexican debt crisis marks the moment when capitalist restructuring is forced to abandon its geographical hierarchies through financial deregulation: "no longer weak rings, but weak networks."[19] By 1982, according to Negri, the recurrent (and often proclaimed) "crises" of capital had become permanent: Trouble could come anytime from anywhere, threatening every node in the web.

Deals had to be struck: Debtors in default would reschedule their payments, sliding the time of their obligations farther into the future. That arrangement proved to be short-lived, for what was really at stake was neither "liquidity" nor "solvency" but structural control. The crisis could be "resolved" only by altering the international political system, not by supplying more circulating cash. By the end of the decade, the Baker Agreement (1987) and Brady Plan (1989), brokered by the United States and IMF, had effected the transition toward increased equity holdings by Western banks and highly selective project-by-project investment. The massive "external" debt accumulated in the 1970s and early 1980s was thus magically "internalized" through the "restructuring" prescriptions of the IMF and World Bank. These financial deals have come to define the fundamental political constitution of many local regimes, shifting the ground of responsibility from "the people" to the global finance markets.[20] A government must answer first to the markets, assuming the eager voice of the people; then it can inform the people of their destiny, assuming the imperious voice of the market. (The political consequences of these restructurings have always been complex and profound; for example, Chomsky has argued that the Polish Solidarity movement came into being because of the austerity measures enforced by the IMF.[21] There have also been famous "IMF riots" in countries around the world.) As for the long-term legitimacy, or rather *viability*, of pro-IMF governments, it is still too early to say yet too late to prevent pervasive misery and wasted years.

In the mid–1980s the old debts were circulating on the market as promissory notes sold at a discount alongside stocks, bonds, and all the other paper instruments of investment that were invented in the wake of deregulation. (By the late 1980s, before his conviction, Michael Milken had a pitch that began, "I've been looking into Third World debt. . . . There are great opportunities there. Take Mexico."[22]) Indeed, the most striking feature of the current expansion of financial frenzy is the way in which deregulation has permitted collective accumulations of value and obligation (pensions, insurances, mortgages, and national debt itself) to be shaped and mobilized as if they were so many "individual capitals" written up as negotiable documents in a process wishfully called "securitization." For this reason, it is clear that international debt and its reconfiguration were never just a matter of finances between elites: With each recalibration and each exchange of new promises for old claims, societies are forced to find new compromises for their internal conflicts and to redistribute burdens, creating impossible binds for those who require minimal monetary stability to survive in a commodified environment. There was never any question of forcing the debtors to pay in full: Neither their export capacities nor the import demands of the creditors could bear the necessary volume. In the course of the 1980s, economic agents and blocs of all kinds had to learn—often by trial, error, and ruin—how to roll with their debts.

The crucial point of this story, as Lipietz tells it, is not that money suddenly became false and ungrounded—because nobody ever knows if there is a solid ground for the values they are using and pursuing—but that the mechanisms and systems that create and "validate" money changed in a fundamental way sometime after 1979. To explain his point, Lipietz refers to the old Roadrunner cartoons, where the hapless Coyote would often find that he had rashly run over the edge of a cliff and, in a moment of suspended self-consciousness, would pull out a sign reading HELP! before falling into the chasm. The total efforts of capitalists, personified by Coyote, can always rush headlong beyond the "ground" (which for Lipietz is the ensemble of social guarantees that composed the secret stability of Fordism). At that point, either the friendly hand of the cartoonist–central banker comes onscreen to sketch in some new turf or Coyote surely falls. But it is not a perfect image, since there are many Coyotes: Some do indeed survive, strolling into thin air; others drop away at the first step.[23]

A better scene, taken from the same source of wisdom, would show Coyote (a particularly cunning capitalist) still hoping to trap Roadrunner (who leads the chase for profits, or rather, abstract wealth). Coyote, well schooled in lures of mimesis, paints a big black spot on a rock wall, framing it to look like the entrance to a tunnel. Then he sits back, waiting for Roadrunner to smash against his image and the all-too-real rock behind it. Instead, Roadrunner cruises through the tunnel, disappearing in a puff of dust. Coyote, now convinced that the tunnel may not be "just" an image after all, begins to chase his prey, hitting the rock and getting knocked silly. For good measure, Roadrunner comes racing back through the tunnel, knocking him flat again. Having learned his lesson, Coyote later tries to trick Roadrunner with the opposite tactic: He places a painting of a broken bridge across the road. Roadrunner rushes past, heedless of the image; when Coyote takes off in pursuit, he enters his own picture and falls off the broken bridge.

This lesson is rather more "objective": There is no way to know which images will serve as a passage onward, and yet there is no other way to go. In this sense, the distant, faceless bankers are the greatest dreamers of our era if only because they think they are dreaming for the rest of us. These dreams display all the classic Freudian mechanisms: the *condensation* of human activity into myriad images of value, the *displacement* of the sites of productivity to avoid the traumas of resistance, the *calculation of representability* that maintains the cohesion of the marketplace logic by means of constant valorization and devalorization of circulating images, and finally the ceaseless *secondary revisions* of economic discourse itself in its mission to justify the ways of Mammon to man. But there is no point in hoping that these dreamers will ever awake, either by total failure or total success: As Freud said, dreams will do everything to preserve the bliss of sleep.

For the owners of capital, there is no such thing as a wake-up call or reality check. The 1987 crash was more an algorithmic nightmare of computer programs than a surprise glimpse beyond the rapt fascination of a careening market. As Lipietz has put it in properly vague terms, the "crash of 1987 merely revealed the obstacles which made illusory the previously attempted solutions."[24] Apparently the breakdown of one illusion does not herald a moment of truth. The 1989 revolutions have not brought to life the senile fantasy of a free worldwide market but rather intensified competition over the institutionalization and regionalization of markets.[25] It has often been remarked on the left that the Western powers and their many mouthpieces have taken the breakdown of "actually existing socialism" in exactly the wrong way: Rather than proclaiming a victory of their side against a weakened and ruined enemy, these critics insist that it would be more wise for the Western powers to see in these sudden upheavals the portents of their own troubles to come.[26] Nowadays Lipietz, who had elaborated his analysis of the "enchantment" of values in the credit system during the period when the spell seemed unbreakable, offers his own urgent solution: not just devalorization of the debts but a rehabilitation of the Keynesian plan for an international currency, discarded at Bretton Woods, revived in the still-distorted form of SDRs, and now ripe for full implementation.[27]

The common thread in all these versions of the eighties can be glimpsed in the image of suspension, where both the capitalist system and its opponents make extravagant claims for the future only by disposing the claims of the past. If from one angle the end of the eighties coincided with the crash of centrally planned economies and the discrediting of the ideologies that defended them, from another angle all of that is a false problem, a red herring. From this transnational capitalist angle, all the cataclysmic events that should have closed an era—the collapse of the Soviet bloc, the defeat of apartheid, the Gulf War, even the violent outbreak of ethnic warfare around the globe—merely prove that the eighties axioms of "productivity" and "competitiveness" are more than just keywords of economic success. They have now been enshrined as the only abiding civic virtues. To be beholden to the world market is, finally, to understand history ever more intimately, as a personal and local fate and judgment handed down from an impersonal deity. When such faiths are built into the most basic mechanisms of planning and social reproduction, history does not end so much as it becomes the invisible hand that we must always bet against.

Perhaps, then, this particular eighties has not yet ended and indeed may never properly end: It marks the moment when debt ceased to be the monetary expression of the romance of development and became the orienting image of social life itself, the specter of an elusive future circulating in the present, forever dashing off toward the dusty horizon. The debt crisis may have ended (according to the *New York Times*, in fact, it ended in April 1994), but the emplacement of debt has continued apace, so that the "opening" of China[28] (ca. 1978) or the "opening" of the formerly socialist countries would appear to be more of the same: the privatization, securitization, and capitalization of all social-political-cultural life. Not even the planet, especially not its nonhuman forms of life, has remained outside this process: The domain and pace of natural history has given way to the futures market, where images of life-to-come can be traded, devalued, and discarded today, now, when the pretext of "foresight" hides countless acts of foreclosure and ruin.[29]

What Next?

From one perspective, these narratives of capitalism are always terribly distressing and remote: Such grand stories say nothing of the many-layered struggles wrapped up with the emergence of new differences and the obstinacy of past ways of life. It is as if money is the only representational medium and events can be said to "happen" only when some movement is registered in the balance sheets and the price tables. This kind of thinking is clearly infectious. It would be hard to tell the official history of debt without suspecting that history telling is itself a kind of official debt, a way of accounting for and thereby preserving duties, obligations, and payments due. There is a blur of debt in every image of history, some oblique plane where bodies are still in motion and our sight is out of sync with the scene. And at the same time, we make images of history precisely to resolve our debts and to halt the preemption of the present by plans, cycles, and claims beyond our reckoning. Perhaps every attempt to seize "the history of the present" faces this dilemma.

That is why the gesture of historicization, so crucial to both the description and the practice of postmodernism, is also a play of images between punctuation and persistence. If "postmodernism" itself announced a break or transformation, other contemporary theoretical programs have searched for hidden continuities or, rather, for images that can be withdrawn from the demands of a localizing historical narrative and used to illuminate disparate eras and situations. One of the most successful examples of this operation (which is for obvious reasons a work of many hands) has been Foucault's notion of surveillance as developed out of the description of Bentham's Panopticon in *Discipline and Punish.* Far from remaining within Foucault's particular account of mid-nineteenth-century social practices, the diagram-scenario of surveillance has taken off as one of the most far-reaching images of modernity itself. (On an even grosser scale, think of the immense success of the dramatic concept-image of Otherness as extracted from Hegel, de Beauvoir, Sartre, or Fanon, which lends itself well to transhistorical usages.) Along the way, "surveillance" has taken on both the nebulous valences of the term "power" and the microscopic inflections of "visuality": As a result, it has become a highly efficient interpretive machine that addresses everything from architecture and cinema to academic discourse and corporate organization. It has become especially prominent in discussions of postmodern media-and-police societies in the 1970s and 1980s, leading to a certain superimposition of historical analysis and contemporary diagnosis: It is as if the image of panoptic surveillance has flown out of its historical situation to watch over and synchronize the present as well. Let me emphasize that I am not trying to reinstate the original Foucauldian time line: Instead, I want to point out that the haphazard fate of this concept-image tells us something about the unformulated needs and appropriative habits of cultural criticism. In order to redirect those appetites toward the question of global economics, we must replace "surveillance" with another organizing figure.

In a brief polemic titled "Postscript on Societies of Control," Gilles Deleuze has proposed just such a way of reperiodizing Foucault's genealogy. He points out that the era of surveillance had been, in Foucault's account, related to a phase of capitalist organizations of labor and mechanizations of production. Now that phase has passed and Foucault's mise-en-scène must be restaged. Indeed, Deleuze discerns a new image sitting on the horizon of history. Here is an outline of his argument.

> Foucault located disciplinary societies in the eighteenth and nineteenth centuries; they reach their peak at the beginning of the twentieth. They proceed by organizing grand zones of enclosure. The individual never ceases to pass from one closed zone to another, each having its own laws: first the family, then the school ("you are no longer in your family"); then the barracks ("you are no longer at school") finally the factory. . . . We are in a generalized crisis of all zones of enclosure, prison, hospital, factory, school, family. . . . [These] are no longer the distinct analogical spaces that converge towards an owner—state or private power—but coded figures—deformable and transformable—of a single corporation that now has only managers. . . . People are no longer enclosed, but indebted.[30]

For Deleuze, the onset of "societies of control" can be dated roughly at the end of World War II, and his examples are all drawn from contemporary capitalist practices—computerization, ceaseless reevaluation of assets, decentralized production practices, and the emphasis on marketing as the logic of decision making. Most striking of all, however, is the appearance of debt as the driving force of social relationships. With this event, two reciprocal tendencies can be visualized together, in an ever-tighter intertwining: the transformation of collective moral obligations and services into economic terms (as charted by Nietzsche's *Genealogy of Morals*) and the transformation of exchange relationships into the moral labor of individual subjects (as charted by Weber's *The Protestant Ethic and the Spirit of Capitalism*). Recognizing the pervasiveness of today's regime of debt makes it easier to imagine that debt may have always been a fundamental line of social mediation, one that definitively constitutes groups, territories, and bodies as conductors and bearers of the movement of value. And given this image of debt, the concept of "value" itself dissolves into a heterogeneous and diffracted flux that is divided among different domains, each with its own rules and processes of reproduction and transmission.

A veritable anthropology of debt can be assembled (with the qualification that this sense of "debt" may extend beyond the human). Pierre Bourdieu, for example, has distinguished between gift exchange, swapping, and lending in terms of their various temporal structures: Whereas gift giving and counter giving follow a tempo of deferment that allows for strategic maneuver, swapping and lending are modeled on simultaneity. In the case of lending, moreover, "the return of the loan is explicitly guaranteed by a juridical act and thus already accomplished at the very moment of the drawing up of a contract capable of ensuring that the acts it prescribes are predictable and calculable."[31] Rather than view these kinds of exchange as historically successive or exclusive, we need to ask how they all remain negotiable possibilities. To say that debt has become more extensive and complex does not mean that every interaction falls under the same rule of debt. On the contrary, since debt (as gift) implies "a deferral and a difference" in what is circulated, all kinds of action can be undertaken in a regime of debt without being reckoned according to the same standard. Indeed, "debt" may be the best way to describe the way in which forces from one domain of value are "transferred" or "translated" into another. This structural notion of debt does not stand opposed to what Marx calls "simple exchange," which is never an exchange of equivalents: It enacts a conjunction of different zones of value, even realms of meaning.[32] At each point in their itineraries, material images of value (money, words, pictures, etc.) are formed precisely in order to shuttle between different activities, different capacities, even different bodies and communities. Debt is the economic verb *par excellence:* Beyond production, *it makes something appear.* Derrida has offered one snapshot of this system, calling it the "*differantial* [*sic*] economy of the tele-facsimile": "[It] does not just mark the interplay of capital. It displaces and deforms all concepts of social ties, as well as all political and juridical history, beginning with what served until now to determine the *res publica* or the (direct or parliamentary) democracy, representation or public opinion, its formation as well as its expression."[33] Now it can be seen that debt is not simply the means by which a particular social-economic system establishes a domain and regulates its crisis; it serves also as the route by which that crisis is transmitted ever onward. Debt puts into play the very imaginary supports (the integrity of the socius, its faith in itself, its capacity for self-regulation) that made it possible in the first place.

This diffusion of crisis makes itself visible in all sectors of everyday existence, beginning with the first "fact" of capitalist life, the commodity. Because the Marxian narrative of commodity production involves a sequence of stages bridged by the metaphysical mediation of money, the object-world of capitalism appears to be filled with the opaque traces of alienated, dead labor. As the processes of production, distribution, and consumption become more thoroughly shot through with credit—which, as we've seen, is nothing other than an image of future time serving as currency in the present—the landscapes and stockpiles of dead labor can be drawn more and more completely into the unending, undead frenzy of exchange. The financial system develops its own rates of obsolescence that become as decisive for production as the rates of technological turnover: This tension will appear only as a competition among different capitals as they jockey from one enterprise to another. For a time, it is even possible for finance to make production itself obsolete, simply too slow for the quickening life span of investment capital, as seemed to happen in the takeover mania in the mid–1980s.[34] When nobody knows what thing may yield some value, every scrap must be brought to market. The work of selling thus becomes an ever more fundamental economic activity, absorbing a greater share of human time whether in the financial capitals or in the makeshift urban markets. (Or, to think of it in spatial terms, every place becomes a possible site of transaction, although the nodes of finance have become ever more concentrated.) Far from validating the old view of a totally rationalized and administered society (whether drawn from Foucault or the Frankfurt School), the passage to prolific debt signals an ever more centrifugal capitalism, its strongest flows skipping around the slightest delay in the valorization process and its weakest flows condemned to slow down until stranded in the wastelands where no other value will try to redeem it.[35]

The image of debt—injected like a glowing liquid into our flow charts of the global body of capital—allows us to question what kind of "reality" is exercised by the newer, grander arrangements of value. In an obvious sense, debt is nothing new, and its imaginary force is already built into the "enchanted world" described by Marx. When it comes to capitalism, nobody minds being metaphysical—just the opposite: Capitalists stake everything on images of value precisely because they recognize that those images are alterable, contingent, transferable. Like Coyote's paintings, what works once may not work again. Marx took pains to show how each individual capitalist seeks to make a particular bundle of money represent Capital itself: By throwing money into the capitalist enterprise, the capitalist makes a wish that quantity will become quality, that this time money will no longer represent something in particular but will come to represent its own power to invest anything with value. At the very moment when the whole speculative process threatens to become all too recognizably concrete—when money returns to the capitalist's hands and there can be no doubt that something has happened out there—at that moment, back from its hazardous campaigns, world-weary money is rechristened as infant Capital and sent out once more. (Marx is fond of childhood images: "A great deal of capital, which appears today in the United States without any birth certificate, was yesterday, in England, the capitalized blood of children.")[36] The arrow of time flips over at the instant of valorization, when the fulfillment of a past investment becomes the power of command over future actions and products. It is as if each capital, each image of value, recoils from its Real, refusing to recognize itself in the limits to movement that alone make it possible. Capital moves by shedding its past, that is, by presenting itself at each moment as sovereign cause rather than contingent effect.[37] That is why, when writing the history of capitalism, it is important to avoid giving capital the history it pretends to have, which is based on the future it wants to own.

This temporal wrinkle in the circulation of money, labor, and commodities is susceptible to disruption at each juncture. With wages, the danger takes the form of working-class resistance and the escalation of general social demands. With commodities, the danger appears as the failure of valorization, the ineradicable suspension of value before the finished product can be sold for a profitable price. But the danger with money reappears at every moment—it can be too elusive, too stable, too fast, or too slow. As capitalists try to hedge against these uncertainties, the coordinates of monetary danger are measured, circulated several times and divided up, so that the commodity chain (and the currency chain) is diverted to so many other games of chance (arbitrage, derivatives, etc.). Thus the moment of valorization always arrives posthumously: The claims already outweigh the promises. In practice, the incommensurability of the promises and the claims need never be revealed as long as the process separates its two vectors of time, the imperfect future tense of production and the prophetic past tense of credit, which spiral around each other without occupying the same moment.[38] Thus the looping course of time in capitalist circulation prevents stability, permits crisis, and sets off inflation and deflation as the unconscious reflexes of the economic collectivity, dream products that combine the traumas of its anxious daytime with its most secret and extravagant desires.

Although debt has haunted all kinds of social structures, appearing both as the god in the temple and as a cohort of household ghosts, the past few decades have brought new images and technologies of debt. The vast machineries of information, the heightened speeds of return, and the proliferation of interfacing zones have enabled the monetary form of debt to serve as the general equivalent of those other debts that had not yet been capitalized. Or to put it in more Marxist terms, debt becomes the "most adequate" and most effective image of the rule of exchange value, capable of flexible transfigurations, more relentless and penetrating than money itself. Capital makes itself most mobile by passing through a variety of transactions, inscriptions, and regulations, all of which transmit value by allowing measures and guarantees to remain as contingent and temporary as possible. The "mobility" of capital in a regime of debt, then, becomes its most determining trait: No longer simply fixed or circulating, capital sets in motion branching detours of calculations and wagers, crossing from one local system of values into another. But the figure of mobility must be specified further: There is no "pure" mobility, no infinite open space or fluid time. Each particle of capital traces its own line of transmission, covering more or less space, taking more or less time. To say that capital becomes more mobile is to suggest that individual capitals may be less discrete, less punctual, and therefore more dependent on the matrix of possibilities cleared by all the other capitals already in motion. Contemporary capitalism can be defined by the way it develops images of value to project relationships between different domains of global existence: not only between worker and boss or between one commodity and another, but between competing currencies, competing environments, and competing hopes for the future.

As long as debt enjoys the transcendence of an unreal temporality, it can conduct its affairs of the day from afar. Marx, however, tried to envision debt as an immanent force binding together the as-yet-unnamed global collectivity. In the remarkable twenty-seventh chapter of *Capital,* volume 3, he summarizes his conclusions about the credit system:

> The credit system has a dual character immanent in it: on the one hand it develops the motive of capitalist production, enrichment by the exploitation of others' labour, into the purest and most colossal system of gambling and swindling, and restricts ever more the already small number of the exploiters of social wealth; on the other hand however it constitutes the form of transition towards a new mode of production. It is this dual character that gives the principal spokesmen for credit, from Law through to Isaac Péreire, their nicely mixed character of swindler and prophet.[39]

This hope that credit may signal a transition to another mode of production may seem ridiculously misplaced in an era so thoroughly marked by social-scale gambling and so well populated by swindlers. Perhaps it could be said that the debt system forces everybody to play those roles or lose out. In this sense, debt becomes an absent structure articulated through its "supports" (as Althusser described capital), for which each subject bears responsibility simply by bearing money (or not). But there is that other chance that the very attempt to see where debt goes and how it works will serve to illuminate all the promises and dangers floated by this movement of history. The eighties presses its claim upon us by virtue of the awesome spectacle it offers, a series of tableaux exhibiting what Alexander Kluge has called "the assault of the present on the rest of time." But this has been a peculiar attack, in which "the present" stakes its claims by hoarding images of "the rest of time," whether in the form of cultural artifacts or financial instruments. Marx would insist that such images, no matter how prepackaged, degraded, or inflated, can still conserve the staying powers of history.

Maybe the eighties are over, maybe not. But before we can say how we will spend the nineties, we need to find out if the nineties have already been spent.

NOTES

1. George Yúdice, "We Are *Not* the World," *Social Text* 31/32 (1992):202–216.

2. The present volume offers abundant evidence of this promising tendency. I also want to cite two already-well-known essays that specifically raise the question of economics and "postcoloniality": Arjun Appadurai, "Disjuncture and Difference in the Global Cultural Economy," *Public Culture* 2, 2 (Spring 1990):1–24; Anne McClintock, "The Angel of Progress: Pitfalls of the Term 'Post-Colonialism,'" *Social Text* 31/32 (1992):84–98. Finally, I would cite the ongoing and indispensable work of Gayatri Chakravorty Spivak, who plies the trade among particularity, peculiarity, and globality. See, for a set of examples, *Outside in the Teaching Machine* (New York: Routledge, 1993).

3. This definition draws directly from the work of Gilles Deleuze and Félix Guattari. In their recent work *Qu'est-ce que la philosophie?* (Paris: Minuit, 1991) they pose the possibility that philosophy (with its distinctive ways of building concepts) can merge with art (which they define as a composition of affects and percepts): "The plane of composition

of art and the plane of immanence of philosophy can be slipped into each other, to the point where the pieces of one would be occupied by the entities of the other. In each case, in effect, the plane and what occupies it are like two relatively distinct, relatively heterogeneous parts. A thinker can thus modify, in a decisive manner, that which signifies thinking, setting up a new image of thought, instituting a new plane of immanence, but, instead of creating new concepts to occupy it, she populates it with other instances, other entities, poetic, novelistic [romanesques], or even pictorial or musical" (65). This spirit of innovation infuses the best cultural work, which does not "culturalize" other domains so much as it seeks to redirect what can still be called the cultural, aesthetic, or imaginary forces already bound up there.

4. See, most recently, Fredric Jameson, *The Geopolitical Aesthetic: Cinema and Space in the World System* (Bloomington: Indiana University Press, 1992), and "Actually Existing Marxism," *Polygraph* 6/7 (1993):170–195.

5. Walter Benjamin, *Das Passagen-Werk,* vol. 1, ed. Rolf Tiedemann (Frankfurt: Suhrkamp), 595.

6. Ernest Mandel, *Late Capitalism,* trans. Joris De Bres (London: Verso, 1978), 560. See also the chart of long waves on pp. 130–132.

7. Fredric Jameson, "Periodizing the 60s," in *The 60s, Without Apology,* ed. Sohnya Sayres, Anders Stephanson, Stanley Aronowitz, Fredric Jameson (Minneapolis: University of Minnesota Press, 1984), 178–209. See also "A Very Partial Chronology" in the same volume, 210–215. This version of the sixties extends from 1957 (Algeria, Ghana, Sputnik) to 1976 (Soweto, Partie Quebecois, the deaths of Mao and Zhao). The chronology makes no mention of any episodes in international finance.

8. Jameson, "Periodizing the 60s," in *The 60s, Without Apology,* 209.

9. Jameson has gone on to develop this antagonism in his essay "Nostalgia for the Present," in *Postmodernism, or the Cultural Logic of Late Capitalism* (Durham, N.C.: Duke University Press, 1991), 279–296. There, "postmodernism" names the impossibility of an eighties that would reclaim the historical energies of the sixties or, indeed, any such energies whatsoever. In this sense, "postcolonial" theory also serves less as a periodizing term with reference to the official statutes of colonialization, dependency, or the survival of imperialism but rather names something like an intellectual prognosis on the recovery or resuscitation of the earlier national liberation and antiimperialist movements (along with the "organic" roles held out for them there). Here again, periodization signals a refusal of certain political determinations, now thought to be absent, unanswerable, or ineffective.

10. Alain Lipietz, *The Enchanted World: Inflation, Credit and the World Crisis,* trans. Ian Patterson (London: Verso, 1983), xvi. For Lipietz's dismissive view on Kondratiev cycles (Mandel's model), see footnote 35 on page 132. He stresses that crisis brings about the "*invention*" of a new system (his emphasis).

11. According to Paul Mosley, Jane Harrigan, and John Toye, *Aid and Power: The World Bank and Policy-based Lending* (London and New York: Routledge, 1991), citing work by Richard Feinberg, the IMF and the World Bank agreed in 1966 to execute different tasks in the international economy, the former taking responsibility for what might be called short-term disciplinary actions and the latter offering the financial means for long-term development (36). Of course, this distinction has not held up in practice, since the different institutions come under different kinds of pressure from governments and private capital. In 1989, after a controversial World Bank loan was extended to Argentina at the urging of U.S. commercial banks (which wanted some of their defaulted loans back) *without*

IMF conditionality, a new concordat had to be written to promise close cooperation in the future (48–56).

12. See the chart reprinted in David Harvey, *The Condition of Postmodernity: An Enquiry into the Origins of Cultural Change* (Oxford: Basil Blackwell, 1990), 144. On the notion of "xenomoney" and the theoretical interest of the futures market, see Brian Rotman, *Signifying Nothing: The Semiotics of Zero* (New York: St. Martin's Press, 1987), 88–97.

13. See Cheryl Payer, *Lent and Lost: Foreign Credit and Third World Development* (London: Zed Books, 1991), 112–114.

14. Michel Aglietta, "World Capitalism in the Eighties," *New Left Review* 136 (November/December 1982):23–25; Alain Lipietz, *Mirages and Miracles* (London: Verso, 1988), 141–144; and Lipietz, *The Enchanted World,* 95.

15. Lipietz, *The Enchanted World,* 122.

16. Even the *Economist,* that faithful mouthpiece of free market purists, admits the absurdity of the monetarist episode, which, in its retrospective gaze, looks like another example of the obsolescence of national governments: "To control money, you must know what 'money' is—and, thanks partly to innovation and growth of international finance, that is no longer clear" (September 19, 1992). Of course, it has never been clear "what money is," least of all to those who operate the levers of international finance. They work best when the multiple determinations of money are obscured from view, the incommensurabilities and double binds transferred somewhere else along the line. The rule of the marketplace may be summarized this way: Make somebody else pay for the structural problems of the system.

17. Mike Davis, *Prisoners of the American Dream: Politics and Economy in the History of the U.S. Working Class* (London: Verso, 1986), 136–138. Davis outlines four components of the restructuring of the domestic American economy: (1) the opening to imports, (2) deregulation of industry and finance, (3) growth of Sunbelt industries with their "right to work" laws, (4) deindustrialization as a deliberate financial strategy. To this last point, we could add that merger mania and massive growth of nonbank financial institutions would be a strong trend well into the 1990s. For his analysis of Proposition 13 as a first step toward Reaganism, see Mike Davis, *City of Quartz: Excavating the Future in Los Angeles* (London: Verso, 1990), 180–186. See also Alan Brinkley, "Reagan's Revenge, As Invented by Howard Jarvis," *New York Times Magazine,* June 19, 1994, 36–37, for an argument that the disconnection between taxes and public services has become an endemic ideological feature of U.S. political life: another strong proof that the eighties are not yet over.

18. Lipietz, *Mirages and Miracles,* 166.

19. Antonio Negri, "Twenty Theses on Marx: Interpretation of the Class Situation Today," trans. Michael Hardt, *Polygraph* 5 (1992):136–170. The quotes are from pages 151 and 153, respectively.

20. For a discussion of constitutionality in a transnational frame, see Gayatri Chakravorty Spivak, "Scattered Speculations on the Question of Cultural Studies," in *Outside in the Teaching Machine* (255–284).

21. Noam Chomsky, *Towards a New Cold War* (New York: Pantheon, 1982), 372, n. 9.

22. George Anders, *Merchants of Debt: KKR and the Mortgaging of American Business* (New York: Basic Books, 1992), 107.

23. It is striking that Slavoj Žižek uses the same scene to illustrate the way a subject can forget the "knowledge in the Real" and "must be reminded" of the Symbolic laws that allow us to deal with the Real in the first place. In this moment of suspension, the Roadrunner

is "between the two deaths." To follow the analogy, we might say that the coyote-capitalist is between the two debts: the debt to the power of the Western banks and the debt to the practical efficacy and necessity of images. See *The Sublime Object of Ideology* (London: Verso), 133–134. There is no space here to use this strange point of contact to investigate a Lacanian conception of money and debt, but it is clear that Žižek will entertain the idea that some law of value (or the Real) will ultimately set to work on the skywalking creature. I am inclined to suspend that judgment.

24. Alain Lipietz, "The Debt Problem, European Integration and the New Phase of World Crisis," *New Left Review* 178 (November/December 1989):37.

25. See Immanuel Wallerstein, *Geopolitics and Geoculture: Essays on the Changing World-System* (Cambridge: Cambridge University Press, 1991), for an argument that the 1989 events brought an end to the hegemonic Pax Americana of the Cold War. In that sense, the events of 1989 are the last episodes of a process begun in 1968: "We have perhaps arrived now in the true realm of uncertainty" (15).

26. The strong version of this thesis is expressed by Robert Kurz in *Der Kollaps der Modernisirung: Vom Zusammenbruch des Kasernensozialismus zur Krise der Weltökonomie* (Leipzig: Reclam Verlag, 1994 [original edition, 1991]). Kurz's work has taken increasingly dire tones concerning the lack of wisdom displayed by both capitalists and radical leftists. See his "Das Weltkartenhaus: Globalisierung der Märkte und fiktives Geldkapital," *Lettre International* 27 (Winter 1994):92–93.

27. Alain Lipietz, *Towards a New Economic Order: Postfordism, Ecology and Democracy,* trans. Malcolm Slater (Oxford and New York: Oxford University Press, 1992), 112–118.

28. The *Economist,* a conspicuously enthusiastic partisan of a Chinese "awakening" to capitalism, argues that the political act inaugurating this transition came in the third plenary session of the Eleventh Central Committee of the Communist Party in December 1978. See "When China Awakes," November 29, 1992.

29. See "Survey of the Global Environment," *Economist,* May 30, 1992:

> "Just between you and me," mused Lawrence Summers, chief economist of the World Bank, in a memo leaked to *The Economist* in February, "shouldn't the World Bank be encouraging *more* migration of the dirty industries to the LDCs?"
>
> Mr. Summers gave three reasons for his controversial proposition. First, the costs of pollution depend on earnings lost through death and injury. These earnings are lowest in the poorest countries. Therefore, "I think the logic behind dumping a load of toxic waste in the lowest-wage country is impeccable and we should face up to that." Second, the costs of pollution rise disproportionately as it grows, so polluting the cleanest parts of the world may be less harmful than making the dirty parts still filthier. Third, people value a clean environment more as their incomes rise. So if polluting industries move from rich countries to poor ones, the costs of pollution will decline.(7)

Anyone needing an example of the way economists perform their "calculations" on a global scale, using the crudest and narrowest notions of value, should study this passage word by word.

30. Gilles Deleuze, "Post-scriptum sur les sociétés de contrôle," in *Pourparlers* (Paris: Minuit, 1990), 240–246.

31. Pierre Bourdieu, *Outline of a Theory of Practice,* trans. Richard Nice (Cambridge: Cambridge University Press, 1977), 5.

32. It is beyond the scope of this rough conspectus to discuss Bourdieu's theories in depth. Two quotes from his *Outline of a Theory of Practice* may prime a further discussion:

"Once one realizes that symbolic capital is always *credit,* in the widest sense of the word, i.e., a sort of advance which the group alone can grant those who give it the best material and symbolic *guarantees,* it can be seen that the exhibition of symbolic capital (which is always expensive in symbolic terms) is one of the mechanisms which (no doubt universally) make capital go to capital" (181, his emphasis).

And: "Symbolic capital, a transformed and therefore disguised form of physical 'economic' capital, produces its proper effect inasmuch, and only inasmuch, as it conceals the fact that it originates in 'material' forms of capital which are also, in the last analysis, the source of its effects" (183, his emphasis). With this passage's careful qualifications and quote marks, it is easy to see that Bourdieu doubts that the distinction between "economic"/"material" capital and "symbolic" capital can be maintained.

33. Jacques Derrida, "Faxitexture," in *Anywhere,* ed. Cynthia C. Davidson (New York: Rizzoli, 1992), 30. Derrida's emphasis on the "differantial"[*sic*] with respect to the thinking of economics is elaborated in *Spectres de Marx* (Paris: Galilée, 1993): There, "tele-technology" is associated with a "general dislocation" in time that marks "our time" (268). All of this will require further elaboration.

34. See Elmar Altvater, *The Future of the Market,* trans. Patrick Camiller (London: Verso, 1993). He argues for the centrality of interest mechanisms in determining profits and wages (94) and speaks of a reversal of capitalist common sense under conditions fostered by a tight or hyperactive credit market: "There is a kind of inversion of the profit-interest hierarchy, such that interest provides a certain and profits an uncertain source of income" (104). The very possibility of such a reversal should indicate the limits to the dynamics of "development" in each cycle of capitalism (however open-ended and unguided it may be).

35. It is becoming common to refer to Africa as a "lost continent," neatly reinstating the trope of absolute Otherness and separation that accompanied the imperialist conquest of the continent, perhaps as a way to prepare a disengagement and a refusal of responsibility for what is unfolding there. See Jacques Attali, *Millenium: Winners and Losers in the Coming World Order,* trans. Leila Conners and Nathan Gardels (New York: Times Books, 1991), 73–74. For optimism regarding the capacity of the World Bank to remake Africa in its own image, see Thomas L. Friedman, "Africa's Economies: Reforms Pay Off," *New York Times,* March 13, 1994, A4.

36. Karl Marx, *Capital,* trans. Ben Fowles, vol. 1 (New York: Vintage Books, 1977), 920.

37. This is indeed the fundamental story behind the Reaganite manifesto, *Wealth and Poverty,* by George Gilder (New York: Basic Books, 1981). Although the book deserves an extended analysis, I will note here that Gilder provides a veritable theology of debt, premised on a dismissal of calculative predictions and a celebration of the capitalist's powers to begin each investment day as if the future remains to be written by his own hand.

He praises the "incalculable and unprovable supply-side responses that are the mustard seeds of capitalist miracles of growth. As Warren Brookes has said, it is only the physical part of our wealth that is finite. Its metaphysical sources (imagination and creativity) are infinite. There are free lunches under capitalism because there are free minds and free men—because of the limitless returns on metaphysical capital, because of the manifold rewards of giving, and because of the magic of the golden rule. But these benefits always elude the computations of aggregate economics.

"If American conservatism can come to terms with the meaning of debt, it will represent a nearly unprecedented intellectual triumph" (228). This conclusion may have been prophetic about the practice of 1980s finance if not about the intellectual capacities of American conservatives.

38. In a survey of the world economy, the *Economist* emphasizes the difficulty in finding useful statistics on capital flows given their volume and speed. With respect to capital account balances, the article notes: "If you combined the capital-account balances of every country in the world, you would expect the sum to be zero. Actually, you would find that the world appears to run a big capital-account surplus with itself. During the 1980s, according to official statistics, an average of $72 billion a year flowed out of national economies and never arrived. In 1991 the discrepancy was $122 billion" ("Survey of the World Economy," *Economist,* September 19, 1992, 6). This cloud of unknowing is related but not reducible to the massive transfers within transnational corporations, long noted to be a crucial unknown quantity in official reports. They have been estimated to be "as much as a third of all trade." See "Survey of Multinationals," *Economist,* March 27, 1993, 9.

39. Marx, *Capital,* vol. 3, 572–573.

PART TWO

OLD EMPIRES AND CONTESTED ZONES

6

Culture and Ideology in the Contemporary Arab World

SAMIR AMIN

IN SELECTING THE TITLE for this research, I intended to surpass the horizon of current analyses dedicated to examining the ideologies upon which political movements in this region of our contemporary world are established. Such analyses—some of which are fine, detailed, and critical—have usually remained confined to political and social realities, as evident from the programs and strategies of political organizations, the economic and social interests regarded as a pivot for such strategies, the echo of such topics within the social reality, and their success or failure with respect to the audience to whom these analyses were addressed. I am assuming here that the immediate analyses of politics and social movements and their ideological and programmatic expressions are known, in order that I may pose the question of their relation to both Arab culture and that of the West, which is present on all levels of reality in the Arab world and all the Third World regions.

The implementation of these ambitious projects implies a visualization of the contents that could be given to the different aspect of reality, classified in the rubrics of civilization, culture, political system, socioeconomic life, and ideology. I have no intentions here of elucidating these issues and proposing definitions for the specific fields that could be studied within these contexts. I shall confine myself to stating that the contents of realities determined by the previously mentioned fields cannot be well defined except through hypothetical theories that explain the interrelations between such realities. In other words, what could the meaning of the term "relative autonomy" in each of these realms (economic, political, ideological, cultural, etc.) signify? What, then, does this relative autonomy—or its negation—signify when we analyze the reproduction of the system as a whole, and its transformation dynamics? And if relative autonomy urges us not to confuse its meaning with the possible meaning given to independence of realms, in relation to one another, or with the meaning we implicitly intend when we discuss causes and effects, then are there nevertheless any hierarchies existing that impose themselves through the dynamics of historic changes? Let us beware here of simplifying and accepting, for example, the fact that the economic system necessarily entails adjustment of the political system and its requirements or, inversely, that culture conveys transhistoric invariants.

How are mutual adjustments of the different aspects of life formed so that they are capable of ensuring the applicability and reproduction of a social system as a whole? How do the permanent maladjustments resulting from a nonequivalent development of the various realms become either absorbed or else explode, obliging society to make a qualitative leap or else, from the absence of a solution, condemning the society facing the dilemma to quit the scene of history? What are the roles assumed by ideologies in producing these necessary adjustments? Under what conditions do they operate as active and positive catalysts and in what cases are they presented as a passive expression of this dilemma?

Certainly, we can proceed to answer through a general theoretical reading of the highest quality, built upon the history of societies. Marx proposed the relevant essential axes while establishing the foundation for historical materialism. He achieved this with what is more than talent. To me it was done with a genius unsurpassed until this very day. Others before him attempted to do the same thing, through what we can call the idealistic philosophies of history, which were all ultimately surpassed by historical materialism. Others have tried to do the same thing after Marx from precisely an adverse angle to historical materialism. Sometimes they did it with talent—as did Weber—but to my mind their proposals remain inferior to those of Marx, being widely phenomenal and even superficial. I am not stating here that the historical materialism of Marx constitutes an accomplished work. On the contrary, I consider this work a launching point that belongs to the successive generations to follow up and examine thoroughly until they reach a point where they might have exhausted its potential and, thus, a new qualitative leap will be necessary.

The best and maybe sole mode of launching historical materialism is to tackle the already cited general issues to see how concrete and precise historical experiences that are carefully analyzed can enrich our stock of reflections in these domains.

The cultural issue, long neglected by active political forces worldwide—in the West and the Third World alike—and reduced upon evocation to a secondary grade within speeches, seems to have resurged with vehemence everywhere. The defense of "authenticity" and commendation of "differences" have become themes in fashion, being, in addition, successful among a diverse and numerous public. Nevertheless, it is ascertained that the cultural speech of our time is not scientifically founded any more than the foregoing silence. This fashionable speech is concomitant with evident political regressions, abandonment of universalistic visualizations, drawing back and even sometimes a mere obscurantism.

Capitalism is not just an international economic system. It is also the prevalent global system in all domains, including the cultural one, as I see it. Hence, a prevalent global culture exists, namely that of capitalism. However, in our current language, we mention "Western culture," whether to defend its superiority or to discard it as being alien. I claim that describing it as Western (or European or Christian or Jewish-Christian) obscures the essence of the matter, which is the capitalist content of this culture. The viewpoint that I defend here emanates from the concept of capitalism as I understand it. In this analysis, capitalism is based on the submission of both the political and ideological realms to the logic of the economic one. I have written on this subject that the law of value not only governs the world of economic relations but, from there, governs society in all its aspects. Hence, the economic domain becomes independent of the organization of power and its ideological legitimacy. The laws of the market become prevalent as autonomous forces similar to those of nature. The essential content of the culture of capitalism finds its definition here: economic alienation. This reflection of dominance of the economic realm accounts for all the phenomenal aspects that define modernity, whether they are considered positive or negative, eternal or historically situated: modern concepts and practices of liberty and democracy; portioned labor and labor force reduced to the state of commodity separation between nature and society, and so on.

The dominance of the economic system in this analysis concerns capitalism. In all the foregoing social systems this dominance is situated on the level of the organization of power. Here power is the source of richness. In capitalism, it is the opposite; richness is the source of power. The inversion in this relation, according to Marx's interpretation, which is mine as well, is essential. The transparency of economic relations in the foregoing societies, in contrast to the opacity that is produced in capitalism through commercial relations, implies that ideology functions in premodern societies as a sort of legitimacy to power, whereas in capitalism it is a sort of legitimacy to richness—the economic system, the market and its efficiency and so on. Hence, the content of the prevalent ideology of precapitalist societies is not defined by economic alienation but by metaphysical alienation.

The precapitalist world is thus multiple. It is divided into distinct cultural domains that are themselves determined through great metaphysics that operate within the boundaries of these domains. Thus, we can discuss cultures in the plural, be they Islamic, Hindu, Confucian, or Christian. If this is so, then metaphysical ideologies belonging to each of these domains assume a similar function in all the discussed precapitalist societies: In the same way they render the tributary power legitimate (in the feudal form in European Christianity, in similar forms in Islamic Orient, Hindu India, Confucian China, etc.). The similarity is so striking that these societies, in spite of their distinctiveness, resemble one another greatly.

The modern world is singular; the foregoing worlds were multiple. Yet societies in the past, defined in their own cultural domains, were relative to one another. Exchanges between them were not negligible and were sometimes even important. The tributary economy does not integrate these local systems in a single international system in the same way that capitalism integrates all global societies in a single international economic system. The unity of the modern world proves the dominance of the economic system. The diversity of the foregoing systems was the product of the metaphysics dominating therein. Hence, the prevalent culture of the modern world—capitalist culture—appeared in its form as an expression of Western culture. It was in Europe that capitalism, which imposed itself throughout the world, was born. But this birth was also a rupture with Europe's past: European capitalist culture is not the heir of the tributary culture of Western Christianity. It is a form of rupture with the latter. Europe did not become a capitalist culture except through being liberated from metaphysical dominance (here in its Christian form). The Western character of capitalist culture is thus a mere appearance—a form in the very sense of the word. Why, then, is the capitalist culture seen as Western by everyone, by its advocates and decriers, by its beneficiaries and victims, and why is it expressed by the Eurocentrism of some and the reversed Eurocentrism of others?

In my view, the reason for this complementary double alienation is to be sought within the reality of capitalist universality. Capitalism has actually conquered and unified the world and created for the first time in history a unique economic system. However, it did not homogenize the operating conditions of this unique system. On the contrary, universalized capitalism was deployed through polarizing the planet and creating a deep contrast between its centers and peripheries. This fact is the root of our cultural problem. Socialism, including historical Marxism, has underestimated this dimension of polarizing capitalism by virtue of its own nature. It was thought that the culture of capitalism would erase all foregoing cultures because capitalism, being an economic reality, would impose itself in all similar modes of reaction everywhere. Hence, in the same way that capitalism imposed a reinterpretation of Christianity in the West, it thought that it could successfully impose elsewhere a similar reinterpretation of Islam and other religions and could gradually erase, with the same efficacy, vestiges of the past: the prevalent metaphysical alienation, nations, and so on. However, the immanent polarization of the system did not operate in this direction but in an opposing one—that of accentuating the contrast between nations and cultures.

Thus, polarization implies that on the cultural level the modern world is both one and many. Capitalist culture is prevalent on the international level, but it failed to absorb the foregoing cultures within its peripheries in the same way it had absorbed the foregoing Eurochristian culture from its centers. In such a condition, the permanence of cultural diversity is not a vestige of the past, on its way to a gradual diminution. It is a product of polarizing capitalist expansion. However, this diversity is not absolute. It proceeds in parallel with the prevalence of the universal capitalist culture.

Polarization did not necessarily stick to the limits of cultural domains. Sometimes it transgressed them both ways. The centers are not all heirs of Europe—Europeans of the old continent, of North America, and of Australia. In Japan, the exception, capitalist culture operates perfectly. This culture has subjected and transformed—reinterpreted—the foregoing culture (here Confucian) in exactly the same way that capitalist culture in the West expressed itself through forms of Eurochristian appearances, notwithstanding the fact that they have been reinterpreted and adjusted to the demands of capitalist prevalence. Further, all peripheries are not of an originally non-European culture. Latin America, the other exception, is a peripheral continent, given its economic position in the global system. Nevertheless, its culture is expressed in forms that greatly pertain to European ancestors even though sometimes these forms have integrated some American traits. The prevalent capitalist culture does not seem to clash here with an autonomous precapitalist culture. Nevertheless, this culture, which seemed satisfactory within the centers, is exercised here with difficulty because society has become peripheral as far as real life is concerned.

According to this analysis, the challenge confronting peoples from the periphery is essentially a real challenge to start with (economic in the first place, before being cultural). Nevertheless, the challenge is exercised as largely a cultural one to the extent that sometimes this dimension obscures the vision of the actual grounds of inequality upon which capitalist universalization is deployed.

The current (or currents) of traditionalist thinking has never ceased to exist in the modern Arab world. If today it is occupying the forefront of the scene and seems to dominate it through the tumult of its manifestations with hardly any competition, this is because nearly all the other currents of thinking are passing through a crisis and not because this one has overcome its own crisis.

Historical Islamic thinking, like all other manifestations of tributary cultures, performed a prevalent function in the premodern society of the region, surpassing sociopolitical conflicts and guaranteeing the reproduction of tributary power, which it rendered legitimate. To do so, historical Islamic thinking presented multiple facets that responded to diverse interests within society. The main axis of its preoccupation was—as in all tributary metaphysics—its obligation of conciliating between faith and reason within a logic that is nonhistorical in principle, but nevertheless it was completed through a great flexibility of practical adaptation to the demands of a historical evolution within the tributary system. I propose a reading for this method of thinking and of the diverse forms of conciliation between faith and reason that it had forwarded, with special attention to the striking similarity between the mode of function of this method and of other tributary ideological systems (the Hellenistic, the Christian, the Confucian, and so on). The flexibility of Islam in adapting to the demands of social life is no less striking. Historical Islam is in fact a progressive construction. It is not found ready-made in the formulation of the religious message from which it originates. For example, the Shari'a (law in the social sense of the term), which is presented by contemporary Islamists as a specific, "not contaminated" product and which is derived only from faith and from sacred texts, is in fact a rewriting in the Islamic language of Byzantine law (particularly in its codification by Justinian) and the Iranian law of the Sassanids. Muslim intellectuals of olden times knew it and admitted it. It is in our times that we have forgotten it. Nevertheless, conciliation between faith and reason does not constitute the sole expression of historical Islamic ideology. In periods that may be described as declining, the apparent faith imposes itself unilaterally through insisting on social submission to rituals while transgressing the purely religious realm (prayers, etc.) in order to include the sheer and simple social rituals (clothes, etc.), relegating the frank and fine interpretation of dogmas to oblivion. For nearly ten centuries, even before the Ottoman conquest of almost the entire Arab world, this shabby interpretation has been constituting the prevalent dimension within the cultural action of the Arab, Turkish, and Persian Islamic world. Islamic traditionalism, prominent since the nineteenth century, is a traditionalism of this declining world.

The birth of the modern world and, consequently, that of the concomitant capitalist culture is distinguished by an abandonment of—and not a return to—the main concern that has dominated precapitalist cultures, namely that of knowing how to conciliate between faith and reason. Here, the European Renaissance ruptures and separates instead of conciliating between faith and reason. I say separates, not opposes: It raises reason to an independent level without referring to faith. Thus, it is concerned with a qualitative severance, which is a prerequisite of modernity (capitalist and subsequently socialist).

The nineteenth-century Arab Renaissance in its best forms—like in those of its successors until this very day—remains within the central problem of tributary metaphysics: conciliating between faith and reason. It intends to *return to the origins,* before the decline that renounced this conciliation in favor of ritualistic traditionalism. Thus, it will fail in its project to modernize Islamic culture. The prevalent Islam within social reality will also remain nothing but a ritualistic traditionalistic practice. Progressively, Mohammed Abdou, Rashid Reda, and then the intellectuals of the Muslim Brothers Movement—which prevailed among the majority—such as Hassan Al Banna and even the pioneers of contemporary extremism, such as Sayed Qotb, all reduced the objective of the Renaissance in order to propose a pure and simple return to the organization of the Arab-Islamic world that prevailed prior to its conquest by European imperialism, that is, a return to the ritualistic traditionalistic Islamist power of the Ottoman decline.

In this sense, we can say that Islamist culture is no longer the culture that actually prevails within the region, despite appearances. In fact, it has become a hollow form that does not eliminate the true dominance, namely that of capitalist culture (and not Occidental culture, as viewed by the Islamist movement). Capitalism, even in its peripheral form, has taken hold both of the social reality governing daily life and of political life in all its various aspects: The economy is governed by private property, capital, and the market. However, the peripheral status of prevalent capitalism aborts all attempts by the society that is subdued to absorb the adequate forms of politics, ideology, and culture that are in demand within central capitalism. Instead of bourgeois democracy, we here have autocracy. Instead of a culture that separates faith from reason, we have a cultural schizophrenia. From one aspect society remains subject to a ritualistic traditionalistic practice. From another, it applies science: It badly teaches it at schools and badly applies it in enterprises.

The drama or dilemma of the Arab world, as well as that of the Third World as a whole, is expressed in the way it is described here. To escape the dilemma, we must simultaneously erase the social consequences—truly dreadful and palpable—of capitalist peripheralization and perform a cultural revolution that allows a separation between faith and reason. A true reinterpretation of religion can be placed within this context.

In the absence of the foregoing, cultural schizophrenia will continue to express itself through the prevalence of capitalist culture under a shabby and mutilated form, on one hand, and the persistence of an appearance of an ancient culture, itself reduced as well to a ritualistic traditionalism, on the other hand. In a caricature form, we find that Coca-Cola, a masculine beard, and a feminine veil can all coexist here without any problem. This mixture responds to the demands of management of a comprador capitalism of an inferior quality—a *bazaar compradorization.* I shall return later to the social base of this phenomenon and the reasons that led to the current situation, allowing them to occupy the forefront of the scene.

The currents of modernist thinking are in turn no less caught in the dilemma. Modernist thinking is defined within the Arab world, as in all other regimes of the Third World, by its objective, which is to catch up with the advanced West and to become its equal on levels of efficiency in production and politics. In fact, the West—as a model—is capitalist. Hence, the project is that of a national bourgeois aspiration even if this aspiration is expressed in different modes according to the times, the social bases supporting it, and applicable methods. The common denominator on one hand and the diversity in modes of expression on the other define not only the currents of modernist actions and their ideological-political expressions but also the visualization of the cultural problem, conciliated here to their own modernization and their national as well as religious peculiarity.

Modernist Arab thinking was formed early in Egypt and Syria during the nineteenth century. It adopted the European model, as a whole, in all its dimensions and values: liberty, individualism, efficiency, the sciences, and democracy. It does not find that this imitation, which it praises overtly, could possibly pose any ambiguity for religious faith or the use of the language. In this, it is perfectly right. If imitation is successful, it will not abolish faith but will impose a reinterpretation of religion. It will not abolish Arabism but, on the contrary, will impose modernization on the tool with which it expresses itself, namely the language. If imitation has not given the expected results, thus seeming utopic, it is not because the standing traditional culture has constituted an absolute obstacle but because the actual system of capitalism does not offer the new peripheries the possibility of escaping from their subordinate positions to become new centers.

Nevertheless, the proposed modernistic project is one of *catching up* through seriously applying bourgeois national politics. From Tahtawi to Taha Hussein, this project has remained one of national capitalism, in the plain sense of the word, establishing the social hegemony of a bourgeoisie after the fashion and equal to that which has established the modern West. The force of the project—its seriousness—is expressed with a courage that will never be found again in subsequent generations: The traditionalist and ritualist form of religion is overtly rejected as being incompatible with modernization; social power is based upon perfectly laic conceptions. The weakness of the project dwells elsewhere: Capitalist development in the reality of its deployment is peripheral here. There isn't a genuine and significant national bourgeoisie that could promote the project. The genuine bourgeoisie—formed of rich peasants and merchants—lacks the courage of the intellectuals of the modernist project. This class—condemned to mediocrity through peripheral capitalism—accepts being subject to the social powers of ritualist religion, to political autocracy, and to foreign domination. As for the superior categories monopolizing local political power, namely the great landlords whose lands were transformed by their adaptation to integration within the international market and who benefited from this transformation, these constituted the tool for capitalist peripheralization. Hence, their modernist convictions remain superficial, and on the whole, the manipulation of ritualistic religious submission seems to be of use to them.

Thus, the modernist project, in its first blend, had to gradually perish and break as the sociopolitical system that it advocated proved its impotence and as the objective of *catching up* gradually became distant just when people expected it to become closer. In the Arab Orient—in Egypt, Syria, and Iraq—the "liberal" modernist project of the big bourgeoisie, which is in fact the project of intellectuals who do not actually represent this class, started to wear out in the period between the wars. Thus, as of the 1950s, the scene was ready for it to be replaced by the Nasserian, Baathist etatist modernist project.

The new modernist project—like its precedent—was defined by the same objective of *catching up*. However, contrary to the project of the foregoing generations, it is itself produced by intellectuals who emerge and even largely represent the new social classes and categories that are mistakenly described as *petite bourgeoisie*. In fact, they are a group of sorts of middle strata begotten by the peripheral capitalist expansion itself. Squeezed between the popular classes and the governing classes of the old system, the new middle classes have rightfully denounced the contradictions of the system, which claimed to imitate the West, its democratic facade, its social injustice, its submission to imperialists, and so on. The Nasserian and Baathist modernist project has its assets of positive and genuine achievements: agrarian reform, education, employment, industrialization, and national control over the productive system through nationalization. Its political ideology can be summarized in a few simple yet strong themes: the unity of the Arab nation, economic development with social justice (described as socialism), and independence in international relations. Their formulation was always based upon a pragmatic philosophy that in fact does not address any of the fundamental questions (the nature of capitalism, that of the socialist objective, and especially, the question of religion and culture). Nevertheless, its advocates thought that actions adopted according to these principles would allow the attainment of the objective of *catching up.* To them, the concentration of exerted efforts justified resorting to the dictatorship of a party and, in the best of instances, a populistic mobilization of popular masses, refusing the autonomy of organization and the self-expression of these masses. History has demonstrated that this modernist project has failed to realize its objectives. It quickly ran out of breath, becoming sclerous and then degenerating into a common dictatorship that finally collapsed. In all cases the project was gradually abandoned: The objective of Arab unity became void of any reality; the real concern of those in power was to remain perpetually within the framework of their country.

The submission to the demands of capitalist universalization eroded the social achievements and reaffirmed dependency. This failure, which in my view was foreseeable, was ultimately attributable to the strictly national bourgeois nature of the project. But the polarization inherent to capitalist universalization does not allow the crystallization of a national bourgeoisie capable of supporting the project, the local bourgeoisie being compradorist in its prevalent tendency. The story of the Bandung Project's failure (1955–1975) demonstrates that compradorization cannot be a national alternative unless it is popular (i.e., liberated from submission to the prevalent logic of the bourgeoisie) and cannot be popular unless it is democratic (i.e., exceeding populist practice). In other words, the nondemocratic option of the Nasserian, Baathist modernistic project has actually proven its strictly bourgeois character.

Concerning the cultural issue, the experiences of applying the project were diverse. In this domain the Baathist ideology has always been overtly laic, but it was laic in Ataturk's fashion, within current practices only. Not for a moment did the ideologists of the project consider the obstacle that could be represented by the ritualist traditionalist culture; nor did they consider the necessity of a cultural or even philosophical revolution within religion itself, where such revolution is necessary for establishing the laicization of society. In this domain, the Baathist states have adopted the same attitude—that of *liberal* bourgeoisie systems of the period between wars: an extreme attitude of apprehension. In addition, the applied antidemocratic methods, interdicting the expression of modern thinking in its liberal and Marxist bourgeois forms, have abandoned the field to religious traditionalism, which never ceased to exist in society and hence the new middle classes themselves were never liberated. In this field, the Nasserian experience was even more retrograde. Undoubtedly, this is because the religious institution in Egypt—symbolized by Al Azhar—was always powerful, organized more or less like a church. After all, the Nasserian regime has given a new push to Al Azhar in "modernizing" it, thus saving the institution from the torpor and insignificance into which it had sunk. But at what price? Al Azhar became a machine for producing lawyers, doctors, economists (!)—all obscurantists—and it set itself up as a new moral and intellectual inquisition. In return for their submission to state policy, state power granted to the Muslim Brothers the monopoly of culture speech. Thus, the theme of laicization was never presented by Nasserism. On the contrary, backward steps were taken in this domain, in comparison to the experience of the foregoing decades, particularly in education.

The new modernistic project—Nasserian and Baathist—as I have just described, contained nothing that clashed profoundly with Arab Marxism in its prevalent currents. Its similarity to the Soviet system is striking: It has the same objective of *catching up* through a nationalistic and nondemocratic etatism. The only approach Arab Marxists could apply to the system was not to proceed too far or too fast in the adopted direction, for example, they could pursue less radical social reformations. Hence, the prevalent Arab Marxism shared the visions of the historical challenge. Moreover, Arab communism used to find its supporting base and its main source of recruitment in the middle classes, which had either produced or adhered to the Nasserian and Baathist project. Nevertheless, it represented a more subtle version—a more intellectual, educated, and cultivated one. Yet it shared with the latter's practice of silence concerning the traditionalistic culture.

The failure of what I designated the bourgeois national utopia (the Bandung Project) explains the powerful return of traditionalism—which always has existed—to the forefront of the scene. To me, this failure is latent in the nature of the project, which is what actually rendered it utopic. Undoubtedly, some important circumstantial considerations have arisen here that render the collapse more conspicuous, to the benefit of traditionalistic thinking. To start with, the military defeat, that is, the victories of Zionist expansionism (1967), obviously count for a lot in the brutal and dramatic character of the change. Saudi oil money, as of 1973, played a significant role in the deplorable turn of events. The concomitance of the financial influx, which delayed the inevitable economic failure of the project, and the emanation of this influx from a most backward Islamic society—where ritualistic traditionalism is concerned—has greatly magnified the illusion of an *Islamic solution.* Then, the Iranian revolution followed. Here, a populist anti-former-regime revolution, similar in many aspects to that launched by the

Nasserian and Baathist project, blended with the Islamic form of this revolution. Thus, this concomitance has also nurtured the illusion that the "Islamic solution" could have been "revolutionary" and "anticapitalist." History proves that such is not the case and that its assets from positive social achievements are even fewer than those of the Nasserian and Baathist projects.

The return of traditionalism has confined the modernistic conception to its three terms: liberal bourgeois, etatist-nationalist, and conventional Marxist. As expected, this confinement was also accompanied by unfortunate attempts of conciliation between the political programs of those strands (democratization, nationalism, social justice, etc., with emphasis on one of these dimensions or the other according to the advocated strategies) and by an Islamic rallying that is sometimes purely opportunist and sometimes sincere, but always superficial in the sense that it never poses the vital issue: that of separating faith and reason.

On the contrary, the neo-Marxist arguments, which begin to find a nonnegligible echo in contemporary Arab literature, probably constitute the sign of a possible outlet from the dilemma in which traditionalistic thinking and bourgeois modernistic thinking have confined the contemporary Arab society. The present analyses have concentrated on the literature released by the Arab Orient. But they do not ignore that of the Arab Occident. It remains that Arab thinking found itself confronted with the challenge of modernization in the Orient long before doing so in the Occident. The nineteenth-century Renaissance is Egyptian and Syrian. The Orient has surmounted the long successive phases of the attempt to update the tributary autocratic state (Mohamed Ali in Egypt, the Ottoman Tanzimat *Regulations*), then the liberal state between the two wars, before embarking on the radical nationalistic etatist experience in 1952. The Arab Occident, hindered by colonization until the 1960s, was not acquainted with similar progress (except for the short-term experience of Kheireddin in Tunisia during the nineteenth century). As I have said before, either etatism (with Boumedian in Algeria) or contemporary compradorization arrived abruptly; there was no previous *liberal phase*. This historical epitome has found its echo in the modern Arab Occidental culture, which is characterized by a sort of compromise with traditionalism and which is highly in favor within the region.

The development of what we could designate cultural hegemony in the Arab Orient—Egypt, Syria, and Iraq—is altogether parallel, typical, and, moreover, remarkable. During the 1940s and 1950s the hegemony of Marxism actually stretched over these three countries. The decline of the liberal bourgeois project gradually subjected it to the demands of compradorization and submitted it to imperialism. Although at first it generated from a national bourgeois ambition, the progressive weakness of its modernistic speeches and the tremendous concessions granted to traditionalism made it lose its original credibility. The only convincing alternative was the one proposed by communists, who were encouraged by socialist revolutions after World War II, particularly the one in China. The strategy of uninterrupted revolution by phases, advocated by Mao in New Democracy, not only seemed to correspond to a genuine objective possibility throughout the Third World between 1945 and 1950–1955 but also seemed to be the sole possibility. Hence, the ideological battle during these two decades was one between the communists and the common petite bourgeoisie of the new radical nationalism, which emanated from the decomposition of the liberal national bourgeois movement. However, the communists were hegemonistic in compelling others—whether through conviction or opportunism—to submit to their stances. The nationalists emanating from Misr Al Fatat (Young Egypt), the Free Officers operating in secrecy, and even the Muslim Brothers had to take into consideration the appeal of the Chinese and Soviet models to the Egyptian popular and middle classes.

The radical etatist nationalistic ideology was imposed during the 1960s and 1970s. If it was the sole occupant of the arena, this was because it exploited the state's authority, which was in the hands of Nasserians and Baathists, and prohibited any other means of expression. Nevertheless, this dictatorship would not have sufficed to ascertain the ideological hegemony of its project had it not been for its assets from actual progressive achievements. However, the dictatorship was responsible for the catastrophes of the subsequent decades. For although the project itself had lost its momentum—revealing the utopic character of any bourgeois national project, be it liberal or etatist—it had not paved the way to surpass itself. On the contrary, it killed its chances. Arab Marxists, the majority of whom endorsed the radical nationalistic project instead of setting boundaries therefrom, are also responsible to a degree in this regard. Although it would be difficult to find excuses for their choices, it is not difficult to explain them: the delusion produced by Sovietism, the genuine support of the USSR in the just combat against Zionist expansion, and the social achievements of the populistic etatist system.

Once more Islamic ideology is hegemonic, just as it was prior to the launching of capitalist modernization. However, the objective reality of contemporary society is so different from that of the centuries preceding capitalism that it is difficult for this ideology to function in the same mode as it used to. Islamic currents are divided and even strongly in conflict with one another. Among the minority of young militants, organized in a multitude of small groups, there is a predominant *revolutionary* conviction that the governing power should be cast down; thus they partially reproduce the forms of loyalty and causes of dissension in sets that were known to us in Arab communism half a century ago. However, these movements do not possess the theoretical implements that would allow them to analyze the reality of the historical challenge. Hence, they have no program with which to approach the actual issues that confront society. For this reason, they risk being manipulated and exploited by the traditionalist powers that predominate—even superficially—in a public opinion that lacks political perception, is void of any culture, and is suppressed by unbounded capitalist exploitations and despised by the compradorized powers that be. The development of the Iranian revolution on this level is full of important lessons that should be known. The two radical Islamic groups—Fida'iyeen and Mujahideen Khalq—that constituted the shock troops in the attack on the Shah's regime were immediately put aside then liquidated by traditionalists, who dominated the state system. This took place while Khomeini was still alive, before Rafsandjani openly put an end to the confusion that arose at the beginning due to the concurrence of the Islamic revolution and the populistic radical nationalist revolution. In the Arab world, where the latter revolution belongs to a bygone past, the chances of a mythological project for a "real and pure" Islamic solution are farfetched. Many traditionalistic leaders of the movement know that the model of power they aspire to exists in Pakistan and Saudi Arabia. This is all they seek. As for the local compradorial bourgeoisie and its advocates in Western governments, the solution we are tackling is hence not unacceptable. It might even be the efficacious means of running the affairs of societies that suffer insurmountable conflicts, at least for a period of time, regarding their people's future.

It is useful to compare the trajectory of the Arab world to that of Latin America and East Asia, where it seems that cultural liaisons, ideologies, and sociopolitical projects have evolved in somewhat different ways.

Latin America survived a pre-Columbian history. Mexico's culture, which lasted a long time, ended by being absorbed by the dominant culture of capitalism. The peasant revolution of 1910–1920 put an end to the relative autonomy of Indian communities, accelerating their integration into the capitalist market and ending in an urbanization of the vast majority. In contrast, in Peru and Bolivia, the absence of a similar revolution prolonged the survival of scraps of such cultures to the present time, although the social destruction emanating from peripheral capitalism has distorted its meaning. But after Latin America was conquered, it never again enjoyed Europe's feudal culture, despite appearances (the position of the church in society, the large private estates, etc.). It was shaped by mercantilism and shared its culture. Moreover, no one was surprised that its ruling classes proclaimed their independence from the Iberic mother country in the name of the philosophy of enlightenment, replaced in the nineteenth century by the positivism of Auguste Comte. It is clear that the dominating capitalist culture within this context is expressed in a conservative and diffident version that is consonant with the prevalent social interests. But let us not be deceived: The fundamental values of this culture are modernistic even when the conservative political speech that conveys them manipulates "tradition." It is doing what the conservative English bourgeois speech, for example, is doing. It is concerned with perpetuating a precapitalist culture. The *tradition* invoked here remains subject to the imperatives of capitalist expansion.

After World War II, when Asia and Africa witnessed the crystallization of what I have designated the Bandung Project, Latin America got engaged in a similar course, namely the project of *Desarrollismo* (developmentalism). Whereas the Bandung Project did not express itself exclusively in terms of an economic strategy but was accompanied by political and cultural speech that restored to it the national dignity that had been flouted by European colonial imperialism, the Desarrollismo Project remains strictly technocratic, that is, Western in the full meaning of the word. Here, the cultural reference was Anglo-Saxon pragmatism, which was prevalent in the United States of America and which superseded continental European philosophies. On the level of its objective social content, the Latin American project combined what had constituted the essence of the liberal bourgeois project with the essence of the subsequent radical nationalist project in the Arab Orient. It is thus situated, within the scale of the Bandung era, to the right of center.

The Desarrollismo Project, in ingenuously ignoring capitalist polarization and likening development as such to capitalist expansion, has assumed that the required modernization had to establish the democratization of society after the fashion in Europe and North America, which were its two inspirational models. What really happened with capitalist expansion in the periphery proved that modernization in Latin America necessitates a violent dictatorship against the popular classes, which become its victims. Yet this same development enlarged the base of the middle classes, whose beneficiaries constituted the supporting forces of modernistic dictatorships. These same middle classes in Asia and Africa formed the base of the Bandung regimes, particularly those of radical nationalism. It is interesting that the dispersion of illusions of the Desarrollismo Project in Latin America originated in an ideological reaction, entitled the School of Dependence, that has revealed ever since the 1960s the reality of capitalist polarization. Although this ideology probably dominated within Latin American intellectual circles during 1960–1970, it was not the direct mobilizer of the social forces that were capable of immediately imposing strategies other than those of Desarrollismo. Nevertheless, it inspired the strategies of the Cuban Revolution, before it became inscribed in the Soviet logic. Then it inspired Guevarrism and finally, after the failure of the latter, it inspired the popular national strategies of the Nicaraguan Sandinistas, the Salvador revolution, the Labor Party in Brazil, and maybe—through some sort of deviation—the Enlightened Path of Peru.

Undoubtedly, Latin America today—on the level of its economic and social reality—is well into the prevalent neocompradorization that characterizes the current phases of contemporary history. Definitely it suffers from the confusion of political ideologies of the historical left, which did not anticipate the collapse of Sovietism. Despite this, there exist indications that the coming together again of a popular national force is a foreseen possibility: The Nicaraguan experience and that of the Labor Party in Brazil, as well as the powerful and genuine democratic movement within the popular and middle classes, are all evidence of this.

Moreover, the emergence of a "theology of liberation" in the bosom of the Catholic church precedes a revolution against the Christian, Euramerican West. In Latin America, the adaptation of faith to the demands of a socialist perspective is the objective deep reflection, which in addition has a genuine and significant social influence.

In East Asia the Confucian trend prevailed during the tributary epochs that preceded imperialist aggression. I thought it useful to attract attention to the relative flexibility of Confucianism, which is attributable to the fact that this tributary ideology is formulated in philosophical, but not sacred, terms. This is the case with Hellenism when compared to its Christian and Islamic successors.

Concerning Japan—the sole non-European country to become a capitalistic center—I have already pointed out the peripheral form of its tributary mode of production (similar to the European feudal form) and its interpretation of Confucianism. In my view, these specificities, both actual and cultural, have undoubtedly favored Japan's prompt and effective adaptation in confronting the challenge of capitalist modernity. Yet accordingly, I consider that in Japan, as in Europe and North America, the hegemonic ideology is purely and simply that of capitalism, which owes nothing to the "tradition" that has disappeared there. The greatly superficial forms that give the impression that tradition still exists have become perfectly integrated into the prevalent capitalist logic and are at its disposal. In this sense, there exists no Japanese model.

In the same way that Japan adapted to the cultural revolution of capitalism without any problems, China attempted to do the same with that of socialism, through adopting Marxist thinking. I do not wish to say here that China has resolved the problems emanating from the challenge of modernity; it has not developed either a hegemonic culture or an ideology that is up to the challenge. Quite the contrary. First, the Marxism adopted by China is that of the Third International, which is itself the outcome of a long history, and I have pointed out what seems to me to be its weak points: an inadequate awareness of the polarizing dimension of capitalism and, consequently, an erroneous view of the problems of *socialist transition.* Second, Maoism, in its attempt to surpass this sclerous heritage, clashed with historical boundaries and came to an end. Hence, China remains confronted with the question that was posed at the onset: Could it invent a popular national strategy for a *lengthy transition* different from the one set by historical Marxism until now? Could it integrate the democratic dimension within this strategy? If it cannot, it risks a deviation toward a pure and simple capitalist construction that would be more or less under control.

It is useful to resort to similar cases in the Arab world for the sake of comparison, such as the visualization of the relation between society's culture and its project in modern Turkey. Turkey is the only Muslim-populated country that has voted from extreme laicism, with an even antireligious tonality, ever since Ataturk. Even the political forces that adopted this "modernistic" choice have sought to conciliate between their people's culture and the requisites of modernization, in spite of being capitalist. They have never thought for a moment that a cultural revolution in the bosom of religion has constituted a launching point for European modernity and that a similar revolution in Islam was possible and necessary. Thus, they were content to *imitate Europe* in a somewhat superficial manner. For this reason, as well as for the more profound reason of their purely bourgeois national conception of modernization, they have not been able to avoid the peripheralization of Turkey within the international capitalist system—though the position of this country in the peripheral system is better than that of other Muslim countries.

Now we should descend from the stratospheres of culture to the grounds of economic and social transformation following the war. I described the postwar period in the Arab world as the period of deployment and integration of the Bandung Project, that is, of a bourgeois national project that proved to be ultimately utopic. Today the recompradorization of peripheries puts an end to the illusions this project could have nurtured. Both the Bandung Project and the similar Desarrollismo Project were expressed in diverse ways from liberal or fascist right to populist or even Marxist left, which have been foremost on the scene of events after World War II. The scrutiny of ideologies that were developed after the war in various sites of the Third World should not be separated from the evolution of economic and social reality, which became permissible through the implementation of the cited projects. The outcomes vary but do have a common denominator. All over Asia, Africa, and Latin America, social changes have been so significant that the image of these continents has been turned upside down. During the three centuries of European mercantilism (1500–1800), which affected America the most, which left Asia and Africa hardly touched—except for some maritime business and a few privileges of some concessions (in spite of the superficial conquest of India at that time)—and which was followed by the long century that stretched from the Industrial Revolution (as of 1800) up to World War II, the Third World (peripheries) remained apparently traditional. Conquered and colonized, Asia and Africa remained—like Latin America—rural and deprived of industries worthy of the name. In contrast, Europe, the United States, and Japan became distinguished by their industrialization. The contrast between the center and the peripheries was practically defined by this difference. As of the 1940s and 1950s, the peripheries embarked on an era of industrialization, uneven in its distribution. Altogether, these processes of modernization, which precisely constitute the objective of the bourgeois national project of the period, led to political independence everywhere; to urbanization, which became prevalent in Latin America and the Arab world and is about to become so in sub-Saharan Africa and in Asia; to uneven industrialization, which is still more inefficient in terms of international competition; to a gigantic leap forward in education in terms of quantity; and to a penetration of commercial and capitalist relations that extended to the remotest corners of the rural world (usually accelerated by an agrarian reform that reduced the vast properties for the benefit of agricultural koulakization). In all these domains, the Arab world is no exception.

As a criterion of the success or failure of this period's projects I have proposed adopting that of worldwide capitalism itself, since the period's outcome is precisely the apparent reaffirmation that there exist no other alternatives for that system. This criterion is competitiveness on the world market. On this basis, I propose to use the Marxist conceptions of an active army and a passive army while adjusting them to the criterion of a capitalist worldwide dissemination and confining the concept of an active labor force to the part used in competitive historical systems, in its given sense (even though this characteristic is evidently relative). Within this context, the contemporary peripheries, upon emerging from the historic postwar phase (1945–1990), found themselves divided into two clearly distinguishable groups. In one group, which included the already discussed Latin America and East Asia, there existed a blend of capitalist countries (South Korea, Taiwan, and Thailand) and communistic countries (North Korea and China). Important openings for worldwide competitiveness were formed among these national productive systems. Hence, the labor force in this group is distributed between the active army and the reserve in variable proportions, yet always leaving an important place for the active category. In the other group—mainly sub-Saharan Africa and the Arab and Islamic world of Asia—nearly the entire local labor force has the nature of a reserve; this applies formally in poorly productive agricultural sectors, in badly designed industries, or in unofficial sectors of the same nature, or simply reduced to a state of unemployment.

I have suggested that the reaction of resistance and popular revolt to social destructions that were the result of the wild expansion of peripheral capitalism has taken different forms according to whether—in the case of the developmental endeavor of the Bandung years—local society found itself in the first or the second group of countries of the contemporary periphery. In countries of the first group, it seems that we are actually engaged in conflicts that emanate from the productive system and the associated organization of power: struggles for a state policy that seeks redistribution and struggles for democracy. In countries of the second group, to which the Arab world belongs due to the absence of real grounds for a struggle, the revolt seeks the sphere of imagination and adopts a form of cultural, religious, or ethnic claim. Hence, these forms of revolt confront the "people" with a "power" that lacks a true legitimacy to which one can resort.

The dilemma that encompasses the cultural and ideological debate within the Arab world is of this nature. The insistence on an identity affirmation is always a sign of such a dilemma. Dynamic societies never pose questions of that kind. From time to time they look back upon their past only to ascertain that society has changed for the better and has developed since. Blocked societies regard their past differently; they are inclined to see a lost paradise. Thus, the ideological dilemma is accompanied by economic, social, and political dilemmas. Actually, in the contemporary international system, the Arab world is regarded as merely an oil producer. The strategic position of the region and its importance within the context of the Cold War is void today due to the Soviet collapse. Under such circumstances the only apparent "realistic" perspective is that the future of the Arab world lies in its becoming a *compradorization bazaar* for the international system. By this I mean a system that has simultaneously renounced being competitive on the international market and embarked on another disconnected and popular development, thus limiting itself to the management of poor mutual relations. The compradorial class, which finds its place in such management, is composed mainly of intermediary tradesmen or financiers, limiting the role that can be assumed by more up-to-date and efficient categories such as entrepreneurs and technocrats. This comprador class, which is composed of traditional tradesmen (from which comes the "bazaar" that I suggested using) and of rich peasants (koulaks), could be a vehicle for an obscurant power that nevertheless is capable—through imposing its dictatorship for at least a while—of controlling a lamentable social situation that is lacking in perspective. The development of Iran on this level is full of lessons that could be derived. The aspirations of an industrial national bourgeoisie, adopted by the shah's autocratic regime, were replaced by the management of the economy through bazaar tradesmen. Naturally, traditionalist Islam, which this class sees as its identity, is quite far from all serious criticisms of capitalism. This is largely evidenced by the writings of adherents to *Islamic economy.* The cultural and ideological alternative has definite potential; its theoretical and practical program should reconcile the contradictory demands of an international penetration and autonomy of action within the global system; the demands of popular management and the relations of a largely capitalist production, and political democratization and progressive social transformations. The alternative should also deepen its strategic vision of the lengthy transition "beyond capitalism" and emphasize not only *catching up* but the launching of another sort of development. Finally, it should inscribe the local, national, and cultural specifications within a universalist perspective.

7

The Archaeology of Banality: The Soviet Home

SVETLANA BOYM

SINCE BANALITY APPEARS to be a phenomenon of global culture, one tends to think tautologically that the banal is the banal is the banal. Yet Vladimir Nabokov insists on the originality of Russian banality and on its untranslatability. In his view, only Russians were able to neatly devise the concept of *poshlost'*—a word that refers at once to banality, lack of spirituality, and sexual obscenity—because of the "good taste in old Russia."[1] (This is perhaps one of the least ironic sentences in Nabokov, one that borders on banal.) In a similarly patriotic manner, distinguished linguist Roman Jakobson claims that the Russian word for the everyday—*byt*—is culturally untranslatable into the "Western" languages; according to Jakobson, only Russia among the European nations was capable of fighting "the fortresses of *byt*" and of conceiving radical alterity to the everyday (*byt*).[2] So the opposition to everyday life is regarded as a heroic trait of Russian identity. One could add to this hypothetical Dictionary of Cultural Untranslatables Walter Benjamin's observation in his 1928 essay "Moscow" about "the abolition of private life" in Soviet Russia.[3] In fact, in Russian there has never been a single word for "privacy." This is not a mere linguistic accident; there has been a sustained intellectual critique of the Western concept of the "private individual" and of "mercantile civilization" from nineteenth-century intelligentsia of both Western and Slavophile conviction to Bolsheviks and leftist avant-garde artists to contemporary nationalist patriots.[4] If in the American cultural mythology, everyday life (the "American lifestyle") and individual self-sufficiency are the foundation of the national dream, in Russia it is a resistance to the ordinary and a belonging to Russian spiritual culture (which could be coupled with a future-oriented Soviet ideology) that until recently has been a national civic religion. (Now both of the national mythologies seem to be waning.) In Russian and Soviet intellectual history, banality and everyday life have become conflated and interchangeable, and both are inextricably linked to the icons of the national ideology and paradoxes of patriotism. So how can we begin to defamiliarize the defamiliarization of the everyday?

Instead of demonizing the banal or discussing the "banality of evil" in a manner that has frequently taken for granted the evil nature of banality, I will explore a comparative "archaeology" of everyday life. It will not perpetuate the idea of Russian exclusivity or Russian exoticism but only acknowledge cross-cultural mistranslations and show that the war against banality can itself become redundant. Russian and Soviet examples point at a different history of the relationships between public and private, "high" and "low," art and life, self and thing, or, rather, civic selflessness and "domestic trash"—to use the Soviet terms of the 1920s.

After his trip to the Soviet Union in 1926 Walter Benjamin suggested that citizens should look at their country on the maps of neighboring states, "but all Europeans ought to see, on a map of Russia, their little land as a frayed, nervous territory far out to the West."[5] Yet in spite of Benjamin's advice, the Soviet Union and the rest of the Second World remained a kind of demimonde of Western cultural studies. It fell in between the cultural maps of the First and Third Worlds and was marginal to recent debates around Eurocentrism. On the one hand, the intellectual romance with the USSR is marred by the memory of the Cold War and by the nostalgia for that beautiful land of Dr. Zhivago (played by Omar Sharif, of course). The USSR became dematerialized; it appeared to some to become merely an evil object of ideology, a media special effect. The journey to Soviet Russia was a mythical topos of several generations of leftist intellectuals in the West, a kind of "spiritual home," a home of the revolutionary communist ideal, as Jacques Derrida reminds us in his recent antitravelogue "Back from Moscow, in the USSR."[6] On the other hand, the dream of the West, of belonging to the "Western democratic public sphere," as well as a vicarious infatuation with Western consumer goods, was characteristic of the leftist intellectuals in the East. While some "Western intellectuals" nostalgically hum "back in the USSR," Eastern European intellectuals wish to go only half as far—"back in the US"—and one rock song popular in post–Soviet Russia happens to be a mirror image of the Beatles' original: "Bye-bye, Amerika—where I will never go." Perhaps it is this mythical idea of home that Easterners locate in the West and Westerners locate in the East—the u-topia that neither side wishes to radically undermine—that prevents a critical dialogue from happening. Both sides were frequently disappointed by the mythical "homecoming" to East or West and frightened by their own uncanny reflections discovered on the other side. Eastern and Western European intellectuals engage in something more subtle and more insidious than the blatant Cold War propaganda; they violate each other's imaginary spaces, tamper with each other's fantasy worlds—shaped but not necessarily predetermined by differences in actual cultural experiences—and continue to "dematerialize" everyday life on the other side of the barely lifted iron curtain. To make cross-cultural communication possible, one needs something resembling Slavoj Žižek's "ethics of fantasy," something that would recognize cultural particularity not in abstract terms but with specific items of cultural hate and cultural enjoyment: "What confers on the other the dignity of a 'person' is not any universal symbolic feature but precisely what is 'absolutely particular' about him that we can be sure we never share."[7] Perhaps the neglected history of Russian and Soviet everyday existence—not the political dramas but the stories of shared collective life and common ways of everyday deviations from law and order—can help to remap the Second World.

In the search for the archaeology of banality, we will not limit ourselves to a polite tour of the spiritual home of Western intellectuals. Instead, we will visit a number of Soviet homes—from the communal apartment represented in a Socialist Realist painting and deemed "ideologically incorrect" to the actual communal apartments in Leningrad–St. Petersburg. There we will eavesdrop on Soviet and post–Soviet domestic rituals and strategies of cultural survival and examine private collections in the corners of communal spaces. The communal apartment, my central archaeological site, is a specifically Soviet form of urban living, a memory of never-implemented utopian communist design, an institution of social control and the breeding ground of grassroots informants between the 1920s and the 1980s.[8] *Kommunalka*—the term of both endearment and deprecation—was a result of postrevolutionary expropriation and resettlement of the private apartments in the urban centers; it consists of individual or family rooms (not living rooms, bedrooms, or studies but all-purpose rooms that can perform any function) and "places of communal use"—a euphemistic expression for the shared bathroom, corridor, and kitchen that usually serve as the neighbors' battleground. Here one encounters endless schedules of "communal duties" and endless scolding from the fellow neighbors. The morning in the communal apartment begins with the difficult awakening of the local alcoholic on the kitchen threshold as he watches neighborly kids riding bicycles in the corridor; it also begins with a line to the communal toilet, accompanied by a critique of everyone's crimes and misdemeanors by the apartment "elders." The communal neighbors, often complete strangers from different classes and social groups thrown together on the whim of the local housing committee, are joined together in a kind of premodern "mutual responsibility" (*krugovaia poruka*)—the old form of collectivity and centralized control practiced in Russian villages since the time of the Mongol invasions. Any communal apartment dweller is scarred for life by that symbolic "mutual responsibility"—a double bind of love and hatred, of envy and attachment, of secrecy and exhibitionism, of embarrassment and compromise.

The communal apartment, which now appears as a nostalgic ruin of Soviet civilization, occupied a special place in Soviet fiction and Soviet oral culture. It is frequently used as a metaphor for a distinctly Soviet mentality. Thus when Stalin was taken out of Lenin's mausoleum in Red Square, people joked that Khrushchev had "resettled Lenin's communal apartment" (which in the post-Soviet time would be further "privatized").[9] More recently, the behavior of Russian national patriots and members of the Russian Parliament was compared in the post-Soviet press to the "communal apartment tactics" of boorish intimidation, conformism, and collective guilt.[10] Communal apartments were not merely an outcome of the postrevolutionary housing crisis but also the result of a revolutionary experiment in living, an attempt to practice utopian ideologies, to destroy the bourgeois *byt* and banality of the old world. The archaeology of the communal apartment reveals what happens when utopian designs are inhabited and placed into history, both individual and collective. My "thick description" of the Soviet home will include an ideal official iconography of the communal apartment, ideological campaigns against "domestic trash," banality, and kitsch, as well as actual practices of daily living and subversive interior decoration, of the carving out of alternative personal spaces and imagined communities where privacy can be equated with kitschy aesthetics. Hence the archaeology of scarce everyday possessions will be explored together with an archaeology of the everyday itself. But the distance of a cultural critic will occasionally be disrupted by my own indelible memories: a former communal apartment resident stuck in the collective closet and frequently scolded by watchful neighbors. This will, I hope, provide a necessary balance between familiarity and defamiliarization, between homesickness and the sickness of being home.

Rubber Plants, or the Soviet Order of Things

Let us begin with a 1952 painting of a Stalinist domestic idyll, entitled *To the New Apartment.* This is a perfect Socialist Realist genre scene, which reminds us of the old Academic paintings, and tells us more about Soviet iconography than about communal apartments and Soviet domestic life. In the center is a middle-aged woman, a heroine of the "Great Patriotic War" and proud mistress of the new apartment, who looks like she is about to break into a Russian folk dance. Nearby is her son, an exemplary good boy and young pioneer, and there is a portrait of Stalin in place of a father. The gazes of this Soviet family do not meet; the mother looks at the viewer as if inviting our approval while the son looks up to his proud mother, and Stalin looks in the opposite direction, as if watching us through the half-open door, guarding the limits of the visible. The scene appears to belong to some familiar totalitarian sitcom: The characters wear appropriate Soviet uniforms and freeze in the established theatrical poses known from films and paintings, as if awaiting the predictable prerecorded applause. This is not merely a private family festivity but a celebration of the Soviet collective in miniature; we see communal apartment neighbors on the threshold, exhibiting their healthy kittens and bicycles.[11] There is little separation here between public and private; rather, the painting depicts a single, fluid ideological space. The furniture in the room is very sparse, and the private objects are limited to Soviet classics, including the work of the revolutionary poet Vladimir Mayakovsky, a radio set, toys, a political poster proclaiming "Glory to Our Beloved Motherland," a globe with the largest country of the world, the Soviet Union, usually colored in bright pink, a balalaika, and a sickly looking rubber plant in the foreground.

Laktionov, To the New Apartment

The painting is neither reflective nor self-reflective: People and objects hardly cast any shadows here, and there is no mirror hidden in the corner. The scene flaunts its perfect bright visibility and its transparency of meaning. The painter of this new apartment is not presenting himself on the canvas, not meeting our glance, and not questioning the rules of representation. *Las Meninas* this is not! Yet *To the New Apartment* is an icon of Soviet civilization in the same way as Velazquez's *Las Meninas,* in Michel Foucault's reading, becomes an icon of the early modern "order of things."[12] This is the way culture wished to see itself and to be seen, without thinking about the act of seeing.

It is difficult to imagine what could have been considered "ideologically incorrect" in this painting that is so carefully and so moderately ideological. Yet its seamless surface was censored twice, from two different sides: first for the rubber plant in the 1950s and then for the portrait of Stalin in the 1960s. When the painting was first exhibited in the early 1950s, it was the sickly looking rubber plant in the foreground that rubbed the critics the wrong way.[13] The painting was accused of celebrating petit bourgeois values, philistinism, and banality, as embodied by the rubber plant (in Russian, *fikus*), and of "varnishing" Soviet reality. Both the exemplary Socialist Realist painting and its Socialist Realist critique are perfect examples of what Milan Kundera calls "totalitarian kitsch" (in *The Unbearable Lightness of Being*); yet the official critics of the Stalinist period are themselves engaged in the war against kitsch, but a different kind of kitsch, its petit bourgeois variety.[14] We see how the critique of kitsch and banality can itself become kitschified. But what is ideologically incorrect and "unnatural" about rubber plants?

As we begin to uncover the ideological roots of the rubber plant, the cultural plot thickens. It reflects many paradoxes in the Soviet construction of the "new everyday" (*novyi byt*). The iconography of the rubber plant is not without ambiguities. It might have been regarded as the last sickly survivor of the exotic palm trees of the imaginary "greenhouses" of the upper bourgeoisie or as a poor relative of the infamous geranium on the windows of the merchant dwellings that were purged and physically eradicated in Stalin's time. Here the Socialist Realist art critics of Stalin's times (they practiced an impossible profession, since one had to "criticize" in order to survive, knowing that criticism could cost the artists' lives) have borrowed a slogan from the radical campaigns "against domestic trash" led by the leftist artists of the 1920s. In 1929 the State Academy of Arts planned to organize an exhibit of petit bourgeois elements in art and antiaesthetic elements in the workers' everyday life. It was a kind of Soviet parallel to the German exhibit of degenerate art, except the style of "degenerate art" was radically different. Moreover the Soviet exhibit was not so much about degenerate art as about degenerate everyday life. The campaign Down with Domestic Trash was launched by the newspaper *Komsomol Truth* in response to Vladimir Mayakovsky's poems, and it proposed to "burn little demons of things" and create a new avant-garde environment. Mayakovsky offers an elaborate iconography of counterrevolutionary flora and fauna, from rubber plants to petit bourgeois birdies of bad taste, from suspiciously chirping yellow canaries to sweetly singing nightingales and three porcelain elephants, symbols of bourgeois happiness on the mantelpiece. (These three porcelain elephants would be among the major "enemies of the Soviet people," purged in ideological campaigns from the 1920s to the 1960s. Colors also play an important role in the iconography of bourgeois philistinism; one can write a semiotic of the shades of red in the postrevolutionary manifestos, where there is a great fear of "watering down" red, thereby turning it into decadent pink or decorative crimson.[15]) By the mid–1930s, the trashing of domestic life and the critique of philistinism temporarily subsided after expunging some of the left intellectuals who attempted to transfer revolutionary art into the practice of everyday life. The new acquisitiveness of Soviet citizens, those heroes of labor, was cautiously encouraged in official writings, partially in order to justify and partially to disguise the legitimation of the new order of social inequality, with special privileges allocated for the Stalinist elite (who usually resided in spacious private apartments).[16] Yet there was a tension in the official acceptance of domesticity, and hence the depiction of its ideal iconography is unstable. The purging of the rubber plant, from 1920s avant-garde to 1950s Socialist Realism, reveals some paradoxical continuities of the utopian vision, although the styles of those two utopias were quite different. It also points to some tragic paradoxes in the Socialist Realist culture, which in a rather cruel manner realized the old dream of the Russian intelligentsia—the dream of creating a unified "people's culture" by abolishing the distinction between "high" and "low."

The rubber plant, an iconographic blemish on the image of Socialist Realist domestic bliss, and perhaps the only true-to-life object in the painting, can function as a trigger of cultural memory and a key to the "archaeology" of Soviet private and communal life. Indeed, there are rubber plants all over the world, but nowhere else, to my knowledge, were they ideologically purged and occasionally physically eradicated. Yet the Soviet "flower of evil," that suspicious-sounding *fikus,* a victim of both avant-garde fire and the Stalinist cold war, has survived on the window sills of many actual and not-so-picture-perfect communal apartments in present-day Russian cities. The archaeology of the everyday offers us neither a complete reconstruction of the past nor its single authorial explanation, neither a comforting taxonomy nor a scientific periodization. It only helps to unearth a few material exhibits, like the rubber plant, that illuminate twisted plots of forgotten cultural history. Walter Benjamin compares archaeological digging to the operations of memory. In his view, the archaeologist "must not be afraid to return again and again to the same matter: to scatter it as one scatters earth, to turn it over as one turns the soil. For the matter itself is only a deposit, a stratum which yields only to the most meticulous examination what constitutes the real treasure hidden within the earth; the images, severed from all earlier associations that stand like precious fragments of torsos in a collector's gallery—in the prosaic rooms of our later understanding."[17] The process of the archaeological search and the collecting of cultural fragments teaches us to be profoundly suspicious of those seemingly transparent, brightly lit, and picture-perfect reconstructions of history like *To the New Apartment.*

The rubber plant is a survivor of both cold climates and ideological battles around different conceptions of the communal home. The archaeology of discourses on banality in modern European history points to a certain crisis in conceptions of community and communality. Here we discover a number of flip-flops—words whose meanings changed drastically sometime around the turn of the nineteenth century. Or, like *unheimlich,* that Freudian Hoffmanesque doppelgänger, they preserve in them two opposite meanings. Among those words are the French and English versions of "banality" and the Russian *poshlost.* In medieval French "banal" referred to something shared and common in the feudal jurisdiction (banal fields, mills, and ovens). After the French Revolution, with the advent of romanticism, what used to be perceived as a "common good" turns into a common place. From a cross-cultural perspective, there is a similarity in the history of the shifting meanings of Russian, French, and English "banality."[18] Initially *poshly* was neither morally nor aesthetically valorized; this, too, is a term of description that was turned into a term of discrimination. "Common" itself, from something shared, becomes something vulgar; as for "commonplace," from a rhetorical topos and the site of the long-forgotten ancient art of memory, it devolves into a cliché, an embodiment of the dangers of modern unoriginality and mechanical reproduction. This crisis in the understanding of communality stimulated a search for a communality lost and its radical reinvention in nationalist and socialist utopias—a Common Place that is at once a good place and a no-place. In modernist critical theory domesticity is often associated with kitsch, pseudoart and pseudolife. "Home" is frequently construed not as a space of artistic revelation of the infinite but, in the words of Hermann Broch, only as a site of "sentimentalization ad infinitum," an artificial shelter, a place of worship of the bourgeois Goddess of Coziness, who satisfies the nostalgia for rootedness and offers illusory protection from exterior misfortunes and an escape from death.[19] Home, in this view, is a communality of kitschmen and kitschwomen. Yet what was a discourse of modernist counterculture in the West, in Russia partly converged with the official postrevolutionary discourse as well as the prerevolutionary Slavophile discourse on Russian "homeless" identity and antimaterialism.

The everyday is a modern concept that has to do with the secularization of the worldview and the division of the spheres of experience into public and private, festive and everyday. The commonplaces of one's everyday life seem so natural to us, so taken for granted, that it is difficult to dislocate them and challenge their borders from a cross-cultural perspective. This "naturalization" can lead to many cultural mistranslations. The appeal to the everyday can perform different cultural functions. In the United States the appeal to the everyday is often perceived, by American intellectuals, as an antiintellectual gesture and a resistance to theory.[20] In French thought this "resistance" is conceived differently.[21] The focus on everyday life has emerged in response to sociological and ideological models of culture and has switched the attention from theory to practice, or at least to the interaction between the two. Michel de Certeau examines the historical separation of "art" in the singular from "arts in the plural, the arts of" (saying, doing, inhabiting space, walking, cooking—all these practices of the body and techniques of the self), as well as the separation between theory and practice, between knowing (*savoir*) and knowing how (*savoir faire.*) He focuses on the rhetoric of everyday practice and on acts of minor subversion of the official codes of behavior.[22] The everyday tells us a different story of modernity, in which major historical cataclysms are superseded by ordinary chores, ways of working and making: the arts of cooking, negotiation, inhabiting space, loving, reading, buying. In some ways, the everyday is anticatastrophic, a precarious antidote to the narrative of death, disaster, and apocalypse.[23] It is a secular labyrinth, a labyrinth without a monster and without a hero and also without a singular thread of authorial narrative.

In the Soviet Russian context everyday life has always been too cumbersome and difficult to describe. Unreconstructed and messy ordinary existence remained outside the intellectual and political debates and discourses on Russian identity or Soviet patriotism; Russian and Soviet everyday practices tended to embarrass political, economic, and sociological projections. In this respect, zooming in on everyday life goes against the grain of many Russian and Soviet intellectual mythologies; at the same time, it helps us understand what was often perceived as Russian social and economic dysfunctioning, as well as tactics of personal survival and unofficial cultural enjoyment during circumstances of oppression. In this respect, Certeau's idea of everyday practice as resistance to written law, metadiscourse, and ideology seems particularly relevant. From the ideal image of Soviet collective bliss, marred only by one ideologically incorrect plant, we will move to its less ideal representation in the communal apartments of the former Leningrad.

A Personal Guide to the Communal Apartment

Here is another version of the Soviet family romance. Instead of a portrait of Stalin, there is a televisual image of Brezhnev, who is not listened to but is merely present as a background noise. The story is partly remembered by me, partly recollected by my mother, as one of our greatest embarrassments. My parents were having foreign guests, for the first time in their lives, in our room in the communal apartment. Our neighbors, "Aunt Vera" and "Uncle Fedia," were home. Russian children call their neighbors "Aunt" and "Uncle" euphemistically, as if they were members of one, very extended, family. Uncle Fedia usually came home drunk, and when Aunt Vera refused to let him in, he would crash right in the middle of the long corridor, the central "thoroughfare" of the communal apartment, obstructing the entrance to our room. As a child, I would often play with the peacefully reclining and heavily intoxicated "Uncle Fedia," with his fingers and buttons, or tell him a story to which he probably did not have much to add. This time, we were all in the room listening to music to tone down the communal noises, and my mother was telling our foreign guests about the beauties of Leningrad: "You absolutely must go to the Hermitage, and then to Pushkin's Apartment Museum, and of course to the Russian Museum . . ." As the conversation rolled along, and the foreign guest was commenting on the riches of the Russian Museum, a little yellow stream slowly made its way through the door of the room. Smelly, embarrassing, intrusive, it formed a little puddle right in front of the dinner. Yet this scene, with the precarious coziness of a family gathering, both intimate and public, and a mixture of ease and fear in the presence of foreigners and neighbors, remained in my mind as a memory of home. The family picture is framed by the inescapable stream of Uncle Fedia's urine that so easily crossed the minimal boundaries of our communal privacy, embarrassing the fragile etiquette of communal propriety. (And it smells too much to turn it into a mere metaphor. It is something hard to domesticate.)

If there was ever such a thing as a Soviet cultural unconscious, it must have been structured as a communal apartment with flimsy partitions between public and private, between control and intoxication. The Soviet "family romance," to use Freud's phrase, now in its melancholic twilight stage, is adulterated by the fluttering sound of a curious neighbor's slippers in the communal apartment or by an inquisitive representative of the local housing committee. It is a romance with the collective that is unfaithful both to communitarian mythologies and traditional family values.

The communal apartment is not to be confused with a kibbutz or merely an apartment with roommates. Although its name and conception bears some resemblance to many projects of utopian architecture—house communes and communist homes—it was technically born out of Lenin's head. Only a few weeks after the October revolution Lenin drafted a plan "for the expropriation of all private apartments where the number of rooms equals or surpasses the number of residents"[24] and assigned ten square meters per person. What might appear striking in Lenin's decree is that it suggests a different understanding of home and space than that of Western Europe or the United States. A person, or rather a statistical unit, was not entitled to a room or a private space but only to a number of square meters. In his memoirs Joseph Brodsky calls his family's living quarters, poetically and quite literally, "a room and a half." The space was allotted bureaucratically as if it were not a living space or a space of preexistent apartments but some abstract architectural model. As a result, most of the apartments in the major cities were partitioned in an incredible and often nonfunctional manner, creating strange labyrinthine spaces.

In the literature and art of the 1920s, the search for the dwelling place lost appears to be an all-embracing passion, and identity is closely linked to the housing crisis. Literature of the late 1920s and early 1930s contains abundant tragicomic images of neighbors persuading each other to commit suicide for their sake, of publicly shamed intellectuals composing iambic tetrameters in the communal closet while their neighbors are busy expropriating the rooms of absent explorers of the North Pole or subletting six single beds in one communal room.[25] By the mid–1930s, the communal apartment had turned into a prominent Stalinist institution of social control.[26] Only in the late 1950s were many communal apartments resettled as individual apartments in the "microdistricts" of the urban outskirts. These building blocks received the unflattering name *Khrushchoby* (a combination of "Khrushchev" and "slums"). But it took forty more years and the fall of the Soviet Union to put an end to the communal apartment as a social institution.

The imposed communality of the apartment had its paradoxical effects. In response to forced collectivism, neighbors exaggerated the marks of separateness—everyone had his or her own bell, gas burner, and electricity switch; yet they also internalized communality as a fact of life, as a guarantee of stability and peaceful stagnation. People who once professed to hate any form of communal interaction now recall these apartments with nostalgia. An elderly woman, a Russian émigré now living in the United States, suffered all her life in the horrendous communal apartments. Now she complains of solitude: "At least if worse came to worst, even after peeing in your teapot, they would still call you an ambulance if you need it, or lend you a little bit of salt for your cooking. . . . It is that little roughly grained salt that I miss."

Once I was asked to describe my earliest memories of growing up in the same room with my parents. The first thing I remembered was the texture of the curtain that partitioned our shared room—heavy, dark yellow, with an ornamental appliqué. It was called *port'era*—from the French for the door curtain, although in the communal rooms there were no doors, only curtains—signs of imaginary privacy. I remember overhearing voices, whispers, and music, but most of all I liked the *port'era* itself. So much for primal scenes.

The central architectural feature of the communal apartment, and its symbolic marker, is the partition. Most of them were made of plywood, and they marked the intersection of the public and private spheres within the apartment. After the expropriation of property, old rooms and corridors were endlessly partitioned and subdivided, creating monstrous angular spaces with a window opening onto a dark backyard or often entirely without windows. But later, residents began to construct their own partitions on top of the official ones. Every tenant exercised his or her imagination in the invention of all kinds of curtains and screens, not so much as protection from the communal noise but rather as a delineation of minimum privacy. A plywood partition was a much more tenuous division than a wall, more a sign of division than a division itself. The partition served not so much to keep intimate secrets as to create an illusion that some intimacy was possible.

Secrecy is one of the most important ways of keeping the illusion of privacy. But secrecy in the communal apartment was a game of searching for alternative communalities. There used to be an unofficial children's game that we played in the kindergartens, called "the game of burying secrets." We would go to the further edge of the park somewhere near the fence, off the public paths, and perform a ritual burial of "secrets" in the ground. The "secret" was a piece of colored glass found in the trash that covered up an old stamp, a piece of the glittering foil wrapping of chocolates, an old badge: all those useless found objects that exerted a peculiar fascination on us. The "secret" was something to be hidden in order to be shared, a bond between friends, a perfect something to be exposed as a seal of another, unofficial, communality. Secrecy is not solitary; it has to be dramatized in public.

The game of secrets was an attempt to escape an imposed collective sociality and create a different one, a sociality by choice, a friendship based on the shared game of concealment, not the official hide-and-seek played with the teacher and the "good girls" of the group, a game in which there was in fact nothing to find and hence also nothing to seek. As for the secret itself, the fetishized, useless souvenir preserved only for the sake of the game, it helps to disclose some styles of personal collecting in the communal apartments.

The Aesthetics of Survival: Aunt Liuba's Still Life

Benjamin wrote, "To live means to leave traces."[27] Perhaps this is the best definition of the private—to leave traces for oneself and for others, the memory traces of which one cannot be deprived. A room in a communal apartment reveals an obsession with leaving traces, with commemoration and preservation in the most ostentatious fashion. The campaign against "domestic trash" did not triumph in the majority of the communal apartments. Instead, the "domestic trash" rebelled against ideological purges and constituted that secret residue of privacy that often protected people from imposed and internalized communality. Entering the communal apartment, one is struck by the contrast between the public areas—the shabby hallways, spaces of transition inhabited by local drunkards and teenage gangs, and the no-less-desolate "places of communal use"—and the private rooms that appear to be oases of domestic coziness, overcrowded with kitschy memorabilia. How are we to frame these ordinary fetishes of Soviet privacy? How to strike a balance between ethnography, cultural critique, and aesthetics? Instead of a critique of kitsch or an ideological critique of commodity fetishism (which often fetishizes the critical concepts themselves), an examination of some collections of dwellers of the communal apartments—as representations of the practice of everyday survival and "common" aesthetic pleasures—might be more intriguing.

Let us enter the room of a sixty-year-old widow, "Aunt Liuba," whom I visited in summer 1991 in what was then still Leningrad, USSR. Liuba works in the coatroom of a student residence. She never moved to the new apartment, like the heroine of the Socialist Realist painting, but continues to live in a communal apartment. Liuba's room appears untouched by the recent changes in taste and ideology; rather, it preserves the sense of a long duration of time, of a certain domestic mentality that has survived historical upheavals. Liuba's room also illustrates almost literally everything that was considered to be in bad taste, from the 1920s to the 1970s, including the infamous rubber plant.

In Aunt Liuba's only room (of approximately thirteen square meters), there is a chest of drawers, a bed, a table, and an old-fashioned television set covered with a special lacy cloth and treated with peculiar reverence. It seems to be an altar of modern conveniences. The decoration of Aunt Liuba's room reminds us of many rural Slavic dwellings as well as of the rooms of merchants and urban dwellers of the nineteenth century. In the center of the Russian village home (*izba*), which perhaps has been framed and idealized by the ethnographers so many times that it has become hard to imagine what it was actually like, there was a stove (*pech'*), the symbol of an old Russian hearth, used for cooking and for sleeping during the cold nights; across from it, one would find another source of light and warmth in the "Red corner" (*krasnyi ugol*), where the icons where kept and the candles for them lit. In Soviet public spaces, the former "Red corner" was preserved but turned into a "Lenin's corner" with a lot of red: the color of blood, the color of the Russian icons, the color of the revolution. In the rooms of the communal apartment, the functions of a stove and a Red corner were taken up by the television set and the display shelf of the commode where all the most precious items were kept. The artificial light of the television is reflected in the glass doors of the commode, casting bluish shadows upon the personal possessions inside.

Aunt Liuba's interior, communal apartment, Leningrad, 1990 (photo by Boym)

The chest of drawers, or commode, is the most important piece of furniture in the old-fashioned communal apartment room. It survived all the ideological purges including the campaign against "domestic trash," which ridiculed it as "fat-assed," curvy, effeminate, and petit bourgeois.[28] The genesis of the commode symbolizes the development both of the bourgeois commodity and of bourgeois conceptions of comfort, home, and interiority, which reached their peak in the middle of the nineteenth century.[29] The middle of the nineteenth century is a moment when, as Walter Benjamin writes, "the private individual enters the stage of history."[30] The mid-1920s in Russia is a moment when the private individual goes backstage. Yet the old and not-so-luxurious commode in the room of the communal apartment remains, as the site of personal pride, an externalized display of one's interior self and an expression of the desire for individuation.

Liuba has carefully arranged the objects on her commode. There is a big plastic apple, brought from her native Belorussian village, a Chinese thermos with bright floral ornaments, a naturalistic porcelain dog, three bottles containing different glass flowers (not without a touch of elegance), a samovar, and a set of folk-style Soviet porcelain cups. "You see I have it all here—it's my still life," she says proudly when I photograph her room. It is curious that she uses the artistic term "still life" to describe it. (She uses, in fact, the term *nature morte*, a gallicism in Russian.) To her, the display is obviously imbued with an aesthetic quality as much as with personal memories.

Aunt Liuba's "still life" is truly memorable. But how is one to imagine a "still life" in a culture where one major devastation follows another: revolutions, wars, housing crises, hunger, Stalinist purges: where habit and repetition, everyday stability, are much more difficult to sustain than a grand style? In Russia, one can speak only about nostalgia for a still life, nostalgia for sustaining everyday materiality in the face of a continuing series of crises. Liuba's collection of Soviet ready-mades—objects of trivial private utopias and of the everyday aesthetic—framed by the glass of the commode as if it were a museum exhibit, is a kind of monument to that desire for a still life, for a life that does not rush anywhere in a torrent of uncontrollable change.[31]

Unfortunately, few sociological theories of popular culture are able to frame Aunt Liuba's still life. In Bourdieu's *Distinctions* there is little place for Aunt Liuba's popular aesthetics, yet surprisingly, one of the central chapters of the book opens with a reference to Russian cultural life in an epigraph from Alain Besançon's *The Russian in the Nineteenth Century:* "And we do not know whether cultural life can survive the disappearance of domestic servants."[32] The seamless passage from the epigraph to the main body of the text, which discusses the French "aristocracy of culture" and "cultural nobility," glosses over the fact that Russian cultural life did survive not only the disappearance of the servants but even the rise and disappearance of a variety of sociological approaches to art and the everyday. Moreover, "culture" itself may be defined in many different ways. Bourdieu contrasts a "popular" movement to translate art into the everyday, into the things of life, with an "aristocratic" movement to "confer aesthetic status on objects that are banal or even common." "Popular taste," writes Bourdieu, "applies the scheme of ethos which pertains in the ordinary circumstances of life to legit-

Aunt Liuba's "still life" (photo by Boym)

imate the works of art, and so performs a systematic reduction of the things of art to the things of life."[33]

Yet as the Russian examples demonstrate, the opposition between aesthetics and ethics, disinterestedness and empathy, "elite" and "popular," does not function so neatly. In fact, the popular aesthetic is often escapist and fantastic rather than entirely realistic; or rather, the elements of fantasy and verisimilitude tend to interact in a complex and ambiguous manner, as in folktales or science-fiction movies. Moreover, popular tastes are eclectic; like urban middlebrow culture, they often preserve a trace of a prerealist or slightly primitive peasant sensibility (which should not be exaggerated lest one slip into folk exoticism yet again). Hence popular tastes frequently include bright colors and fantastic ornaments. In Russia, the culture of icons—not only in their spiritual but also in their pictorial and ornamental quality—influenced both popular tastes and the avant-garde elite.

Bourdieu makes two reductive steps, first by assimilating popular culture to ethical projections and then by equating those ethical projections with realistic representation. For the French sociologist, this double reduction of popular culture to realism and ethics becomes an attempt to confer to it some kind of morality, to valorize it in contrast with the supposedly agnostic and amoral Kantian and modernist aesthetics. This approach to popular culture is sensitive to the class distinctions specific to the French society of the 1960s yet indifferent to the aesthetic ones; further, it does not take into account the diversity of cultural practices nor address the strategies of cultural survival. It reifies scientific distance from "the objects of study," which translates into indifference to their pleasure and pain, minor aesthetic escapes, and enjoyment—not of inner beauty but of interior decoration. In the everyday, especially in the highly politicized and semioticized Soviet everyday, the aesthetic and the ethical were often indistinguishable in minor ordinary practices. Besides, it can be unethical to deny the aesthetic experience of impoverished neighbors in the communal apartment.

Aunt Liuba's personal domestic objects resist any single sociological approach because they offer an eclectic mix of old-fashioned urban middlebrow culture, peasant sensibility, and attraction for what is bright, colorful, and ornamental, as well as nostalgia for the coziness of the petit bourgeois or merchant's home. They are private yet not deprived of cultural myths; they suggest status, but their role is not reducible to it. These objects are difficult to theorize. They are too useless both for use-value and exchange-value theories, neither authentically primitive nor exotic enough for "transgressive" modern theories, and too trivial and banal in a nonfatal manner to be turned into a simulacrum à la Jean Baudrillard. In other words, they are impure and outmoded on all grounds.

In her book *The Body in Pain,* Elaine Scarry talks about the object in the world surviving pain, where materiality is fragile and not taken for granted.[34] It is this conception of the object that is always on the verge of being unmade, private on the verge of being deprived of, that is particularly applicable to thinking about the everyday of ordinary Soviet citizens, characterized by material scarcity. Unlike "kitsch" in Broch's definition, this affirmation of artifacts does not simply "deny death"; rather, it refuses to succumb to it and to the apocalyptic narrative of perpetual alienation and metaphorical homelessness. The artifact on display in the communal home is a sort of souvenir, an object of private memory and a souvenir of privacy itself, a memory of an old preindustrial and possibly prerevolutionary world. The notion of its being a souvenir displaces the object from common into individual history. The souvenir supplants the narrative of the object's production by the narrative of its acquisition. The buyer becomes the author who reinvents the use of the object, makes it memorable, refuses the accepted "system of objects" whether that system is one of capitalist commercialism or of frugal collective ideology, and places it into a different context in which it becomes memorable. As Susan Stewart points out, the tragedy of the souvenir is the death of memory, the nightmare of the "unmarked grave."[35] It comes with the impossibility of, in Benjamin's phrase, "leaving traces." It is the "profane glow of the commodity," a part of ordinary magic that cannot be taken for granted.

In the rooms of Soviet intellectuals we find similar "still lives" of personal souvenirs. Usually they can be found in the cupboard-commodes or on the bookshelves, since the possession of bookshelves is in itself a matter of status for a member of the intelligentsia. The space between the folding glass on the bookshelf, an ephemeral space, served for the display of one's most personal objects: photographs, images of travel, baby pictures, portraits of Hemingway or the Soviet bard Vysotsky (both with beards and with or without a cigar), snapshots of faraway friends, occasional toys or souvenirs from Crimea or Susdal', envelopes with foreign stamps, loose pages from disjointed old books, dated newspaper clippings. This narrow, nearly one-dimensional space behind the glass of the shelf is a flat image of the owner of the room; it is his or her carefully arranged interface with the world. The narrative of these treasured objects cannot easily be reconstructed by an outsider; it is nonlinear, unreadable with many blank spots, oddly meaningful banalities, and minor obsessions. It is a history of one's life, not a biography but rather a biographical legend, a story of "inner life" externally fashioned, a story of what really matters, what "leaves traces" and survives the drudgery of dailiness. Often, it is also a story of travels, real or imaginary—of journeys to exotic places and escapes into wishful thinking. In the 1960s and early 1970s, when traveling abroad was nearly impossible, one used to engage in "virtual travels" via a television program that was popular then, *The Club of Cine-Travelers,* a Soviet version of *National Geographic,* a transit to the "West" via foreign stamp-collecting or the collecting of portraits of a few Western writers, artists, and intellectuals.

The objects on personal display on the bookshelves are not completely individual: There appears to be an unwritten law of fashion that tells everyone when Hemingway is out and Vysotsky is in, when Pasternak is out and Solzhenitsyn is in. Then Solzhenitsyn himself is out, supplanted by the photoreproduction of the exotic and apolitical Nefertiti, the mythical beauty queen of ancient Egypt inherited by the Soviet intelligentsia from the traveling exhibit of the treasures of Tutankhamen, to which hardly anyone could purchase tickets. Now side-by-side with Nefertiti is a half-dressed foreign pinup girl with a non-Russian smile who seems to supplant political and poetic heroes, past and present.

In the 1960s, the intelligentsia of the "thaw generation" rebelled against the "bad taste of the 1950s" that smacked of Stalinism and philistinism and rediscovered in a somewhat distorted form the heritage of revolutionary modernism. It returned to a certain less radical version of the campaigns against domestic trash, in the satirical wars against soft furniture, plush curtains, and in the "journeys in search of the fog and the smell of taiga," as the popular song of the time had it. In the eclectic age of Gorbachev, both the "totalitarian kitsch" of the "high Stalinism" of the 1930s and the old *poshlost'* of the time of the New Economic Policy (NEP), 1950s middlebrow art, and the neomodernist euphoria of the 1960s reappeared as different aesthetic and political styles, occasions for nostalgia and explosive laughter. Yet there was no attack on privacy in the 1960s comparable to that of the 1920s. Once private life had been nearly eliminated, both through the official discourse and by the housing shortage, the forbidden privacy was reconstituted in a different manner: by the minor aesthetic pursuits of the communal-apartment dwellers. They carved imaginary spaces of their own through poetic escapes, a few unofficial guitar songs shared in a crowded kitchen, and the personal collections of domestic trash put on display in the private corners of the communal apartments.

The analysis of these private displays at once reveals everyday resistance to metatheories and can tell us a lot about eclectic Soviet cultural mythologies. They are not about defamiliarization but rather about the familiarization of estranged ideological designs. The objects in the personal display cases are not bare essentials; neither are they merely objects of status and conspicuous consumption. If

Interior of the communal apartment, 1991 (photo by Mark Shteinbok)

Interior of the communal apartment, 1991 (photo by Mark Shteinbok)

they do represent a need, it is first and foremost an aesthetic need, a desire for beauty met with minimal available means, or the aesthetic "domestication" of the hostile outside world. A kind of empathetic aesthetics of everyday is needed to account for the cultural significance of ordinary precarious possessions. This aesthetics should not be ahistorical and universally human; on the contrary, it should preserve cultural particularity and help to confront the problem of the everyday in those catastrophic moments in history when the everyday itself is in danger. Those moments are often blind spots of many coherent topographies of modernity.

The communal apartment in itself was a peculiar common place of Soviet civilization, a kind of ruin of the modernist utopia of communal living. The archaeology of the communal apartment reveals what happens when utopian designs are put into practice, inhabited, and placed into history, both individual and collective, that reminds one of the imposed communality. The communal apartment is like a Soviet society in miniature, a leap of faith from utopian theory into the everyday. It offers a sadly deconstructive allegory of what happened to revolutionary constructivism and how the Socialist idyll turned into a social farce. The problem is that any utopia, perhaps most fundamentally, is a u-chronia; in other words, it assumes a certain atemporality, a ceasing of time flow and the immutability of life. What an architectural utopia does not take into account is history, both in the broad sense of social history and in the sense of individual history, with their multiple narratives of inhabiting the world.

In the 1990s, the decade of radical perestroika, many of the partitions of the former communal apartments have been broken. Before the coup, only a few apartments had been taken over by the artists and then—almost like in downtown Manhattan—they were reconquered by newly emerging shady cooperatives and businesses, branches of heretical Buddhist sects prospering in Russia, or some other astrologists anonymous. After the adoption, in 1991, of the law allowing for the privatization of domestic property, a new wave of gentrification of the communal apartments began; but it turned out to be one of the most intricate exercises for the emerging post-Soviet legal culture, which inevitably stumbled against the unpredictable (or rather, very predictable but never legally accounted for) webs of Soviet everyday practices.[36] Privatization followed a crooked path between new democratic laws with no precedent as of yet and old practices of bureaucracy and bribery (which had many precedents and unwritten rules). In general, it appears that many post-Soviet reforms continue to operate on the abstract level of written law, which nobody knows how to put into practice; there is very little consideration of how those reforms translate into everyday life. If this continues, "free market" and "democracy" will remain empty foreign terms, like "communism" before, implemented in a typically unpredictable Russian manner.

The imposed collectivity that reigned in the old communal apartments is now supplanted by new forms of communality. Now, the words "communal" and "collective" are extremely unpopular. Instead, the new metaphor of post-Soviet communality is "cooperative" or "joint venture" (*sovmestnoe predpriiatie*), but the games of secrets are still played out in all branches of post-Soviet commercial communication.

Now in the time when the prefix "post" has become excessively fashionable, in this post-Soviet, postcommunist, postmodern time, all the formerly untranslatable words have entered Russian in their stylized, markedly foreign forms—*mental'nost', identichnost', menedzher, sponsor,* and so forth. Moreover, many of these new collective enterprises of the former USSR are called "international," or at least they bear the foreign prefix "inter." If before there was very little private life, now there is privatization; and if private life used not to be brought into public, now there is a newspaper called *Private Life,* which specializes in personal ads, cries of loneliness and searches for "Western" husbands and wives. One woman reader wrote a funny teasing line in response to the newspaper's verse contest, reflecting all the ambiguities and paradoxes of the new and still untranslatable (or at least unprecedented in any Western language) post-Soviet everyday: "What is to be done? I don't despair. I have no personal life but I have a 'private' one." Here "private life" is used in quotation marks; it is only the name of a newspaper, a new cliché of the post-Soviet language and not yet a property of still-deprived Russian citizens.

Finally, one should not despair that there are so many foreign words in contemporary post-Soviet Russian and that some of them appear to be unfaithful (or else too faithful and, therefore, uncritical) translations of "Western concepts."

Jacques Derrida mentions that at a recent meeting with Moscow philosophers his term "deconstruction" was inaccurately translated as "perestroika" and that words like "democratization" were frequently employed without proper critical understanding.[37] (One of the Moscow philosophers commented in reference to "deconstruction" that it was merely a joke that for the distinguished "Western" guest might have gotten lost in translation.) Perhaps the responsible choice for "Western" cultural critics is neither to go "back to the USSR" nor to celebrate "the end of history," victory in the Cold War, and other such ideological videogames but rather to acknowledge new cultural hybridity and diversity in experiences of modernity, some of which might upset both First and Third World cultural paradigms. It is important not to succumb to the apocalyptic theories of either total global homogenization or radical cultural untranslatability and, instead, to dig out some ruins and fragments of each other's everyday culture, uproot a few rubber plants, and examine each other's fictions of the self and dreams of escape. One does not have to sacrifice "the principle of hope" in questioning some of these totalizing utopian visions; rather, one has to distinguish carefully between the two.[38] Questioning the power of the totalizing dream can bring a new understanding of history and the possibilities of social change that are not predicated on the willful oblivion of the other's historical experiences.

The first traveler to the island of Utopia, in Sir Thomas More's fictional travelogue, had the peculiar name Raphael Hythlodaeus, which can be translated as "expert in trifles" or "well-learned in nonsense."[39] Trifles, particular details and ordinary occurrences, can provide an important perspective on the utopia of communal life, and a feel for the nonsensical can help one understand the imaginary collectives of the Soviet communal apartment. Although evil can be banal, we do not necessarily have to demonize banality—attempt to sublate/sublimate/overcome or defamiliarize the everyday—and rejoice in our own critical distance from it. The war against kitsch and banality ensures a dynamism of cultural forces and a constant questioning of clichés, but it also fosters a certain kind of moral snobbism. The word "snob," incidentally, or perhaps not incidentally, is another one of those flip-flop concepts linked to the discourse on taste, art, and common place. According to the *American Heritage Dictionary,* it initially referred to "a person of the lower classes"—*sine nobilitas*—but later came to signify something different: "a person who is convinced of and flaunts his or her social superiority."

But then again, who are we to feel superior to snobs?. . .

NOTES

1. Vladimir Nabokov, "Philistines and Philistinism," in *Lectures on Russian Literature* (New York: Harcourt Brace Jovanovich, 1981), p. 313.

2. Roman Jakobson, "On the Generation That Squandered Its Poets," in *The Language in Literature,* ed. Krystyna Pomorska and Stephen Rudy (Cambridge and London: Harvard University Press, 1987).

3. Walter Benjamin, "Moscow," in *Reflections,* trans. Edmund Jephcott (New York: Harcourt Brace Jovanovich, 1978). "Bolshevism has abolished private life." Benjamin rushes to explain that he is not for any "bourgeois coziness" or "completeness of bourgeois interiors" that leaves no space to breathe, but even so, the abolition of private life appears to him to be a rather radical revolutionary measure.

4. Privacy is equated with banality, philistine ideals, and petty middle-class individualism, inconsistent with the Russian personality as dreamed by Dostoyevsky and Herzen and with the Soviet New Man as designed by early revolutionary pedagogues. I provide a more detailed discussion of the comparative intellectual history of "privacy" in Russian and French–Anglo-American contexts and the way in which the conception of "Russian soul" could not have "private life."

5. Benjamin, "Moscow," p. 118.

6. Jacques Derrida, "Back from Moscow, in the USSR," in *Politics, Theory and Contemporary Culture,* ed. Mark Poster (New York: Columbia University Press, 1993), pp. 197–237.

7. Slavoj Žižek, *Looking Awry: An Introduction to Jacques Lacan Through Popular Culture* (Cambridge: MIT Press, 1991), p. 156. What Žižek calls the "absolute particular" can be determined by both individual and cultural experience.

8. According to Soviet statistics, until the 1980s 40 percent of Leningraders lived in communal apartments. It is usually perceived that communal apartments survived only until the 1970s. Even in 1991, when the process of gentrification had already started, in Moscow there were more than 300,000 communal apartments (*Ogonek* no. 38, September 1991, p. 18). My "fieldwork" in the communal apartment was done primarily in 1990 in former Leningrad and in Moscow. In summer 1993 the official Russian news agency announced that 30 million people continued to live in communal apartments.

9. The anecdote is taken from *Istoriia SSSR v anekdotakh* (Smolensk: 1991), p. 77.

10. Alexander Kabakov, "Na chuzhom pole," *Moskovskie Novosti* no. 49, December 6, 1992, p. 5.

11. Moreover, the painting is not about domestic bliss as such but rather about *moving* to a new, Soviet domesticity, an award presented by the Party. Unlike in Nazi Germany, we find hardly any depictions of private or domestic life in the Soviet art of the 1930s and 1950s; it is dedicated primarily to epic sites.

12. Michel Foucault opens his discussion of the "order of things" with an "icon" of early modern civilization—Velazquez's *Las Meninas*—that tests the rules and limits of representation, exposes visual trompe l'oeil, and at the same time pays hommage to the patrons of art, in his case the royal couple. (Michel Foucault, *The Order of Things: An Archeology of Human Sciences,* New York: Vintage, 1973.)

13. For a discussion of the painting, presented at the All-Union Art Exhibit in 1952, see *Iskusstvo* (1953–1954). I am grateful to the art historian Musya Glanz for helping with my research on this painting. However, the iconography of the rubber plant is ambiguous. In many images of idealized domesticity and communal spaces the rubber plants (which were among the most common domestic plants) are represented positively. This reveals a certain precarious position of the socialist realist criticism as such and its frequent ideological inconsistencies and involuntary eclecticism.

14. Milan Kundera, *The Unbearable Lightness of Being,* trans. Michael Heim (New York: Harper and Row, 1989), p. 256.

15. After his suicide in 1930 Mayakovsky was proclaimed by Stalin to be "the greatest poet of our epoch" and officially canonized; no wonder his book appears in the program-

matic new apartment of the picture-perfect Soviet family. Yet Mayakovsky's own suicide note enigmatically—or perhaps melodramatically—ciphers his failure in the war on the everyday, the untranslatable Soviet-Russian *byt:* "The love boat has crashed against the daily grind [*byt*]." See Svetlana Boym, *Death in Quotation Marks: Cultural Myths of the Modern Poet* (Cambridge: Harvard University Press, 1991).

16. On the "new deal," Stalin's style, and the "new acquisitiveness" in the 1930s see Vera Dunham, *In Stalin's Time* (Cambridge: Cambridge University Press, 1976). See also Sheila Fitzpatrick, "Becoming Cultured: Socialist Realism and the Representation of Privilege and Taste," in *The Cultural Front: Power and Culture in Revolutionary Russia* (Ithaca: Cornell University Press, 1993), pp. 216–217.

17. Walter Benjamin, "A Berlin Chronicle," in *Reflections,* p. 26. For the notion of archaeology in contemporary theory see Michel Foucault, *The Archeology of Knowledge,* trans. M. Sheridan Smith (New York: Pantheon Books, 1982). For the critical discussion of the concepts of history and archaeology see *Modern European Intellectual History,* ed. Dominick LaCapra and Steven L. Kaplan (Ithaca: Cornell University Press, 1982.)

18. Russian banality, *poshlost',* comes from *poshló*—something that has happened or something that has been and has arrived. (Vladimir Dal', *Tolkovyi slovar' zhivago velikorusskogo iazyka* (St. Petersburg: Volf Editorial, 1882). *Poshly,* like banal, has to do with the feudal communality and order.

19. Hermann Broch, "Notes on Kitsch," in *Kitsch: The Anthology of Bad Taste,* ed. Gillo Dorfles (London: Studio Vista, 1969).

20. Stanley Cavell confronts the "uncanniness of the ordinary" and questions the separation between everyday and philosophy by both thinking about the everyday philosophically and shifting philosophical hierarchies. Stanley Cavell, *In Quest of the Ordinary: Lines of Skepticism and Romanticism* (Chicago: University of Chicago Press, 1988).

21. The everyday has been defined as a "residue resisting analysis" or "whatever remains after one has eliminated all specialized activities." Henri Lefebvre, "Quotidien et quotidienneté," in *Encyclopaedia Universalis,* reprinted in *Yale French Studies* no. 73, pp. 7–8. The *Annales* School, which began to promote the interest in the everyday, "long duration," and the history of mentality, emerged after the war and reacts against teleological conceptions of history and the privileging of modernity. At the same time, many artists following in the Surrealists' footsteps, such as the situationists, were interested not merely in studying the everyday but in transforming it; hence the study of the everyday can turn from contemplative to interventionist.

22. Michel de Certeau, *L'invention du quotidien/Arts de Faire* (Paris: Union Générale d'Éditions, 1980).

23. See Fernand Braudel, *On History,* trans. Sarah Matthews (Chicago: University of Chicago Press, 1980). Henri Lefebvre, *Everyday Life in the Modern World,* trans. Sasha Rabinovitch (New Brunswick, N.J.: Transaction Press, 1984). For the development of Lefebvre's theories see the special issue of *Yale French Studies* on the everyday (no. 73, ed. Kristin Ross and Alice Kaplan [New Haven: Yale University Press, 1987]); and de Certeau, *L'invention du quotidien/Arts de Faire.* On the situationist conception of the everyday see Raoul Vaneigem, *The Revolution of Everyday Life,* trans. Donald Nicholson-Smith (London: Aldgate Press, 1983). In contrast to that, in the German context, where the cult of domesticity is a crucial part of national and nationalist iconography, recent histories of the everyday have an opposite purpose. They often recover the tradition without rewriting it, perpetuating its blind spots, which can lead to historical omissions, and forgetting the disasters of World War II and the Holocaust. The "non-Aryans," primarily Jews in

Germany, did not share the same history of everyday life as did the Germans and hence cannot partake in the same forgetting. In Germany the debate about representation of the everyday and history reopened after the showing of *Heimat* (1984; director, Edgar Reitz). See Martin Broszat et al., *Alltagsgeschichte de NS-Zeit, Neue Perpektive oder Trivilisierung?* (Munich: Oldenbourg, 1984); Martin Jay, "Songs of Experience: Reflection over the Debate over Alltagsgeschichte" *Salmagundi* 81 Winter 1989, pp. 29–41; and Anton Kaes, *From Hitler to Heimat: The Return of History as Film* (Cambridge and London: Harvard University Press, 1989), pp. 161–193.

24. Quoted in Vladimir Paperny, *Kul'tura Dva* (Ann Arbor, Mich.: University of Michigan Press, 1984), p. 83.

25. I refer specifically to Il'ia Il'f and Evgenii Petrov's satirical novels *Twelve Chairs* and *The Golden Calf,* Nikolai Erdman's play *The Suicide,* and Mikhail Zoschenko's short stories. I offer a more detailed examination of the literature of the communal apartment in *Common Places: Mythologies of Everyday Life in Russia* (Cambridge: Harvard University Press, 1994), chapter 2.

26. Control was also maintained with a number of laws that enforced the passport system, resident permits that linked the individual to a specific place, and the establishment of new privileges that allowed certain groups of the population—Party apparatchiks and intellectual and artistic elites who collaborated with the regime (and were not arrested)—to have additional "living space." Living in a separate apartment was a mark of prestige. Yet elements of Soviet communal mentality persisted beyond communal apartments. A more detailed examination of both the utopian architecture and house communes and of the psychopathology of Soviet everyday life can be found in my *Common Places.*

27. Walter Benjamin, "Paris, the Capital of the Nineteenth Century," in *Reflections,* p. 155.

28. At the end of Erdman's play *The Suicide,* the main character, suicide-to-be Semion, begs his communal apartment neighbors and friends to spare him and not force him to kill himself. He is ready to give them everything he owns—to refuse food, to send his mother-in-law to work in the mines, and even . . . to sell his commode.

29. According to Mario Praz (*An Illustrated History of Interior Decoration from Pompeii to Art Nouveau* [London: Thames and Hudson, 1981]), the commode was invented in the early eighteenth century out of the "confluence of bourgeois and patrician tastes," and it contributed greatly to giving rooms "a more intimate character" (p. 56). In the nineteenth century the glass cabinets turned into a home *kunstcamera,* a private collection of curios, a privileged site of a brico-bracomania, bibliomania, and occasionally rarefied and morbid fin de siècle erotomania. See Emily Apter, *Feminizing the Fetish,* (Ithaca: Cornell University Press, 1992).

30. Benjamin, "Paris, the Capital of the Nineteenth Century," p. 154.

31. Liuba's room is full of artificial flowers—Soviet Victorian roses on the communal wallpaper, exotic red glass flowers and simple plastic daisies on the shelf, stylized golden and yellow daisies on the porcelain, and red floral decorations on the wooden "khokhloma" spoon—all those impure objects that do not belong either to authentic folk culture or to the high culture and that subvert many sociological categories and mythologies of authenticity. The only "natural" flower is a little rubber plant on the windowsill—I was glad to find it there. But by now even the rubber plant has already turned into a flower of ideology.

32. Pierre Bourdieu, *Distinction: A Social Critique of the Judgement of Taste,* trans. Richard Nice (Cambridge: Harvard University Press, 1984), p. 9. Bourdieu proposes to his-

toricize conceptions of taste and aesthetics according to class and social group. Although he criticizes Kantian aesthetic universals, "sensus communis," and the disinterestedness of the beautiful, he ends by reclaiming both aesthetic disinterestedness and formalist "de-familiarization." Although he is a scientist and sociologist, he forgets to historicize his own discourse. By demystifying art, he seems to mystify the "science of sociology."

33. Ibid., p. 5. Such a conception of popular culture is a metanarrative in its own right that does not consider the operations of the everyday and the minor arts of everyday ethics that go against many totalizing designs, including the sociological ones.

34. Elaine Scarry, "The Interior Structure of the Artifact," in *The Body in Pain: The Making and Unmaking of the World* (Oxford: Oxford University Press, 1985), pp. 278–326. The object is treated not as a commodity or fetish but rather as an artifact, a product of human creativity that helps to make the world and undo the suffering. In the context of alienated labor and economic production, thinking about things is displaced into the context of reception, projection of reciprocity, responsibility, and responsiveness. The object is seen as a projection of human sentience, as a projection of the awareness of aliveness. The denial of the object is not only a social deprivation but also a sensory deprivation, a thwarting of sentience, human contact, powers of projection, and reciprocity. It is this conception of the object that is never reified and objectified but always on the verge of unmaking, private on the verge of deprivation. Although Scarry does not wish to draw a clear distinction between art objects and artifacts, it seems that a creative impulse is crucial for her reading, and this creative impulse and affirmation of aliveness constitute the aesthetics of daily existence.

35. Susan Stewart, *On Longing: Narratives of the Miniature, the Gigantic, the Souvenir, the Collection* (Baltimore: Johns Hopkins University Press, 1984).

36. For a more detailed account of the post-Soviet fate of the communal apartments and paradoxes of privatization, see my "Soviet Everyday Culture," to appear in *Russian Culture at the Crossroads: Paradoxes of Postcommunist Consciousness,* ed. Dmitri Shalin (Boulder: Westview Press, 1996). For accounts in the Russian and American press see *Ogonek* no. 38, September 1991, p. 18; and Celestine Bohlen, "Moscow Privatization Yields Privacy and Problems," *New York Times,* February 28, 1993.

37. Derrida, "Back from Moscow, in the USSR."

38. Blaming Russian and East European intellectuals, as well as communal-apartment dwellers, for tampering with utopian dreams of "Western intellectuals" appears—to say the least—a bit one sided (if not unethical.) After all, in Marx's own dictum "material existence determined conscience," and Eastern Europeans had to live the everyday life that was a consequence of the beautiful utopian vision while some of their nostalgic "Western" counterparts could afford to preserve the utopian vision only in theory.

39. Sir Thomas More, *Utopia,* ed. Edward Surtz (New Haven: Yale University Press, 1964), p. 12.

8

Brazilian Critical Theory and the Question of "Cultural Studies"

NEIL LARSEN

TWO THINGS SET ME THINKING about the conjunction named in the title of this chapter. One was a meeting I had a year or so ago with a Brazilian social scientist on research leave at a Boston-area university who was eager to compile a bibliography of "cultural studies" titles to take back with him to Brazil. He had been given the job of obtaining this information by several colleagues back home, among them a well-known social and political analyst whom I inferred to be Octavio Ianni. In a very private, almost secretive tone, it was confided to me that at least some left intellectuals in Brazil were having doubts about Marxism and were curious as to whether "cultural studies" might be a radical alternative. Together with an anthropologist friend at my own university, I did the best I could to provide the desired list of titles. But I was nervous about it, both because the request had cast me in the role of the "metropolitan" intellectual granting a "third world" counterpart access to the latest and most "advanced" intellectual commodity and because I myself was and remain skeptical of much of the intellectual work that often goes on under the name of "cultural studies." To compound the irony of my position, then, I presented my Brazilian colleague with a list of titles, together with a warning to be very cautious—"tenha muito cuidado"—with their contents.

The second was the recent publication, in English translation, of a collection of essays by the Brazilian critic Roberto Schwarz.[1] I had known and admired Schwarz's essays in their Portuguese originals for some time, especially the writings on Machado and the long essay entitled "Cultura e Política, 1964–69." But my rereading of Schwarz did more than refresh my memory. It was positively revelatory and convinced me that Schwarz is, notwithstanding the relative paucity of his published work, the most important Latin American critic of his generation. It struck me, moreover, that the theoretical positions mapped out in essays such as "Culture and Politics" and "Brazilian Culture: Nationalism by Elimination" are, despite the absence of the buzzwords themselves, important contributions to the current debates around questions of postmodernity, postcoloniality, and, indeed, "cultural studies" itself. Thinking back to my quandary over how to respond to my Brazilian friend's interest in cultural studies, I was chagrined to realize that Schwarz had been left off my proffered list but also gratified to have discovered, however belatedly, what should have been my accompanying caveat: not just "muito cuidado" but a pointed reference to "as idéias fora do lugar," or, indeed, to Schwarz's mode of cultural criticism itself not only as a Brazilian alternative but even more so as a possible foil to the cultural studies paradigm as such. It is this latter possibility in particular that I wish to explore in what follows.

But, "misplaced idea" or not, what is entailed by the said paradigm of "cultural studies"? The names on my list included critics once associated with the Centre for Contemporary Cultural Studies (whence the rubric itself derives), or Birmingham School, above all Raymond Williams and Stuart Hall; North America–based critics who have worked on mass and popular culture more or less in the Birmingham style, including Andrew Ross, John Fiske, Constance Penley, and Janice Radway, inter alia; Arjun Appadurai and others associated with the journal of the Society for Transnational Cultural Studies, *Public Culture;* the "science-as-culture" critiques formulated by people such as Donna Haraway and James Clifford; and, in the area of Latin Americanism, the work, say, of Néstor García Canclini and José Joaquín Brunner, as well as the metropolitan-based writings of William Rowe and Vivian Schelling, George Yúdice, Jean Franco, Marc Zimmerman, María Celeste Olalquiaga, and others.

But beyond the obvious concern for "culture" as opposed merely, say, to "literature," what, if anything, joins these various strands? Here I would point to two shared theoretical modulations: The first and most visible is the suspension of the categories of aesthetic judgment that underlie the hierarchy of cultural values—"high-," "low-," "middlebrow," and so on—in the traditional practice of humanistic criticism. Thus the afternoon soap opera and the gossip column become no less valid as objects of critical analysis than novels or poems. In this regard there appears to occur a gravitation of humanistic studies toward the critical methodologies of the social sciences. And yet "cultural studies" is not just a new name for the sociology of culture. For this disciplinary shift is at the same time a movement from the opposite direction as well, suggesting that what is under way is a more general reordering of disciplinary boundaries themselves. In the work of an anthropologist such as Clifford, for example, it is explicitly denied that in studying "culture" the social scientist places himself or herself outside the space of the cultural. The work of the cultural analyst and critic drops its "strong" epistemological claim to objectivity and concedes its own, sometimes problematic, status as a cultural intervention. Culture moves from the right-hand side of the subject/object binarism to bracket the relationship as a whole. Here, then, the conventional social-scientific orientation toward culture as the object of empirical study moves more in the direction of the humanistic disciplines, in which culture has been theorized as an essentially hermeneutic realm—one of "discourses," "meanings," "narratives," and so on—that the critic not only "studies" but interprets and even "resignifies."

It would be an error, however, to suppose that these trends have all emanated from the "metropolitan" intellectual circles in which issues of mass culture have assumed so high a profile in recent years. Take, for example, the work of García Canclini, a Mexico-based social and cultural theorist. In an essay also recently published in English translation,[2] García Canclini proposes that the fundamental conceptual oppositions that have long dominated cultural criticism in Latin America—not only high versus low but modern versus traditional, center versus periphery, foreign versus autochthonous, and so on—have lost their purchase on contemporary reality. A "global restructuring of society and politics" (*OE*, 31) has undermined the older cultural paradigm linked to dependency theory. Rather than continuously referring back to a "patrimony," or a site of fixed cultural essence or identity, culture now becomes simply a process of "reconversion," of constant "negotiation" and "hybridization" across the multiple political, economic, and ethnic divisions of Latin American societies.

Here, in fact, García Canclini openly asserts what is often merely an unconscious implication of European and North American cultural studies, namely that culture, in freeing itself from the purportedly precultural social structures that had previously furnished the criteria for its conceptualization and critique, becomes, in the words of Rowe and Schelling (whose *Memory and Modernity* largely follows on the work of García Canclini) "the decisive area where social conflicts are experienced and evaluated."[3] Not only the center/periphery opposition but, in García Canclini's words, the very "idea of community" as the "abstraction of a cohesive national state" (40) has become obsolete. Extrapolating from this we might then go on to add, as perhaps its third dimension, the general tendency of cultural studies to insist not merely on the *globalization* of culture—whereby, say, sushi bars become as familiar a part of life in Seattle as in Tokyo but still retain their "Japanese" identity—but on its *de-* or *postnationalization.* That is, cultural nationalism itself, based on a logic in which "culture" is (or, in an ex-colonial setting, would some day become) a predicate of "nation," grows outmoded in the face of processes that have rendered culture so fungible, so fluid and free-floating a "sign system," that the very spatial fixity of categories such as "nation" can no longer contain it. If anything, this relation is reversed: It is now "culture," as a generative, symbolic process, that predicates "nation."

It is in connection with this third, postnationalist, dimension of cultural studies—its rethinking of culture as a reality that has transcended the limitations of the nation-state—that Schwarz's work in critical theory becomes especially pertinent. In his essay "Brazilian Culture: Nationalism by Elimination" (which first appeared in Brazil in 1986) Schwarz takes up the phenomenon of the seemingly "imitative nature" of Brazilian cultural life, arguing in an ingenious twist that the very *perception* of foreign imitation as a *problem* is ideological, reflecting the

Brazilian elite's historical alienation from the culture of the masses it exploits. The problem of imitation is, according to Schwarz, a false one because it "concentrates its fire on the relationship between elite and model whereas the real crux is the exclusion of the poor from the universe of contemporary culture" (*MI*, 16). In the course of this argument, Schwarz notes the widespread opposition of contemporary intellectual radicalism in Brazil to the cultural nationalism that characterized the Goulart years on the grounds that the reality of globalized culture now makes this goal an anachronism. "The argument," writes Schwarz,

> is irrefutable but it must be said that in the new context an emphasis on the international dimension of culture becomes no more than a legitimation of the existing mass media. Just as nationalists used to condemn imperialism and hush up bourgeois oppression, so the anti-nationalists invoke the authoritarianism and backwardness of their opponents, with good reason, while suggesting that the reign of mass communication is either emancipatory or aesthetically acceptable. . . . [But] the imposition of foreign ideology and the cultural expropriation of the people are realities which do not cease to exist just because there is mystification in the nationalists' theories about them. (5)

One sees immediately here the implicit challenge to the theoretical revisions of García Canclini and perhaps to cultural studies generally. It is one thing to deny that culture emanates from a national "patrimony," but to proceed from this directly to the premise of the total globalization and fungibility of culture and of the obsolescence of a cultural critique centered on "fixed," structural inequalities such as imperialism and the state[4] appears merely to be a replacement of one mystification by another. To be sure, its defenders may challenge the idea that cultural studies is, as Schwarz claims of the Brazilian antinationalists, "no more than a legitimation of existing mass media": Is this not once again to portray the "reign of mass communications" as a monolithic "culture industry" à la Adorno and Horkheimer, when in fact the very point of cultural studies was to rethink the cultural sphere itself as a contested and contestable one, characterized not only by the brainwashing effects of commercial and state propaganda but just as much by the subversive "reconversions" of consumers themselves? Perhaps so. Yet the thrust of Schwarz's critique of what he terms the "mass media modernists" is that even in such seemingly oppositional practices as "reconversion" there persists a utopian faith in the power of a globalized culture to stand in for the emancipatory social aims that cultural nationalism once looked to the "nation" to carry out. *Both* cultural nationalism *and* a postnationalist cultural studies rest on a common ideological ground insofar as *both* think culture, whether "patrimonial" and fixed or "transcultural" and decentered, in isolation from its economic basis in labor and class relations. The leap from cultural nationalism to the deterritorialized world of constant border crossings and cultural hybrids remains no less a confinement within an effectively reified notion of culture as a strictly symbolic, spiritualized realm. If cultural studies discovers within this realm a power to subvert dominant cultural forms, this in no way undoes the effects of this reification. As Schwarz says, "It is a question of choosing between the old and new error, both upheld in the name of progress" (*MI*, 5).

I have spoken of "reification" here, mindful of the fact that Schwarz himself seems to avoid using the term. Nor, for that matter, does the term "alienation" make any very prominent appearance in the essays of *Misplaced Ideas*. Nevertheless, I think it must be clear that it is precisely these concepts that constitute the point of departure for Schwarz's mode of cultural critique. Given his personal links to the tradition of the Frankfurt School and Adorno in particular, this should come as no surprise. The point here, however, is to note how, by forcefully posing anew the question of culture's *alienated* character in the present social and historical context—what he bluntly terms the "exclusion of the poor from the universe of contemporary culture"—Schwarz throws into high relief a dimension of cultural studies that goes almost entirely unremarked in the course of present-day "debates." For however justly cultural studies may claim to have freed the concept of culture from its bondage to "essentialist" categories such as the "nation," the price it pays for this undoubted liberation would seem to be total, if often unconscious, acquiescence in its alienation. In his essay "The Affirmative Character of Culture," Marcuse wrote of a

> fairly widespread usage of the concept of culture, in which the spiritual world is lifted out of its social context, making culture a (false) collective noun and attributing (false) universality to it. This . . . concept of culture, clearly seen in expressions such as "national culture," "Germanic culture" or "Roman culture," plays off the spiritual world against the material world by holding up culture as the realm of authentic values and self-contained ends in opposition to the world of social utility and means. Through the use of this concept, culture is distinguished from civilization and sociologically and valuationally removed from the social process.[5]

It is this concept of culture that Marcuse dubs "affirmative," in which, according to him, the alienation of labor and social life generally in bourgeois society finds perhaps its most seductive form of ideological recompensation. Now, cultural studies, having emerged in the wake of the antihumanist revolutions of Althusser and Foucault, will naturally have nothing to do with the antediluvian notions of "spirit" or "authentic values." Thus it may seem perverse to suggest any affinity between "affirmative culture" and the conceptual object of cultural studies. Still, despite the fact that it eschews the conventionally "humanist" discourse of culture in preference, say, for a culture that embodies "resistance" or "hegemony" or for culture as the site of a struggle over "meanings," the "culture" of cultural studies strikes me as no less "sociologically and valuationally removed from the social process." This is certainly the case with García Canclini, for whom culture has been narrowed down to little more than the object of the purely descriptive norms of positivist sociology. The fact that García Canclini adds a certain theoretical novelty to this object by stipulating its "deterritorialized" and effectively semiotic rather than semantic property or by proclaiming the total reordering of cultural space itself in the wake of "global restructuring" does nothing to alter its ultimately reifying effect. (Insofar as it is unable to think culture-as-object except in a conventionally empiricist sense, cultural studies, notwithstanding its epistemological relativism, may even be considered to represent a step *backward* from the classically "humanist" affirmative concept of culture analyzed by Marcuse.) The deterritorialization of culture in no way alters the alienated condition of the social whole of which it is in integral part. "Transculturation" does not equal the transalienation of culture. And García Canclini's references to what would appear to be radical transformations on the level of culture's material base suffer from the same sort of vagueness and grandiosity that afflicts so much of the current shoptalk regarding "postmodernity," "late capitalism," "postindustrial society," and so on: In the end, there seems to be little if any convincing evidence that such "global restructurings" as have actually occurred add up to a rupture of truly epochal proportions.[6] As to García Canclini's claim that the concepts of a capitalist periphery and a cohesive national state have now become outmoded—this strikes me as blatant nonsense.

But if the fundamental drawback of cultural studies is its tendency to reify culture, to falsely divest it of its alienated, negative determination, why, the question may be asked, turn to a critic like Schwarz for the antidote? Why not resort directly to Frankfurt School–style Critical Theory as the critical alternative?

In the first place, to elevate "Frankfurt" over "Birmingham" has its own serious drawbacks. For it will be recalled how Adorno, Marcuse, and company, in the wake of European fascism and disappointments with both the Popular Front and "existing" Soviet socialism, proposed to restore negativity to the culture whose affirmative character they so relentlessly exposed: through the purely abstract, hypothetical, and nonpolitical subversions of the modern "work of art." Frankfurt School critique, in its historical despair, could only answer the false promises of industrialized culture with the unfathomable and ineffable negations of the aesthetic avant-garde. I have argued elsewhere[7] that much of the radical impulse behind cultural studies stems from a sometimes poorly understood but nevertheless totally comprehensible exasperation with the left aestheticism of the Frankfurt School and its many local offshoots. If nothing else, the experience of the 1960s inaugurated a state of permanent skepticism regarding the supposed emancipatory role of vanguard aesthetics.

But Schwarz, despite sharing the Frankfurt School's hostility to the debased values of capitalist mass culture, does not share its radical aestheticism. And herein lies his genuine importance as a critical theorist. To the classical Marxist critique of capitalist forms of reification and alienation, Schwarz joins not only the critique of the culture industry but likewise the *critique of imperialism*—something he most assuredly did not learn from Adorno! For Schwarz, as for Marx, the road to the disalienation of culture and social life itself is that of social, not artistic, revolution, and its potential agents are the exploited classes themselves, in Brazil and elsewhere. This potential is something that the Frankfurt School tradition, albeit perhaps sorrowfully, had long since regarded as a falsehood. The possibility that the repeated disappointments of social revolutionary hopes in metropolitan Europe and North America might be internally linked to the structure of imperialism itself—something that Lenin was the first to propose and that achieved a certain general currency in the 1960s with the popularization of Maoism—did not enter the thinking of an Adorno, or if it did, it found no echo there. Schwarz, in contrast, premises critique if not on a note of revolutionary optimism, then nevertheless on the clear recognition that it is the contradictions of capitalism as a world system—its necessarily uneven and unequal division of labor and wealth—that determines the course of development, whether political or cultural.

This, of course, is a perspective that Schwarz shares with an entire generation of radical intellectuals in Latin America and the third world. What distinguishes Schwarz in this respect is his consistently critical attitude toward the radical nationalisms and populisms that, beginning in the 1950s and 1960s, proposed themselves as the revolutionary alternative to imperialist domination. As we have seen in his treatment of the "imitation" complex of Brazilian culture, Schwarz insists on rendering a class critique not only of imperialism but of its nationalist antagonists as well. (It is unfortunate to have to say so, but this rigorous fidelity to the demands of class analysis, even when the answers it points to are highly controversial, makes Schwarz a rarity in both North and Latin America.) The terms of this left critique of anti-imperialist populism and cultural nationalism emerge already fully elaborated in "Culture and Politics, 1964–1969," an essay now more than twenty years old. Here Schwarz straightforwardly points to the Brazilian Communist Party's policy of alliance with the "patriotic" national bourgeoisie as a principal factor in the counterrevolution of 1964 and as crucial to the "mistake . . . at the centre of Brazilian cultural life since 1950" (*MI,* 130). The essay proceeds to a critical exploration of a wide variety of cultural and political developments in post-1964 Brazil (literature, architecture, theater), the acuteness and subtlety of which invite comparison with Marx's *18 Brumaire.* "Culture and Politics" remains, for me, the best piece of critical prose on the 1960s.

It is important to point out, however, that, even while exposing the limitations imposed on cultural practices by the politics of populism and nationalism, Schwarz does not simply condemn these practices out of hand. "Culture and Politics" is, in large part, an effort to identify and analyze what Schwarz calls the "disparity between reformist practice and its cultural results" (*MI,* 133). An example of one such disparity is the Movement for Popular Culture (MPC), active in Pernambuco before 1964, out of which grew Paulo Freire's radical pedagogy. Schwarz invites a comparison of this development (noting its immediate suppression by the military government) to the subsequent literary and artistic phenomenon of *tropicalismo,* in which there can be seen a superficially similar practice of bringing together the rural and the urban, the traditional and the modern, and so on. Despite this similarity, however, there is, says Schwarz, "nothing less tropicalist" than Freirian pedagogy. "Why? Because the opposition between its terms can be resolved—people can be made literate. For the tropicalist image, on the contrary, it is essential that the juxtaposition between old and new—either between content and technique or within the content itself—should make something *absurd,* should be an aberration" (142). That is, although both the activities of the MPC and tropicalism count as "culture" in a broad sense, for the former "transculturation" takes on a genuinely emancipatory character; for tropicalism it has become a mere formality, no longer concretely linked to progressive social ends. The crucial thing here is that Schwarz *is able to draw this distinction,* whereas the "cultural studies" approach of a García Canclini is effectively limited to observing the abstract generality of transculturation, drawing from this, moreover, the ultimately false conclusion that transculturation itself outmodes the very notion of integrating "old and new." Cultural studies, that is, looks not a little like a continuation of tropicalism as Schwarz portrays it—suggesting perhaps that it operates within an analogous, if not identical, set of political and ideological constraints.

To reframe this in terms of nationalism we might say that whereas Schwarz, along with cultural studies, rejects the ideology itself, he is careful not to dismiss but rather to assess in a more dialectical spirit the cultural expressions to which it has given rise, expressions in which, *because he analyzes them in class terms,* he can look for the prefigurations of a higher form of, shall we say, postimperialist social being.

One question remains to be touched on here; namely, is there a connection to be drawn between Schwarz's critical-theoretical perspective and its Brazilian context, in which the latter would be the former's "condition of possibility"? I suggest there is such a connection, insofar as Brazil has been the site, over the past one or two generations, of major developments in the social critique of imperialism and "dependency." (Think, here, of the tradition of Cardoso, Marini, Ianni, Fernandes, Weffort, et al.) Thus Schwarz becomes heir to precisely the more progressive aspects of Brazilian populism and radical nationalism even while acting as perhaps their most persuasive critic. But perhaps there is still more to it than this. In the title essay of *Misplaced Ideas,* Schwarz, with reference once again to the Brazilian "imitation" complex, writes:

> Our ideological life . . . did vary: at a distance, it followed in the steps of Europe. . . . The tenacity of the basic social relationships [the "combination of latifundia and unfree labour"] and the ideological volatility of the "elite" were both a part of the dynamics of capitalism as an international system, the part that it was ours to live out. The latifundia, little changed, saw the baroque, neoclassic, romantic, naturalist and modernist cultures pass by, cultures which in Europe reflected immense transformations in its social order. We could well suppose that here they would lose their point, which in part did occur. But this loss, to which we were condemned by the working of the international system of colonialism, condemned the working of that very system itself. (*MI,* 27–28)

This same "international system of colonialism" has, of course, undergone significant changes; and contemporary Brazil, no longer dominated by the reality of latifundia and slavery, boasts an industrial infrastructure and a mass communications sector that make its place within this "system" look, if less than "central," then more than "peripheral." But Brazil also "boasts" one of the lowest wage levels in the world and continues to witness massive peasant migrations and even the wrenching violence of modern capitalism's encounter with tribal society. Thus if the imported cultural paradigms of the past could, in the Brazil of the latifundia, discover the material conditions best positioned to expose their false universality, how much more true is this today in a Brazil in which all the extremes of contemporary world capitalism present themselves so emphatically? Brazil may be as fertile a soil as any for the fetishized thinking of "cultural studies." But the very fact that the contradictions of modern imperialism take so manifest a form here surely makes these fetishes all that easier to "mis(dis)place."

NOTES

1. Roberto Schwarz, *Misplaced Ideas: Essays on Brazilian Culture,* trans. John Gledson et al., ed. John Gledson (London: Verso, 1992). Further citations are given in the text as *MI.*

2. Néstor García Canclini, "Cultural Reconversion," in *On Edge: The Crisis of Contemporary Latin American Culture,* ed. George Yúdice, et. al. (Minneapolis: University of Minnesota Press, 1992), pp. 29–43. Further citations are given in the text as *OE.*

3. William Rowe and Vivian Schelling, *Memory and Modernity: Popular Culture in Latin America* (London: Verso, 1991), p. 12.

4. "The dense web of cultural and economic decisions leads to asymmetries between producers and consumers and between diverse publics. *But these inequalities are almost never imposed from the top down, as is assumed by those who establish Manichaean oppositions between dominating and dominated classes, or between central and peripheral countries.*" (my emphasis) "Cultural Reconversion," 34.

5. Herbert Marcuse, "On the Affirmative Character of Culture," in *Negations,* trans. Jeremy J. Shapiro (Boston: Beacon Press, 1968).

6. See, in this regard, Alex Callinicos, *Against Postmodernism,* (New York: St. Martin's Press, 1990), especially chapter five, "So What Else Is New?" pp. 121–153.

7. See "Latin America and Cultural Studies: An Overview," *Latin American Literary Review* 20, July–December 1992, pp. 58–62.

9

It's an X-Thing: The Culture of Black Nationalism in Contemporary South Africa

GRANT FARRED

It is in the modality of race that those whom the structure systematically exploits, excludes, and subordinates, discover themselves an exploited, excluded, and subordinated class. Thus it is primarily in and through the modality of race that resistance, opposition, and rebellion first expresses itself.

—Stuart Hall et al., *Policing the Crisis*

Living in the Interregnum

South Africa is a society currently suspended within its own peculiar interregnum, located in the transitional moment between the demise of the apartheid state and the inauguration of a postapartheid one. Historically, such moments are characterized by a complex of futurity, the past, tensions, possibilities, fears, anticipations, and, not least of all, profound uncertainty. It is a time when new narratives of nation, community, and self come into confrontation with declining, though not yet eclipsed, narratives. It is also a time when traditions, cultural practices, modes of struggle, and ideologies are discarded, created, or recovered for new tasks—often following anticipated trajectories, sometimes taking more unusual paths. The interregnum is a period in which the future requires a reconsideration and a reinscription of the past and in which the two phases of a society's history renegotiate their relationship to each other. South Africa is a society poised so precariously between two epochs that the pressures of the interregnum are all too manifest, though perhaps nowhere so obviously as with the assassination of Chris Hani, secretary-general of the South African Communist Party (SACP). Since Hani is the most important political figure to be slain in this period, it is appropriate, we could even say inevitable, that many of the issues associated with the interregnum should have cohered around his death. Hani's death is a social event remarkable less for its insistence that South Africans confront the dominant problematic of the era—how to effect the transition from institutionalized racism to democracy—than for its ability to demonstrate that these concerns will have to take into account the ways in which culture, resistance, and ideology have conjoined to produce a redefinition of South African politics. The circumstances surrounding Hani's death have unsettled established modes of political understanding, especially concerning what constitutes political sites and acts, what counts as political indicators, and where the boundaries of national electoral politics end and international cultural politics begin.

On April 10, 1993, the SACP leader was gunned down outside his home in Boksburg, a predominantly white suburb just outside Johannesburg, by Janusz Walus, a Polish immigrant. Walus, police investigations reveal, had been acting on the policies of the Wit Wolwe (White Wolves),[1] an extremist right-wing group to which he belonged. Hani's national status, however, means that Walus's actions cannot be conceptualized as simply another instance of white South African violence and street justice. In fact, one of the more telling political effects of Hani's death was that it included accounts of his ideological dissidence within the upper echelons of the African National Congress (ANC) leadership. In a political context where the ANC can best be described as an organization struggling to reconcile its revolutionary history with the demands of the democratic electoral process, Hani took up that challenge by attempting to incorporate the former process into the latter moment. Hani believed that the provision of housing, education, medical facilities for black communities, and a certain notion of land and wealth redistribution should be an integral part of the ANC's election platform. This position was too far to the left of the ANC platform, and Hani was thus rendered somewhat anachronistic within the ranks of the movement's leadership. Although the tenets of Hani's radical agenda are acknowledged as key to the ANC's revolutionary past, a past that has been and continues to be strategically invoked, those tenets are no longer deemed organic or necessary to the ANC's electoral future.

Therefore, when Comrade Chris (as he was popularly known in the townships), the one tenuous link between the ANC leadership and the grassroots struggle, was gunned down, black South Africa's patience snapped. For many blacks, inside and outside the ANC, Hani represented the last hope for genuine social reorganization. An unknown black protester, in an angry exchange with the police on Cape Town's Grand Parade on April 14, 1993, made this point with rare force: "You have killed our leader [Hani] and therefore you have declared war on us."[2] Hani's status within the township is an articulation of the paradoxes emerging from the interregnum, representing an uncertain moment when a black national leader, recently returned from exile, had integrated himself into the fabric of township struggle while living in a white suburb—beyond the ken of the township's politically troubled and materially deprived environs. This scenario becomes even more complex if we remember that Hani's checkered history as former chief of the ANC's armed wing, Umkonto we Sizwe (Spear of the Nation), included an implication in the maltreatment of his troops. All this, however, left his township stature undiminished. On April 14, 1993, the day of the Hani commemorations, black South Africans turned on their white counterparts not out of unmitigated racial hatred but out of a sense of historical futility: Black South Africa's future prospects resemble the ravages blacks endured in their apartheid past. From the vantage point of the township, there appears to be no difference between the apartheid and the postapartheid South Africa.

At this moment it would appear that Steve Biko's 1969 categorical reminder to blacks has never been more timely. Biko, who led the Black Consciousness movement in the late 1960s and early 1970s, held that whites are a "homogeneous community" when it comes to their privileges: "a community of people who . . . enjoy a privileged position that they do not deserve."[3] On April 14, 1993, just four days after Hani's assassination, this Black Consciousness insight seemed to pervade the thinking of disenfranchised South Africans as they gathered across the nation to honor Hani. It is paradoxical that in a South Africa preparing for democracy, conditions vastly different than those in which Biko and his fellow students developed the theory of black consciousness, a Manichean paradigm—black versus white—was temporarily set in place. These base categories of apartheid became the terms of struggle as blacks attacked whites in the major urban centers of Cape Town, Johannesburg, and Durban. The Hani commemorations produced an unprecedented scene in South African history: white people running for their lives by ducking into alleys, hiding behind barred doors, cowering in public toilets, seeking refuge anywhere, everywhere; blacks attacking whites simply because they were white. Ironically, Cape Town, the South African city with the most liberal traditions, witnessed a particularly brutal and bloody display of black anger, a violence matched only by the regime's history of brutality against blacks. Tony Yengeni, secretary of the ANC's Western Cape office, was in the forefront of expressing this new militancy. Black people, declared Yengeni, "want revenge for Chris Hani."[4] Yengeni, who was supported in his assertions by the ANC Youth League leader Peter Mokaba[5] and Winnie Mandela, went on to warn of the possibility of insurrection: "He [Yengeni] warned that Cape Town centre could be burnt down, and accused the ANC of negotiating itself into the grave."[6] If nothing else, the events that shook Cape Town's Grand Parade and downtown Johannesburg demonstrated to the country's enfranchised community how deeply the memory of apartheid's effects was still embedded in the nation's black psyche. In the act of transforming the Hani commemoration into a violent protest, the township youth were simultaneously demolishing and reenacting the imaginary and historical barriers between black and white, albeit this time with the intention of inverting the traditional balance of power.

The critical feature of Hani's death, however, was that it drew attention to the constituency he had created and the process by which he had constructed himself as a political leader who forged real and symbolic links with the street culture of black township youth. Although it is possible to speculate whether Hani fully grasped the developing connections among street culture, community activism, and the emergence of black nationalism as an ideology that has pertinence and cachet in this moment of the interregnum, he has become in death a martyr for this amalgam of social forces. The salient feature of Hani's last public appearance before his assassination was thus, appropriately, the black baseball hat he wore, one marked "Rebel." Within the environs of a township culture where the youth are increasingly taking on the look of their inner-city counterparts in the United States of America, through the consumption of Chicago White Sox and Los Angeles Dodger baseball hats, basketball paraphernalia such as high-top Nike sneakers and New York Knicks and Chicago Bulls T-shirts, and the array of Malcolm X garments, Hani literally took on the politics of the street. Hani's immersion in transnational street culture may constitute only a qualified (or surface) investment in those practices, but his willingness to represent himself in its accoutrements positions him as an activist engaged in, at the very least, a minimally reciprocal relationship with his community. Hani's position attends to the processes by which the township images (imagines) itself. In adopting this self-representation, Hani became an icon for the township youth's particular brand of resistance because he, at least politically and culturally, was in sync with the thrust of their energies. Hani's baseball hat is thus a powerful metaphor, at once articulating his own dissidence within the ANC national leadership and suggesting an affiliation with the township constituency, which has historically supported the movement (and may continue to do so) but sees itself as increasingly alienated from Mr. Mandela and his colleagues.

Hani and the township's cultural politics, however, locates them at an unusual historical juncture. Black township youth, previously (and occasionally still) the shock troops of the ANC-led insurrection, find themselves at once enfranchised and marginalized by a South African body politic that is rapidly reconstituting itself. Township youth are located simultaneously at the outskirts of the new political arrangement (where the universal franchise does not promise to dramatically alter their living conditions) and at the intersection of local and global cultural practices—practices dominated, of course, by the United States. South African township youth thus represent what Paul Willis calls the "complex synerg[y] of culture and commerce."[7] Township youth negotiate a series of subject positions, positions that are always strongly impacted by their immediate experience but also informed and shaped by the effects of global culture. In an international context where popular culture has established itself as "America's second-biggest export after aircraft,"[8] it is of secondary importance that we engage the effects of U.S. cultural hegemony on South Africa; the primary task is to explore the relationship between South African township and American inner-city youth and the ways in which culture and ideology travel back and forth across the Atlantic. This chapter traces the roots of black nationalism in South Africa, offers a critique of the phenomenon, and, most important, focuses on the means by which cultural products are consumed and reinscribed, the process by which these U.S. artifacts (in reality a misnomer, since they are, in the main, produced outside U.S. national boundaries) transform and reconfigure other spaces, the ways in which imported cultural products renovate and sometimes resuscitate local political campaigns. Since all culture is ideological, what we are principally concerned with is identifying how ideologies encode themselves in, mediate themselves through, and render themselves indistinguishable from, cultural practices. The informing problematic here is the means by which black nationalism and its various cultural manifestations locate themselves in certain practices and how the ideology translates from one site to another—namely, from the United States to South Africa and, to a lesser extent, vice versa. I will trace the cultural and ideological trade routes of what Paul Gilroy has named the "black Atlantic world"[9] through the development of a black nationalist discourse in South Africa, a phenomenon largely unattended to up to now in that society.

Black Consciousness in South Africa

Historically, it is incomprehensible that in a country so uniquely polarized and stratified along the lines of race, black South Africans have never produced a fully fledged nationalist movement. The Black Consciousness grouping, founded in the late 1960s principally by students at segregated black universities and led by Steve Biko, represents the most serious effort to form such an organization. As a political force, the Black Consciousness movement was most active in the early- and mid-1970s. After Biko's death in 1977 its appeal waned somewhat and its ideology and agenda were taken up by the Azanian People's Organization (AZAPO), which has its base primarily in the Eastern Cape region (as did Biko's movement) and some parts of the Transvaal. The outstanding feature of Black Consciousness to date, however, has not been its containment to certain regions, though that too is undoubtedly a valid perception, but the historical neglect to which the organization has been subjected. According to the historian Tom Lodge, Black Consciousness (or BC, as it is known colloquially) is so grossly underresearched that there are "no scholarly biographical studies of the leading figures of the movement, an essential prerequisite for any understanding of why men like Steve Biko, Barney Pityana, or Harry Nengwekulu developed intellectually when they did in the way they did."[10] In *Bounds of Possibility: The Legacy of Steve Biko and Black Consciousness*, a collection of essays edited by Barney Pityana and a few of Biko's other colleagues, some of the movement's leaders have tried to redress the situation.[11]

The Hani commemorations of April 14, 1993, thus represent a watershed event in South African history, a moment in which the country's populace was confronted with a "new" political agency, one founded upon an essential notion of blackness that resonates with the ideological energies of Biko's movement. "Black nationalism," explains Wahneema Lubiano in an essay on the phenomenon in the United States of America, "in its broadest sense is a sign, an analytic, describing a range of historically manifested ideas about black . . . possibilities that include any or all of the following: racial solidarity, cultural specificity, religious, economic and political separatism.[12] The "possible" articulations of black nationalism that Lubiano lists should not be read as a hierarchy, though there is a certain appeal in tracing a nationalist trajectory in which "racial solidarity" forms the basic building block of such a political arrangement and the various kinds of "separatisms" represent the apex of such a movement. There is no narrative of progression, if we may call it that, where racial solidarity becomes a ubiquitous social experience because it takes on increasingly more nuanced and varied manifestations. Instead, what we have is a black nationalism founded upon a complex "separatism" that affects the shape that nationalism takes. Racial separatism, to be sure, cannot be written out of racial solidarity and cultural specificity, but then neither does it singularly determine how black nationalism expresses itself—resources and conditions of struggle, to name but two factors, impinge on how any variant of black nationalism manifests itself. Black nationalism may not have an even trajectory or progress neatly, but this does not mean that it has not set an end goal for itself. Black nationalism, Lubiano holds, is predicated upon a "fantasy": "Nationalism articulates a desire—always unfulfillable—for complete representation of the past and a fantasy for a better future."[13]

Black nationalism in South Africa demonstrates how nationalism can take on the most basic and final expressions. South Africa's primary brief is the "fantasy for a better future," a future where blacks will share equitably in the wealth and resources of the country and where they will dominate the nation's political structures. The only way in which this future can be achieved, nationalists believe, is by forging racial solidarity among the country's black (which excludes coloreds and Indians, the other disenfranchised groups) communities. Black South Africans are conscious, as Biko asserts, of the "need to rally around the cause of their suffering—their black skin—and to ignore the false promises that come from the white world." Black solidarity, then, will depend on a narrative that "members of a social, political, ethnic or 'racial' group tell themselves, and which is predicated on some understanding—however mythologized or mystified—of a shared past, an assessment of present circumstances."[14] The "present circumstances" in South Africa lend themselves to the creation of such a mythologized narrative, a narrative where the black masses (as opposed to an emergent, growing middle class) can invoke a "shared past" of disenfranchisement, exploitation, and deracination as they close ranks against what is rapidly being perceived as an elitist, ideologically "nonblack" ANC leadership. To be "black" is thus to conform to a profile of blackness that is uniformly proletarianized. To be black is, in the terms of the Pan-Africanist Congress (PAC) interim constitution, to be a member of the "African working masses" and to be opposed to the "new elite drawn from the ranks of the oppressed . . . [an] elite which will not advance the cause of our struggle in any manner whatsoever but will be looking to its own interests."[15] The PAC paradigm is premised upon black nationalism and is in many ways synonymous with the phenomenon's current populist manifestations. "PAC" and "black nationalism" are of course not always interchangeable terms, and they do not function as such in this chapter; what is engaged here, however, are the effects of a shared ideological basis and the PAC's preparedness to incorporate black nationalist tendencies into its agenda. In many ways the PAC functions, sometimes despite itself, as the official organ of black nationalism even though the phenomenon, as I argue later on, often contradicts and frustrates the normal functioning of both the state and the black political structures. Despite the several overlaps and the many conjunctures between the PAC and the black nationalists, there is no easy commensurability between the two political groupings. At the moment it is perhaps adequate to say that their discreteness is variable and that the distinction derives from the problematic positioning of one organization in the realm of electoral politics while the other impacts that arena from an "informal" political base. Both the PAC and the nationalists agree, however, that black class bifurcation cannot be tolerated because it undermines race solidarity. In the nationalist view, intrarace class divisions constitute nothing less than race betrayal, the ultimate act of disloyalty, because they equal consorting with the enemies of the "African working masses." Within this nationalist paradigm, race and class fuse to become interchangeable political descriptions: "Race" and "class" are reduced to categories that can all too easily stand in for each other. The race-class fusion represents a powerful variation of the nationalist fantasy, one where the Single Great Black Community is in and of itself an articulation of the future black South African state. The events of April 14, 1993, were a violent, preliminary expression of this black nationalist dynamic. The most potent effect of that event was the announcement of how nationalist blacks want to change their society, a vision that has little in common with the ANC's rhetoric of racial inclusion. The ANC envisions a society where whites, blacks, indians, and coloureds can occupy the same space with some degree of postapartheid harmony.

Black nationalists seek to divide South African society racially rather than make it cohere. Hence, the discourse of loss that followed in the wake of the Hani assassination and commemoration registered very differently in (the different sections of) the two sides of the racial divide. Blacks converted the death of a political leader into a politically enabling moment, one in which they rediscovered an ideology. Whites had no such transformative mechanism available. Instead, whites lost their sense of security and the knowledge that their privileged spaces would no longer be inviolate. All that whites gained, it would seem, was the guarantee of future racial conflict. A stunned white South Africa publicly measured the costs of Hani's violent demise in strictly quantifiable terms—those of property damage and of foreign investment opportunities squandered. Against the backdrop of an economy ravaged by international sanctions, the white response is not without a certain validity. Within the context of a society in political and ideological flux, however, this overreliance on an economistic discourse was inappropriate. For its part, the black community transformed Hani's assassination into a compound metaphor, one that stood for complete loss—economic, political, and ideological. Above all else, however, the SACP chief's death registered, in Cornel West's phrase, the "eclipse of hope."[16] In the face of the overwhelming devastation of their communities through systematic unemployment, state-sponsored violence, and what many disenfranchised viewed as the capitulation of the ANC, blacks turned inward. The act of turning inward, however, did not incorporate the ANC leadership or include strategies to counter the effects of ethnic violence that was devastating communities in the province of Natal and in Johannesburg. More than anything, however, Hani's death marked black community members off from their white counterparts.

As the Black Consciousness movement demonstrates, black nationalism has long been a feature of South African life. In 1959, ANC members disaffected by the appointment of nonblacks to leadership positions left to found the PAC; this rupture was certainly the most formative political moment since the inauguration of the apartheid state in 1948. Currently, black nationalist militancy is a phenomenon characterized by elusiveness (its ability to transgress organizational boundaries) and hybridity (its ability to forge new, unlikely ideological and political formations). Although it is historically appropriate that black nationalism has been embraced most publicly by the PAC, political developments in the post-April 1993 phase indicate that it is an ideological force that is not the exclusive property of any one organization. Black nationalism has proved infinitely capable of blurring all political party affiliations, presenting itself as the most viable and radical alternative to the government and its security forces, to say nothing of the ANC leadership. The black youths who killed American Fulbright scholar Amy Biehl in a township in August 1993 make this point amply. The fourteen youths charged in the case possess any number of political identities; only four have been identified as PAC members, and for the rest one can but speculate as to whether they support the ANC, AZAPO, or even Inkatha. The key, of course, is not to link those youth accused in the Biehl murder to their political organizations; indeed, if we name their party affiliations it should be with the intention of understanding how the youth are representative of contemporary South African black nationalism. If some of these youth are affiliated with Mr. Mandela's organization, as a number of them almost certainly are, they are possibly disaffected ANC members who have appropriated the militant imperatives of black nationalism in an effort to radicalize their (and their organization's) politics. In the process of creating a township-oriented politics, black youths have created a South African political hybrid that uses the ANC organizational structures as a basis but is infused with a rival's ideological strain. By incorporating black nationalism, the ANC youth have forged a radical brand of township activism. In contrast, the four PAC youths involved in the Biehl murder could simply be party members acting out the black nationalist imperatives that undergird their organization's ideology.[17] To complicate the situation even further, it is entirely possible that several of the youths are institutionally nonaffiliated, members of a growing black constituency whose actions are informed in part by their historical condition (unemployment, unemployability due to deliberate undereducation by apartheid, devastated community structures) and in part by what members regard as the most viable political strategy of the day for their community. With all these possible variants, it is extremely difficult for the state, the ANC, or the PAC leadership to monitor these youth and to control their political activities. The youths who committed the Biehl murder, in reality, have produced an alliance that is specifically class-, generation-, and location-based.

The youth are, to invoke the terms of the 1980s insurrectionary rhetoric of the United Democratic Front (UDF)–ANC alliance, "ungovernable." Since the UDF and the ANC exhorted their members to render South Africa "ungovernable" through militant opposition in the 1980s, the current generation of township youth has appropriated that legacy of resistance to combat the National Party (NP), Mr. Mandela, and his national executive. Most important, however, the township youth are quite literally "ungovernable" because they operate within, outside of, and in between—as well as back and forth between—the formal and the informal political structures of the townships. It is thus impossible to identify the youth politically, or to assert that they wear their black nationalism in any one way—in their X hats or their ANC flags, or indeed if they wear their nationalist colors at all—since their allegiances always seem to be shifting and in constant flux. We can say with certainty, however, that a new kind of political militancy has arrived on the South African political scene, one that will require us to identify, read, and anticipate the effects of this particular militancy. Deductively speaking, we can assert that this variant of nationalism has an ideological core, black nationalism, to which it adds and subtracts other organizational components as the moment demands. Because of the havoc this phenomenon plays with party affiliations, we can only surmise the potential effects of this "black nationalist" identity. It is clear, however, that the 1990s version of BC has already made its impact felt both locally and across the globe. And, like its 1970s predecessor, the current generation of black nationalists relies as much on conventional antiapartheid strategies as it does upon forms of cultural resistance.

Imported Culture, Local Nationalism

Although Black Consciousness's effect on "real" South African politics was only minimal (Biko's movement, for example, never seriously rivaled an organization such as the ANC in terms of size or support), it was certainly a crucial element in black resistance in the early- and mid-1970s. Politically, it underwrote many acts of labor resistance early in the decade, and it was also particularly influential in the 1976 student revolt. Black Consciousness's major impact, however, was felt in black culture. Out of the ideological milieu of BC emerged a group of poets (Mongane Wally Serote, Mbuyiseni Oswald Mtshali, Sipho Sepamla, Mafika Pascal Gwala, and Don Mattera) and short story writers (Mothobi Mutloatse and Mtutuzeli Matshoba) whose work was grounded in the urban experiences of 1970s black South Africa.[18] These artists captured the tenor of Black Consciousness; black pride, beauty, and self-worth is expressed everywhere in the poems and stories of the period. "Alexandra," a poem by Wally Serote, the preeminent poet of that era, provides an affirmation of blackness even amidst the harshness of township life: "I silently waded back to you / And amid the rubble I lay, / Simple and black." Amongst the ruins of township life and the disenfranchisements of apartheid, Serote's black subject still retains a sense of a self, a self rooted in blackness.

The Black Consciousness poets (poetry was the genre of the movement) and their community came into their own, not coincidentally, at a moment when nationalist movements in sub-Saharan Africa and Asia were struggling to achieve postcoloniality and the black nationalist movement in the United States of America was flourishing. The anticolonial campaigns in neighboring Angola, Mozambique, and Rhodesia were at or approaching their peak at that time, and the radical 1960s politics of Malcolm X and the civil rights movement readily lent themselves as models for the struggle against a hegemonic white state. BC in South Africa circa 1970 demonstrates both the intersection and the interplay between the postcolonial world and the black nationalist movement in the United States of America. The struggles of African Americans in the 1960s—the Student Non-Violent Coordinating Committee's drive to register black voters in the South, the student movement's attempts to establish a "participatory democracy," and the larger cultural revolution—were all informed by the critiques of postcolonial intellectuals such as Frantz Fanon, Amilcar Cabral, and C.L.R. James and by the sustained resistance of blacks in places such as Kenya, Ghana, and Tanzania. Fanon, for instance, figured prominently in the thinking of the Black Panthers. All of these struggles impacted, in different ways, the Black Consciousness movement's local campaigns. The anticolonial battles provided a political impetus, and the African American struggle served as a cultural corollary in the battles against apartheid; of course, sometimes these roles were reversed or consolidated. The Black Consciousness movement demonstrates that despite massive repression by the apartheid regime in the 1960s, some forms of resistance remain not only elusive but also incredibly mobile. In this case, resistance traveled via the most circuitous route: from its African origins to the United States and back to the southernmost tip of the continent, setting up a bicontinental axis with three distinct points. BC shows that despite attempts by the NP government to quite literally cut the disenfranchised population off from the postcolonial world, blacks were nevertheless in sync with the global spirit of 1960s resistance. In Paul Gilroy's terms, this is the black Atlantic world at work, exchanging cultural practices, political ideas, and theories of resistance. Black Consciousness is an expression of this mode of traveling resistance (to amend Edward Said's phrase), one uniquely imprinted by the conditions of apartheid but still representative of transatlantic black nationalism. And traveling resistance, we find, is usually a compound of politics, ideology, and culture. In the decade that has become synonymous with cultural resistance, dashikis and T-shirts bearing slogans such as "Black Is Beautiful" and a clenched black fist (the Black Panther symbol) adorned the bodies of young blacks across the globe, not least of all in South Africa. BC was thus a period in which black South Africans exchanged fashion tips with their counterparts in newly independent Nairobi and the inner city of New York.

In a South Africa where cultural politics is broadly accepted as a set of secondary social tasks, Black Consciousness's cultural legacy and its implication in the international exchange of practices suggest that the society's cultural/real politics split is a problematic dichotomy. South African society operates according to a strict political hierarchy: "Real" politics (electoral politics, guerrilla warfare, and antiapartheid protests, to name but three of the most obvious practices) is at the apex, and various cultural activities (sport,[19] music, fashion, and so on) take their place in the reduced, nonstratified political space beneath. This binary does not suggest that cultural politics does not inform and impact "real politics"; rather, it makes clear that the role of cultural politics, insofar as it is acknowledged, is to support "real politics." When disenfranchised South Africans organized international sports moratoriums[20] and the boycott of homeland cultural venues such as Sun City in the days of Grand Apartheid, these activities were regarded principally as a supplement to the liberation struggle. In that antiapartheid moment, such an understanding of the role of cultural politics was no doubt thought adequate, if not entirely accurate; what it means now, however, is that sports and entertainment, as well as the struggles around gender and sexuality, are seen as having no independent "political" purchase. South Africans do not have to develop a cultural politics; rather, it is necessary to dismantle and reorganize the hierarchical political structure that is in place. In a moment when the history of antiapartheid resistance is written, account should be taken of the full repertoire of that resistance, both the political and the cultural. Antiapartheid resistance included strains of both, shifting from one to the other (from boycotting the tricameral elections to securing the sports moratorium) depending on the conditions of struggle and the efficacy of the strategy. A reconceptualization, we might even say a democratization, of what constitutes the South African "political" sphere is crucial at a juncture where black nationalism has announced its reentry into the country's ideological scene not in the form of "real" politics (even though there were plenty of "real political" slogans, the most forceful of which is the PAC's "One settler, one bullet") but in the form of cultural signs.

Black nationalism's reemergence in South Africa took on an uncharacteristic, but not unexpected, sign: the latest fashion imports from the United States of America. In the past couple of years there has been a dramatic increase in the number of X baseball caps and T-shirts worn by black youths on the streets of urban South Africa. By summer 1992–1993 in South Africa the fashion trend reached its peak; X baseball caps and Malcolm X–emblazoned T-shirts were everywhere, an obvious staple of black youth's wardrobe. Even then, however, should South Africans have known that the symbolic presence of America's Malcolm on African streets presaged the ideological resurfacing of Steve Biko's Black Consciousness movement? How were South Africans to know whether the ubiquitous X designated Spike Lee's movie, then just released in that country, or the "alien" political phenomenon that El Hajj Malik El-Shabazz represented? The links—real, imagined, direct, and oblique—between Malcolm's X and the powerful resurgence of black nationalism on South African streets are difficult to forge. In Paul Willis's terms, making the connections between the culture of the street and its political effects is always a particularly daunting challenge. Willis argues that the act of producing a cultural artifact and a community that shares in its use is marked by unpredictability and a series of negotiations among unlikely social forces: "They [cultures and communities] start and form not from intentional purposes, political or other, but from contingency, from fun, from shared desires, from decentered overlaps, from accidents."[21] In South Africa, of course, there exists among black (as among youth anywhere) a "desire" to partake of the latest fashion trends, to represent themselves in its accoutrements, and to have "fun" in doing so. To mark yourself with an X is, in the township, to demonstrate both your street-wiseness and your fashion hipness. That such cultural activity takes place in an environment where there is increasing dissatisfaction with the coming political elite, the point where historical "accident" "overlaps" with "desire," produces a new set of political potentialities. Conditions have been created in South Africa such that imported cultural products and historical contingency can combine to enable a different kind of oppositionality, one in which culture represents the first phase (/face) of the challenge to the incoming government. In a situation where the elusiveness and largely antiorganizational nature of the political force makes it hard to pin down, Willis's succinct exhortation has a particular usefulness: "Let's look to the streets, to the common culture, not to the towers, for what is to be learnt."[22] South Africa's history of rarely engaging culture or cultural activism as a serious site of resistance, especially in a moment when there is an obvious continuum along the culture-politics line, lends Willis's call to "look to the streets" an especial urgency.

The politics of the streets, in this instance, has to start with the self-representation of the black body, an engagement with the aesthetics of the black body. What is being articulated by black youths in their self-representation? Where do these cultural messages originate? How are they adapted to the particular articulations of township youth? Why do black youth embrace, appropriate, and embellish certain fashion phenomena and disregard others? How do we account for the fact that although South Africa has been isolated from the world community for so long—diplomatically, economically, and culturally—certain international cultural influences have continued to permeate the society? How do all those Xs, which appear equally visible on the street and at political rallies and which move easily between the two venues, impact and transform political events? Do the Xs have any impact at all? The newest street fashion does not, of course, always coincide with or predict a major ideological rupture or development. Nor is there an easy convergence between an X hat and a black nationalist ideology. An X hat, worn backward by a black youth in downtown Cape Town or Johannesburg, or on the streets of the Cape Flats or Soweto for that matter, does not necessarily mark the individual as a radical black nationalist. The X is a cultural potentiality, not an ideological guarantee, and the street prominence of the hats and T-shirts is a complex cultural phenomenon. The X marks the intersection of culture and "real politics," the divergent ideologies of the township youth and the ANC national leadership, and the (momentary) "affinity"[23] of political opponents in the black community. (Within the sign of the X, all these events can take place simultaneously.) The X T-shirts can temporarily invalidate the differences between political affiliations, rendering the ANC, the PAC, and even Inkatha momentarily indistinct from each other. The street popularity of X garments can cut across class, race, gender, and generational boundaries, contingently producing a political community that is, shall we say, fashion-based; the X garments are equally capable, however, of cohering a racially and locationally exclusive community, one restricted to township members and capable of acting quickly and effectively. The events of April 14, 1993, made that very plain.

The X thus remains, despite its ability to mediate, sublimate, and resolve all kinds of political conflict, a sign of difference. To cite the most obvious example, white suburban youth who wear X hats and kids from the townships who wear Malcolm T-shirts share little common political ground. The main similarity between these two constituencies would be the fashion value of the garments and their age. (In the longer view, these are not inconsequential similarities, since these youth will be the first generation to come to maturity in a postapartheid society, no small commonality.) The township youth effected the most militant appropriation of X garments, drawing on and politically reinforcing the X accoutrements and establishing a symbiotic relationship between the various sectors of the township youth. It is black youth who have made Malcolm's face a definite presence at political rallies and other political venues, both formal and informal, and so a link has to be forged between Malcolm's newfound prominence and the rise of black nationalism on the country's streets. The X speaks a new kind of politics in South Africa, one that takes its cue from African American fashion and ideology. The township street, for decades a site of struggle with the repressive apparatus of apartheid, continues to be such a site except that it has changed its self-representation and mode of struggle, much like the postapartheid arrangement has done or promises to do. The struggle in South Africa has changed irrevocably, and the cultural element of that campaign may very well be the pivotal one.

Township youth, in possession of very few cultural resources, appropriated Malcolm X, the "undisputed deity of black nationalism,"[24] because his dynamic nationalist image precisely fits their needs as they symbolically oppose the apartheid regime and the ANC leadership. With limited cultural resources, the youth have made their own sense of Malcolm. They focused on Malcolm's nationalism, so that his political cachet was maximized for their purposes. The African American revolutionary was claimed as an icon, and for that reason, as with all icons, his history has been strategically pared: Malcolm X's past has been shorn of his career as pimp, petty criminal, and religious leader. As local ideological options were reduced because of an increasing fraternity between the ANC and the NP, so the Malcolm X baseball hats and T-shirts became the couture of radicalism, the battle garb of the township youth: These garments were invested by township youth with the hopes of black nationalism. The T-shirts and hats became bearers of a specific political code, one that resembled the symbolic importance the X sign had on the streets of, say, New York. The political memory of Malcolm, dormant in the black South African political imaginary for more than two decades, was quickly revived and invigorated, though not proportionately complicated, by the items of clothing that bore his likeness—or symbolically implied it. (To a lesser extent, Malcolm was recovered by the publicity that surrounded the release of Spike Lee's movie in South Africa.) "Malcolm" embodied, for Hani's mourners, radical oppositionality to whites.[25] The clothing of the township youth was, if anything, more of a political statement than an index of their fashionableness. Malcolm X, who spoke so eloquently of his African heritage in an effort to imbue his African American audience with pride and self-worth, has been invested with an ideological significance by the township youth that makes public their discontent with the ANC-NP alliance. Most important, however, "Malcolm" has become a symbol of the township youths' vision of a South Africa different from that of Nelson Mandela's ANC and F. W. de Klerk's government: Their future is etched as a black nationalist imaginary where continued white privilege will not be accommodated, in sharp contrast to what the negotiations promise to deliver. As cultural artifact, Malcolm is particularly useful in the moment of the South African interregnum because he enables the township youth to fight effectively in a new battle against an unfamiliar adversary—the ANC-NP alliance—that is itself a very recent political hybrid. The plethora of X-marked garments in the huge crowd that gathered on Cape Town's Grand Parade, the scene of the most violent attacks on whites, should thus have been harbinger enough of the black anger to be unleashed against whites around the country on April 14, 1993.

In the aftermath of the Hani assassination it is, for all political intents and purposes, impossible to disentangle the cluster of icons that have come to be associated with the event: Hani is the principal icon, of course, but the specters of both

Biko and Malcolm X also loom large. In death, Hani was symbolically handed Steve Biko's mantle: that of a black nationalist leader who is organically integrated into the struggle of the townships. Like Biko, Hani is perceived as a black statesman distinguished by his hard-line opposition to the white regime, a leader committed principally to the struggle of the black masses—one who privileges the black community's position above that of the ANC's tradition of a nonracial, democratic mode of struggle. The similarities between Biko and Hani's deaths encourage the analogy. Hani, like Biko, was a victim of white street justice—the former died on the street outside his home in a white Johannesburg suburb, the latter allegedly committed suicide while in police custody in a Johannesburg prison. Black nationalists, old, new, and recently converted, experienced the 1993 assassination with a sense of *déjà vu* because it reverberated so chillinglly the 1977 "suicide." In death, then, black youth aggressively introduced the white public to Hani's esteemed status in the township. In terms of South African cultural iconography, Hani's assassination is now inextricably linked with the image of Xs and the symbolic rebirth of Biko's Black Consciousness movement. Black nationalism made its 1990s debut at the Hani commemorations on the streets of such towns as Soweto, Alexandra, and Guguletu. Ironically, the very racist act designed to eliminate a prominent black leader provided the public spark that announced the resuscitation of black nationalism, an ideological rebirth marked as much by a volatile potentiality as by a series of political lacks.

Whither Black Nationalism?

Notwithstanding black nationalism's potency and its apparent ubiquity in the townships, it constitutes a political identity inadequate for the demands of a South Africa in the midst of social upheaval. As an essentialist political identity it is, in a uniquely South African manifestation, not only potentially but in practice racially exclusive. South African black nationalism has not yet overcome the problematic of apartheid's racial categories, an obstacle that will prevent it from accommodating those disenfranchised communities named, by law, "coloured" and "indian." This is a critical ideological deficiency because it evacuates the historical importance of "black" as an inclusive political category, artificially setting those other disenfranchised communities off from *the* black constituency and thereby reinforcing apartheid's racial divisions. This is, of course, not to suggest that the "coloured" and "indian" communities do not have a different relationship (we could even say "more privileged" within the South African racial strata) to apartheid. That is undoubtedly the case. However, to insist on black as an exclusive identity is to make the term narrowly derivative of apartheid's racial classification in a way that does not bear resemblance to the realities that coloureds, blacks, and indians share—a common history of disenfranchisement, deracination, oppression, and exploitation. The artist Richard Rive, for example, entitled his autobiography *Writing Black,* though apartheid law named him "coloured," in an effort to give voice to precisely these communal disenfranchised experiences. Rive and Bessie Head joined with "black" writers such as Ezekiel Mphahlele, Nat Nakasa, and Bloke Modisane to create a tradition of "black" urban writing that recorded the struggles of their people during the formative years of apartheid. Sections of the Indian community, like sections of the white, black, and colored communities, have a tradition of forging broad antiapartheid alliances in an attempt to overcome the divisiveness of the regime's racial categories. This tradition has a long history. In this regard we can think of the UDF as a recent example, but also of the 1950s Congress of the People, which invited South Africans of all racial groups to attend and draw up a charter for a postapartheid society. Out of this process emerged the Freedom Charter, the central ANC constitutional document. Black nationalism's essentialist racial basis, not surprisingly, makes little room for those white constituencies—such as radical intellectuals, feminist groups, and the anticonscription movement—that have a tradition, albeit an uneven one, of resisting apartheid. The only way in which black nationalists can engage white South Africans is through confrontation, dealing with each nonblack group as though it were a solid, coherent, unproblematic bloc. There exists, of course, no more unfissured a black identity than there does an essential white one. Inasmuch as a resurgent black nationalism has revived a restrictive notion of blackness, it will have to develop that black identity in contestation with other disenfranchised identities that have transmuted differently. Here fracturings in the black community along the lines of class, ideology, party affiliation, and gender during the decades of apartheid and in the interregnum will have to be accounted for by the nationalists.

In this historic interstitiality, black nationalism reemerges at a conjuncture when issues of gender are just becoming part of the broader public debates in the society. To wit, for the first time, women's rights have just been inscribed as an article in the new constitution. The reemergence of black nationalism presents a particular challenge to South African women because it is so deeply rooted in the violence of the society's patriarchal past (and present). Even though women number among its cadres, black nationalism is specifically gendered male—"township youth" is a code word for young black men. (It is not surprising that in so deeply patriarchal a society there is a disturbing commensurability between the articulation of violence as an ideological weapon—across the political spectrum—and the high rate of domestic violence. More South African women, across the racial spectrum, are raped than in the United States, a country six times more populous.) In a context where black nationalism predicates itself upon racial difference, women's issues stand to become an early casualty of the war against whites and that constituency in newly postcolonial societies that Fanon identified as the "national bourgeoisie." In order to make an intervention against black nationalism's expected antifeminist trajectory, the women's movements will have to utilize tragic events (as they did the Biehl murder) to foreground their campaign against male-dominated violence.[26] The publicity generated by such a brutal occasion enables feminists to turn attention to the ways in which all the country's political structures, regardless of race, operate within a patriarchal system that is saturated with violence. As devastating a phenomenon as black nationalism is, it provides South African women with the opportunity to convert the feminist rhetoric of the interregnum (where universal enfranchisement is marked by a recognition of the particularities of women's experiences) into a platform for several antipatriarchal critiques. However, as urgent as these interventions against the South African patriarchy and violence are, such critiques must not omit the different histories of the different groups of women.

Women's issues apart, the aspect of disenfranchised life that nationalists have thus far been unable to properly account for is the class divisions within the black community. This is a matter, one can safely assume, that will only assume greater significance as the black middle class expands under the aegis of postapartheid capitalism. Black nationalism's class deficiencies are of course directly related to its race essentialism. Despite their many critiques of the ANC leadership, black nationalists still regard their community as one bound together by a common history. Race and class are interchangeable categories, common denominators of a singular experience. The interregnum is an unsettled period, one conducive to race fracturing such that the nationalists' anger and vituperation are aimed both inward and outward—at those blacks who undermine *the* community's solidarity and at those external forces (whites) who facilitate and encourage blacks to break ranks. As an ideology founded upon race and class singularity, black nationalism finds itself confronted with a pronounced lack of congruence between the two political categories it has endeavored to render seamless. Not all blacks, the nationalists are learning, either regard themselves as or act as members of the proletariat.

Black nationalism is caught in a contradiction not of its own making: a historical moment that reinvigorates racial solidarity while simultaneously engendering the disruption of that unity. Black nationalism has attempted no encounter with the ethnic strife that has ravaged the black community for almost a decade now precisely because it is located in a moment when its ideological basis is both firm and fault-ridden. The Zulu-Xhosa ethnic conflict has, as well, been going on for some ten years, claiming thousands of lives in the process while destroying rural and urban communities from the hinterland of Natal Province to the black townships that outlie Johannesburg. Ethnic uniformity, or a refusal to acknowledge the politics of ethnic difference as it currently manifests itself in South Africa, is a cultural variation on the nationalist's proletarianized conceptualization of race. Unless black nationalism addresses these pressing issues, engages these ambivalences and contradictions, it will reduce itself to a momentary phenomenon, one with the potential to strike lethally but only sporadically in times of extreme crisis. Stuart Hall argues, as part of a broader discussion on Foucault, that discourses "go on unfolding, changing shape, as they make sense of new circumstances. They often carry many of the same unconscious premises and unexamined assumptions in their blood-stream."[27] As a discourse, black nationalism has "unfolded" and "changed" in dynamic ways, demonstrating the capacity to "make sense of new circumstances" in an unsettled historical moment. However, what black nationalism has failed to do is bring into critical focus its "unconscious premises and unexamined assumptions." Black nationalism, as Paul Gilroy insists, will have to produce an understanding of the "aesthetic and political plurality of blackness—its shades, nuances and uneven contours, its inner contradictions and internal fractures. Blackness is riven by class, gender and generation."[28] Black nationalism's relationship to the core issues Gilroy outlines, as well as to ethnicity, will have to be addressed if those ideological toxins are to be cleared from its "blood-stream." However, for all its ideological insufficiencies, black nationalism has proven itself a potent force within the South African context, one capable of exploding anywhere at any time with both fatal and dynamic consequences. Black nationalism may very well prove the X factor on the road to negotiating a new South African social dispensation. Black nationalism is a latent, unarticulated, volatile force, one always capable of being summoned at a moment's notice. Black nationalism's ability to be ideologically, politically, and culturally efficacious in a period of extreme contingency may depend, in the last instance, both on a full articulation of itself and on a complex knowledge of the conditions under which it is trying to (re)make history.

NOTES

This chapter forms part of a larger engagement with the politics of black nationalism in South Africa that I have been working on in the aftermath of Chris Hani's assassination. I have written on this issue in terms of space, "Downtown Cape Town: That's Where Black South Africans Are Headed" *Architecture New York* (no. 3, November/December 1993), and in terms of the effects of the Hani and Biehl murders, "Black Nationalism Reemerges on South African Streets," *New Politics* (4, no. 4, Winter 1994); both previous essays were crucial to the final form of this chapter. Several people contributed to this project at different stages. I would like to thank Laura Kurgan, Tom Keenan, and Lindy Roy for their incisive questions about the spacial arrangements of apartheid. Jim Murray provided useful comments on the *New Politics* paper, and Andrew Ross encouraged me to explore these issues from the first. Henry Schwarz provided a thorough reading and useful editorial comments. Finally, special thanks to Gitanjali Maharaj for her several readings of all three essays.

1. Walus's assassination of Chris Hani was part of a broader right-wing attack on those persons, institutions, and organizations—journalists, community activists, certain newspapers, and of course political organizations—that supported the principle of negotiations. The government and the ANC, the principal parties in this process, were singled out for special attention. The "hit list" discovered by the authorities contained the names of several members of the ANC's executive committee, including Nelson Mandela. Also on the list was the minister of foreign affairs, Pik Botha, a key member of the government's negotiating team. For a fuller list, see "Mandela, Pik on 'hit list,'" *South,* April 17–April 21, 1993.

2. "'You Have Killed Our Leader,'" *South,* April 17–April 21, 1993.

3. Steve Biko, *I Write What I Like* (New York: HarperCollins, 1986), p. 19.

4. *South,* April 24–April 28, 1993.

5. During the furor surrounding Hani's death, the ANC official Mokaba, in an interview on national television, revealed the extent of his own immersion in the rhetoric of black nationalism. Angered by Hani's assassination, he urged his ANC Youth League colleagues to "kill the Boers [whites]." See *South,* April 17–April 21 and April 24–April 28. Mokaba was publicly rebuked by the ANC leadership and made to apologize, again on national TV.

6. Ibid.

7. Paul Willis, *Common Culture,* (Boulder: Westview Press, 1990), p. 130.

8. Paul Willis, "The New Colossus: American Culture as Power Export," *New York Times,* January 30, 1994.

9. Paul Gilroy, *The Black Atlantic* (Cambridge: Harvard University Press, 1993), p. 3.

10. Tom Lodge, *Black Politics in South Africa Since 1945* (Johannesburg: Ravan Press, 1987), p. 324.

11. Barney Pityana, Mamphela Ramphele, Malusi Mpumlwana, and Lindy Wilson, eds., *Bounds of Possibility: The Legacy of Steve Biko and Black Consciousness* (Atlantic Highlands: Zed Books, 1991) is particularly useful for providing an overview of Black Consciousness. See especially the chapters on the history of the organization (Wilson), culture (Ramphele), and gender (Ramphele).

12. Wahneema Lubiano, "Standing in for the State: Black Nationalism and 'Writing' the Black Subject," *Alphabet City* 3 (Winter 1991–1992), p. 20.

13. Ibid.

14. Ibid.

15. "PAC Says It As It Is," *People's Express: The Alternative View of Township News,* February 23, 1994, p. 1.

16. Cornel West, *Race Matters* (Boston: Beacon Press, 1993), p. 5.

17. The earliest speculation, according to police reports, was that the youths were members of the Pan-African Students' Organisation (PASO). The initial suspicions were of course unfounded, but they indicate that the authorities, like the major political organizations, believe that there is a natural ideological home for youths who commit acts such as the Biehl murder—the PAC. The complexity (and "unreliability") of political affiliation, however, is revealed when it is alleged that the youth were acting on the strategies of Operation Barcelona, a campaign orchestrated by the ANC affiliate—the Congress of South African Students (COSAS). It is telling that Operation Barcelona, which advocated the destruction of government property in support of striking teachers who were demanding a pay raise, was not endorsed by the ANC. (See *Worker's Vanguard,* June 4, 1993, for a fuller critique of the ANC's stance in regard to the striking teachers.) Finally, I should note that the "Barcelona" in Operation Barcelona refers to the venue of the 1992 Summer Olympics—the city that marks South Africa's entry into the Olympics as a nonracial society in formation. The codename Operation Barcelona serves as a metaphor for the youth's athleticism and their ability to strike quickly at state apparatuses and then to escape detection.

18. The most important collections of poetry to come out of this period were Mtshali's *Sounds of a Cowhide Drum* (1971) and Serote's *Yakhal'inkomo* (1972). See also Matshoba's *Call Me Not Man* and the collection of short stories edited by Mutloatse, *Forced Landing.*

19. As far as cultural political struggles go, women's issues are gaining greater public access than the lesbian, gay, or bisexual movements. This trend can be accounted for in terms of the work done by feminists who have recorded the struggles of black women. See, for example, the critical work of Cheryl Walker, *Women and Resistance in South Africa,* the political biographies of Frances Baard (*My Spirit Is Not Banned*), Emma Mashinini (*And Strikes Have Followed Me All the Days of My Life*), and Miriam Makeba (*My Life*) as well as the fiction of Lauretta Ngcobo (*And They Didn't Die*). There was evidence of the growing political importance of women's issues in the aftermath of the Biehl murder when several mourners held up feminist placards, one of which read "Amy a Fighter for Women's Rights" (see the *Cape Argus* weekend edition, August 28–29, 1993). Protests such as this one occurred at several rallies held in the Western Cape and nationally.

20. The work of the South African Council On Sport (SACOS) was particularly crucial in this regard. See Cheryl Roberts, ed., *Sport and Transformation: Contemporary Debates On South African Sport* (Cape Town: Township Publishing Co-operative, 1990); and Roberts, *Challenges Facing South African Sport* (Cape Town: Township Publishing Co-operative, 1989).

21. Willis, *Common Culture,* p. 141.

22. Ibid.

23. Donna Haraway, "A Manifesto for Cyborgs, Sciences, Technology, and Socialist Feminism in the 1980's," in *Feminism/Postmodernism,* ed. Linda Nicholson (New York: Routledge, 1990), p. 196.

24. Jacquie Jones, "Spike Lee Presents Malcolm X: The New Black Nationalism," *Cineaste* 19, no. 4, p. 9.

25. It is remarkable that in a review of two works on Malcolm X in the *Weekly Mail,* the premier South African leftist newspaper, no connections are made between the racism, white supremacy, and anticolonialism that Malcolm struggled against and the processes of transformation in South Africa. ("From the Bottom of the Black Experience," *Weekly Mail Review/Books,* June 1993).

26. The ways in which the Biehl murder has created a political opportunity for women by allowing them to mobilize against violence and patriarchy are briefly noted in note 19. See also *New York Times,* August 19, 1993; *Cape Times,* August 27, 1993; and *Cape Argus,* August 28, 1993, all of which attend, to a greater or lesser degree, to the question of female empowerment that emanated from the Biehl murder.

27. Stuart Hall and Bram Gieben, eds., *Formations Of Modernity* (Oxford: Polity Press, 1992), p. 314.

28. Paul Gilroy, *Small Acts: Thoughts on the Politics of Black Cultures* (New York: Serpent's Tail, 1993), p. 116.

PART THREE

NARRATION AND THE SENSE OF PLACE

10

"Invented" Histories: Cultural Production in George Lamming's *Season of Adventure*

SUPRIYA NAIR

This book is based upon facts of experience, and it is intended as an introduction to a dialogue between you and me. . . . Magic is permissible. Indeed, any method of presentation may be used. There is one exception. Don't tell lies. From time to time, the truth may go into hiding; but don't tell lies.

—George Lamming, The Pleasures of Exile

Such a mass of ignorance and falsehood has surrounded these islands for so many centuries that obvious truths sound like revelations.

—C.L.R. James, *The Black Jacobins*

IN A LECTURE READ to the University of Miami American Assembly on the United States and the Caribbean in April 1973, Derek Walcott made what at first seems a startling claim: "In the Caribbean history is irrelevant, not because it is not being created, or because it was sordid, but because it has never mattered; what has mattered is the loss of history, the amnesia of the races, what has become necessary is imagination, imagination as necessity, as invention."[1]

Walcott's statement seems to echo the disavowal of native history asserted in colonialist historiography. However, his valorization of what stands in place of history—"imagination as necessity, as invention"—suggests that it is precisely the claims of colonialist historiography that he is refuting. Walcott's apparent dismissal of Caribbean history addresses the issue not of historicity but of historiography. The writing of colonial history has not been devoid of mythification, of ideologies posing as timeless truths. Hence its rewriting should appropriate the potential of invented traditions and imagined communities,[2] except that in this case the status of truth and lie is more self-reflexively combated, not in order to assert a final truth but to choose a particular history.

The work of the imagination in the formation of national identities has generally been relegated to the sphere of false consciousness and irrationality.[3] In such readings, myth corresponds to falsehood and nationalisms are contradictorily and uselessly invested in a bourgeois, ethnocentric reversal to a mythic past. My own reconsideration of nation and imagination focuses not on the visible, distinct, and homogeneous claims to ideological and geographic territoriality but on a practice that emerged as a subculture in the colonial period. In spite of acceptance in some communities, Vodoun continues to enact in its underground rituals the fragmentation and elusiveness of a submerged diasporic history. George Lamming first witnessed the Vodoun ceremony of the Souls during a visit to Haiti in 1956. He uses this experience in the first section of his fourth novel, *Season of Adventure,* published in 1960.[4] Written six years before Lamming's native island, Barbados, achieved independence, the novel continues the allegory of the fictional, composite West Indian[5] island. Although the focus on black communities runs the risk of essentializing a hybrid and multivalenced culture as it exists today in the Caribbean, I will eventually argue that Vodoun is used to recall and ritualize the memory of slavery as a specific passage in black history. Although Vodoun is a local Caribbean practice, it is significantly and predominantly connected with African rituals. Given its close ties with early slave revolt, the experience of Vodoun as a residual and an emergent subculture[6] relocates *traces* of Africa in the elsewhere of the imagination. My use of invention in the discussion of *Season* will be inflected by a variety of meanings as they come into play in the novel. To invent is to discover obscured details, to fabricate a new history, to create a fictional story, to experiment ingeniously, to produce something from nothing (as against finding or discovering something from what is already there). The associated sense of making an inventory, of compiling the traces of the past and giving it a clearer shape or form, is also relevant, particularly since many Caribbean intellectuals such as Edouard Glissant[7] and Kamau Brathwaite[8] have emphasized its importance in the putative formation of a Caribbean identity.

Lamming's use of Africa as a diasporic link figuratively represents the nation, which is also continental, as a "zone of occult instability where the people dwell."[9] His ameboid notion of the nation corresponds to the mental as well as material distribution implied in Bhabha's concept of "dissemiNation" and Gilroy's emphasis on "circulation" and "mutation."[10] The slipperiness of the imagination explodes the totalizing boundaries of the existing nation, allowing it to travel across the rigidities of geopolitical mappings. Brathwaite captures the itinerary of one leg of diaspora in representing its course through the metaphor of seasonal winds blowing in from the African coast into the Caribbean, bearing with them reminders of earlier winds and earlier currents that brought populations from African countries into the Caribbean islands.[11]

Specifically in the formation of the black diaspora, retrieving the past has involved its own difficulties because the degradation and violence that marked the forced scattering recorded a mangled heritage. The argument that the past is a wreck in Caribbean history has not been restricted to colonialist dismissals. Writers such as Wilson Harris, Derek Walcott,[12] and V. S. Naipaul have also agreed that slave culture had little that was productive to offer. Naipaul's infamous remarks on the Caribbean islands are informed by his conviction that past events of slavery and indentured labor have irredeemably skewed the history of the West Indian diaspora and drained current history on the islands of any productive potential. Confessing that he was often awakened by nightmares that he was back in Trinidad (after nodding off by a fireside in English bedsitters), Naipaul explains that his fear of Trinidad was the result of his belief that the island was "unimportant, uncreative, cynical. . . . We lived in a society that denied itself heroes."[13]

Lamming believes that a similar shame directs the fear of Africa expressed by James Baldwin in *Notes of a Native Son* and offers an explanation for the latter's oppressive sense of past history: "The backward glance is painful for it offers him [Baldwin] nothing but a vision of the bush, primitive, intractable, night-black in its inaccessibility. . . . We know what is meant by bush. It is the tom-tom and the axe: the tom-tom always loud with noise, and the axe for ever suggestive of blood."[14] Lamming's attempt to recuperate a more energizing vision of Africa in *Season* is not without a certain idealization, but it is also complicated by an awareness of the difficulty of maintaining a connecting thread when several historical factors had served to weaken it. Apart from the uprooting of clans with varying cultures and languages, once the slaves were relocated into plantation culture, cohesive organization was difficult. Although her circumstances are different, Fola's unawareness of her real father in *Season* has its historical roots in plantations where slaves constituted the master's chattel and not family units that required affiliation. Differences in ethnic and linguistic groups and labor functions also made slave unification a tenuous process.

In addition to the problem with logistics, Fanon's critique of "the return to Africa" addresses not just its Eurocentric reiteration of a generalized continent but also the teleological blunder it records. It is not identification with but alienation from national culture that makes the colonized, educated, alienated intellectual grasp at the (illusory) "secure anchorage" of a pan-African identity, Fanon argues. In spite of attempting to justify this desperate recourse to "mummified fragments," Fanon ultimately censures the invocation of a mythic Africa, which he likens to a "cult or ... religion."[15] Derek Walcott is equally dismissive of resuscitating dead gods, a metaphor he uses to critique what he considers a bankrupt intellectual romanticism that only succeeds in trivializing and commercializing the African connection.[16] It is interesting that both writers use the image of religion to reprove the invocation/evocation of Africa, because religion has been the sphere defined as premodern, traditional, unscientific, all qualities stereotypically associated with the African past before the intervention of the scientific, modern, secular West. And yet the meeting with dead gods, Lamming would argue, is not entirely outside the sphere of the living, the modern, the revolutionary. Nor is it simply a question of class and national alienation. Indeed, in the case of Vodoun, largely a lower-class practice, the dead cannot speak except through the voices of the living, and very often they speak of matters that concern the material here and now. Ventriloquism does not make puppets out of living beings. The first section of *Season* is titled "Arriving and Returning," emphasizing dynamic circulation rather than stasis. In Lamming's preference for the words "glance" and "presence" to indicate a return, he is also careful in suggesting temporality rather than timelessness, diffusion rather than rootedness. Rather than a definitive migration backward to Africa, the movement is metaphorical, strategic, and selective.

The Tropology of Africa

Since *Season* is ultimately concerned with the locality of the Caribbean, it is not with the tom-tom but with its more contemporary Trinidadian (and now internationalized) counterpart, the music of the steel drums, that the novel opens. The novel itself is dedicated to Ghana, which Lamming had visited shortly after it had gained independence in 1956, before any other African nation. The Ceremony of the Souls that the drumbeats announce signals the tropological presence of Africa through rites of religion and celebration. As Lamming argues elsewhere, "If that presence be no more than a ghost, then it is like the ghost that haunted Hamlet, ordering memory and imagination to define and do their duty."[17] The directing role that the ghost plays in the Shakespearean drama, sternly exhorting Hamlet to seek retribution now that he has revealed the "true" history of his murder, makes Lamming's use of the ghost as a marker of African presence particularly appropriate. Although the ceremony is concerned with recalling the spirits of the ancestors, the point of this resurrection is not nostalgia, sentimentality, or a necrophilic obsession. The spirits are invoked with the specific purpose of guidance for the future based on "a full and honest report on their past relations with the living": an explanation of the familial and communal past and a public revelation of hidden secrets.[18]

The nonlinear narrative of Vodoun encodes the speech and image patterns peculiar to the enactment of possession: chants, songs, fragmented responses to questions, visions, swoons, dances, and so on. "Possession" resonates with a multiplicity of meanings within the colonial context that conditioned the birth of Vodoun. Fanon invokes two possible possessions in *The Wretched of the Earth:* one socioeconomic and political, the other psychoanalytic and therapeutic. In the first case, the native's "dreams of possession" embrace the affluent settler's space and stimulate the attempt to usurp the settler's ownership.[19] The second use of possession is also marked by the defining role of the colonizers. "In under-developed countries," says Fanon, "the occult sphere is a sphere *belonging* to the community which is entirely under magical jurisdiction. By entangling myself in this [sphere] I find the everlasting world which *belongs* to me" (emphasis added).[20]

It is this "imaginary maze" that, according to Fanon, entraps one in the unproductive phase of possession. I use the word "unproductive" because although the repressed violence of the natives "is canalized by the emotional outlets of dance and possession by spirits,"[21] Fanon seems to find the expulsion of pent-up energy ultimately futile: The violent native only grapples with a shadow boxer. The only positive aspect of possession in Fanon's account is minimized, since it releases frustrations without always effecting a change in the social structure that is responsible for the native's condition. Further, Fanon's reference to the magical notion of "belonging" implies his critique of the fantastic world that allows the natives to delude themselves with the consolation of possessing at least one sphere that is beyond colonialist control. The constant retreats to unreal locales apparently distract from the very real conditions of material dispossession in the colonial world.

Many cultural critics would object to Fanon's ambivalent attitude toward Vodoun as a significant political rite.[22] C.L.R. James draws the link between Vodoun as a conspiratorial, organizational political strategy and as a creative, oppositional, cultural system. "In spite of all prohibitions, the slaves travelled miles to sing and dance and practise the rites and talk . . . and make their plans," he points out.[23] James reveals why the discomfort with Vodoun within the colonial framework was not restricted to its supposed lack of moral value. A more secular and material reason behind banning such practices was that they were often used to promote revolutionary struggle. The Haitian revolution was believed to have been inaugurated by Boukman's Vodoun ceremony in 1791. These otherworldly rituals offered the possibility of more than spiritual salvation and physical or libidinal release to the devotees. Interwoven in the worship of ancestors was the promise of earthly liberation as well, especially through the magic of rituals that were said to protect the rebelling slaves from harm. Interestingly, the ancestral souls were themselves dependent on the success of the Ceremony of the Souls—the truth being told and grievances redressed—for their own release from the watery purgatory, according to Vodoun mythology, the preliminary stage of the soul's ascendance. The frequent recurrence of the sea as location and image in Caribbean literature reminds us of the "long, wet hell of the Middle Passage,"[24] the historic slave past, the dissemination from one coast to another. Using an example of what he calls "the literature of reconnection," Brathwaite argues that Paule Marshall's description of the sea as a raging burial ground for drowned slaves insists on "recognizing African presence in our society not as a static quality, but as root living, creative, and still part of the main."[25] Brathwaite's metaphor recapitulates Lamming's in charting not just a move outward but its return inward in a continual chain. The emphasis on death and on the past underline not so much the incarnate but the incorporeal grasp of African presence in the Caribbean. Paradoxically, the unmarked sites of watery genocide give witness to one of the areas of the absent presence of African ancestry.

Vodoun itself takes its name from *vodun,* the Dahomean word for spirit. The spirit of the corpse temporarily returning to the material enters through the crossroads between times, locations, and cultures. The *loa* themselves are a diasporic community of spirits, wandering from one group to another as their servitors summon them to appear. "When the gods left Africa, they taught their people how to live the epic of displacement," says Joan Dayan. She points out that the metaphor of mounting a horse, as the *loa* "rides" the servitor, underlines the mobility of possession, because the "*loa* are in the people not in the place."[26] Not only are the gods themselves multiple, they are also diverse in their manifestations across national and domestic affiliations, like the very people they both serve and are served by. In its circulation of diasporic traffic, Vodoun operates through a series of aporia: Those who reenter are already departed, new birth emerges from painful partition, and the traditional ritual is also culturally contaminated as it adapts to everyday events.

Popular Western images of the the Vodoun ritual exploit its fetishization of the dead, indicated by its stereotypical representation in sensationalized horror films of the macabre and the undead.[27] But we should bear in mind Michael Taussig's cautions against an all-too-easy assumption that fantastic responses to nonfantastic realities are necessarily non-Western and backward. Far too many modern perceptions of reality are fetishized for us to target religious fetishism as a "primitive" mode that needs conversion to more rational thinking. Using Marx's characterization of market relations, Taussig draws attention to the ubiquitous presence of fetishes in a capitalistic, urban, industrialized, "advanced" society. And yet to the general public, the word "fetish" conjures up visions of primitive tribes and exotic figurines.

The critique of fetishism is based on the presupposition that qualities such as "life, autonomy, power, and even dominance" are drained from the animate to the inanimate in the process of exchange.[28] I want to argue that fetishism need not render the live subject passive or invisible. Folk superstition and magic have been criticized for the unreflected, uncritical beliefs they invoke and for the concrete acts of irrationality and injustice that such beliefs can generate. Much labor and time, it would seem, is expended on wasteful and wishful thinking. But religious and magical practices, like other ideologies, are not beliefs that inherently lack value, although they need constant critique and grounding in social relations. A fetishistic practice may cocoon the living in a fantasy world, but it can also utilize symbolic rituals and rites in order to engage productively in everyday life. The emergence of Vodoun within the context of slave revolt, its association with social practices such as oral communication and collective critique, and its carnivalesque rituals of singing, dancing, and drumming make it a unique personal and communal narrative grounded in rather than dislocated from a particular history.

The return to Africa in *Season* does not skip the history of slavery but uses it as a point of literal and metaphorical entry into the Caribbean. As Crim says to the background of the drums, "Perhaps contradiction help . . . but is the way you forget. Is not simple forget, is forget to remember."[29] Within the colonial system of education, what one was taught to forget was the arrival from Africa. Thus, the schoolboys in Lamming's *In the Castle of My Skin* are hazy about slavery and, although comically misunderstanding British history, they are more grounded in the latter than in the former.[30] When Lamming recounts his first impressions on arriving at Accra, school is what provides the "first shock of familiarity" as he watches the Boy Scouts rehearse the welcome of an English dignitary. But almost as soon as he recollects his childhood in the performance of the Ghanaian boys, the moment of connection is immediately and stridently ruptured when they begin to speak in Fanti and Ga: "The voices clashed like steel; and their hands were like batons conducting the wild cacophony of their argument."[31]

Lamming's attempt to commemorate the past in *Season* is similarly traumatic. Fola's return to an immediate as well as historical past is also initiated by wildness and cacophony, disconnection and confusion, as she watches the *hounsi*[32] dance to the music of the drums. Her "fearful encounter with her forgotten self" at the *tonelle* where she witnesses the Ceremony of the Souls initially holds the terror and alienation pictured in one version of Lamming's backward glance. Her first reaction is to be repelled by the spirit possessions and by her unwilling sense of kinship with the dancing women. In spite of her attraction to the white history teacher, Charlot, who introduces her to the ritual, Fola is uneasily aware of her bond with the illiterate, lower-class black women.

At the same time, Fola's shame proves that she has absorbed Charlot's history and shares his educational background. Ironically, she does not probe her fear of hypnosis and white rats to consider the implications of being possessed by a hostile and often alien culture and history. Her condition would therefore be more dangerous to the possessed women in the *tonelle.* They would regard Fola as a zombie whose physical power and psychic powerlessness emerges out of the slave context, since the living dead represent the dreaded condition of unfeeling servitude in a being whose soul has been stolen by the one now controlling it. Fola's, and by implication the Republic's, independence is meaningless because they are still controlled by the colonial paradigms of superior and inferior culture and history.

In a scathing indictment of middle-class intellectuals who sell their "talents" and isolate themselves from the laboring classes, Lamming presents a topsy-turvy world in an informal talk he gave on Emancipation Day, 1986, to a village audience in Buxton, Guyana, which has a largely Afro-Guyanese population of slave ancestry. On the one hand is the revolutionary history of the slaves and the laborers that continues to stay alive even if they are ignored or dead in official accounts. On the other hand are the incipient "mercenaries," the native middle class that claims to be the most productive class even as it cuts itself off from that revolutionary consciousness. "It's the dead going through all the motions of living. The system of institutions—school, extension of school, church, law courts, all these institutions were in some way designed to turn the overwhelming majority of the population into zombies," Lamming concludes.[33] In his scheme of history, the established and the institutional discipline the subject into willing compliance with the state. Antihegemonic potential, according to the novelist, lies in officially unrecognized sites whose very invisibility allows them to escape the fossilization of institutional politics and culture.

In *Pleasures,* Lamming refers to Prospero's magic as one example of cultural power. The sheer spectacle of Prospero's conjuring freezes Ferdinand and Miranda into a captive audience. Lamming's analysis of Prospero's magic constitutes a discursive challenge to more than a literary drama. The tragic upheaval of the Middle Passage and the collective enslavement of the African peoples were believed to be the result of sorcery. Caliban, therefore, can be read as the zombie, the monster-slave "created" by Prospero. Hence Caliban must reject his interpellated identity and Prospero's invented history in order to enact his eventual resistance. It is not surprising that Lamming draws a parallel between Caliban's abortive revolt and Toussaint's more successful and collective "transformation of slaves" in the Haitian Revolution (1789–1804), during which the supposedly infallible superiority of the Europeans over black people was profoundly shaken. *Season* is engaged in a dialogic response to the Haitian Revolution as well as to the genesis of Caribbean and pan-African nationalisms. The reference to the Haitian ceremony and to C.L.R. James's *The Black Jacobins* in Lamming's discussion of *The Tempest* emphasizes the importance of folk rituals and revisionary history in the drama of revolution.[34] Lamming's strong emphasis on the practice of Vodoun as an emancipatory project challenges the dominant perceptions of both Haiti and black populations as uncontrolled sites of gruesome exploits and anarchic misdirection.

Fola's visit to the *tonelle* ultimately revolutionizes her sense of her individual and collective history and provides the stimulus for concerted action. In fact, her witnessing of Vodoun is an educative experience, reorienting her sense of historical placement. As Fola herself realizes, "she would make her own history" in the process of relearning her past.[35] Although Fola, who is alienated from her mother, needs at first to turn to the "Boys" for her revolutionary initiation, she emerges as more decisive than the Reserve Boys themselves and intervenes at a critical moment to save them from police harassment. Her own conception is problematically "creolized" through the literal act of her mother's rape in order, it would seem, to represent the bastardized and violent parentage of the island. Her eventual acceptance of folk traditions on the Reserve and her active bid to save the drums from extinction finally place her in direct opposition to the patriarchal, neocolonial elite represented by her stepfather, Piggot, the chief commissioner of police and head of a committee in charge of "raising the moral tone of the country's name abroad."[36] Piggot's revulsion for the drummers and the Vodoun rituals mimics the language of the colonial administration in its anxiety to distance itself from the backward mentality of the masses. As Brathwaite sums up in his introduction to Melville Herskovits's *Life in a Haitian Valley,* "The darkness of the night of ignorance, of voodoo drums and human sacrifice, of zombies, Congo gutturals, Dagon, Ogun, paingan women carnalized by gods. It was all of a piece, really, with what the Establishment thought of Africa and Africans in the New World; dumb, drumming, demoralized boyoes up to no good, inconsequential but needed."[37]

But the "moral" image alone is not the sole concern of Piggot and his lot. The Reserve on which the drummers and their families live and practice their rituals is also a valuable piece of real estate. It is therefore in Piggot's economic interest to ban the drums and rid the land of the lower-class practitioners whose rituals are tied to the land. The conflict between the native middle class and the people on the Reserve is, however, couched in the language of development and rationality, common strategies used during the period of colonization. The refusal of the lower classes to cooperate with the allegedly progressive, capitalist entrepreneurs by giving up their land, and with it their practice, is translated into moral profligacy; the profit-making agenda of Piggot and his lot is disguised as moral rectitude. The middle classes encourage an emphasis on folk or local culture only when it seems free of the risk of economic or political threat and when it can serve to invent a homogeneous nation. Since essentialist discourses such as negritude and Afrocentrism have often been appropriated by the alienated middle class to deemphasize class and gender issues, the novel's insistence on their explosive contiguity distances its reading of culture from the safer notion of ethnic or national similitude. The practice of Vodoun inscribes the internal divisions within the nation even as it serves as a connecting link between diasporic communities. Whereas the hegemonic interruption of the state reveals class tensions, Vodoun practices themselves dispel the rhetoric of community even within the same class when charms are used against members of the same group.[38] The recourse to the "modern" secular nation-state of San Cristobal as a unifying, progressive, and mediating unit of diverse and competing cultures and countercultures is thus a tactic used to control fringes such as the Reserve.

Nation and Imagination: Invented Narratives

Lamming describes a similar tension in the opening lines of *Pleasures.* The peasants in Haiti, threatened with imprisonment if caught participating in Vodoun ceremonies, play a game of hide-and-seek with the authorities that the slaves on plantations had played in different ways with the overseers and slave patrols. The elaborate and almost stylized rituals extend beyond the banned ceremony to include the police as unwitting participants in a street drama. Forced by fear of a police raid to move from the relatively secluded space of the *tonelle,* the peasants move to the anonymity and open space of the street. The *ververs,* the sacred symbols that indicate divine presence and initiate the opening of the ceremony, are quickly drawn in the dust. When the police make a sudden swoop, Lamming goes on to say with unconcealed enjoyment, no arrests can be made because of the lack of evidence. Even as the police descend on the peasants, the latter arise to greet the law while their feet swiftly erase the marks in the dust. "But the moment the police depart, the signatures will be made again; the gods will return, and prayer will assume whatever needs those peasants whisper," concludes Lamming.[39]

The imaginative inventiveness of the peasants who inscribe their practice on available spaces and then remove those signs provides a new theory of writing and textuality that is literally deconstructed, literally under erasure. As Lamming points out, Prospero's magic is countered by the peasant "magic that vanishes and returns according to the contingencies of the moment."[40] The erasable but reappearing text refuses to be pinned down because the narrative and performative strategies of the dominated populations are rigorously monitored. Since the disguise of critiques of power is essential in social structures where open opposition can be life threatening, the rebellion is withdrawn to the outskirts of the legitimate space and inscribed in what James Scott calls the "hidden transcript."[41] The hidden transcript assumes many forms in Lamming's novel. The *tonelle,* for instance, serves as the "sequestered" space in which the lower classes engage in a celebration that is their own. The code language that the drummer "Boys" use to baffle the police is another signifying system that refuses to be read by those in power. The spirit possessions counter the condition of being "possessed" by the dominant groups by moving away, although only briefly and temporarily—a fact Scott does not emphasize enough—from dominant social control.

But none of these rituals establishes the power of the masses institutionally. Like the marks in the dust, these subcultures are not solid and concrete like the "monuments, cathedrals, important graves; the whole kingdom of names and faces which had been kept alive" for Charlot and his North American friends.[42] Fola herself has no sustained or visible manifestations of historical agency and presence. Her confrontation with the Vodoun ritual serves as a jolting introduction to a history that still remains largely screened from the public gaze. But Vodoun itself becomes an invented tradition that proposes its own "kingdom of names and faces. . . ."

The critical rupture with the past is precisely what gives the islands a unique culture and the possibility of renewed transformation and new beginnings. Therefore, even as connections are made with that point of rupture, it also serves as a point of entry into creative historiography. Just as Vodoun makes up its narrative as it goes along, often introducing new *loa* based on historical figures rather than gods, Fola's familial narrative is open to imaginative interpretation because it does not bear the weight of a long tradition. In the novel, justifying his "act of invention" in painting Fola's unknown father as he imagines him to be, Chiki declares, "Where nothing is known . . . it is easy to make invention credible."[43] The very nature of the gaps and spaces in West Indian history and, metonymically, in Fola's biographical knowledge provides ample material for a "new" name and face. The impetus behind Fola's "season of adventure" is that she has been lied to about her past. Extending the lie to her larger history reveals the novel's oppositional stance to the lies told in an earlier, imperial adventure, colonization. Hence her "need to invent and leap beyond her past" is an intervention in two critical moments: colonial as well as neocolonial histories.

Fola's strategic act of accusing her supposed father of the murder of the vice president, Raymond, and her use of the painting as evidence of her father's return push a private exercise of the imagination into the public gaze of the nation, where rumor and reality, truth and falsehood, personal and communal, merge. The painting is reprinted and disseminated as copies are pasted in every public space in order to hunt down the culprit. So familiar does the painting become and so shared, at least in desire, is the act of murdering the hated vice president that men go to absurd lengths not to look like the invented face that stares out at them from mass-produced posters. "Some people described how they would notice a change in the shape of a mouth or eyes, and got the feeling that their faces had started to take on the shape and expression of the assassin's."[44] Mimesis operates in reverse here as art begins to slide out of the canvas and imprint itself on reality. It also alters the course of events by allowing the real murderer from the Reserve to escape while the law sets off on a wild-goose chase to find Fola's nonexistent father.

The multiple reproduction and repetition of constructed narratives (and of mass culture) also facilitate the second and more democratic republic and save both the Forest Reserve and the drums, a class-informed cultural expression in the novel. "People in Piggot class don' need the Bands . . . except for special celebration an' so, 'cause it have radio an' all class o' music box in their house. But the bands is all we got," claims Jack, the brother of the famous drummer Jack o' Lantern, who was killed in a police encounter over his drum.[45] Piggot's resolve to silence the drums has its historical antecedent in colonial reactions to slave drumming, which was banned because it provided a communal framework for possible revolt.

The steel drum was invented in the mid–twentieth century by black street gangs in Trinidad who fashioned drums out of empty fifty-five-gallon oil barrels, transforming industrial waste into cultural expression. This process of magic, Lamming would say, applies to West Indian history in general. Waste itself has value in an impoverished world that continues to use or recycle what may be easily discarded in more prosperous worlds. Even the Vodoun gods, Dayan points out, have no objection to the miscellaneous leavings on their altars,[46] brought by a people who are as much of a cultural patchwork as their gifts of appeasement.

Lamming draws upon a history of silencing the subcultures but goes on to present the explosive effects of musical practice among the masses. The attempt to ban all drumming in *Season* mobilizes the lower classes and leads to the massive demonstration against the corrupt First Republic. Once again Fola and Chiki exploit print culture and improvise with laboring-class materials. Before the ban becomes official, the "national rumor" is pasted on the back of gin boxes and spread by fishermen and factory workers to organize a mass revolt. But what initiates the demonstration is Jack's vow to play the drum over his brother's grave. Great Gort goes a step further: He digs up Jack o' Lantern's drum from his grave and uses it to lead the march.

I want to move from the drum as vehicle of social protest and instrument of revolution to its function in the novel as agent of historicity. The act of retrieving the drum from the grave parallels the act of recalling the voice of an ancestor to guide the living. In this case, the beating of the drum at the head of the procession multiplies into the protesting "voices" of hundreds of household implements such as kettles and spoons, which are beaten together as the sheer mass of people overwhelms the police. Artistic production is performed in conjunction with political praxis. The polyphonous "cacophany" strategically uses elements of ritual religion and musical tradition, modern print culture and working-class labor, in order to communicate its mass protest in both oral and written, verbal and nonverbal, forms. Although the possibility of a massacre is not entirely out of the question in a neocolonial nation, Lamming's construction of a successful revolution may have been inspired by C.L.R. James's account of the Haitian revolution. Encouraged by the promise of liberation during Vodoun ceremonies, the slaves recklessly threw themselves into an initially unorganized armed struggle by fighting the formidably armed and organized French troops with "knives, picks, hoes, and sticks with iron points."[47] But as in the case of its historical predecessor, the revolution in the novel foreshadows not a future of unmitigated glory but a period of dashed hopes and continuing struggle. The novel's conclusion situates it in the transitory period between colonial and neocolonial governments when the upbeat nationalism of the 1950s, the economic optimism of the 1960s, and the emergence of black consciousness as a politically viable movement were soon to be followed by fresh crises and uncertainties.

Since the Ceremony of the Souls demands the intervention of the past for future direction, the ceremony itself is a historical conduit for activist performance. In other words, history comes alive both in narrative and in performance through the folkloristic traditions of Vodoun, which serve an educational and, in the Gramscian sense, a directive role.[48] In the essay "On Education," Gramsci apparently approves of the child's insertion into state and civil society because it transforms her or his "magical [folkloristic] conception" into a more modern, scientific worldview.[49] Clearly, Gramsci's Marxist valorization of the social discipline of work enables him to elevate the supposedly more adult progression into the rational over the childlike stage of magic and superstition. But within the context of slave history, it was the magical world of the impossible and the superstitious that dispossessed populations turned to in order to seek respite from the drudgery of thankless and poorly compensated labor. Music, too, played a role in alleviating the brutal conditions of labor. The sugarcane laborers' often subversive chants were synchronized with the rhythm of the machete, the whiplash, and the overseer's abuse. But this is not to argue that the playful and artistic imagination was absolutely outside the realm of politics and labor. On the contrary, what needs to be emphasized is the inextricable connectedness of the imagined and the real, the spiritual and the material, the aesthetic and the political, the sacred and the profane.

In another, more receptive, reading of the potential of folklore, Gramsci urges a serious approach to the "surviving mutilated and contaminated documents" of what amounts to subaltern histories.[50] Whereas Gramsci considers only intellectual scholarship on folklore in this case, Lamming's novel is invested in folklore as an active producer and not just as a narrator (or narrative document) of history. Although the irrational aspect of the imagination is clearly important in Lamming's project, since it counters constructions of the logical and the rational, the imagination is also valued for its contribution to intellectual labor. Unlike Gramsci, who sees a division between work and folklore, between theoretical and practical activity and magic and superstition, Lamming foregrounds the work of Vodoun as a magical theory and practice.[51] Additionally, contrary to Gramsci's separation between folklore and education, the former, for Lamming, also functions pedagogically. Fola's witnessing of folk rituals initially distances her from the class she is merely observing at that point. But that encounter directs her later participation in the revolt, since it enables her to reconstitute herself in relation to a particular history. When Kofi James-Williams Baako rebukes Chiki for using his people in his art without giving something back to that community, Lamming explores another possible meaning of return—an intellectual's return to the people not just as artistic but as activist source. In Baako's definition, politics itself becomes art, an "art of the possible," and it is the responsibility of the intellectual to open up the possibilities of the future to the community that inspires or nurtures her or him.[52]

Returning to the trope of the "Lie" in the controversial "Author's Note," a section in which the authorial voice interrupts the fictional world of the narrative, the unidentified author assumes responsibility for Powell's disappearance. This brief aside seems to be the foil for the main plot, which asserts an alliance between the educated intellectuals and the Reserve rather than the division that alienates the author from Powell. The nostalgic, sentimental tone of this interruption is at odds with the directed endeavors of Chiki and Fola. Their return to the past, unlike the author's note, involves a more active retrieval of memory, which is open to more imaginative transformation.

NOTES

1. Quoted by Edward Baugh in "The West Indian Writer and His Quarrel with History," *Tapia* 7, no. 8 (February 1977), 6.

2. Although both Benedict Anderson and Eric Hobsbawm examine invention and imagination predominantly from the dominant cultural perspective, neither of them foreclose their potential for resistance and subversion. See Anderson, *Imagined Communities: Reflection on the Origin and Spread of Nationalism,* (London: Verso, rev. ed., 1991); and Hobsbawm and Terence Ranger, eds., *The Invention of Tradition* (Cambridge: Cambridge University Press, 1983; reprint, 1992).

3. Partha Chatterjee critiques the too easy dismissals of nationalism in "enlightened" thinking and offers a more nuanced reading of nationalisms in *Nationalist Thought and the Colonial World: A Derivative Discourse* (Minneapolis: University of Minnesota Press, 1993), 1–35.

4. George Lamming, *Season of Adventure* (London: Michael Joseph, 1960; reprint, Allison & Busby, 1979).

5. The term "Caribbean" is increasingly preferred over the more colonial title for the islands stretching from Jamaica to the Leeward and Windward islands, Barbados and Trinidad, as well as for the mainland territories of the British Honduras and Guyana. But I will also use the terms "West Indies/Indian," particularly when emphasizing colonial implications specific to the area and period of study in this discussion.

6. Raymond Williams, *Marxism and Literature* (Oxford: Oxford University Press, 1977), 122–123.

7. See Edouard Glissant, *Caribbean Discourse: Selected Essays,* trans. Michael Dash (Charlottsville: University of Virginia Press, 1989).

8. Kamau Brathwaite, "The African Presence in Caribbean Literature," in *Roots* (Ann Arbor: University of Michigan Press, 1993), 190–258.

9. Frantz Fanon, *The Wretched of the Earth,* trans. Constance Farrington (Middlesex: Penguin, 1963), 183.

10. See Homi Bhabha, "DissemiNation: Time, Narrative and the Margins of the Modern Nation," in *The Location of Culture* (London: Routledge, 1994), 139–170; and Paul Gilroy, *The Black Atlantic: Modernity and Double Consciousness* (Cambridge: Harvard University Press, 1993), 199. Both Gliroy and Bhabha articulate the nation from within a postmodern, postindustrial space in which geographical borders are not absolute.

11. Brathwaite, "The African Presence," 190–191.

12. Ibid., 232.

13. V. S. Naipaul, *The Middle Passage: Impressions of Five Societies—British, French, and Dutch—in the West Indies and South America* (New York: Vintage, 1962; reprint 1992), 41.

14. George Lamming, *The Pleasures of Exile* (Ann Arbor: University of Michigan Press, 1960; reprint, 1992), 32–33.

15. Fanon, *The Wretched of the Earth,* 175, 180.

16. Derek Walcott, "What the Twilight Says: An Overture," in *Dream on Monkey Mountain and Other Plays* (New York: Farrar, Strauss and Giroux, 1970), 8.

17. George Lamming, "Caribbean Literature: The Black Rock of Africa," in *African Forum* 1, no. 4 (1966), 52.

18. Lamming, *Pleasures,* 9.

19. Fanon, *The Wretched of the Earth,* 30.

20. Ibid., 43.

21. Ibid., 45.

22. See, for instance, Selwyn R. Cudjoe's *Resistance and Caribbean Literature* (Athens: Ohio University Press, 1980); Michel Laguerre's *Voodoo and Politics in Haiti* (New York: St. Martin's, 1989); and Patrick Taylor's *The Narrative of Liberation: Perspectives on Afro-Caribbean Literature, Popular Culture, and Politics* (Ithaca: Cornell University Press, 1989).

23. C.L.R. James, *The Black Jacobins: Toussaint L'Ouverture and the San Domingo Revolution,* 2nd ed. (New York: Vintage Random, 1989), 86.

24. Lamming, *Pleasures,* 12.

25. Brathwaite, "The African Presence," 255.

26. Joan Dayan, "Vodoun, or the Voice of the Gods," in *Raritan* 10, no. 3 (Winter 1991), 36, 40.

27. The film *Angel Heart* (1987) is one such example. Maya Deren's documentaries on Vodoun counter such stereotypical depictions.

28. Michael Taussig, *The Devil and Commodity Fetishism in South America* (Chapel Hill: University of North Carolina Press, 1980), 31.

29. Lamming, *Season,* 16.

30. Lamming, *In the Castle of My Skin* (Ann Arbor: University of Michigan Press, 1991), 56–57.

31. Lamming, *Pleasures,* 162.

32. The *hounsi* are the female servitors who participate in the ritual. Women also function as priestesses, the *mambo,* counterparts to the *houngan.*

33. Lamming, "The Makers of History," in *Conversations: George Lamming Essays, Addresses and Interviews, 1953–1990,* ed. Richard Drayton (London: Karia Press, 1992), 292.

34. See "A Monster, a Child, a Slave," and "Caliban Orders History," in Lamming, *Pleasures,* 95–150.

35. Lamming, *Season,* 175.

36. Ibid., 102.

37. Brathwaite, introduction to *Life in a Haitian Valley* (New York: Anchor Doubleday, 1971), xii–xiii.

38. Vodoun, like many other ideologies of popular resistance, has been co-opted by the ruling elite. During the rule of "Papa Doc" (François Duvalier) and "Baby Doc" (Jean Claude Duvalier) in contrast to the repression that Lamming describes in the opening lines of *Pleasures,* Vodoun was used as a tool of the Haitian state.

39. Lamming, *Pleasures,* 10.

40. Ibid.

41. James C. Scott, *Domination and the Arts of Resistance: Hidden Transcripts* (New Haven: Yale University Press, 1990).

42. Lamming, *Season,* 73.

43. Ibid., 278.

44. Ibid., 308.

45. Ibid., 314.

46. Dayan, "Vodoun," 39.

47. James, *The Black Jacobins,* 108.

48. Antonio Gramsci, *Selections from the Prison Notebooks,* trans. Quintin Hoare and Geoffrey Nowell Smith (New York: International, 1971), 10.

49. Ibid., 34.

50. Gramsci, "National-Popular Literature, the Popular Novel, and Observations on Folklore," in *Communication and Class Struggle,* vol. 2, ed. Armand Mattelart and Seth Siegelaub (New York: International General, 1983), 75.

51. Gramsci, *Selections,* 34.

52. Lamming, *Season,* 324. Baako's politicization of folk art and its influence on the educated intellectual can also be seen in Fanon's essay "On National Culture," in *The Wretched of the Earth,* pp. 166–199, and in Ngugi's account of the Kamiriithu experiment in *Decolonizing the Mind: The Politics of Language in African Literature* (London: James Currey, 1986), 34–62. However, Fanon, like Gramsci, makes a distinction between folklore and historical struggle and labor, a distinction that limits folklore merely to the narrativization rather than to the enactment of history.

11

Rethinking Migrancy: Nationalism, Ethnicity, and Identity in *Jasmine* and *The Buddha of Suburbia*

SANGEETA RAY

THIS CHAPTER WAS ORIGINALLY WRITTEN for an MLA conference panel in 1992 organized by the division designated as "English Literature Other than British and American."[1] The creation and naming of this particular division reminds us yet again of the interconnections between the practices of a global economy and the significations deployed in academic worlds. The West continues, albeit precariously, to rehearse its neoimperial policies on the global stage even as it is intermittently jolted out of its determined complacency by the reverberating aftershocks of the catastrophe of colonialism. A singular manifestation of the epistemological distortions produced by the violent insertion of the English language into the linguistic economy of colonized worlds is the ongoing production of literatures in English from societies geographically and culturally characterized as non-Western. Even as the debates about multiculturalism in American higher education continue to rage, one can at least believe that the study of English and American literature can no longer be restricted to white writers. The inclusion of African American, Asian American, and Chicana/o literatures as well as postcolonial literatures, despite all the attendant problems of ghettoization, tokenism, and "minoritization," has visibly altered the whitewashed facades of English departments across the country. And this change is equally manifested in the constructions of divisions and panels in various conferences.[2]

Despite the seeming urgency of the desire to implement and document change through the invention of previously nonrecognized categories, the distancing of the ever-encroaching presence of the "other" persists. The deterritorializing capability of the middle term "Other" in the MLA division "English Literature Other than British and American" is contained by the fixed positions of the standard-bearers of the larger constituency. The signifiers English, British, and American function as guardians of the expanding borders of literary studies, a constant reminder not only of the way things were but also an indication of the tenuous status of existing epistemic formations.

A further indication of the ties between critical discourses saturating cultural institutions (such as the university) and concrete agendas permeating public spheres in various global spaces is made apparent in the title of the session organized by the division in which this chapter was originally accepted—"Imaginary Homelands: (Inter)national Writing." The title underlines certain significant tenets of our new worldliness: a recognition of the constructedness of cultures, the inventions of traditions, and the creations of new political identities that circumvent and subvert the boundaries of an essentially demarcated nation.[3] But this "new worldliness" that charts the repetition of the same in global spaces that have hitherto been seen as different—First Worlds as nonnationalistic and Third Worlds as hypernationalistic—has not been able to overcome the legacy of an epistemological incommensurability that continues to haunt contemporary poststructuralist and postcolonial theories that rightly seek to question, challenge, and undermine the various forms of epistemic foundationalism of Western philosophical discourses. For example, a number of critics of postcoloniality continue to persist in delineating the national context in their examination of the various "intellectual" and "popular" projects issuing from previously colonized worlds. I am not advocating an end to such critical examinations; but any nonreflexive critical enterprise focusing entirely and too easily on an explanatory model based on nationalist determinations for certain sections of the globe may inadvertently efface the resurgence of nationalist strains in self-aggrandizing Western democracies. Thus a session such as the previous, despite its good intentions, does underline the presence of a spurious and debilitating nationalist discourse as the common theme that binds English literatures other than British and American. Perhaps one way out of this conundrum is to adopt a position advocated by Madhava Prasad, who argues that since "the institution of literature is closely bound with the history of the nation-state . . . [i]t would be more accurate to reinscribe all literatures in their national context, and then begin the analysis of the invisibility of the national framework in the western context and its hypervisibility in the Third World context."[4]

Perhaps, then, we should look at the title of the session slightly differently. We could argue that it evokes the resurgence of nationalism across the globe even as it seeks to put it under erasure by putting the prefix "inter" in parentheses. This is a utopian gesture that is perhaps further borne out by the phrase "Imaginary Homelands," which in its repetition of the title of Rushdie's collections of essays and in its echoing of the title of Benedict Anderson's manifesto *Imagined Communities* highlights the paradoxical nature of the juxtaposition of the two terms—a signifier that suggests the not-real with the hyperreal signifier echoed in current nationalist discourses. The valorization of the homeland, no longer referenced merely as the land of one's birth but as the land that is marked by certain religious and ethnic signifiers and as the land to which one lays political claim by identifying with those religious and ethnic states, has assumed a kind of ontological stability in the discourses of the fundamentalist prophets of religion and ethnicity.

The interruption of this forced stability by the term "imaginary" allows for a demystification of the ideologies of nation and for an awareness of the retroactive nature of national affiliations. If nationalist discourse celebrates the conjunctive, seamless nature of the bonds forged between peoples, places, and religion/ethnicity, the prefix "inter"—variously defined as "between," "reciprocal," "within," and, for our purposes, as "carried on between"—can be interpreted to emphasize the disjunctive and seamed nature of geopolitical spatial configurations. One can choose to visualize international as somehow breaking through the limited borders of nation formations or even as transnational, whereby national boundaries are transcended through the celebration of various "spatial histories of displacement" that complicate the unidimensional referential graph imposed by nationalists or "nativists."[5] I would, however, like to interrogate the persistent presence of the term "nation" in our discourses—even as we seek to delegitimize, deconstruct, and devalue its significations—by looking at two texts that attempt to address and perhaps subvert the viability of national alliances by implementing precarious and often equally problematic spatial revisions in their remappings from within the interstices of a homogeneous national landscape. Before proceeding to the analysis of the two novels *Jasmine* and *The Buddha of Suburbia,* I would like to engage with a seminal essay by Homi Bhabha that explores the temporal dimensions in the "cultural construction of nationness as a form of social and textual affiliation."[6]

In his essay "DissemiNation: Time, Narrative, and the Margins of the Modern Nation," Homi Bhabha celebrates the liberatory capability of the performative resignification of a national narrative by marginal migrant subjects whose occupation of interactive spaces are marked internally by "cultural difference and the heterogeneous histories of contending peoples, antagonistic authorities, and tense cultural locations" (*DTN,* 299). Thus, according to him, the pedagogical fullnes of national space-time is made possible only by a repression of the oppositional performances of noninterpellated, nonnational subjects. These subjects reenter and disrupt the national space-time continuum by introducing a "dialectic of temporalities" (*DTN,* 303) that displaces and supplements the master narrative of monolithic, linear, national identifications. Bhabha's essay describes the construction, deconstruction, and reconstruction of certain configurations of the nation through narrations that compete with each other for ascendancy in the metropolitan arena. And the genre that he returns to again and again to exemplify the disruptive powers inherent within the contending forces of these narratives is the novel. It is interesting to note the consistent manner in which a form utilized mostly by an educated elite—be it Nadine Gordimer and J. M. Coetze in South

Africa or Toni Morrison in the United States or Salman Rushdie in postcolonial Britain or even Rabindranath Tagore in colonial India—becomes the site for the exploration of the manner in which the "foreignness of languages" articulates the traumatic personal and political psychodramas of the marginalized who will radically alter the existing nation by writing in their alterity. Thus, in Bhabha's readings of the novels by these writers, ex-centric characters confront the totalizing narrative of a nation by interrupting it with a "supplementary movement of writing" (*DTN,* 305). Bhabha's complex analysis of *The Satanic Verses* or *Beloved* or *My Son's Story* underscores the "double writing or dissemi-*nation*" (*DTN,* 299, emphasis in the original) of/by the "other" as the inscription of the subversion of the modern liberal nation. However, he fails to suggest how these powerful textual moments of double writing can be mobilized outside of the scene of writing by, say, an illegal female worker in the garment district in New York or an Indian woman abused by her coworkers for wearing a sari to work in a factory in Manchester. When Bhabha does move to another genre, this time a film, *Handsworth Songs,* produced by the Black Audio and Film Collective, he scarcely pauses to analyze the impact of the actual events marking the uprising of 1985. Moving immediately to the level of the symbolic, Bhabha's beautiful metaphor-laden language encrusts the suffering of the working-class woman who fails to perceive the future any differently from the past, and the persistent presence of pain expressed in the last line of a song sung by another woman—"When I stand it fills my bones" (quoted by Bhabha in *DTN,* 307). Bhabha's desire to valorize the performative aspects of the language used in the poem is revealed in his concluding sentences: "From the archaic world of metaphor, caught in the movement of the people she translates the time of change into the ebb and flow of language's unmastering rhythm; the successive time of instaneity, battening against the straight horizons, and then the flow of water and words" (*DTN,* 307). However, Bhabha's analysis of the poem, privileging its tendency toward movement and disruption, is undermined by the sense of stagnancy and burden evoked in the image of a woman feeling her bones filling up with salty seawater.

Bhabha is accurate in pointing out that the exorbitant power enacted via the metaphoricity of migrancy reveals the tenuous ideological and temporal cohesion necessary for the narrativization of nation by the putative autonomous subject. But when Bhabba situates this power in the discursively embodied migrant and locates this discursive migrant site as the place of contestation of a hegemonic construction of the national subject, Bhabha reveals his overarching intellectual and political desire to recognize in the migrant an uninterrupted capacity for decentering fixed positions and recasts the migrant as having only one possible subject position. Even more dangerous, there seems to be a suggestion that this particular subject position could be mobilized similarly in very different locations—as a counter to the consolidation of a racist British nation, as an interrogation of the politics of an apartheid South African nation, and/or as a supplementary incursion into the writing of a history of the United States. Bhabha also neglects to acknowledge the desire for stability in many migrants that often involves a migrant's positioning herself at the very nodes of the hegemonic institutions of the nation she is assumed, by Bhabha, to automatically challenge because she can never acquire fixity given her migrant "identity." In other words, he fails to recognize the desire for a (mis)perceived autonomy that an identification with the average citizen of the nation-state grants the migrant. Migrant groups move back and forth, often with great difficulty and encountering immense loss, between spaces that demand the kind of "politics of identity" (raised by psychoanalysis, Lacan, and in this particular essay by Bhabha) and spaces that reinscribe territorial subjectifications based on the "politics of identification" (with a nation, tribe, culture, and/or community). Spivak's cogent argument, mandating a crucial rethinking of the relationships between the acrimonious yet critically overlapping terrains of the postcolonial bourgeois feminist and the metropolitan feminist, is equally applicable in the context of the rearticulation of the structures of address governing the notion of "natural" and "virtual" *belonging* to/within a nation:

> I have come to think that there can be an exchange between metropolitan and decolonized feminisms. . . . [T]he radical element of the postcolonial bourgeoisie must most specifically learn to negotiate with the structure of enabling violence that produced her; and the normative narrative of metropolitan feminism is asymmetrically wedged in that structure. Simply to resist it as white feminism is to yield privilege to the migrants' and the diasporics' struggle *on* [emphasis Spivak's] their terrain, and to forget that *they too want to inhabit the national subject by displacing it: Black Britain, Arab France. . . .*[7]

If the totalizing, immanent narrative of national hegemony is undercut by imminent and contending narratives that continuously remember the presence of cultural difference, the recuperation and often violent annihilation of difference, in a world increasingly dominated by the kind of libidinal investment in nationhood that Andreas Huyssen speaks about in the context of Germany,[8] demands that we not overemphasize the power of the "wandering peoples" to disrupt the frontiers of the modern nation by speaking "the foreignness of language" and therefore "splitting the patriotic voice" (*DTN*, 318). In the case of nation-states such as Britain, France, and even the United States, the Machiavellian practices of the existing state are constantly engaged in defusing the explosive power latent in the hybrid's desire to legitimize his or her narration of a potential nation-state formation. Bhabha's preoccupation with the larger group—described as postcolonials, migrants, minorities—elides the specificity of *the* migrant as a gendered, raced, classed agent who, even as he or she enacts the modern reality of migration, is often fettered by the real and imagined baggage that accompanies her *only potentially liberatory* "perspective of the signifying singularity of the 'other' that resists totalization" (*DTN*, 312). Bhabha tends to celebrate this migrancy tout court as an always already empowering hybridity.

Since Bhabha himself often reads novels to illustrate the epistemological veracity of his theoretical propositions, I would like to turn to two novels, one by a self-designated American writer, Bharati Mukherjee, and the other by Hanif Kureishi, a black British screen- and fiction writer. I choose to foreground the placement of these two writers, one in her own words—"I left India by choice to settle in the U.S. I have adopted this country as my home. I view myself as an American author in the tradition of other American authors whose ancestors arrived at Ellis Island"[9]—and the other captured in/by my descriptive (prescriptive?) categories to suggest the ways in which one narrativizes one's or an-other's occupation of a space by linking elements to produce a coherent nationalist subject. One could read Mukherjee's statements as empowering, since she claims American nationality by reversing the process of adoption—the immigrant adopts America rather than America benevolently accommodating the immigrant. However, her narrative of nationalism—by producing a linear progression from the early European immigrants arriving at Ellis Island to those who were actually screened, given documents, and allowed to enter America under the aegis of the inscription on the Statue of Liberty to those who now arrive *legally* and succeed in living the American dream—colludes in what Mary Layoun has called "the third-person and often implicitly omniscient perspective" of the official grammar of the nation. This grammar "seeks to construct its history, or to posit a narrative past (*usually as continuous and uninterrupted* [my emphasis]) in an assertion of legitimacy and precedent for the practices of the narrative present. And this narrative of nationalism postulates a narrative future or constructs a telos, presumably one deriving from the structure and content of narrative—and the nation—itself."[10]

In his various interpretations of the representational aesthetic characteristic of the texts he chooses to read, Bhabha constantly reiterates the potential for the new immigrant to assert her agency via a hybridization of the old order that disrupts official, hegemonic narratives decisive in policing the borders of the nation. This reading is severely undermined by Mukherjee's particular discursive movement of identity construction. Her refusal of the labels of postcolonial or Asian American or a writer of the South Asian diaspora does not lead (as it might in certain other more critical instances) to an interrogation of the "efficacy and desirability of [the] terms and of the 'natural' relationship between those terms"[11] that constitute the hegemonic narrative of the United States as a nation. It does, however reinforce the distinctions between the inside and the outside, fundamental to the totalizing principle governing the teleology of the official construction of the political identity of a subject of a pluralist American nation. It is possible for writers from and in the margins to successfully represent the complex intersecting perspectives that accompany the realization of the acute political complications resulting from one's multiple disclocations vis-à-vis one's gender, sexuality, race, ethnicity, postcoloniality, and migrancy. However, both Mukherjee's enunciation of her own migrant-American identity and that of her heroine Jyoti in the novel *Jasmine* are celebrations of the condition of migrancy as a proviso for the boundless possibilities of assimilation, and not that which "opens up a void . . . that at once prefigures and pre-empts the 'unisonant,' which makes it [the national Heim] *unheimlich;* analogous to the incorporation that becomes the daemonic double of introjection and identification" (*DTN,* 315, emphasis in the original).[12]

In contrasts, my characterization of Kureishi as a black British artist, even as it accepts the existing division of spaces along national lines, does suggest the impossibilty of ignoring or forgetting the manner in which historical and political circumstances have irrevocably altered the human topography of Britain, especially some of its metropolises. But even more significant, the term "black British," because of the racial policies of Britain, allows us to include a whole body of immigrants who are not white in a way that the term "black American" does not. It not only allows us to group Kureishi among the black writers of Britain but suggestively alters the connotation and denotation of being British itself by fundamentally yoking Britishness to everyone in Britain who is not of Anglo-Saxon origin. The term "black British," inextricably linked to the nonwhite migrants inhabiting Britain, is capable of the kind of positive "dissemiNation" of a hegemonic writing of a British nation expressed so eloquently by Bhabha.[13] One could go even further and argue that the term "black British" is closely linked to "black English," which in syncopating its two meanings (nationality and language), suggests coalitions that can be forged across and beyond national boundaries, forcing us to acknowledge the fragility and permeability of national borders even as it reminds us of the enduring legacy of imperialism and colonialism. Kureishi, of course, would easily fit into the pantheon of brilliant writers populating the pages of Bhabha's texts. His novel depicts the social pathology of one forced to inhabit a London and its suburbs where the transposition of immutable modern, civilized values in the name of a common humanity via a sublation of the other is repeatedly and violently questioned.

The two novels *Jasmine* and *The Buddha of Suburbia,* then, could be read side by side in order to illustrate both the promises and the shortcomings of Bhabha's emphasis on the performative aspects of the writing of the nation from the interstitial spaces occupied by the migrant, the minority, the postcolonial, and so on. Even though nationalisms all over the world share certain common features, the specificity of a migrant experience to rendingly rewrite an entrenched inscription of a normative national "I" is contingent on numerous political, social, and human factors that often elude Bhabha's critically aesthetic manipulations of representations of migrancy, hybridity, and cultural difference. These differences gain greater clarity not only in the manner in which the two writers identify themselves but also in their representations of an America and an England trying to recoup from the perceived onslaught of unwanted immigrants. It would be inappropriate of me to even suggest that a politically astute postcolonial critic such as Bhabha is not aware of the singular nature of every sociopolitical situation. What I am arguing here is that in Bhabha's own beautifully orchestrated performative narrative the nonlinear trajectory plotted by that which is anomalous, extra-ordinary, hybrid, or ex-centric in the representational domains from/in the margins subsumes and erases the other side of migrant experience that is conformist, regular, unexceptional, and ordinary. In order to subvert the epistemological foundation of the production of the West's "others," it is not enough to only make visible the political rationality behind a nationalism represented in the image of the Enlightenment. Bhabha clearly juxtaposes a pedagogical chronology articulated by the dominant group and a performative migrant chronotope that responds to the hegemony of the pedagogical national will by introducing a "differential and iterative time of reinscription" that in turn breaks down the "unified present of the will to nationhood" (*DTN*, 310). He thereby casts the migrant chronotope in an inevitably responsive mold, which might account for the excessive privileging of the motility of the migrant in Bhabha's critical discourses on migrancy. The efficacious precision of Bhabha's careful and at times brilliant formulations of the recrudescent power of the performative to wrest with the significations of the pedagogical in "writing the nation" (*DTN*, 297), and his emphasis on the "temporal dimension in the inscription" (*DTN*, 292) of political entities, is at times breathtaking.[14] However, I don't think he adequately takes into account the enduring legacy of a linear logic that imbues most narrative acts. Despite the synchronicity of the double time in Bhabha's version of the plotting of national temporalities in the postcolonial moment, national time continues to persist in its manifestation as narrative linearity and imposes a causal progression between past, present, and future tenses as it seeks to forcibly surmount the contingent, the nonlinear, and the accidental.

An enthusiastic valorization of the migrant as an agent of disruption can be said to characterize Jasmine, the eponymous heroine of Bharati Mukherjee's novel.[15] But the dissident presence of an East Indian woman in America who retreads the footsteps of the early immigrants moving west in search of a new home and land is reterritorialized in Mukherjee's valorization of her heroine as adopting and reflecting the adventurous spirit characteristic of the American. This particular Americanness, which for Jasmine seems to be embodied in Taylor, is directly opposed to the "documented rectitude" of the life of the Indians in Flushing. The American and the America she falls in love with embody an "ease, [a] careless confidence and graceful self-absorption."[16] The one similarity between the India and the America described in the pages of the novel is the constant presence of violence that shatters the innocent lives of ordinary people. In India, the violence debilitates Jyoti and leads her to envision a modern sati-like finale for her existence on the campus of the International University at Tampa, Florida; in America, inexplicably, the even more gratuitous acts of violence (such as her rape by Half-Face) imbue her with an "American" resiliency, allowing her to transmogrify herself from Jyoti and Jasmine to Jazzy, Jase, and Jane Ripplemeyer.[17] If, as a critic in a recent essay suggests, "America is celebrated as the mythic center of an emergent world,"[18] the romance of the new world mapped out by Jasmine is juxtaposed with a textual re-presentation of an India by now familiar to the West—a regressive world stricken by poverty, communal violence, and oppressive social practices; a world where dead dogs float in water that people use for household chores, where women are ritually beaten by their husbands for expressing their opinion, and where young widows pour kerosene over their bodies and set fire to themselves.

In the India unfolded in the pages of *Jasmine,* the emphasis on communal identity, the identification of the "pure" Sikh as opposed to the "impure" Sikh, and the extension of this purity as an indication of an unequivocal distinction between the Hindu and the Sikh lead to violent acts intent on disfiguring or dismembering the body of the impure individual. The schoolmaster, who identifies himself as "a good Sikh, a pious Sikh" (85), has his turban ripped off and his head shaved before he is shot thirty times by the Khalsa Lions, the soi-dissant bearers of a unique Sikh identity. The Hindu woman who wears a sari is a whore because she bares certain portions of her body. She symbolizes the degeneration of the Hindu nation, which, according to the discourse of the Khalistanis represented in the text, has sought to systematically undermine the purity of the Sikhs. The Hindu woman becomes the repository of an essentialized, threatening difference and needs to be literally written out of existence for the survival of the Sikh nation. Unfortunately, the best-laid plans fail to produce desired results. A bomb meant for Jasmine in a crowded Amritsar bazaar accidentally kills her husband, Prakash. Although such an incident was probable, it is then utilized to simplify and unjustly hypostatize a complex historical relationship between the two ethnic communities. The Khalistanis are reduced to savage murderers who go around killing harmless, innocent Hindus, and Mukherjee's denunciation of the movement is thoroughly partisan.

I am not indicting Mukherjee for her aesthetic indulgence of excess. Neither am I suggesting that these depictions are totally innacurate; it is the lopsided nature of her representations of the two worlds that reinforces the binary opposition between the stagnancy of India and "the infinite possible geography [and] licence" of America and that, I believe, fails to produce the kind of questioning of the "homogenizing myth of cultural anonymity" envisioned by Bhabha in his essay. If the will to nationhood "unifies historical memory and secures present-day consent" (*DTN*, 310), the forging of the national narrative depends largely on the subject's "obligation to forget" certain other narratives that undercut the constructed syntactical origin that begins the writing of the nation successively reproduced in the unambivalent space of an homogeneous empty time. Bhabha suggests that this obligation to forget becomes the basis for a new remembering that will allow "other contending and liberating forms of cultural difference" (*DTN*, 311).

Perhaps. In *Jasmine* the presence of cultural difference is assimilated in a manner that fails to transform or question the myth of the American metropolis as a place of tremendous possibilities. Even as Jasmine confronts the images of illegal immigrants working in a "windowless shed the size of a two-car garage" (26) and brutally handcuffed and dragged off by INS officers; even as she is enraged at the American housewife who blames her failure to attain the American dream on the presence of "too many of them" (27); even as she is disgusted at the condescending attitude of Du's (her adopted Vietnamese son) teacher, Mr. Skola, who "tried a little Vietnamese on him" and was surprised when Du "just froze up" (29)—"How dare you? What must he [Du] have thought? His history teacher in Baden, Iowa, just happens to know a little street Vietnamese? Now where would he have picked it up?" (29)—Jasmine ultimately represses the desire to intervene and impugn the ubiquitous discourse of the establishment interpretation of cultural difference. This suppression of the "complex realities of the economic, political, and historical exigencies of immigration" by Jasmine, along with Mukherjee's situating her "authorial self 'in the tradition of other American writers whose parents or grandparents had passed through Ellis Island'"[19] prevents this latest migrant minority from challenging the monolithic imaginary presentation of the American nation as the triumphant melting pot. Except for her expressed empathy with Du and his sufferings in Vietnam, Jasmine consistently separates herself from every other minority collective in America—the Kanjobal Indian women given refuge in Lilian Gordon's house, the Indian community reliving their "lost home" in Flushing, or the "day mommies" she encounters while looking after Duff. For Jasmine the extraordinary links that can be forged through the restoration of forgotten memory between diverse marginal communities is abandoned for the insular solitude that is the effect of the "absolute ordinariness" (131) of mainstream American existence she aches for. If as James Snead points out, hybridity necessarily challenges the desirable goal of universality, Jasmine, as a hybridized figure, fails to adequately meet this challenge. Samir Dayal argues that "Jasmine instinctively grasps that self-assertion does not necessarily imply a confidence in a stable reified self. Her struggle to maintain her precarious sense of self registers the effectivity of violence in the continual articulation of her precarious subjectivity in the world" (80). I would argue otherwise. Even if we grant that Jasmine has abandoned a notion of a unified self and has resigned herself to a nomadic existence, the end of the novel unequivocally reintroduces the familiar trope of the American epic romance. The scattered family regroups in its onward march to unknown territory in a repetition of the path charted by the early pioneers. Substituting a transformed Asian subaltern woman for a European can hardly be deemed an occasion for the celebration of a radical self or national transformation.[20]

In Jasmine's America the enunciation of cultural difference is reduced to pleasant exchanges of exotic recipes and alien gods. Cultural difference in this text is reinscribed as oppositional practices and antagonistic traditions of cultural value that travel in a parallel fashion; and if they intersect at all, they do so in the most benign fashion, without the "sudden shock of the successive, nonsynchronic time of signification" (*DTN*, 313) suggested by Bhabha. In fact, the novel *Jasmine* celebrates the pluralist ideal of America where the immigrant can attain health, wealth, and happiness. *Jasmine* celebrates a neoimperial space where the "missionary dispensing new visions and stamping out the old" (131) is replaced by the arch "facilitator," Lilian Gordon, who, with her "low tolerance for reminiscence, bitterness or nostalgia ... made possible the lives" (131) of the wretched of the world through sheer ingenuity. In pluralist America, the logic of individualism conceptualizes difference in terms of respect for individual characteristics and attitudes, and "group differences are conceived categorically and not relationally, as distinct entities rather than interconnected structures or systems created through repeated processes of the enunciation of difference."[21] In this kind of revisionist space, becoming American demands a rejection of both community and a politics of collectivity, and a validation of the official bourgeois authorization of America as the supreme melting pot.

Hanif Kureishi's *The Buddha of Suburbia,* in contrast, is a carnivalesque celebration of the composite realities of bastard identities rather than a nostalgic longing for a remote paternity.[22] The reader is subjected to repeated subversions of the politics of an old and rigidly conforming order struggling to survive in what one reviewer of the book has called "a frayed and aimless menopausal Empire."[23] The novel plunges directly into the bizarre—the traditional family with a twist (Indian father, English mother, bisexual son) becomes even more Rabelaisian when Karim's father and his cohort, Eva, a frustrated suburbanite enamored with all things exotic, exploit the English penchant for the mystical East by selling Haroon's yogic abilities and knowledge of eastern religions from books read in English translations as authentic Buddhism. The description of the sexual union of Haroon and Eva witnessed by Karim captures the first of many sensational and incongruous alliances forged in this text. As he watches his father and Eva, Karim, the irreverent voyeur, imagines his own moment of conception: "I knew it was Daddio because he was crying out across the Beckenham gardens, with little concern for the neighbors, 'Oh God, oh my God.' Was I conceived like this, I wondered, in the suburban night air, to the wailing of Christian curses from the mouth of a renegade Muslim masquerading as a Buddhist?"[24] The masquerade continues with every attempt at the "staging of experience—in-identity"[25] rooted in the idea of origin either being displaced or replaced. Thus the fruitful union between Changez and Jamila as envisaged by her father—daughter and grateful, hardworking son-in-law freshly imported from India who would jointly assist in the running of the family-owned business—is never realized in the novel. Jamila refuses to sleep with Changez, who in turn, obsessed with the sexual titillations offered in the pages of Harold Robbins, appeases his desire with Shinko, a Japanese prostitute. This triad not only is complicated by Changez catching Jamila and Karim having sex but achieves a new plateau when Jamila and Shinko strike up a relationship. Changez, a traditional Indian Muslim, is in the end living in a commune taking care of the "daughter of the house," a baby girl named Leila Kollontai, and cooking and feeding his wife, who when her lover Simon is away, has an affair with a documentary filmmaker, Joanna. Even though Changez finds it difficult to acknowledge his wife's bisexuality and is abjectly degraded when his desire for Jamila is repeatedly repudiated, the unusual community is visualized as one possible site for the expression of a new home and a different familial configuration. The final depiction of the lives of Changez, Jamila, and their various partners remains problematic in its ultimate denouement, but it cannot be annulled precisely because, even as Changez desires to identify himself as the one normal person living in London (normal in this case signifying a person burdened with a few racial and sexual prejudices, not a tyrannical fascist!), he continues to be stripped of his self-representations, an important step for ethnicity to become culturally and politically productive in the West.

In the London and its suburbs depicted in Kureishi's novel, the official marginalization of the topos of immigrant spaces as instances of local eccentricity is replaced by a chaotic, carnal, aesthetic vision of incompleteness. Those very isolated sites are transformed into potential locations for the articulation of a revolution permanente and for the expression of new exuberant relationships among body, language, and politics. The narrative, via an exaggerated simulation of cinematic techniques, provides a marvelous ocular itinerary of the transgressive possibilities of hitherto unimagined communities. Every effective conglomerate contains the possibility of resistance against the efforts at balkanization by the conservative regime because it opens up spaces marked by a kind of piling up of issues that unsystematically collates various levels of experience revolving around culture, class, race, and sexuality, exposing a reality, that, even as it is being scattered, returns "not to some immutable state of Being, but . . . to the point of entanglement from which one is forcefully turned away."[26]

In the end, Mukherjee's vision reinforces and continues the polarized thinking produced by a Cartesian epistemology grounded in ontological dualism. The excess that marks the site of the migrant seeks to elude this binary logic; however, subversions of hegemonic social formations that could be effected through the transgressive, flamboyant representations of this excess are constantly harnessed, in *Jasmine*, by the desire of the immigrant woman to function effectively within the institutional limits dictated by a dominant nationalist ideology. Jasmine acquires agency by participating in the objectification of the "other" that is the hallmark of the epistemology of individualism. Here, not only is an assertion of the triumph of the postcolonial individual dependent on a negation of collective action but the very survival of both the nation and the immigrant rests on a violent othering of herself as an East Indian woman. The other as East Indian woman is then offered to the American palate as a desirable exotic product for consumption. Jasmine fails to grasp the "ambivalent temporalities of the nation-space" (*DTN*, 294). She sways to the rhythm of the "continuist, accumulative temporality of the pedagogical" (*DTN,* 297) and by the end of the novel has been assimilated by a political ideology that claims a transcendental authority.

Jasmine fails to listen, or is incapable of listening, to the contradictions that exist between the rhetoric of nation and the grammar of nation (Layoun). In contrast, Karim, in *The Buddha of Suburbia,* gradually begins to scrutinize the "gaps, the telling spaces"[27] that emerge in the contradictions between the two and exercises his agency through a recognition of the possibilities that lie in alternate performances that "need not postulate the existence of some transcendentally integral narrative or narrator."[28] As an upcoming actor on the British stage, Karim is forced to objectify the other as and in the role of a typical Indian-Paki—first in the image of Kipling's Mowgli and second in the image of the new postcolonial immigrant, Changez. His presence on the stage is not a testimony to his abilities as an actor; as Shadwell, the director, puts it: "Karim, you have been cast for authenticity and not for experience" (147). That this authentic Indian-Paki has to cover himself in "shit-brown cream" (146) and mimic an "Indian accent" in order to realize authenticity is never acknowledged by the director or the other actors. Karim's Indian father makes him Indian despite the fact that he has an English mother, has never been to India, and dresses and talks like any other white Englishman. Karim succumbs to pressure and performs his Mowgli with great panache. The reactions of his family members and friends allow us to gauge the various levels of libidinal and political investments in cultural and ethnic identity that the postcolonial condition generates. Karim's mother "wept with pride," and "Jean, who hadn't wept since the death of Humphrey Bogart, laughed a great deal" (156). Karim's father can only splutter with rage at such "bloody, half-cocked business. . . . That bloody fucker Mr. Kipling pretending to whity he knew something about India! And an awful performance by my boy looking like a Black and White Minstrel!" (157). Jamila is alternately saddened and appalled by Karim's apparent political naïveté and capitulation to English prejudice:

> You looked wonderful. . . . So innocent and young, showing off your pretty body, so thin and perfectly formed. But no doubt about it, the play is completely neo-fascist. . . . You were just pandering to prejudices. . . . And cliches about Indians. . . . I expect you are ashamed, aren't you? [Karim replies] "I am, actually." [But Jamila refuses to sympathize with him.] She didn't pity [him]; and mimicked [his] accent in the play. Only Changez "had chuckled all through the show. 'Good entertainment,' he said. 'Take me again, eh'" (157).

Jamila represents the alternative mode of radical subjectivity; an occupant of the embattled zone of an Asian Britain, she refuses to be subjected to and objectified by "a new, ethnically absolute, and culturalist racism" that manifests itself in "an irreducible cultural difference."[29] When we are first introduced to Jamila she is described by Karim as "being more advanced" than him (52). He records Jamila's education by listing the various people, books, and music that profoundly influenced her. At different points in her adolescence Jamila read Baudelaire,

Colette, and Simone de Beauvoir; listened to Billie Holliday, "Bessie, and Sarah and Dinah and Ella"; carried around a photograph of Angela Davis; and wore black clothes. For "months it was Soledad this and Soledad that. Yeah, sometimes we were French, Jammie and I, and other times we went black American. The thing was, we were supposed to be English, but to the English we were always wogs and nigs and Pakis and the rest of it" (53). But Jamila's politically conscious repudiation of a social topography based on a discourse that "aligns 'race' closely with the idea of national belonging"[30] simultaneously validates a circumscribed ethnic definition of identity. What is interesting about Kureishi's text is the cacophony generated by the multiplicity of heterogeneous positions. Jamila's desire to counteract the debilitating effects of this new cultural racism by arguing for an accurate, noncliched representation of Indian identity is problematized by the positions articulated by both Karim's father and Changez. Kipling's identity as a respected British imperialist writer is attacked by Karim's father, who reduces Kipling to a sycophant and British imperialists to an undifferentiated mass—"whity." In a curious move, Karim's father, who is completely self-absorbed, ignorant of the political ramifications of being an "other" in Britain, and prejudiced against people of African descent, evokes the rhizomatic connections made possible by a yet-inarticulated diasporic intimacy. When he compares Karim's theatrical presentation of Mowgli to exaggerated depictions of black minstrels (with painted faces), the possibility for retrieval of any specific form of authentic identity is called into question. Furthermore, a simple, mechanistic correspondence between an Indian and the Mowgli represented on stage is completely undermined by Changez's (the latest Indian immigrant to enter England) unequivocal enjoyment of the play as sheer entertainment. No one position is favored, and yet the various voices arguing and interfering with each other do question both the structures of the nation-state and the constraints of ethnicity and national particularity.

Kureishi's bildungsroman, depicting the travails of a young Indian British male, constantly engages with the conundrums of identity and subjectivity. If in his role as Mowgli, Karim allows himself to be objectified by a director who doesn't hide his intentions, in the second play, directed by an avant-garde playwright who couches a similar desire to deny cognitive capacity to an ethnic minority by using left-wing, jargon-loaded clichés, we see Karim actively trying to resist the clutches of a paternalistic and tyrannical racist discourse. The intervening time has changed Karim. Jamila's father makes him realize that these "strange creatures . . . the Indians . . . in some way . . . were my people, and that I'd spent my life denying or avoiding that fact. I felt ashamed and incomplete at the same time, as if half of me were missing, and as if I'd been colluding with my enemies, *those whites who wanted Indians to be like them*" (212, emphasis mine).[31] This awareness does not cause him instantly to rush off and attack Pyke, the director, for his inimical ethnocentrism. He continues to play the role of an Indian immigrant, but this time, he "uncovered notions, connections, initiatives, I didn't even know were present in my mind. . . . I saw that creation [of an identity] was an accretive process which couldn't be hurried, and which involved patience and, primarily, love. I felt more solid myself, and not as if my mind were just a kind of cinema for myriad impressions and emotions to flicker through" (217).

Karim had drawn on Changez for his creation of Tariq, the character he plays in the production. The success of his realization of the accumulative process of creation is brilliantly depicted by Kureishi in Changez's reaction to the performance. Karim, scared that Changez would be extremely upset by seeing himself caricatured on stage, tries to avoid him. However, Changez accosts him and, in a brief moment that transcends the attempt that seeks to erase contradictions, registers the potency of cultural value that can emerge from a realization that hybridity is not merely the "admixture of pre-given identities or essences" (*DTN*, 314). "'Come a little closer, top actor,' [Changez] said. 'And listen to my criticism. I am glad in your part you kept it fundamentally autobiographical and didn't try the leap of invention into my character. You realized clearly that I am not a person who could be successfully impersonated'" (231). Reading this enlightening passage as an instance of Changez's willful blindness is both naive and incorrect.

In *The Buddha of Suburbia,* unlike in *Jasmine,* the achievements of a progressive individualism are revealed in the last analysis to be putative; party politics such as Terry's Trotskyite affiliations are shown to be equally self-serving; the intellectual elitism of Mathew is nothing more than a transparent veneer disguising his narcissism. Karim is confronted with all these fragmenting, isolating, dividing and yet creative epistemological fields in his passage through the conflicting ideological minefields that constitute metropolitan London. The last lines of the novel celebrate "an unsullied event" where Haroon, Eva, Allie, Changez, and Shinko gather to toast Karim's success and where the Buddha of Suburbia announces his upcoming marriage to Eva. The prose lapses into sentimental reflection as Karim "sat in the centre of this old city that [he] loved, which itself sat at the bottom of a tiny island" hoping for a future he "would live more deeply" (284). However, this moment of nostalgia and hope does not lead to an unmitigated celebration of a utopic future with an imaginary family in an imaginary homeland, as it does in *Jasmine.* Karim does not wish to repress memory, and as he sits surrounded by people he loves "he felt happy and miserable at the same time" (284), knowing that the "mess" of the past would always enter the flow of current life. Cultural dissensus and alterity, nonconsensual terms of affiliations and articulations, continue to inform the ambivalent terrains of previously homogenized national landscapes. Unlike *Jasmine, Buddha of Suburbia* is more successful in relating the traumatic ambivalence of a personal, psychosocial history to the wider disjunctions of political existence.

In conclusion, I would like to revisit Bhabha's essay, through which I read both novels. As Sara Suleri points out, the "vocabulary of cultural migrancy . . . helpfully derails the postcolonial condition from the strictures of national histories"; yet the metaphorization of migrancy, as it travels a world beset with neoimperialist and racist policies accompanying the globalization of capitalism, can "become so amorphous as to repudiate any locality for cultural thickness."[32] I would argue that Bhabha's reading of *Satanic Verses* (the penultimate section of his essay) as a particular example of the attempt "to redefine the boundaries of the western nation, so that the 'foreignness of languages' becomes the inescapable cultural condition for the enunciation of the mother-tongue" (*DTN,* 317) is a brilliant enactment of the cultural thickness saturating a local site. The same is true to a large extent of Kureishi's novel. However, the radical dynamism of Bhabha's theoretical exploration is often mitigated by its vexing imbrication in the amorphous yet homogeneous rhetorical zone that unilaterally privileges the cultural analytic of an always already unsaturated migrant identity. It is this much easier and less problematic depiction of a supposedly radicalized national sphere that is valorized in Mukherjee's *Jasmine.* Bhabha's theoretical speculations do allow for the possibilty of challenging the "coherence of all national perspectives [by pointing] to the spurious invocation of ethnic particularity," but they equally make room for the reification of the "binary opposition between national and diaspora perspectives" that could reassert itself as an "overt and cultural nationalism."[33]

NOTES

1. This divison also incudes English literature from Australia, New Zealand, and Canada. The inclusion of English literatures from these countries necessarily problematizes the use of the term "non-Western," which I use in this chapter. I use it loosely to identify the various other countries that can be encompassed by the division, such as India, Pakistan, Bangladesh, Sri Lanka, Philippines, Malaysia, Singapore, the Anglo-Carribean, and Africa.

2. In critiquing the ways in which non-Western English literatures get categorized, I am not minimizing their importance in changing the canonical nature of English literary studies.

3. For example, Bruce Robbin's essay "Comparative Cosmopolitanism," *Social Text* 31/32 (1992), pp. 169–186, provides an eloquent appeal for the need for academics dedicated to multicultural education to move to a "stage of conscious self-definition, self-legitimation, or self defense" (170) rather than always being forced to respond to the right from a defensive position.

4. Madhava Prasad's essay "On the Question of a Theory of (Third World) Literature," *Social Text* 31/32 (1992), pp. 57–83, is the latest missive in the ongoing discussion fueled by Jameson's essay "Third World Literature in an Age of Capitalism," *Social Text* 15 (1986), pp. 65–88. See my essay "Gender and the Discourse of Nationalism in Anita Desai's *Clear Light of Day,*" (Genders 20 [1994], pp. 96–119) for a critique of the methodologies of a number of male theorists who ignore the implications of a gendered discourse such as nationalism on the status of women as political subjects.

5. See Homi Bhabha's essay "Freedom's Basis in the Indeterminate," *October* 61 (1992), p. 47.

6. Homi Bhabha, "DissemiNation: Time, Narrative, and the Margins of the Modern Nation," in *Nation and Narration,* ed. Homi K. Bhabha (New York: Routledge, 1990), p. 120; hereafter cited in the text as *DTN.*

7. Gayatri C. Spivak, "French Feminism Revisited: Ethics and Politics," in *Feminists Theorize the Political,* ed. Judith Butler and Joan W. Scott (New York: Routledge, 1992), p. 58.

8. See Andreas Huyssen's essay "The Inevitability of Nation: German Intellectuals After Unification," *October* 61 (1992), pp. 65–73.

9. Alison Carb, "An Interview with Bharati Mukherjee," *Massachusetts Review* 29 (1988), p. 650.

10. Mary Layoun, "Telling Spaces: Palestinian Women and the Engendering of National Narratives," in *Nationalisms and Sexualities,* ed. Andrew Parker et al. (New York: Routledge, 1992), p. 411.

11. Layoun, "Telling Spaces," p. 411.

12. In a different context, Smadar Lavie points out that Bhabha's migrant figures are based on a construction of "hybridity as mimicry in the form of hegemonized rewriting of the Eurocentre. This is a response-oriented model of hybridity. It lacks agency, by not empowering the hybrid. The result is a fragmented Otherness in the hybrid. The fragments of the Other, however, can be mended together, forming seams, so that they can be narrated in a Cartesian linear manner." See her essay "Blow-Ups in the Borderzones: Third World Israeli Author's Gropings for Home," *New Formations* 18 (1992), p. 92.

13. This argument is solely based on the uses of a particular terminology in the two countries. I do not want to suggest that being a black immigrant in Britain is inherently a liberating process or that there are no interracial problems among the various groups lumped together under the rubric black; or that the nation itself does not have various policies to constantly harness the disruptive energies for its own purposes or that it is not always coming up with policies and projections that seek to both distance and mitigate the perceived threat of and by the other. One cannot forget the title of Paul Gilroy's book: *There Ain't no Black in the Union Jack.*

14. His critique of Benedict Anderson's failure "to locate the alienating time of the arbitrary sign in his naturalized, nationalized space of the imagined community" (*DTN,* 311) and his reading of *The Satanic Verses* are exemplary. In contrast, his analysis of the British film *Handsworth Songs* seems to linger too long in the domain of the angst of the perplexing quotidian lives of the oppressed and does not quite arrive at the conclusion he draws, that is, that a minority discourse that acknowledges the "contentious, performative space" of national culture can "inscribe a 'history' of the people [and] become the gathering [point] of political solidarity" (*DTN,* 307).

15. The status of Bharati Mukherjee as a postcolonial or immigrant writer in the United States is confirmed by the publishing of a critical anthology on her writings. The concluding paragraph of the editorial introduction is particularly relevant: "[This] publication is also an unequivocal acknowledgement of Mukherjee's emergence as a major American writer with an international audience. Her works, collectively, provide us with a poignant chronicle of her own personal search for home, wholeness, and stability. Her greatness, however, derives from her discovery in our immigrant lives of an occasion for art of epic dimensions" (*Bharati Mukherjee: Critical Perpectives,* ed. Emmanuel Nelson [New York: Garland, 1993], p. xvii). A stronger encomium is difficult to imagine.

16. Bharati Mukherjee, *Jasmine* (New York: Viking, 1989), p. 171. Subsequent citations of this work are included in the body of the text.

17. Samir Dayal offers what seems to me a highly problematic analysis of the various forms of violence in *Jasmine* in his essay "Creating, Preserving, Destroying: Violence in Bharati Mukherjee's *Jasmine*," in Nelson, *Bharati Mukherjee*, pp. 65–88.

18. Craig Tapping, "South Asia/North America: New Dwellings and the Past," in *Reworlding: The Literature of the Indian Diaspora*, ed. Emmanuel Nelson (Westport, Conn.: Greenwood Press, 1992), p. 43.

19. Anindyo Roy, "The Aesthetics of an (Un)willing Immigrant: Bharati Mukherjee's *Days and Nights in Calcutta* and *Jasmine*," in *Bharati Mukherjee*, p. 130.

20. For an interesting critical examination of the erasure of subalternity in *Jasmine*, as well as Mukherjee's "claims to represent the Other as the *wholly other* in her writing" (p. 146) see Alpana Sharma Knippling's essay in *Bharati Mukherjee*, pp. 143–160.

21. Joan Scott, "Multiculturalism and the Politics of Identity," *October* 61 (1992), p. 17.

22. My examination of this novel concentrates on a few key moments in the text. I do not attempt, in this chapter, to explore the ramifications of the various manifestations of sexualities and different kinds of sexual objectifications that permeate the novel. The Buddha's attraction to Eva, Jamila's relationship with Changez, Karim's sexual encounters with Charlie, Charlie's indulgence in painful sadomasochistic sexual rituals, Karim's subject position as a voyeur, and the representation of various forms of mutilated bodies could provide interesting possibilities for other kinds of imagined coalitions and identifications.

23. Bob Shacochis on the back cover of the Penguin edition of the novel.

24. Hanif Kureishi, *The Buddha of Suburbia* (London and New York: Penguin, 1990), p. 16. Subsequent references to this work are incorporated into the body of the text.

25. See Gayatri Spivak's essay "Acting Bits/Identity Talk," *Critical Inquiry* 18 (1992), p. 781.

26. In citing Edouard Glissant (*Caribbean Discourse*, trans. J. Michael Dash [Charlottesville: University Press of Virginia, 1989]) at this point, I might be accused of too easily transposing an acute observation made by him regarding the particular political situation of the population of Martinique vis-à-vis France to characterize the depiction of the complexly intertwined sexual lives of Kureishi's characters living in a London consumed by xenophobic racism. However, as Spivak has written, despite the problems encountered in the unmooring and transference of specific terrains, one must at times be able to put "identity in parenthesis [to] show that [a specific] context is also saturated and open, like all contexts" (Spivak, "Acting Bits/Identity Talk," pp. 781–782). Thus, despite the risks involved in this transposition, the emphasis on cultural performance in the two texts *The Buddha of Suburbia* and *Caribbean Discourse* allows me to critically read the textured nuances of the various geopolitical and sociosexual collective bodies depicted in Kureishi's novel.

27. Layoun, "Telling Spaces," p. 420.

28. Ibid., p. 414.

29. Paul Gilroy, "Cultural Studies and Ethnic Absolutism," in *Cultural Studies*, ed. Lawrence Grossberg, Cary Nelson, and Paula Treichler (New York: Routledge, 1992), p. 190.

30. Ibid.

31. Hanif Kureishi, in his autobiographical essay "Rainbow Signs" in *My Beautiful Laundrette and the Rainbow Sign* (London: Faber and Faber, 1986), raises similar questions

concerning the construction of ethnic identities in a Britain reeling from the violence unleashed by Enoch Powell's racist diatribes in 1960, which were viciously endorsed by the conservative Thatcher regime.

32. Sara Suleri, "Woman Skin Deep: Feminism and the Postcolonial Condition," *Critical Inquiry* 18 (1992), p. 759.

33. Gilroy, "Cultural Studies and Ethnic Absolutism," p. 197.

12

Homeboys: Nationalism, Colonialism, and Gender in Rabindranath Tagore's *The Home and the World*

MICHAEL SPRINKER

There is only one history—the history of man.

—Rabindranath Tagore

CAPITALISM, WE KNOW, is the first genuinely global socioeconomic system. Marx and Engels's evocation of its irresistibly expansionary drive in the *Communist Manifesto* set the tone for all subsequent attempts to describe capitalism's tendency to become a world system. In the most recent period, this more or less banal fact has become something of a fixation for many on both the left and the right who may disagree violently about what conclusions to draw but who seem generally to concur that we are witnessing a distinctive and wholly unprecedented epoch in world history. This epoch has been variously described as that of consumer society, late capitalism, or the triumph of liberal or democratic capitalism (over socialism or communism). Its leading features (already matured or tendentially present) are the revolution in global communication and transportation technology; the disappearance of the classical industrial working class; the dissolution of the nation-state as a viable political form (superseded either by transnational corporations or by multistate organizations such as the European Community); and the dissemination of a common cultural idiom (generally derived from the middle-class consumer culture of the United States). These developments can be lamented (Schiller et al.), celebrated (Fukuyama), or observed with a mixture of fascination and horror (Jameson). What is rarely in doubt, however, is that (1) capitalism in the contemporary period has assumed a new and unprecedented form; (2) this latest stage in capitalism's history demands equally unprecedented modes of theorization (post-Marxist, poststructuralist, neo- or postliberal).

It is not my purpose here to contest this view of our world in any systematic way, although I'm extremely skeptical of many of its specific claims and of the overall drift it follows. I do, however, wish to recall that as Immanuel Wallerstein has insistently held, capitalism has *always* been a world system; globalization was, as it were, written into its very program. Without some more sober reckoning of the long history of capitalist development (around half a millenium or so), without, that is, the kind of reckoning Marx himself made in order to determine capitalism's laws of motion, we are in no position to judge whether the current period marks a wholly new departure in that history or whether it is governed by principles already familiar to us, however disguised these are by the phenomenal forms that social relations have assumed in what is now held to be the post–Cold War era.

My own view is that although the velocity of capital's valorization has increased noticeably since the 1960s, thereby exacerbating commensurately the system's potential instabilities, its underlying structures of accumulation, the twin linchpins of the wage relation and the commodity form, remain pretty much as Marx understood them more than a century ago. Moreover, the specifically political consequences of capitalism's restless pursuit of cheap labor and raw materials and expanded markets, namely, imperialism and international rivalry among the leading capitalist nation-states, is probably not much altered in nature from the time of Lenin's classic treatise, written at a moment when the contradictions of interimperialist competition had attained explosive intensity.

Such, at any rate, is the rationale for including this chapter in a volume on international cultural studies. I assume that the questions of colony, empire, and nation that motivated significant amounts of Rabindranath Tagore's writing during the first two decades of this century are still very much with us. And I further assume that the solutions he proffered to the conundrum of nationalism in colonial South Asia, however inadequate and compromised they now appear, are of some continuing relevance to the politics and ideology of contemporary India, and more generally to postcolonial nationalism around the world. As always, the history of the British Empire is not without its lessons for understanding subsequent places and times. The particular complexities of the British-Indian encounter command our attention still, not least because they powerfully shaped the world with which we have to contend.

It is probably fair to assume that most readers of this chapter have some knowledge of Rabindranath Tagore. But I'll wager not so many already know of, much less have read, the text I'll be discussing, his novel *Ghare Baire,* or *The Home and the World.* For like the overwhelming majority of subcontinental authors who have written in one or more of its indigenous languages—even those whose work has been translated into English (Tagore's has been generally available since the 1910s)—Rabindranath has signally failed to achieve the same notoriety as more recent Indian and Pakistani authors who write primarily in English.[1] Among his major writings, if we except the selection in *The Tagore Reader,* only *The Home and the World* remains in print in an inexpensive paperback edition here in the United States or in Britain, and that only sporadically. This contrasts with the general circulation of texts by Salman Rushdie, Anita Desai, Bharati Mukherjee, V. S. Naipaul, Vikram Seth, or Ruth Prawer Jhabvala (the latter not of Indian descent, but since the publication of *Heat and Dust,* one of the "voices" most prominently licensed in the West to speak authoritatively about India and Indians). Although earlier in the century Rabindranath was much celebrated around the world, his writings, having once migrated from their homeland, in recent years have been returned there stamped "unclaimed."

This is not the place to recount the causes for the decline in Tagore's Western fame, which would require telling a complex story about the rise and fall of the Indian subcontinent as a focus of attention for the Anglophone world, the fortunes of the English language on the subcontinent itself, and the migration of people and texts to the imperial metropole and their uneven assimilation into the dominant cultures in the United States, Canada, and Britain. It would appear that history has passed Rabindranath by, that his universal humanism has been more or less swamped in the tidal wave of postcolonial nationalism; his continuing attachment to the localized subjects of Bengali culture and society strikes Western readers, I imagine, as merely quaint.[2] Rabindranath's novels have particularly suffered in their Western reception for being suffused in the lifeworld of Indian civilization while not appearing sufficiently exotic to Westerners, who are inclined to want "Eastern mysticism" from such figures as Tagore—and of course they have managed to extract that in abundance, as even a cursory glance at the Tagore bibliography will attest, but not from his novels. In short, reading Tagore's fiction, we are unlikely to get anything like the standard story of massive poverty and ignorance, matched by spiritual transcendence, that has been a staple of Western accounts since Kipling and Forster established the basic coordinates for "imagining India." Instead, we are faced with the more mundane problems of everyday life among the Hindu upper castes and classes, set in quite particular historical situations that seem to us remote in time and experience.

Yet it is worth recalling that Rabindranath was deeply immersed in the nationalist struggle during an important period, that his life and his art were firmly imbricated in the historical conditions of colonial India, and that therefore one has a perfect right—indeed, an obligation—to consider him as part of the canon of colonial writing that has become the focus of so much attention in the West in recent years.[3] If his texts, having migrated to the West, failed to become rooted in the Western imagination, this has less to do with their intrinsic interest than with the fortunes of the ideological program with which they were identified. It is with the ideology of Tagore's novelistic practice, in particular with his views on Indian nationalism, that I am primarily concerned here.

I begin somewhat obliquely with an oft-quoted letter from Joseph Conrad to his friend the socialist R. B. Cunninghame Graham. It offers a convenient point to enter the problematic of colonial history and writing:

> There is a—let us say—a machine. It evolved (I am severely scientific) out of a chaos of scraps of iron and behold!—it knits. I am horrified at the horrible work and stand appalled. I feel it ought to embroider—but it goes on knitting. You come and say: "this is all right; it's only a question of the right kind of oil. Let us use this—for instance—celestial oil and the machine will embroider a most beautiful design in purple and gold." Will it? Alas, no. You cannot by any special lubrication make embroidery with a knitting machine. And the most withering thought is that the infamous thing has made itself; made itself without thought, without conscience, without foresight, without eyes, without heart. It is a tragic accident—and it has happened. You can't even smash it. The last drop of bitterness is in the suspicion that you can't even smash it. In virtue of that truth one and immortal which lurks in the force that made it spring into existence it is what it is—and it is indestructible!
>
> It knits us in and it knits us out. It has knitted time, space, pain, death, corruption, despair and all the illusions—and nothing matters. I'll admit however that to look at the remorseless process is sometimes amusing.[4]

This text has characteristically been interpreted—in the first instance by Conrad himself—as a metaphysic. But it is well to recall the context in which Conrad was writing. He was responding to Graham's pressure to become involved in socialist politics, a mission on Graham's part that in retrospect seems almost risible. Conrad expresses his skepticism in metaphysical terms, but the basis for his doubts is determinately political. These issued, we may surmise, from some quite specific historical experiences: in the first place, the memory of his father's failed revolutionary romanticism, but more proximately his own experiences in the Congo Free State, where the high-minded rhetoric of improvement and civilization had been revealed to be, as Marlow says of Kurtz in *Heart of Darkness*, "hollow at the core."

I am suggesting, then, that we can more profitably construe this passage's stark pessimism as having to do with imperialism. Further, it is possible, although Conrad himself probably did not intend it, to take the image of the cosmic knitting machine itself to be a figure for the imperial project as a whole not only during the era of colonialism but into the contemporary period of postcolonial history and writing. For "the most withering thought" suggested by the legacy of imperialism, particularly for those who have suffered most from its depredations, is not just the memory of what was done in the past but that "the infamous thing . . . has happened," and that "it is indestructible." I mean by this not that imperialism cannot be overthrown but that the fact of its having happened cannot easily be erased. This is the situation of anticolonial writing that I wish to consider in this chapter. The text I discuss is Rabindranath Tagore's *The Home and the World,*[5] written during World War I but dealing with the previous decade when, in the wake of the partition of Bengal, the movement for *swadeshi,* or self-development, swept across British India and seemed to threaten the political stability of the Raj. My purpose is to situate this text in the history that produced it, which stretches from the period from 1903 to 1908, when *swadeshi* was in full swing, through the subsequent decade, during which Rabindranath's relationship to the mainstream nationalist movement altered decisively and permanently, and nationalism itself would begin to assume its better-known guise of Gandhian *satyagraha.* Without further preamble, then, let us consider this history and Rabindranath's place in it.

By 1915, when *The Home and the World* was first published, Tagore had become a staunch opponent of the Indian nationalist movement. Only two years later, he would denounce nationalism globally in a famous series of lectures, arguing that only a universal humanism could possibly solve the social problems that lay at the heart of his country's misery or indeed any political problem pitting one group of people against another. While condemning any and all nationalist feeling, Rabindranath comes down especially hard on two instances, as it happens the very ones then opposing each other in his native land. Of the so-called Extremists in the Indian National Congress, he has this to say:

> Their ideals were based on Western history. They had no sympathy with the special problems of India. They did not recognize the patent fact that there were causes in our social organization which made the Indian incapable of coping with the alien. What should we do if, for any reason, England was driven away? We should simply be victims for other nations. The same social weaknesses would prevail. The thing we in India have to think of is this—to remove those social customs and ideas which have generated a want of self-respect and a complete dependence on those above us,—a state of affairs which has been brought about entirely by the domination in India of the caste system, and the blind and lazy habit of relying upon the authority of traditions that are incongruous anachronisms in the present age.[6]

The Extremists' failure derived from their inappropriately importing Western political ideals into the Indian context; it lay above all in their incapacity to grasp the solidity and perdurance of the caste system, which constituted the fundamental obstacle to any social reformation in India. David Kopf is probably correct to locate Rabindranath's implicit program for social change in this period—exemplified in the statement made just prior to his condemnation of Extremism: "It was my conviction [during the early years of the Indian National Congress] that what India most needed was constructive work coming from within herself"[7]—in the context of his lifelong association with the Brahmo Samaj, cofounded by Rabindranath's grandfather Sir Dwarkanath Tagore and reformed by his father, Debendranath.[8] What is more difficult to account for is the poet's equally fervent espousal of the nationalist cause during the previous decade; little in his previous writing and training could have prepared one for the zeal with which he embraced *swadeshi* from 1903 until around 1906–1907.[9]

One possible clue to the source for this curious and generally atypical moment in Rabindranath's career comes in the poet's characterization of the nationalism that the British introduced in India:

> Before the Nation came to rule over us we had other governments which were foreign, and these, like all governments, had some element of the machine in them. But the difference between them and the government by the Nation is like the difference between the hand loom and the power loom. In the products of the hand loom the magic of man's living fingers finds its expression, and its hum harmonizes with the music of life. But the power loom is relentlessly lifeless and accurate and monotonous in its production.[10]

The analogy here is far from innocent or fortuitous. In his famous tract of 1909, *Hind Swaraj,* Gandhi had condemned British rule in India for having subjected the subcontinent to the dominance of modern industrial civilization, thereby warping—albeit not irreversibly in Gandhi's view—India's natural development. Rabindranath, although never so determinedly anti-Western as Gandhi, nonetheless participates in this passage—and indeed throughout the lectures on nationalism—in the essence of the Gandhian program, which rejected modernization and cultivated indigenous crafts as an alternative developmental path for contemporary India.[11] So-called constructive *swadeshi,* of which Rabindranath was an early advocate and fervent adherent, anticipated much that was considered novel and distinctive in the Gandhian program of social reform and political resistance.[12]

Gandhi and Rabindranath would divide over many issues—including, famously, the former's interpreting the 1934 Bihar earthquake as divine retribution for India's failure to reform itself spiritually—but both joined in seeing the introduction of industrial technology and the modern state form aligned with it as unmitigated disasters for the subcontinent. They also agreed that the key to India's future lay in constructive village work.

Of course, everything in politics hangs on the specificity of programs, and in this Rabindranath and Gandhi would differ in virtually every particular, especially after the former's withdrawal from the nationalist cause in 1908. One cannot but agree in general with Sumit Sarkar's observation that "anti-traditionalism in fact was to pervade virtually all of Tagore's post-1907 writings,"[13] a commitment that would separate him from the cultivation of traditional clothing, handicrafts, and Hindu customs so powerfully invoked in the popular imagination of Gandhism.[14] At the same time, one is compelled to register the considerable complexity of the problem, particularly as Rabindranath's attitudes altered in the shifting political and ideological winds that swept across the nationalist movement between 1908 and 1920. Sarkar points directly to the final pages of *Gora*

(1907–1910) to indicate Rabindranath's "vision of an India united on a modern basis transcending all barriers of caste, religion and race."[15] But this text was written in the midst of the poet's recoil from the communal violence of 1906–1907, and it is quite understandable for him to have emphasized modernity as the ideological counterweight to Hindu revivalism. For the latter, he felt (and he was not wrong), was in large measure responsible for communalism's resurgence. With the advantage of distance from the immediate events, he would come to judge somewhat differently the emergent nationalism of the *swadeshi* movement he himself had embraced. It is to his laconic portrait of the *swadeshi* era, *The Home and the World,* that we must now turn.

For readers unfamiliar with the novel, a schematic recounting of the plot and the substantive ideological issues it presents may be useful at the outset. The story, which is told alternately in three voices, Bimala's, Nikhil's, and Sandip's, opens with Bimala, wife to the prominent *zamindar* Nikhil, addressing her mother (in a letter? in her diary?) and recalling the events of her marriage, including her husband's insistence that she be educated and liberated from many of the *purdah* restrictions. Her narrative quickly shifts to the arrival on the scene of Sandip, longtime friend to Nikhil and currently a *swadeshi* leader. Nikhil insists, against Bimala's initial resistance, that his wife meet his friend, and in so doing he sows the seeds of disunity in his home. Sandip seduces Bimala (quite literally in the Satyajit Ray film of the novel; more on the divergences between novel and film further on) into involvement in *swadeshi,* exhorting her to purloin some money from her husband to support the cause. Nikhil, who has backed *swadeshi* industry in the past—much to his own disadvantage—consistently resists Sandip's attempts to be enlisted in the current struggle, maintaining that the movement has turned into a coercive campaign that unfairly victimizes the poor, especially his predominantly Muslim tenants. Sandip's perfidy is ultimately exposed, in part by the minor character Amulya, who apprises Bimala of his master's hypocrisy, but too late for Bimala to repent successfully of her betrayal of her husband. The novel ends with Sandip's banishment from the household, Amulya's shooting death, and the probably mortal wounding of Nikhil, who has ridden off to prevent further violence against his tenants.

On first inspection, the novel would seem unproblematically aligned with the forces of modernization. Nikhil's insistence that his wife, Bimala, receive a Western education and that subsequently she come out of *purdah* to meet his friend Sandip marks the text with the modern reforming social vision that Rabindranath clearly identified with and that was one legacy of his Brahmo heritage. Moreover, to the extent that the text unequivocally condemns Extremist nationalism in the morally dubious Sandip, it rejects all the trappings of Hindu revivalism that played a significant role in Extremist ideology.[16] It has often been thought that Rabindranath's views can be identified with Nikhil's, and certainly there is warrant for this claim. But the text's ideological structure is far from stable, its conclusions highly troubled. That *The Home and the World* condemns nationalism no one can seriously doubt; that it recommends a thorough program of modernization and universal humanism—which is how Tagore's post-*swadeshi* thought is customarily understood[17]—is less certain.

To begin to come to terms with this text's ideological specificity, we may turn to Sumit Sarkar's lapidary judgment on the trajectory traced by Rabindranath between 1907 and 1915: "The unity of humanist values and socially effective action which had been Rabindranath's ideal in *Gora* has broken down, and we are faced instead with the stark *Ghare-baire* dichotomy of Nikhilesh and Sandwip."[18] This characterization has the merit of posing the text's basic ideological opposition clearly and without equivocation, and yet it does not quite capture the manifest complexity of the home/world tension as this latter is figured in the narrative. To the extent that Sandip is associated with political activism and is the principal agent disrupting the household, Sarkar's description holds. But as we learn early on, the domestic space of the home is itself sharply divided between the *purdah* quarters of the women and the household's public spaces, where only men are allowed. Nikhil's insistence that Bimala, who resists at first (p. 23), come out of *purdah* and thereby complete her liberation from the traditional woman's role suggests that "the world" is not just the domain of political action but equally the site in the home itself where the affairs of men are discussed and conducted. Later on, Nikhil himself presents a further complication of the home/world dichotomy when he explicitly opposes the domestic realm, where commerce occurs, to the inner life, where he believes truth and authenticity properly reside (p. 65). At stake here is a familiar inside/outside opposition that, after Derrida and de Man, we readily recognize as a powerful tropological structure, reversible, flexible, and ultimately totalizing.

The power of this figure is dramatically realized in Nikhil's meditation near the center of the text (pp. 109–110), the upshot of which is his decision to let the cards fall where they may. The passage is too long to quote or explicate in detail here, but the main thrust can be grasped economically enough. It opens with the stark opposition between morality and politics, seemingly that posed in the characters of Nikhil and Sandip, respectively, though in the context Bimala embodies political values against her husband's commitment to ethical right. Nikhil asserts that correct political action can issue only from sound moral principles; Bimala claims that political necessity overrides ethical duty. As is apparent, the opposition can be overcome only by privileging one term over the other, thereby foreclosing a truly dialectical resolution of the tension. But the text continues as Nikhil experiences a sudden illumination—his recognition that Bimala has been dressing up in order to seduce him into ordering his tenants and dependents to support *swadeshi*—that liberates his soul and concomitantly transforms the world (here, nature). Nikhil's illumination is a liberation from the self (i.e., from his selfish passion for his wife) to a recognition of his proper place in the world:

"I seemed to have come closer to the heartbeats of the great earth in all the simplicity of its daily life." Nikhil thus apparently reconciles the two antagonistic values, proclaiming: "An anthem, inexpressibly sweet, seemed to peal forth from this world, where I, in my freedom, live in the freedom of all else."

By the end of the passage, Nikhil is satisfied that he has at last found the true path in life and that in doing so he has attained freedom while acknowledging the freedom of others—specifically, the world. But this ostensible liberation of the self, accomplished through introspection, retains some curious features that render Nikhil's untroubled acceptance of his newfound wisdom more fragile than he knows. Nikhil's discovering the secret of self-liberation discloses that the subject, which is the agent of its own freedom, depends on the world to realize its freedom: "In my work will be my salvation." The means to personal salvation turns out to be the instrument by which the world itself must be transformed in such a way that freedom (presumably the same freedom Nikhil attributes to himself) is equally available to all. As Nikhil puts it: "I shall allow freedom to others." On the testimony of this very passage, however, freedom is that which cannot be given by one to another; one can only achieve it for oneself. Nikhil never notices the contradiction, and for good reason: The ideology of liberation he embraces here and throughout the text is no Kantian kingdom of ends where all are equally empowered to realize their freedom; it is, rather, the paternalist ideal of the enlightened and wise patriarch extending freedom to others—even when, as in Bimala's case, doing so violates their explicit wishes in the matter.

Sumit Sarkar and others are surely correct to counterpose Nikhil to Sandip. The latter's first appearance in propria persona clearly establishes him as the ideological foil to the former's moral integrity (pp. 45–46). The text overloads the ethical charge on Sandip by imaging the revolutionary brigandage he advocates (and later authorizes when he convinces Bimala to purloin a large sum of money from her husband's treasury) as a rape, an overturning by violence of domestic tranquility. And of course he does just that, for Nikhil's and Bimala's marriage is permanently disrupted with his arrival. At the same time, it would seem that Sandip is intended to represent less an ordinary criminal or sinner than the quite different figure of the Nietzschean superman, the transvaluer of all values who, in this instance, subordinates morality to political necessity. It is therefore not immorality that he figures but amorality.

One interpretive commonplace of *The Home and the World* is to identify Bimala with India (or Bengal), the female figure in nationalist iconography of the period leading up to *swadeshi.*[19] Sandip makes the connection explicitly and often, so there can be little doubt about Tagore's having consciously mobilized this ideologeme in his portrayal of Bimala. But the figure itself was far from uncomplicated, as a splendid article on the subject by Tanika Sarkar demonstrates.[20] Symbolizing the nation in its mission to overthrow British rule, woman was at the same time the repository of traditional values. In fact, insofar as nationalism was deeply imbricated in traditional Indian (or, more narrowly and not infrequently,

Hindu) values and practices, its ideological program was less revolutionary than restorative, to invoke the useful categories Sumit Sarkar hazards in his study of the relations between elite leaders and the popular masses during the independence struggle. As Tanika Sarkar argues, there was little recognition of any conflict in this figure prior to the emergence of Gandhian mass movements. But in Rabindranath's novel, one cannot ignore the tension between the modernizing values associated with the world, the nation, and politics and the traditional commitments of women to family, husband, and home, in a word, to a conventional concept of wifely and motherly duty. Despite her momentary embrace of nationalist politics (and, in the magnificent Satyajit film, her literal embrace of Sandip), Bimala remains tied to many sanctioned forms of domestic subservience, symbolized most powerfully in the text by her continually brushing the dust from her husband's feet. And as the plot reveals, she regards her theft of 6,000 rupees as sinful (pp. 138–140); her ultimate repentance is represented by her willingness to undergo "public humiliation" (p. 186) after having once again subordinated herself to her husband. (In the Ray film, her reversion to the traditional woman's role is brilliantly figured in the film's final image when Bimala appears with her hair shorn and attired in the Hindu widow's plain white sari.) Seduced into politics by Sandip, Bimala cannot entirely free herself from conventional moral bonds; in the end she is ashamed of what she has done and attempts, vainly it would appear, to rekindle her husband's love by submitting to his will.

The exposition thus far has produced sufficient data to generate a structural description of the text's underlying semic or ideological system on the familiar Greimassian model (Fig. 12.1).

A brief word about the Bara Rani, Nikhil's sister-in-law and the figure that interpretations of this novel customarily slight. If at the outset Nikhil, by virtue of being male and a *zamindar* (not to mention his previous involvement in constructive *swadeshi*), signifies the paternalist/patriarchal order of traditional rural

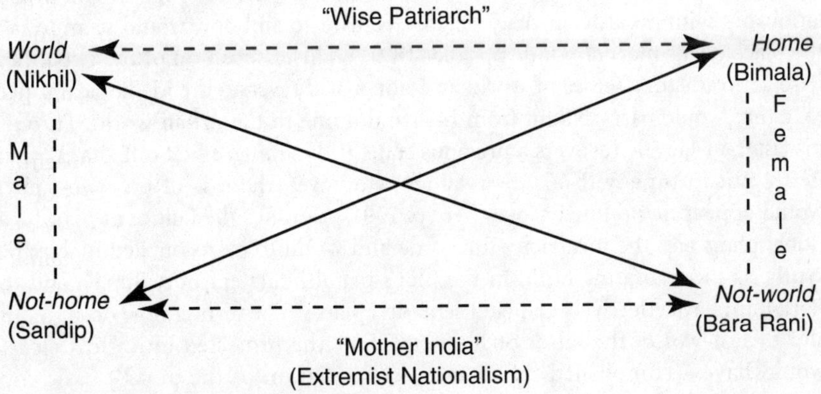

FIGURE 12.1 The Greimassian Model

Indian society, the semiotic negation of that order can only be the isolated, enclosed domain of the *purdah* quarters whose presiding deity is the Bara Rani, the conventional Hindu widow and defender of tradition. She it is who perpetually plagues Bimala for violating the norms of woman's role and who sees no reason why her sister-in-law should be educated, much less that she should be allowed to breach the boundaries of *purdah* and circulate among men.

That the so-called neutral term would be nationalism, symbolized by that oft-repeated nationalist cry "Bande Mataram" (Hail Motherland), accords not only with the historical situation in which "Mother India" predominated in nationalist discourse but also with Rabindranath's avowed political position after 1908, which was consistently antinationalist, as we have seen.[21] The so-called complex term presents rather greater difficulties. Although the novel surely projects an ideal resolution of the antinomy between home and world, nothing could be plainer than that the transcendence demanded by its system of values is undermined by the plot's final destiny. Although the novel remains ambiguous in this regard (Ray's film is more explicit), it seems likely that Nikhil has been mortally wounded in attempting to quell communal violence in the neighborhood. This raises a decisive problem: to wit, what are we to make of the ending? For strictly speaking, the diagram represents only the initial state of the system, not its ultimate disposition.

The novel's conclusion has several components. First is the projected abandonment of the home as it has generally been defined in the text, namely, Nikhil's household and his rural estates. Prior to his wounding, Nikhil announced his intention to leave the estates and to repair to his house in Calcutta, which can be taken to symbolize the world at large—as indeed it did for Rabindranath himself, who never felt comfortable in any modern urban environment. Nikhil's decision to go to the city is therefore an admission of defeat, a flight from home to the world. Moreover, there is no indication, despite his wife's desire for it, that Nikhil has in any useful sense effected a reconciliation with Bimala.

Second, and directly relevant to the last point, is the rekindling of Nikhil's relationship with his sister-in-law, which was prior to and now would seem to take the place of his marital bond (pp. 188–189).[22] This disposition of the two otherwise contradictory semes of world and not-world reverses the ideological trajectory that would carry Nikhil from his rural home to the urban world. Through his sister-in-law, he recovers a previous state of the home, albeit one that is manifestly not in tune with his own values. Moreover, the loss of his wife—for it would appear he no longer loves her (p. 199)—signifies the failure of his educational plans and the incapacity for home and world to be reconciled in a higher synthesis incorporating both. In the plot's penultimate episode, Bimala and the Bara Rani have effectively changed semantic places: The former now occupies the slot of not-world, the latter of home.[23] Thus, the projected move to Calcutta would have accomplished the desired reconciliation of the novel's basic contraries, but only at the price of regressing to absolutely traditional male and female roles—obviously an unacceptable solution for Tagore. Moreover, the solution fails to be realized in the text. I'll return to this point in a moment.

Third, and a consequence of what has just been said, Sandip has been effectively banished from the household. Nikhil concedes Sandip's freedom to visit them in Calcutta, but the latter's residence in the home will no longer be tolerated. In order to recover the formal propriety of his marriage, Nikhil is forced to expel the immediate threat to domestic peace. Sandip's rootlessness is simply too disruptive, a force that the home cannot tolerate.

Finally, we have the communal violence itself, which there is every reason to believe was the efficient cause for Tagore's withdrawal from active political involvement in 1908.[24] It is responsible for the death of Amulya, Sandip's disciple and Bimala's devotee, and, as I've observed, probably Nikhil's as well. If I am correct in assuming this latter, then the main narrative action might be crudely summarized as follows: By inviting the antithesis of the home (Sandip; politics) into the household, the representative of progressive humanism (Nikhil) has destroyed any possibility for domestic harmony, leaving both the domestic space of the household and the public environment of the estates ultimately bereft of patriarchal authority.

But why should things have to turn out this way? Why could Rabindranath not realize any other than the tragic solution to the tensions thrown up by *swadeshi* and by the nationalist movement generally? What, in short, is the objective blockage in the text's ideological system that forecloses any alternative denouement to this episode in the eventual overthrow of British rule?

One possible answer would be that history went this way, that *The Home and the World* is no more than a perspicuous accounting of *swadeshi*'s demise and Indian nationalism's degeneration into senseless (and for the most part ineffectual) terrorism. Sumit Sarkar's massive study of the period would in part bear out such an inference. Sarkar unstintingly criticizes the movement's middle-class leadership, which signally failed to strike roots in the peasant masses and mobilize them in favor of political resistance.[25] His conclusion is that because an effective alliance between the mostly urban intellectual leadership and the rural masses was never forged, *swadeshi* could not seriously challenge British rule. Its defeat left the middle-class elites with only two options: Return to previous forms of Congress mendicancy or resort to terrorism. That the latter was not without its positive role Sarkar concedes,[26] but he is quick to point out that ultimately it was a dead end. He cites favorably Rabindranath's terse judgment on the political limitations of such a revolutionary strategy: "My impatience never makes any road in the world shorter, nor does time lessen itself for my special benefit."[27]

Sarkar goes on to observe, however, that "it would be wrong to credit Tagore with an alternative entirely cogent or satisfactory. . . . Rabindranath could not really suggest any concrete social or economic programme with which to rouse the uneducated masses. His constructive rural work amounted to little more than humanitarianism, the appeal to zamindars was surely utopian, and the basic problems of land relations remained untouched."[28] There was, in short, a fundamental contradiction in nationalist ideology at this period that Rabindranath was unable to overcome or circumvent save by utopian appeals to morality and enlightenend humanitarianism.

One strand in recent debunkings of Tagore attributes this impasse to the poet's objective class position. Thus Hitendra Mitra writes:

> Tagore was born in a social class which collaborated with the imperialist rulers and acted against the anti-imperialist struggles of the people. He was conscious of the fact and tried to fight against it in his own way when he was young, not socially rooted and practically neglected by his close relatives. He could not succeed to go beyond his class position because he imbibed the thought and perception of his feudal family which appropriated him to its own use after his initial success as a poet.[29]

Mitra later locates the shift in Tagore's ideological position from antiimperialist to comprador at the moment when the poet was sent off to manage his father's estates in 1891.[30] The difficulty with this account is not so much its methodological crudity, which draws a direct line from an objective class position to a set of ideological beliefs. Such examples are not difficult to find. Sarkar himself makes much the same point about the educated *bhadralok,* who composed the bulk of the nationalist movement's leadership during *swadeshi.*[31] Rather, the weakness in Mitra's critique lies in its failure to come to terms with the genuine complexity of Rabindranath's thinking, which was composed of a curious amalgam of different ideological positions, not all of which derived from his remaining a substantial landholder throughout his life. Ideologies, we may say with some assurance, always ultimately serve certain class interests, but they rarely are shaped unilaterally by economic considerations.

To begin to sketch out a more satisfactory explanation of the ideological impasse figured in *The Home and the World,* we need to return to an issue that has hovered on the margins of this chapter but that I have not yet fully articulated. It is, to be brief, the question of gender. I referred earlier to the article by Tanika Sarkar on the function of female iconography in Bengali literature and in images of Indian nationalism on the eve of *swadeshi.* It will be recalled that woman's position in this discourse as embodiment at once of perdurable traditional values and revolutionary hope created a tension, evident in the figure of Bimala, between the domestic sphere and political activism. But this opposition was not just the "natural" outcome of gendered social relations in Hindu households. (We can omit for the moment the question of the conditions obtaining among Muslims, since *swadeshi* nationalism was overwhelmingly a Hindu affair, as the communal riots of 1906–1907 would make plain enough.) The contradiction in woman as ideologeme resulted from a quite specific set of historical circumstances imposed by the colonial situation.

In a useful essay on the genealogy of the concepts *ghar* (home) and *bahir* (world) during the nineteenth century, Partha Chatterjee argues that British rule produced among its subjects a separation between inner and outer aspects of social life as a defensive measure against the manifest superiority of European material practices:

> The colonial situation, and the ideological response of nationalism to the [British] critique of Indian tradition, introduced an entirely new substance to these terms and effected their transformation. . . . The world was where the European power had challenged the non-European peoples and, by virtue of its superior material culture, had subjugated them. But, the nationalists asserted, it had failed to colonize the inner, essential, identity of the East which lay in its distinctive, and superior, spiritual culture. . . . in the entire phase of the nationalist struggle, the crucial need was to protect, preserve and strengthen the inner core of the nationalist culture, its spiritual essence. No encroachments by the colonizer must be allowed in that inner sanctum.[32]

Chatterjee goes on to show how this ostensibly modernizing and liberatory discourse did effect changes in (almost exclusively middle-class) women's potential sphere of action, opening up opportunities for self-emancipation, particularly in education;[33] but he is quick to point out how these new freedoms functioned simultaneously to restrict woman's activity to its proper sphere: the home. He writes:

> Education then was meant to inculcate in women the virtues—the typically bourgeois virtues characteristic of the new social forms of "disciplining"—of orderliness, thrift, cleanliness, and a personal sense of responsibility, the practical skills of literacy, accounting and hygiéne and the ability to run the household according to the new physical and economic conditions set by the outside world. . . . The new patriarchy advocated by nationalism conferred upon women the honor of a new social responsibilty, and by associating the task of female emancipation with the historical goal of sovereign nationhood, bound them to a new, and yet entirely legitimate, subordination.[34]

Indian nationalism was in this respect (albeit not in many others), to recall the terms of Chatterjee's earlier work, "a derivative discourse." And it is precisely this derivativeness that may help to explain the ideological impasse in *The Home and the World.*

For the *narrative* problem in that text is determined by the extent to which Bimala can be brought out of the confines of the traditional home into the modern world without destroying her distinctively female virtues. Or if we follow convention and read Bimala as a figure for India itself (and after Tanika Sarkar's work it seems entirely legitimate to do so), then it can be said that the novel is about just that puzzle which nationalist discourse as a whole set for itself: the possibility for the strengths of indigenous culture to be maintained while altering the traditional functions and forms of female identity in order to signify the resistance to colonial rule. The difficulty, as the novel presents it, lies in the conflict, irresolvable in principle, between the honorable but ineffectual Nikhil and the powerful but unprincipled Sandip. Bimala's initial choice in favor of the latter signifies on one level Rabindranath's negative judgment on the nationalist movement's turn toward Extremism. At a deeper level, that of the ideological system that governs the text from the outset, Bimala's choice is to some extent unavoidable. The text cries out for but cannot produce the combination of power and justice that is the ideal figure demanded by the semiotic system: the authoritative, wise, and powerful patriarch. By splitting the necessary qualities for its ideal resolution between two male protagonists, the novel acknowledges the impossibility of fulfilling its own ideological fantasy.

The error, if one may call it that, in this ideological structure is at one with nationalism's self-representation. Nationalist discourse, both Chatterjee and Tanika Sarkar suggest, was trapped by its figuratively representing social and political relations in the symbolic garb of familial relations. Whatever progress had been achieved in this sphere for middle-class Bengalis during the nineteenth century, the family remained a determinately patriarchal institution. Moreover, as Sarkar and Chatterjee also maintain, prior to the emergence of Gandhism, women occupied a position in nationalist discourse homologous to that of another group for whom the nationalists claimed to speak but whose real conditions of existence they scarcely addressed: the peasantry.[35] Recent historiography on the independence struggle has revealed the extent of Congress's failure to resolve the basic contradiction between an elite leadership and its programs and the aspirations of a mass-based movement to overthrow British rule. Gandhi's capacity to mold a popular mass movement that remained firmly in the control of middle- and upper-class elites is by any standard one of the extraordinary success stories in the politics of this century. That it ultimately exacted a high price has become increasingly evident since 1970 as the capacity of Congress to unify the nation has steadily eroded.[36]

Something of the contemporary relevance of Tagore's novel can be gleaned by briefly considering Satyajit's film version. In his informative if overly hagiographic study of Ray, Andrew Robinson observes: "If non-Bengalis know Tagore at all today, it is mainly by virtue of Ray's interpretations of him on film."[37] These include film versions of the three short stories strung together in *Three Daughters*, of the novella *Nastanir* (*Charulata*), and, most famous, of *Ghare Baire* itself, as well as a documentary (sponsored by the Indian government) on Tagore's life. Ray's lifelong fascination with Rabindranath extends well beyond the familiar forms of Bengali piety for the national poet. Both men were reared in prominent Brahmo households and rebelled against the sect's more puritanical practices. Rabindranath was a close family friend, a great admirer of Sukamar Ray's (the filmmaker's father) nonsense verse, and a frequent visitor to the household in which Satyajit was raised. After graduating from Presidency College in 1939, Ray's mother sent her son to Santineketan to study art.[38]

Other affinities between poet and filmmaker run still deeper, and it is on this level, that of the fundamentally antipolitical nature of their art, that their similarity can be most clearly discerned. In response to the Naxalite uprising in West Bengal, Ray made *The Adversary,* which portrays a young bomb-making revolutionary in an unfavorable light. In *Company Limited,* Ray is said to have recorded the following remark of George Steiner's in his directions for shooting: "The evil of politics lies precisely in the separation of the human person from the abstract cause or the strategic necessity."[39] Characteristic of his ambivalence toward politics—Robinson is probably not wrong to attribute to Ray generally left-wing sympathies, however vague—is the following incident, related by Robinson:

> Around this time [the mid–1960s] he also agreed to take part in a rally against the Vietnam War and to read out an international appeal. Ray says he would not have gone along, given the choice. "I would probably have stayed at home, because I'm built differently. But there were so many of my friends involved, I said, 'All right. I'll come.' I believed in what was being done. I wasn't merely assuming an attitude. It's not that. But it is just not me. I don't like taking part in public rallies. I'm very much a private person."[40]

It is difficult not to read such comments back into a film like *The Chess Players,* where the metaphorical significance of the nawabs' refusal to suspend their game in the face of the British incursion has a clear autobiographical resonance with Ray's own desire to protect his art from the pressures of political commitment.[41]

Ray contemplated making a film of *The Home and the World* as early as 1948,[42] and he seems to have kept the idea alive over many years.[43] By the time the project was finally realized in the 1980s, Tagore's novel had been overlain in Ray's imagination with a great deal of political history, including the Naxalite episode that had torn Calcutta apart in the early 1970s. When Ray describes Tagore's attitudes toward the nationalist movement in the first decade of the century, one cannot help but hear the echo of Ray's own sentiments about the political violence he himself had lived through:

> Tagore's essays on the terrorist movement and some of the other things that he wrote are actually put in the mouth of Nikhil—exact sentences even. He represents Tagore's attitude to the terrorist movement and its ultimate futility. It's a very valid viewpoint, very rational. It was really a middle-class movement with no connection with the lower strata of society at all. So ultimately it just fizzled out, and in other cases it turned into very violent riots between Hindus and Muslims. It was a failure and Tagore could see it was going to be a failure, although the political leaders didn't see it his way.[44]

In the film, communal violence figures much more prominently than it does in the novel. In addition, there is an unmistakable allusion to Naxalbari when Amulya justifies his theft from the local treasury to Bimala by reference to the Naxalite slogan that money is "mine one day, the moneylender's the next." In general, the politico-ethical allegory projected by Rabindranath is displaced into the purely erotic: Bimala has a real love affair with Sandip, punctuated by those scandalous kisses about which Ray was so nervous that he didn't even reveal his intentions to the actors until shooting the scene. There are some other notable differences between film and novel—a much greater role for the Bara Rani in the former than is warranted by Tagore's text, the clear reconciliation between Bimala and Nikhil just before the latter's death in the film, and the complete excision of Nikhil's transformation from the film—but in general, Ray has captured much of the novel's spirit, not to mention carefully reconstructing its period atmosphere in dwellings, furnishings, and clothing.

Ray has also reproduced the essentially antipolitical intentions that guided much of Tagore's writing in the aftermath of *swadeshi*. But he has, in my view, seriously underplayed the sociopolitical allegory that remains at the novel's core. Indeed, he has made the antipolitical aspects so dominant as virtually to eliminate one of the major tensions complicating the novel's ideological system. Victor Banerjee's utterly feckless Nikhil seriously undermines the power this character wields in Rabindranath's conception, rendering nugatory both his political significance and his ethical value. Omitting the scene in which he experiences a personal transformation and resolves (for himself and implicitly for the ideological system that the text enacts) the contradiction between home and world on which the novel is founded was thus no mere oversight on Ray's part. It was a strategic decision, crucial to the filmmaker's recoding of the novel's political allegory. Ray was surely correct to see the close relationship between Nikhil's opinions and Rabindranath's, but he was just as surely wrong to see both as insipid, and powerless to act when faced by the violence of *swadeshi* politics. The temptation to read this alteration in terms of Ray's, rather than Rabindranath's, character is all but irresistible.

To return to *The Home and the World*, it may be said that its narrative of *swadeshi*'s failure speaks to a deeper historical and ideological impasse shared by *swadeshi* and the Gandhi Congress alike. The latter successfully mobilized peasant masses to overthrow British rule, but without altering the basic structures of agrarian exploitation and domination that were the ultimate cause for the peasant discontent upon which it was able to draw.[45] Gandhi's appeal was never to the peasantry as a class; on the contrary, as Sabyasachi Bhattacharya has observed, the Congress managed to appear "as a supra-class entity, an arbitrator or mediator, a consensus-making body."[46] This prepared Congress for the transfer of power; it did not secure its ultimate authority as a party of the people, since by its very nature Congress could speak only of, not for, them. In maintaining the fundamental class relations bequeathed by the British Raj, Congress reinforced the underlying contradictions, explosive at times, that the Raj had created in the transition from Mughal rule.[47] To recall the image drawn from Conrad at the beginning of this chapter, both Rabindranath's exclusive emphasis on constructive *swadeshi* and Gandhi's appeal to the sanctity of traditional village practices were attempts to "oil the infernal knitting-machine" of British imperialism on the subcontinent. As one of Gandhi's near contemporaries would have said, the real task would have been to smash the machine itself.

Looking backward into the past for models of a future social order (not for nothing was Gandhi an admirer of Ruskin) could only reinscribe those forms of domination that the colonial administration itself had so skillfully exploited: caste distinctions, communal tensions, regional and class differences, and, as we have seen specifically in Tagore, gender discrimination.[48] Marx once famously observed of earlier revolutionary moments in Europe that in them "the resurrection of the dead served to exalt the new struggles, rather than to parody the old."[49] To some extent, this is what Gandhism and constructive *swadeshi* sought in India. But Marx went on to argue that in the modern world of industrial capitalism, a world that was already on the horizon on the subcontinent, such reverence for the past was anything but revolutionary:

> The social revolution of the nineteenth century can only create its poetry from the future, not from the past. It cannot begin its own work until it has sloughed off all its superstitious regard for the past. Earlier revolutions have needed world-historical reminiscences to deaden their awareness of their own content. In order to arrive at its own content the revolution of the nineteenth century must let the dead bury their dead.[50]

Or as one writer from another underdeveloped hinterland of the capitalist world system put it, "You can't go home again."

NOTES

1. Throughout, I refer to Rabindranath Tagore indifferently as "Rabindranath" or as "Tagore." Both are, to my knowledge, acceptable, although in some contexts—where other members of his family are in question—use of his given name is required. I have been told by a knowledgeable friend that custom and decorum dictate that only Bengalis use the given name alone. I hope my own usage will give no offense; none is intended. I merely follow standard practice in the secondary literature.

2. Recently, Tagore has figured among the pantheon of anticolonial nationalists proposed by Edward Said in his *Culture and Imperialism* (New York: Knopf, 1993); see pp. 215, 219, 232, 264. Such a characterization is not wholly wrong, of course, but as I shall be arguing at some length, it fails to capture the complexity—and mutability—of Rabindranath's views on nationalism and colonial resistance.

3. Gayatri Spivak has drawn attention to Tagore's "colonial prose," describing how in his fiction composed during the last years of the nineteenth century he "fashion[s] a new Bengali prose" in a "stunning mixture of Sanskritized and colloquial Bengali." ("The Burden of English," in Rajeswari Sunder Rajan, ed., *The Lie of the Land: English Literary Studies in India* [Delhi: Oxford University Press, 1992], pp. 280–281).

4. *Joseph Conrad's Letters to R. B. Cunninghame Graham,* ed. C. T. Watts (Cambridge: Cambridge University Press, 1969), pp. 56–57.

5. Rabindranath Tagore, *The Home and the World,* trans. Surendranath Tagore (1919; reprint, Harmondsworth, Middlesex: Penguin, 1985); hereafter cited in text parenthetically by page number.

6. Rabindranath Tagore, *Nationalism* (London: Macmillan, 1917), p. 135.

7. Ibid., p. 134.

8. David Kopf, *The Brahmo Samaj and the Shaping of the Modern Indian Mind* (Princeton: Princeton University Press, 1979), pp. 287–310. Rabindranath's relation to Brahmo culture was far from straightforward. Perhaps the best indication of his views at this period is to be gleaned from his novel *Gora* (1907–1910), where both strict Brahmos and orthodox Hindus are held up to scorn.

9. Tagore's involvement in antiimperialist politics predates the *swadeshi* period. He wrote a number of anti-British articles during the 1880s, including an attack on the Chinese opium trade; see Krishna Kripalani, *Rabindranath Tagore: A Biography* (New York: Grove Press, 1962), p. 99; and Hitendra Mitra, *Tagore Without Illusions* (Calcutta: Sanyal Prokashan, 1983), pp. 127–138. Nonetheless, Susobahn Sarkar's overall judgment still stands fifty years after it was first pronounced: "In truth Rabindranath had no firm faith in a radical programme of action, any institution or apparatus for administration; Sudhindranath Datta was quite correct in his remark that even the upheaval at epoch's end did not provide to Tagore sufficient impetus for liberation from certain traditional values" (Susobahn Sarkar, "'Progress' and Rabindranath Tagore," in Sarkar, *Bengal Renaissance and Other Essays* [New Delhi: People's Publishing House, 1970], p. 141).

10. Tagore, *Nationalism,* p. 29.

11. As Partha Chatterjee argues, however, the project announced in *Hind Swaraj* is less nationalist and specifically anti-Western than "a total moral critique of the fundamental aspects of civil society." *Nationalist Thought and the Colonial World—A Derivative Discourse?* (London: Zed Books, 1986), p. 93. On the dialectic between "traditionalism" and "westernism" in Tagore, see Susobahn Sarkar, "Rabindranath Tagore and the Renaissance in Bengal," in *Bengal Renaissance,* pp. 148–183. On the pitfalls of such a schematization, see Sumit Sarkar, "Rammohun Roy and the Break with the Past," in Sarkar, *A Critique of Colonial India* (Calcutta: Papyrus, 1985), pp. 15–17; and K. N. Panikkar, "Culture and Ideology: Contradictions in Intellectual Transformation of Colonial Society in India," *Economic and Political Weekly* (December 5, 1987): 2115–2120.

12. See Sumit Sarkar, *"Popular" Movements and "Middle Class" Leadership in Late Colonial India* (Calcutta: Centre for Studies in Social Sciences, 1983), pp. 69, 76–78, 94; and *Modern India: 1885–1947* (Delhi: Macmillan, 1983), p. 112.

13. Sumit Sarkar, *The Swadeshi Movement in Bengal 1903–1908* (New Delhi: People's Publishing House, 1973), p. 85. See Susobahn Sarkar, "Rabindranath Tagore and the Renaissance in Bengal," pp. 173–183.

14. On Gandhi's appeal to the popular masses, see Chatterjee, *Nationalist Thought,* p. 110; Sumit Sarkar, "The Conditions and Nature of Subaltern Militancy: Bengal from Swadeshi to Non-Cooperation, c. 1905–22," in Ranajit Guha, ed., *Subaltern Studies,* vol. 3, (Delhi: Oxford University Press, 1984), pp. 307–320. But see especially Gyan Pandey, "Peasant Revolt and Indian Nationalism: The Peasant Movement in Awadh, 1919–22," in Guha, ed. *Subaltern Studies,* vol. 1 (Delhi: Oxford University Press, 1982), pp. 143–197; and

Shahid Amin, "Gandhi as Mahatma: Gorakhpur District, Eastern UP, 1921–2," in *Subaltern Studies,* vol. 3, pp. 1–61.

15. Sarkar, *The Swadeshi Movement,* p. 85. The decisive moment, after Gora has discovered the truth about his Irish origins, comes in the hero's speech to Anandamoyi, the woman who has raised him: "'Mother, you are my mother!' exclaimed Gora. 'The mother whom I have been wandering about in search of was all the time sitting in my room at home. You have no caste, you make no distinctions, and have no hatred—you are only the image of our welfare! It is you who are India!'" (Rabindranath Tagore, *Gora,* trans. W. W. Pearson under the supervision of Surendranath Tagore [1924; reprint, Madras: Macmillan, 1980], p. 407). Gora then requests a drink to be brought him by Lachmiya, the Christian servant whose touch he has hitherto shunned for fear of losing caste.

16. Here again, *Gora* provides the relevant gloss, for the titular hero's strict observance of traditional Hindu customs throughout the novel is directly linked to his patriotism. Extremism is not yet on the horizon in the novel itself, which is set in the late 1870s or early 1880s, but Tagore composed it after the demise of *swadeshi* during the Moderate/Extremist Congress split. Interpreting the narrative in the light of its contemporary context is surely justified.

17. See, for example, Chatterjee, *Nationalist Thought,* p. 100; and Sarkar, "'Progress' and Rabindranath Tagore," p. 141.

18. Sarkar, *The Swadeshi Movement,* p. 502.

19. See Anita Desai's introduction to *The Home and the World;* and R. P. Bhaskar, "The Novels of Tagore," in Mehendra Kulasreshta, ed., *The Genius of Tagore: Tagore Centenary Volume,* Part 1 (Hoshiapur: V.V.R. Institute, 1961), p. 100.

20. Tanika Sarkar, "Nationalist Iconography: Image of Women in 19th Century Bengali Literature," *Economic and Political Weekly* (November 21, 1987):2011–2015.

21. Once more, comparison with *Gora* is instructive. Anandamoyi is explicitly identified as both Mother and India in the final chapter. Throughout the novel, although she scorns any strict, sectarian application of Hinduism to social life, she nevertheless embodies the domestic virtues of womanhood that underwrote nationalist iconography. *Gora* thus provides proof *a contrario* of Rabindranath's subsequent disillusionment with nationalism, for in *The Home and the World,* the world is consistently and unequivocally condemned, the cry of "Hail Motherland" ringing hollow by the end.

22. It is generally agreed that the relationship between the Bara Rani and Nikhil was in part determined by Rabindranath's relations with his own sister-in-law, his companion in youth who committed suicide. But the central issue in the text is less the psychological charge this situation bore for the author than the structure of familial relations representing the political problematic.

23. Benita Parry read an earlier draft of this chapter and suggested that Bimala's shifting position in the novel's semantic system makes her a "floating signifier" and that this is a significant fact for understanding how gender discourses operate in the text. She is doubtless correct, but the decisive question remains: Why should gender have functioned in this manner at this historical moment both for Tagore and for nationalist discourse generally? My treatment of patriarchy attempts a preliminary exploration of this problem.

24. See Sumit Sarkar, *The Swadeshi Movement,* pp. 82–87.

25. Ibid., pp. 78, 90, 333. See Rajat Kanta Ray, *Social Conflict and Political Unrest in Bengal 1875–1927* (Delhi: Oxford University Press, 1984), who argues that the dependent

position of landed and professional elites in the colonial economy held these latter hostage to the existing mechanisms of surplus extraction that exploited rural cultivators, thereby rendering the objective interests of elites and masses necessarily contradictory. Tagore himself seems to have understood this situation perfectly well: "In the realm of politics [Rabindranath] bitterly criticised from the beginning habits of 'mendicancy'; the 'atmasakti' (self-help) which he invoked is indeed of priceless value in political life. He grasped the main shortcoming of our earlier political efforts—the lack of contact between our educated classes and the common people" (Sarkar, "'Progress' and Rabindranath Tagore," p. 146).

26. Sarkar, *The Swadeshi Movement,* pp. 89–90.

27. Ibid., p. 90.

28. Ibid., pp. 90–91.

29. Mitra, *Tagore Without Illusions,* pp. 51–52.

30. Ibid., p. 138.

31. Sarkar, *The Swadeshi Movement,* p. 334–335.

32. Partha Chatterjee, "Colonialism, Nationalism, and Colonialized Women: The Contest in India," *American Ethnologist* 16, 4 (November 1989):624.

33. Ibid., p. 628.

34. Ibid., p. 629. Chatterjee's general view is supported by Ghulam Murshid's *Reluctant Debutante: Response of Bengali Women to Modernization, 1849–1905* (Dhaka: Sahitya Samsad, 1983), who observes: "The movement for the 'emancipation' of Bengali women was initiated by men. Therefore, in the true sense, it was not a movement for 'liberating' women from the authority. . . . Men's attempts to uplift their women were not meant for women's welfare alone, they were, at the same time, motivated by men's aspirations for the fulfillment of their own lives" (p. 60). See also Meredith Borthwick, *The Changing Role of Women in Bengal 1849–1905* (Princeton: Princeton University Press, 1984), pp. 38, 270. Borthwick's study is the most extensive in English.

35. On women's role in the struggle for Indian independence, see Manmohan Kaur, *Women in India's Freedom Struggle* (New Delhi: Sterling Publishers, 1985); and Vijay Agnew, *Elite Women in Indian Politics* (New Delhi: Vikas, 1979), especially chapter 3, "Mahatma Gandhi and the Participation of Women in Nationalist Politics," pp. 34–61. Both books discuss Sarla Devi, Rabindranath's niece and a prominent figure in the nationalist movement in Bengal and in the Punjab from 1897 until her death in 1945. The former quotes the following passage from Valentine Charol's *Indian Unrest* (1910), which bears interestingly on the Bimala-Nikhil-Amulya relation in *The Home and the World:* "The revolt seems to have obtained a firm hold of the zenana and the Hindu woman behind the purdah often exercises a greater influence upon her husband and her sons than the English woman who moves freely about the world. . . . In Bengal even small boys of so tender an age as still to have the run of the zenana have I am told been dressed up as little Sanyasis in little yellow robes preaching hatred of the English" (Kaur, *Women in India's Freedom Struggle,* p. 107, n. 12).

36. See Achin Vanaik, *The Painful Transition: Bourgeois Democracy in India* (London: Verso, 1990), especially chapters 2–4.

37. Andrew Robinson, *Satyajit Ray: The Inner Eye* (London: Andre Deutsch, 1989), pp. 47–48.

38. Ibid., pp. 13–55. The comparison between Ray and Tagore is one of the leitmotifs of Robinson's study.

39. Cited in ibid., p. 209.

40. Ibid., pp. 203–204.

41. Ray's passion for chess during the 1940s and 1950s is well known. Robinson notes that Ray sold his collection of chess books to raise funds for his first film, *Pather Panchali* (see ibid., p. 241).

42. Ibid., p. 66.

43. See ibid., p. 270, for details about Ray's thoughts during the 1960s on casting this film.

44. Cited in ibid., p. 267.

45. See Ray, *Social Conflict in Bengal;* Ravinder Kumar, "Class, Community, or Nation? Gandhi's Quest for a Popular Consensus in India," in Kumar, *Essays in the Social History of Modern India* (Delhi: Oxford University Press, 1983), p. 68; and Sarkar, *Modern India.*

46. Sabyasachi Bhattacharya, "The Colonial State, Capital and Labour: Bombay 1919–1931," in S. Bhattacharya and R. Thapar, eds., *Situating Indian History* (Delhi: Oxford University Press, 1985), p. 192.

47. See Chatterjee, *Nationalist Thought,* pp. 124–125.

48. See the essay "Woman," written contemporaneously with *The Home and the World,* where Rabindranath proclaims the world-historical role women have been called to play by modernity, basing his ideas on a clear distinction between properly male and distinctively female spheres. Rabindranath Tagore, "Woman," in Tagore, *Personality* (New York: Macmillan, 1917), pp. 201–218.

49. Karl Marx, *Surveys from Exile,* ed. David Fernbach, trans. Ben Fowkes (New York: Vintage, 1974), p. 148.

50. Ibid., p. 149. The figure is perhaps not so unproblematic as I've indicated here. Jacques Derrida has recently commented in extenso on the oddity of the image of the dead burying the dead and on the general economy of ghosts, spirits, and specters in Marx's writing, early and late; see Derrida, *Spectres de Marx* (Paris: Galilée, 1993).

13

Sexing the Pundits: Gender, Romance, and Realism in the Cultural Politics of Colonial Bengal

HENRY SCHWARZ

THIS CHAPTER CONCERNS the importation and appropriation of European literature in colonial India from roughly 1835 to 1915. It specifically examines the ideological construction of the concept of literature by English theorists employed by the East India Company who found in it a softer route to improvement than those proposed by earlier reformers such as utilitarian radicals like Jeremy Bentham and James Mill, who aimed to revolutionize Indian society through wholesale social reorganization. The concept of literature is important here for several interrelated reasons. First, the modern practice of producing literature was an activity that indelibly characterized indigenous Indian society during its colonial period, especially in Bengal, where it became an activity remarkable for its ubiquity, copiousness, and achievement. European forms of narration such as the novel, romance, and autobiography are among the most visible and durable of India's European legacies. Second, the gender dynamics of both the importation of literature and its indigenous reception and appropriation in the colony shed light on two related subjects that have occupied historians and literary critics of the nineteenth century, though never in tandem: the construction of a semimodern colonial patriarchy from disparate elements of traditional, orientalist, reformist, and nationalist discourses and the crucial and problematic place of woman in the literature of the so-called Bengal renaissance.[1] Finally, the creation of modern literature in India can inform us about the historical role of English literature as an agent of domination and perhaps advise us about the continuing relevance of English studies in a postcolonial world.

An important body of research has arisen in recent years that investigates the question of culture and gender as it informs the development of nationalist discourse in colonial Bengal. In a problem familiar to historians of the period, a curious silence hovers over "the women's question" in the last decades of the nineteenth century. By this time, writes Partha Chatterjee, Bengali "nationalism sought to resolve the women's question in accordance with its historical project."[2] In Chatterjee's view, the Indian nationalist movement at a certain point closed off further discussion of women's social reform, partly in order to more effectively confront English rule in its political, public face. After several decades of heated debate over the role of women in the modernizing reforms of the early and mid-nineteenth centuries, "the women's question" makes a "sudden disappearance . . . from the agenda of public debate. . . ."[3] The disappearance of the debate does not mark a successful resolution of the question of women's place in a rapidly changing society so much as a decision to discuss it no longer, a consensus generated by nationalist leaders who hoped to build a solid defense against undesirable elements of Western cultural penetration into Bengali social life.

The impulse behind this separation of public and private spheres, according to Chatterjee, stemmed from a selective appropriation of modern European thought itself. By the terms of this selection, Bengali elites sought to compete in the European-dominated "public sphere" of conversation, debate, and, most important, political argument by actively taking part in the "worldly" affairs of the nation. At the same time, this attempt to engage the rulers in the public sphere resulted in a countermovement by which the true essence of Bengali culture—its superior spirituality and cultivation—was protected from European contamination by being safely confined to the home. On the one hand, this confinement was necessary to preserve the distinctiveness of a uniquely "national" culture. If Bengali identity too closely imitated the West in its acquisition of European forms of public conduct and political debate, "the self-identity of national culture itself would be threatened."[4] In this sense, Indian nationalism could count as a "success" its situating of the women's question "in an inner domain of sovereignty," for in relegating the question of woman's reform to the private sphere, it precluded the further contamination of domestic—or spiritual—life by Western influence.[5] On the other hand, however, the very positing of an essentialized sphere of private culture was itself influenced by European Orientalists and liberal reformers who had determined, in debates surrounding sati, purdah, and other issues, that one of the defining traits of Indian society was its relegation of women to "degenerate and barbaric" conditions of near enslavement in the home and their confinement within a tightly guarded domesticity.[6]

Thus the separation of public and private spheres, and with it the construction of sharply delimited and essentialized gender roles, can be seen to mark a decisive step in the construction of what I would call a "semimodern" colonial patriarchy. "Semifeudal" was a term coined by radical economists in the 1960s and 1970s to describe the stunted form of capitalist relations instituted under the early years of English commercial activity in India, forms that introduced new market mechanisms within the shell of older modes of land tenure and exchange.

Semimodern can be used to designate forms of social modernization based on their distinction from discursively constructed notions of tradition. As Chatterjee and others have observed, such "invented traditions" are often constructed to justify reform retroactively; in many cases they are severely limiting, since they posit dubious interpretations of the past as facts and then use these empirical "facts" as the basis for justifying reforms that are already irrevocable.[7]

"Literature" was a central element in the larger ensemble of semimodern constructions in colonial India. The particular blend of qualities associated with the term during the eighteenth and nineteenth centuries in England provides us with only a partial indication of how English thinkers imagined its usefulness in helping to maintain control of the colony while furthering the "improvement" increasingly used to legitimate its continued control. In exchanges on the function of literature in the education of colonial Indian subjects, we can begin to glimpse the attitude toward public and private spheres, political and domestic discourses, and masculine and feminine roles advanced by English reformers as they sought to maintain the loyalty and improve the mind of the Indian student. To be sure, the English teaching of literature in government-supported schools reproduced to some extent the separation of which Chatterjee speaks by explicitly gendering the accessibility of education. Women's education was essentially unsupported by English initiative until John Drinkwater Bethune opened his school for girls in 1859, fully half a century after the beginnings of English education in Bengal and forty years after the East India Company had stated its support for "the revival and improvement of literature and the encouragement of the learned natives of India" in the Charter Act of 1813.[8] Not until 1883 are any women recorded as passing the B.A. at Calcutta University. This does not mean that certain images of woman or the feminine were unimportant to English interests. Without explicitly singling out women for educational reform, however, government policy implicated its male students in gendered behavior in interesting and contradictory ways. When we begin to examine the complications of gender markings and their appropriations by English and Indians within the history of their colonial engagement, new alignments suggest themselves that cut across more static and traditional oppositions of the differences between East and West, ruler and ruled, male and female. Although I do not disagree with Chatterjee, I find it productive to complicate his argument by passing it through the optic of literature. Were nationalist reformers wholly successful in resisting contamination of the subjective, inner space of Bengali identity by European ideology? Were European ideologies of the political and the cultural spheres themselves so clear cut, or not crucially ambivalent on questions of gender? Did the cultural expressions available in the newly emerging discourse of literature in colonial India faithfully reproduce the representations of gender found in either English educational institutions or in the discourse of official nationalism? We should perhaps begin with a new provocation: If Bengali nationalist discourse settled "the women's question" to its own satisfaction for its own pragmatic ends, the displacement of this question onto the cultural sphere—the realm of the home and its working out in the sensitive realm of the literary—may have reactivated its tensions.

In order to do so, it is first necessary to make a point about literature that is often overlooked in the histories of its development both in Europe and India. Although many attempts to define the nature of literature have been made throughout the English tradition, the practice of definition became almost obsessive during exactly this phase of England's domination of India, what in English studies is usually termed the romantic period. According to Raymond Williams, the transition within English usage from "literate" to "literary," from a condition of being well read to the acquisition of distinct qualities of taste and perception in the matter that is being read, is manifestly a development of the late eighteenth to early nineteenth centuries. According to Williams's definition, the distinct form of textual practice we now call literature arises within a very definite type of capitalist modernity when certain mechanisms of private property, mechanical reproduction, leisure time, market dynamics, and nationalist aspirations conspire to create a unique new form of textuality to which properties of "literariness" can be attributed.[9] To extend this definition to Chatterjee's framework, the very concept of literature in this period is intertwined with that of the rapidly expanding public sphere of discussion and debate—increasingly conducted in print—against which literature often became defined as a counterspace of interiority, private contemplation, self-expression, and inner creativity. But since the private sphere arises only in distinction to the increasingly invoked notion of the public (such as is conveyed in democratic institutions, trade unions, newspapers and publishing houses, and the other institutional apparatuses of communication that characterize modernity in Habermas's sense[10]), it is only in and through the notion of the public that it can be articulated. Rather than using purely formal efforts to deduce the prevalence of certain rhetorical figures or other forms of linguistic usage as the provenance of the literary, Williams usefully shifts the discussion toward a contextual approach in which the idea of literature can be seen to emerge in relation to an increasingly cluttered and codified world of public discourse, and to which it then forms something like an antidote. Thus the romantic elevation of the process of individual creativity, for example, or the theorization of the symbol as the organic, harmonious reconciliation of word and thing, subject and object, can be read as imaginative resolutions to actual social contradictions: to the loss of individuality in mass commodity production, on the one hand, and to the technological domination of nature and the alienating effects of urbanization on the other. The very idea of literature can be interpreted as an imaginary relation to real conditions of existence, a kind of fantasy of wholeness and organicity when such notions are increasingly under attack in the world outside.[11]

Terry Eagleton's complementary account of "the rise of English" in this period illustrates how such values became concretized in national institutions. According to Eagleton, English literature became institutionalized as a university discipline through a complex series of transformations in which the new definitions of literature proved remarkably flexible in accommodating the increasingly severe antagonisms within English modernization. The emerging themes of individuality and interiority emerging in discussions of the romantic symbol, coupled with the very public anxiety over the failure of religion and the increasing class stratification brought about by industrialization, produced a discursive field perfectly suited to the amelioration of such tensions within the ongoing discussion of English national destiny.[12] "Literature [as such] does not exist"; it is rather a category that is invented or produced through competing definitions of intellectual property and identity. Following Williams, Eagleton asserts that our modern definition of literature begins to take hold somewhere between the philosophical exploration of "literariness" as intense performances of individual subjectivity in the romantic period and the actual implementation in schools of a subject called English literature in the 1860s. Although the story begins in the late eighteenth century, the concept of literature does not really come into being in England until Matthew Arnold sets out to "Hellenize" the middle classes by calling for the establishment of national institutions of culture in the second half of the nineteenth century. Arnold saw English literature as "the poor man's classics," a substitute for the moral and philosophical truths learned through higher education, now available for wider consumption by those who could not be expected to study Latin and Greek. The creation of English literature became a socially interested means of cultivating a common "inner life" when the appeal to religion began to seem irrelevant in holding the nation together, and of healing the individual's alienation from the realm of nature when mechanized commodity production replaced the organic relations of worker, object, and community. As in Williams, there is no necessary essence of literature: The supposed autonomy of private life, which literature is often seen to immediately "express," is reciprocally linked to the changing needs of the public. More radically, Eagleton's argument proposes that literature is in fact a tool of social regulation, a concept invented as a disciplinary subject by reformers to secure the compliance of disparate groups to the very idea of England.

This contextualist approach to understanding literature has distinct advantages over the art-for-art's-sake definition that would characterize the study of literature as creative expression or disinterested contemplation. It elides one crucial historical development, however. As Gauri Viswanathan has shown, to put it bluntly, English literature as a discipline was invented in India. Between the romantic doctrine of the symbol, which in the early 1800s elevated the idea of literature into something "gloriously useless, an 'end in itself' loftily removed from any sordid social purpose,"[13] and the actual institution of English literature as a discipline that served to congeal the organic homogeneity of the English nation in workers' colleges, women's schools, and much later in the universities, Eagleton leaves a gap of some sixty years that his story does not fill. The history of the beginnings of English literary education in India sheds light on the use of the concept not only in India but in England as well.

Romancing the Empire

Thirty years before Arnold's call to arms in the 1860s, an attempt was made to anglicize the educational institutions in India supported by revenues of the East India Company and, in doing so, as some protested at the time, to "annihilat[e] . . . all the languages of India, vernacular or classical."[14] The reformers' dreams of "the universal use of our native tongue throughout the East"[15] were prompted by that oft-repeated code of early English imperialism, "improvement," but improvement of a particular kind. In contrast to earlier utilitarian aspirations put forth by such prominent thinkers as Jeremy Bentham and James Mill to undertake a wholesale renovation of Indian society according to the radical reform of its legal, political, and economic systems, liberal reformers of the 1830s proposed a softer method of improvement that relied first of all on generating sympathy between the native subjects and the aims and intentions of the "benevolent despotism" of colonial rule. This would occur, in short, through emulation of the great examples of the Englishmen before them. Improvement by example implied that the uplift of Indian civilization from what they considered its stagnant condition could be effected most simply by its adopting the habits, morals, and values of England through education. For twenty years, debate raged over the most expeditious means to effect this result, usually boiling down to how to best employ the funds allotted for the purpose. With surprising consistency, both those who argued in favor of anglicization and those who opposed it agreed that the general aim of education in India ought to be a gradual, internal improvement of customs, manners, and learning effected through the promotion of feelings of attachment and emulation among the ruled for their rulers.

In 1835, Thomas Babington Macaulay penned the infamous lines that were to direct the English educational policy in India for two decades. The purpose of education, he wrote, should be to "form a class who may be interpreters between us and the millions whom we govern; a class of persons, Indian in blood and colour, but English in taste, in opinions, in morals, and in intellect."[16] The most effective way to inculcate English tastes, opinions, morals, and intellect was through the study of English literature. "Literature" in the colony was by no means a stable term, as it was not in England at the time, and the fact that it was almost obsessively invoked within the debates on education points to the force it wielded on behalf of competing claims to power, culture, civilization, and freedom. One thing is fairly constant between these claims: English literature, whatever that is, was seen as the indispensable tool used to create this class of persons designed to become the internal rulers of India. Those who sought to define and use the term were romantic both in their period and in their inclinations, but the definitions they produced oscillated between various poles of the romantic literary legacy.

Macaulay thought his object could be attained exclusively through the medium of the English language, and one month after his speech to the Committee on Public Instruction in Calcutta, Governor-General William Bentinck signed the proposal into effect by redirecting all the company's revenues allotted for education to the promotion of English alone: The "great object of the Government ought to be the promotion of European literature and science among the natives of India; and . . . all the funds appropriated for the purpose of education would be best employed on English education alone."[17] Macaulay's was not a lone voice, nor was Bentinck's decision uncontested. Debate simmered for several years between India and England in what has come to be called the Anglicist-Orientalist controversy. Several longstanding members of the committee resigned in protest, and Macaulay himself threatened resignation if his proposal was not adopted. Noted Orientalists predicted insurrection in the countryside if government subsidies to education in the native languages were suspended and foresaw with dread the "annihilation of all the languages of India, vernacular or classical, and the universal use of our native tongue throughout the East." (Charles Trevelyan himself had recommended a plan to romanize the scripts of the Indian languages.) H. H. Wilson wrote in disgust, "The measures . . . appear to me to involve the most mischievous consequences: impressing upon the minds of the natives the conviction that they and their rulers have conflicting feelings and incompatible interests,—contributing to destroy their respect for the British character, which, it appears from recent melancholy events, has lost already much of its weight in native estimation, and tending to defeat the very purpose in view,—to retard indefinitely, if not altogether to prevent, the intellectual, moral, and religious improvement of the people of India."[18]

John Stuart Mill agreed, and in spring or summer 1836 he penned a dispatch, "Recent Changes in Native Education,"[19] that strongly rebuked Macaulay and the committee for reversing the "cautious and deliberate measures" the company had taken for years to achieve "a great public end."[20] In a letter to Henry Taylor he referred to Macaulay as a "coxcombical dillettante litterateur who never did a thing for a practical object in his life," and who had "upset in a week" the plans of decades. Mill's dispatch, however, was never sent, and the Bentinck Resolution effectively directed educational policy until the Despatch of 1854 substantially widened the scope of instruction and reverted its priorities more in line with the intentions of Mill and the Orientalists. With surprising consistency, both those who argued in favor of anglicization and those who opposed it agreed that the general aim of education in India ought to be a gradual, internal improvement of native customs by promoting feelings of attachment and emulation among the ruled for their rulers. I will return to Mill's intentions in a moment. But first it is worth recalling Macaulay's pronouncements, for they direct us to a definition of literature that informs all subsequent accounts of the subject in India: "A single shelf of a good European library was worth the whole native literature of India and Arabia" (*MIE,* 241). "Whoever knows that language, has ready access to all the vast intellectual wealth, which all the wisest nations of the earth have created and hoarded in the course of ninety generations. It may be safely said that the literature now extant in that language is of far greater value than all the literature which three hundred years ago was extant in all the languages of the world together. *Nor is that all*" (*MIE*, 242, my emphasis). Beyond the sublime bigotry and ignorance that informs these statements, a larger conceptual horizon is apparent that meshes interestingly with Williams's descriptions of the romantic period. Among the most complex ideologies of romantic "literariness" is the competing claim that literature simultaneously captures the fullness of life ("full, central, immediate human experience," as Williams phrases it) while being also able to transcend life ("access to a truth 'higher' or 'deeper' than 'scientific' or 'objective' or 'everyday' reality"). Macaulay does both. In his words, English literature

> abounds with works of imagination not inferior to the noblest which Greece has bequeathed to us; with models of every species of eloquence; with historical compositions, which, considered merely as narratives, have seldom been surpassed, and which, considered as vehicles of ethical and political instruction, have never been equalled; with just and lively representations of human life and human nature; with the most profound speculations on metaphysics, morals, government, jurisprudence, and trade; with full and correct information respecting every experimental science which tends to preserve the health, to increase the comfort, or to expand the intellect of man. (*MIE*, 241–242)

And this is the justification for India's necessary submission. English literature proves the superiority of English civilization; India's historic mission will be to experience "revival" at this vivifying touch. Indeed, the sun cannot possibly set on such a panorama.

It is interesting here that histories can be read *either* as "narratives" *or* as "ethical and political instruction"; they work both ways. Both "just and lively" *and* profoundly speculative, Macaulay's definition of English literature harmoniously reconciles empirical reality with revealed truth into a unified entity reminiscent of some descriptions of the romantic symbol. English literature is literally everything to Macaulay, combining the highest degree of empirical accuracy with the profoundest sense of spiritual "depth." But according to Mill, this was not at all what England wanted to confer on India. The mission was much more modest and the process, more discreet. It was true that India needed improvement, but before that could occur it needed love. Whereas Macaulay thought in terms of educating individuals, Mill's inclination was to create communities.

Macaulay missed the point even though his rhetoric carried the day. It was the other Coleridge whom Mill endorsed in his great plan for India, the conservative social thinker who elucidated the irrational bases of sympathetic connection among the people that neither utilitarian social theory nor romantic arrogance could account for. Mill did not want transcendence, he wanted compliance. In two remarkable essays published in 1838 and 1840, he worked out this conception of culture more fully in the context of the English nation. In Coleridge's theory and practice of history in *The Constitution of the Church and State*, according to Mill, the value of empirical knowledge was secondary to the feeling of sympathetic connection that the narrative generates. The problem with older utilitarian notions for reforming India, such as those of his father and Jeremy Bentham, was that they lacked that special faculty of imagination "which enables us, by a voluntary effort, to conceive the absent as if it were present, the imaginary as if it were real, and to clothe it in the feelings which, if it were indeed real, it would bring along with it. This is the power by which one human being enters into the mind and circumstances of another."[21] This was to be the goal of literary education in India: not the "supererogatory harmonizing of the cognitive faculties,"[22] as Michael Sprinker has described the romantic symbol, but rather the other romantic legacy that could generate "imagined communities" from the stories and legends of a people's common history. Coleridge's particular contribution to the contemporary definition of literature was to illustrate the "connaturaleness" of English law and history with the genius of the English people; in this way, according to Mill, he has "at once given history, even to the imagination, an interest like romance, and afforded the only means of predicting and guiding the future, by unfolding the agencies which have produced and still maintain the Present" (*BC*, 131). Teaching the history of the nation to its citizens in the pleasing form of literature is an integral part of the "national education," the ineffable stuff that holds the nation together, "at once the principal cause of its permanence as a society, and the chief source of its progressiveness" (*BC*, 132). Coleridge's historicism, it is worth emphasizing, is valued not so much for its "accuracy" about the past but for its ability to impart a sense of meaningfulness to the nation by ordering historical facts into sequences of cause and effects and, in this sequential narration, to vividly illustrate to people their "intelligible place in the gradual evolution of humanity" (*BC*, 132). The value of Coleridge's insight, as applied to teaching English in India, is thus not the innate superiority of the Western learning, as Macaulay would have it, but the possibility of generating emotional cohesion between the empire and its subject-peoples, a possibility afforded by the sense of a common history and destiny such as can be generated in sentimental romances.

Compare this to Wilson's arguments for the continued instruction of Oriental languages at government schools and for the limited but crucial role of English literature in Indian education. "It is highly desirable to encourage the resort of students from the villages and provinces [to schools as a] means of becoming acquainted with the persons, character, or conduct of the ruling authorities. Hitherto . . . they have seen close at hand the principles and practice of English sway, and they have been brought into personal intercourse with many of its principal functionaries,—an intercourse which as yet has tended to dissipate prejudice, attract confidence, and beget affection, and which has sent forth hundreds of well-instructed young men to disseminate similar feelings amongst their countrymen" (*ENI*, 4). Macaulay too stresses the exposure of Indians to English example as fostering a desirable connection; only for him, this exposure could be greatly multiplied and carefully controlled in the form of the English book. As Trevelyan put it, "The Indians daily converse with the best and wisest Englishmen through the medium of their works, and form ideas, perhaps higher ideas of our nation than if their intercourse were of a more personal kind."[23] To the Anglicist mind, as Vishwanathan asserts, "the English literary text functioned as a surrogate Englishman in his highest and most perfect state."[24]

But Wilson's idea was rather more ingenious, as Mill agreed in a letter commending him several months later.[25] Beyond this positive personal contact, writes Wilson,

> it is . . . vain to seek to extend very widely a profound acquaintance with English literature. . . . Yet it may be so cultivated . . . by assisting in . . . the formation of an indigenous literature. It is not by the English language that we can enlighten the people of India; it can be effected only through the forms of speech which they already understand and use. These must be applied to the purpose . . . by the presentation of European facts, opinions, and sentiments, in an original native garb. . . . [We must] *give to the people of India a literature of their own, the legitimate progeny of that of England, the living resemblance, though not the servile copy, of its parent.* . . . We shall never wean them . . . from the congenial imagery and sentiments of their poetry. (*ENI*, 12–14, my emphasis)

"Original native garb" is a particularly apt phrase here, for the Indianized English literature intended is far from unique, new, or distinctive. Wilson's conception of an original literature is closer to the illusory feeling of autonomy generated by the simulacrum in Plato's allegory of the cave. For this practice of literature, "freely entered into" is in reality a gift of servitude in which Indian consciousness and identity is designed to be mirrored back from an English "original," over which the Indian material is merely "native garb." For Mill, Wilson's improvement upon the principles of Macaulay and Trevelyan is located precisely in the difference between surrogate and new creation. In Trevelyan, the synonomy between English man and English book is too close; it cannot account for the barely perceptible slide between copying and re-presentation, the rearticulated shadow of English meaning that is produced anew in the act of articulation.[26] Mill agrees that the mere "servile copy," or too-close aping of English manners, is undesirable in forming the ultimate act of emulation; what must be elicited from the native is precisely the difference of his own speech in an original production of meaning.

The oddity of this unnerving intention pervades Mill's language, which guiltily shadow's Wilson's in his official-dispatch draft. He agrees (without referring to Wilson) that among the primary virtues of subsidizing education in India is the opportunity for Indians to meet Englishmen face-to-face: "It is highly desirable to encourage such resort [of students to schools, who develop a] feeling of gratitude towards the Government, and to a knowledge of the British character."[27] Wilson considers the project of importing "English literature along with English cottons into Bengal chimerical and ridiculous. If the people are to have a literature, it must be their own. The stuff may be in a great degree European, but it must be freely interwoven with home-spun materials, and the fashion must be Asiatic" (*ENI,* 14) Mill concurs. "It is altogether chimerical to expect that the main portion of the mental cultivation of a people can take place through the medium of a foreign language." Indian scholars superficially trained in English can have "no taste for our literature, no participation in our sentiments, no impression of our principles. . . . We cannot expect any extensive or solid improvement from the multiplication of this class of English scholars."[28] His final recommendation is as uncharacteristic of English policy as it is effective, as strange as Wilson's advocacy that Indians should write even more of their superstitious nonsense. Mill indeed advocates a large-scale transfusion of European thought into the colony, but gradualness will be the surest guarantee of its effectiveness. In helping to promote the development of a European-based Indian literature, "the legitimate progeny of . . . England," Mill is cautiously ambivalent. "We direct your attention to this object as one of the highest importance, although it is one in which little, we think, can be for some time effected, beyond the encouragement of *independent and voluntary exertion.* In this, however, much discretion is requisite, as original works adapted to the taste of the natives and to their wants are scarcely to be procured. . . . It is premature to lay down any rules for systematic translation, and the committee in the promotion of this part of their work must rather follow than lead the demands of the native public."[29] Strikingly, Mill is willing to temporarily sacrifice control in order to provoke an authentic native voice. Exertion is more effective than coercion; the practice of *making* literature, of voluntarily entering into the reproductive labor of imitation to produce a "living resemblance" would be the truest act of submission to improving principles.

One such "native voice" is articulated in the person of Calla Chand Bose, a fellowship student at Hooghly College in 1846. Responding to an examination question on "the tendency of literature to improve and elevate the mind, with especial reference to the benefits now resulting to this country from the diffusion of English Literature," Bose writes:

> As an instrument of civilization, literature is the most effectual means of refining the manners and customs of a people. It softens their disposition, represses their most rancorous feelings, and awakens sympathy with generous conduct. It teaches men to feel for others' distresses. No science . . . has ever drawn a tear. . . . While on the contrary, a beautiful pathetic poem can instantaneously excite our most benevolent feelings, move charity in the highest sense of the word, and, as it were, melt our heart at the miseries of our fellow beings. . . . Indeed, if there is any one class of instructions that is alone able to effect the mental development of the youthful reader, it is literature.[30]

"Sympathy," "feeling," and "charity" are the highest rewards of literary acculturation, emoluments far removed from the sublime visions of romantic poetry. Does this statement indicate the "success" of a colonizing intention? Indeed, it could be read against the grain to elicit a kind of ironic mimicry and distortion of the government's stated position. Yet dependent as he is on its patronage for the subsidy of his education, what else could this student say?

If one wished to examine the rewriting of vernacular history occurring under these auspices, one could turn to Bankimchandra Chatterjee's statements on the history of Bengali literature, written in 1870. Bankimchandra reiterates the Orientalist feminization and racialization of the Indian past when he disparages the pre-English Bengali vernacular for its lack of "manly feeling—of *womanly* feeling there is a great deal" and denounces the nationalist icon, Jayadeva,[31] as "the poet of an effeminate and sensual race. . . . His exquisitely sounding but not unfrequently meaningless verse echoed the common sentiments of an inactive and effeminate race. And since then all Bengalis who have ventured on original composition have followed in his footsteps."[32] Not only does Bankimchandra rewrite the history of Bengali literature as a narrative of cause and effect[33] but, more tellingly, he summarizes and discards traditional Indian literature by feminizing it in contrast to the manly vigor associated with modern European rationality. In fact, according to Bankimchandra, most of precolonial Bengali culture exhibited such effeminacy (one exception being the Nyaya system of philosophy, which never reached the masses), and he conclusively identifies effeminacy as the overriding cultural habit of Bengal under Mughal rule. "Indolent habits and a feeble moral organization gave birth to an effeminate poetical literature; and then for ages the country fed and nourished itself on that effeminate literature."[34] He sees Bengalis coming into their own as a virile "race" only in the nineteenth century. Because of their weak past, however, they can be as yet only the vehicles rather than the beneficiaries of European improvement: "It is possible to imagine that the Bengalis . . . are now doing a great work, by, so to speak, acclimatising European ideas and fitting them for reception hereafter by the hardier and more original races of Northern India." Bengalis are the "Italians of Asia," similarly "supple and pliant," and through them, "the revival of learning" in India will begin.[35] Of course Bankimchandra's statements are polemical; if we read them as a reaction to the educational program, they seem self-conscious, rhetorical rejoinders to the overt intentions of the colonial mission.

Such evidence constitutes a matrix of acceptance for the interpellative calls of literature and urges us to rethink the history of modern Bengali literature in terms of romance. Traditional literary histories of Bengal ascribe a large influence of English ideas to the development of modern Bengali prose forms. None, to my knowledge, have traced the continuity of the theme of romantic attraction, and its ironic appropriation, through this history. Chatterjee claims that Bengali modernity selectively appropriated European influence through an "ideological sieve" that allowed it to posit its identity "on a difference with the perceived forms of cultural modernity in the West."[36] In the semimodern realm of literature, I would argue, it is possible to observe a surprising degree of negotiation with the dominant forms through which this cultural modernity was presented and mobilized in the colony, a negotiation that in some cases registered the aims and intentions of English acculturation perhaps even more explicitly than stated by English reformers themselves.

Before returning to a more recognizable definition of literature, it is necessary to make another amendment to the concepts posited by Williams and Eagleton. Just as their contextual definitions of literature neglected to account for the historic place of empire, their arguments equally elide the role of gender in defining its function as a discourse of national consolidation. The gendering of literature in England in the period also affected its function in the colony. As Nancy Armstrong has observed, the image of the middle-class English woman formed a crucial site of national cohesion during this same period, both within and by means of fiction. Certain representations of women as figures of domestic stability and familial love became instrumental to fostering the romantic connections through which Englishness could assert itself as a national force: "The power of the middle classes had everything to do with that of middle class love. . . . Middle class authority rested in large part upon the authority that novels attributed to women and in this way designated as specifically female."[37] To view the rhetoric of reform in Indian education in the 1830s as a part of this gendered romance, to see the construction of "a class of . . . interpreters" as influenced by the construction of middle-class domesticity in England, will necessarily complicate Chatterjee's separation of colonial Bengali culture into public and private spheres. Literature as a category is ambiguous and flexible in this period, as we have seen, and part of its very definition includes crossing the divide between home and world. Before Indian nationalist thinkers in the late nineteenth century strategically decided to further demarcate these two realms of culture, English educational ideology had done much to unite them, positing the "world" of public, political debate very much within the province of "culture" and "the literary," since it was in and through literary education that the Bengali male was to receive his primary lessons in the emulation of English society. The statements of educators such as Macaulay, Wilson, and Mill, despite their differences, emphasized literature's ability to create romantic bonds of attraction in the colonial relationship and, in doing so, to propagate a kind of colonial domesticity or middle-class love in India.

In what follows, I read the figure of romance by a dual logic. I began by examining the use of love in the construction of power. What I want to explore further is the contradictory movement by which the literary romance genre, one of the preeminent forms practiced by Indian writers in the nineteenth century, got taken up in a concerted attempt to reproduce the bonds of affection cultivated through literature between the colonizer and the colonized, but now for alternate ends. Indian romance will began from the premise of identity rather than hierarchy—an identity that, because of its construction within the anxious gaze of imperial power, is both racialized and sexualized as a second-class subject in its own homeland. Romance in this sense will be read as both genre and ideology—both as the irrational logic of connection that binds communities in acts of mutual concern and as the formal means by which this imaginary connection is narrativized in the minds of countless and dispersed subjects who, as in Benedict Anderson's "imagined community," never have the opportunity of meeting face-to-face. Thus my analysis shifts to consider themes of more general sociohistorical importance. When and how is the romance genre and its ideology of national connection established in the colony? How is the sense of romantic connection in nationalism overdetermined by the gender hierarchy inscribed at its origin in the imperial romance? How does literature promote expressions of love alongside the fact of domination, and how can that love be turned against the dominating object of its attraction?

Heterosexual love has of course long been seen by Western feminists as a relationship of domination, most pointedly in the material inequalities of women's work and social reproduction, no less so in the phallocentrism of the symbolic order. It has become something of a cliché to see the colonial relationship as a replication of this gendered inequality. The imperial romance, introduced into India through English education and the translation of European classics into the vernacular languages, and designed to elicit "a literature of their own," was explicitly formulated as a vertical bond of love that essentially reproduced the hierarchy of male dominance in modern European patriarchy. This argument encounters an important asymmetry in actual practice, however: In the colony, literary love had more to do with relations between English and Indian men than with the "proper" heterosexist script of domestic fiction.[38] The educational programs, manuals, and fictions designed to train English women into acceptable domesticity that Armstrong cites had close correlates, directed toward both men and women in Bengal, as Chatterjee and Dipesh Chakrabarty have recently explored.[39] Appropriately, these manuals often advocated behavior that could reconcile the demands of European conceptions of time and work in the world while preserving the sanctity of tradition in the home. But if the public sphere of English education, bureaucratic service, and political debate was already fashioned as a realm of imperial romance between English and Indian men, what did that imply for gender roles in the world? And how were Indian men to behave in the household if their education itself dictated concerns of emotional sympathy, connection, and obedience, attributes of modern European domesticity nominally feminized within the English tradition? If men's training in English morals, opinions, and intellect was originally intended to operate on the hearts as much as on the minds of colonized subjects, how strongly did that training determine the eventual shape of the public sphere? If indeed we can follow Armstrong in believing that the English novel originated as part of a program to construct middle-class domesticity through affectionate, national connections, how did it differ in acculturating the Indian male into his role as second-class citizen of the empire?

It is important to recognize the acute differences between the colonial relationship and the gender hierarchy of modern European patriarchy. The imperial romance assigns gender markings within the overdetermined relationship of a tacit economic and military dominance and alongside the contradictory assignments of "race" (the Westernized Oriental Gentleman). In the process, identifications that might seem self-evident in the European context become troubled. Colonial Indian subjects are feminized in their innate poeticalness: If however, as Trevelyan writes, "their highest ambition is to resemble us,"[40] how exactly are they to resemble their masculine colonial masters? How closely do Indians aspire to resemble the English when simultaneously admonished that they can never be English? What happens to the English self-image when it confronts this distorted resemblance? Perhaps Macaulay was not being merely rhetorical when he exhorted this "class of persons" to be *both* "Indian in blood and colour" *and* "English in intellect," a dual subject designed to constitute itself as both itself and as other, both "resembling" European masculinity while accepting the charge to remain secondary. The colonial subject interpellated by the affectionate discourse of English literature in the imperial romance is directed to occupy conflicting positions: both English *and* Indian, resembling but not being, masculine *and* feminine, symbolically split along the age-old axis of the body and the mind. Where Homi Bhabha cites the fracturing of authority in its construction of the "racist stereotype—the simian Negro, the effeminate Asiatic male—which ambivalently fix identity as the fantasy of difference,"[41] he outlines a central structure of address that, however, neglects to mention the ambivalence of gender attribution and its repercussions for mimicry, the appropriation of and resistance to the call of imperial romance. For colonial authority also produces a gendered supplement in its disavowal of the instability of power, an addition that returns with a difference in the act of enunciation. The imperial romance in India was designed to exact submission among its subjects by advocating a domesticated, middle-class love through the exaggerated reinstatement of the hierarchy of masculine dominance at the core of modern European patriarchy. What this meant for its Indian subjects was another matter.

Romancing the Nation

> *Before this Bankim's pen had produced . . .* kahinis, *which in English they call romances. The background of these romances was very far away from our everyday life.*
>
> —Rabindranath Tagore[42]

When Indian nationalists turned their attention toward creating the imagined community of India in the second half of the nineteenth century, like their English educators before them, they seized on the romance genre as a privileged vehicle of national integration. Given the rules of the game, however, by which in the preceding half-century the importation of English ideas had already established to some extent a public sphere of newspapers, textbooks, publishing houses, and distribution networks resulting in the creation of something like a national taste with a reading audience (however small) whose preferences were dictated by Europe, the vernacular romance was forced to work within a channel already deeply cut. The colonial romance (as I term its indigenized version) soon became an effective form in which to provoke a *rhetorical* challenge to English imperialism. In the absence of a popular mobilization against foreign rule, it could do little more than that. The fascinating challenge to this form of nationalist literature, from the perspective of gender, was that the romance mode itself was a European import that had already been used to inspire a hierarchical attraction between the colonizers and the colonized. Colonial romance, in contrast, was compelled to forge its connections horizontally. In the terms dictated by the imperial romance, this implied (logically if not practically) a relation of feminine to feminine. Unlike the new middle-class domesticity under construction in the English novel, which attempted to instate imaginative principles of heterosexual reciprocity and reproduction, the colonial romance began from a different premise: European heterosexist laws of reproduction had already scripted the literary Asian male as feminine subordinate, and any answer to the question of native solidarity at the national level had to take the instability of that representation into account.

The great popularity of the romance novel among the Bengali reading public is established in both numerical and personal accounts.[43] The importance of registering the appearance of genres such as the romance within the Bengali literary system is that the repetition and regulation implied by genre attests to a certain standard in the construction of a public "taste." As Fredric Jameson asserts, "Genres are essentially literary *institutions,* or social contracts between a writer and a specific public, whose function is to specify the proper use of a particular cultural artifact."[44] Vincent Leitch has recently reiterated the importance of genre study for a poststructuralist literary criticism, arguing that "because genres amalgamate linguistic and social with literary conventions, they are linked with social formations, including the institutional and ideological elements of such formations."[45] Within the colonial context, the appearance of recognizable European genres in vernacular form gives us some indication of the extent of import and absorption of foreign literary conventions into the vernacular tradition, and of the influence of imported literary conventions on the formation of the Bengali readership. Thus the emergence of European generic classifications signifies not merely an idiosyncratic mimicry of styles by certain authors but also the development of a readership dictating to some extent the kinds of literary entertainment and instruction it expects to receive. The rise of recognizable European genres from within the experimental registers of Bengali prose around the middle of the century, I would argue, marks a structural and institutional appropriation of European ideology that indicates a far wider audience for the reception of European forms than that generated by the adoption of either the English language or European content alone. It also indicates a wider audience than reached by formal English-style schooling, for the vernacularized romance is now available to anyone who can read or can hear the new literature read aloud, a tremendously important consideration in a society whose literacy rate hovered at less than 10 percent in the period under consideration. The emergence of the European romance genre within the Bengali vernacular thus takes us simultaneously in two directions: toward a quantitative increase in the interpellative possibilities for European ideas and toward the possibility for mobilizing those ideas for alternate ends. The rise of romance does not of course imply the extinction of older popular traditions within the production of Bengali literature. What it does signify is the definitive emergence of a new cultural mode that would struggle with and eventually supplant the dominance of the precolonial tradition by the end of the century.[46]

By the early 1860s, the romance genre began to make itself available for literary appropriation to later generations of English-educated Bengalis. Bankimchandra, an avid reader of Mill,[47] self-consciously employed the romance theme to generate a particular vision of Indian history in which bold pictures of vanished Hindu glory would reawaken the martial spirit (*bahubol*) of a defeated "race." Much as literature had been used to generate cohesion among the middle classes in England and much as it was being used to forge sympathy between the colonizers and the colonized, Bankim reinvented it for an alternate nationalist purpose, "to speak to the masses in the language which they understand."[48] In attempting to foster a sense of unity among the readers of the Bengali language, Bankim mobilized a strategy for national cohesion that had been in use in India for the preceding sixty years: Solidify the identities, reify the types, and present, as forcefully as possible, those images "which enable . . . us, by a voluntary effort, to conceive the absent as if it were present, the imaginary as if it were real, and to clothe it in the feelings which, if it were indeed real, it would bring along with it."[49]

Bankim's picture of the nation and his conception of literature within it, enunciated from his first Bengali novel, *Durgeshnandini* (1865), to his last, *Sitaram* (1887), is a decidedly militarist and masculinist construction that combines the moral firmness of the neo-Hinduism emerging after the Sepoy Mutiny with secular English science and efficiency, a combination to be realized in the world by rhetoric, persuasion, intellectual and verbal force. Paradoxically, however, and in fascinating anticipation of the present-day spectacle of avenging feminine deities thrown up by Hindutva, Bankim frequently vested this rhetorical combination in the historically "impossible" female characters of his romance novels—the preternaturally cunning and resourceful Bimala of *Durgeshnandini,* the stealth-warrior Shanti of *Anandamath,* and the self-disciplined captain of robber bands in the eponymous heroine of *Devi Chaudhurani,* to name only a few—in a willful disregard for the real constraints of colonial power, much less the traditional degredation of women supposedly found in Hindu scripture. These romance heroines are larger than life and, despite vague references to their representative stature in some vanished era of Bengali autonomy, were as impossible to realize as exemplary models of action under British colonialism as they were in any historical past on record. Bankim instead invented a "usable past" for these idealized figures that combined images of conservative Hindu tradition with an old staple of the English educational program: romance.

With some historicization, the canonical typology of literary forms given in Northrop Frye's *Anatomy of Criticism* can be adapted across cultures as a useful tool of reference for categorizing large-scale literary structures. Precisely because Frye's system is so reductive and noncontextual, its classifying procedures can be moved between cultures with relative ease. The dangers of such application are in many ways obvious: There is nothing to be gained, and much to be lost, from orientalizing gestures that reduce substantial differences to recurrences of the same. If genre is to remain a useful category of literary analysis, however, especially in the context of an acculturation process as deep as England attempted in India, Frye's panorama of forms is almost inescapable in registering degrees of compliance and deviation from the English intention to create "a literature of their own."

Romance for Frye is among the most elemental narrative forms, mobilizing natural and supernatural forces rather than historically specific individuals. "The enemy is associated with winter, darkness, confusion, sterility, moribund life and old age, and the hero with spring, dawn, order, fertility, vigor and youth."[50] The anthropomorphized hero of romance, according to Frye, is a projection of these antinomies (winter vs. spring, good vs. evil) onto human form. Romance is distinguished from the older form of myth by markedly different conceptions of temporality and agency, namely its entrance into secular time and its concretization of the amorphous and presubjective actors of myth—the wily coyotes and protean tricksters—into stable hierarchies of value, suggesting that this genre, in contrast to myth, takes an active role in transforming the world rather than merely explaining it. In romance, the binary oppositions of myth take on solid and dependable "characters" in the world. In this social projection, as Jameson glosses Frye's account, romance functions as "a wish-fulfillment or Utopian fantasy which aims at the transfiguration of the world of everyday life in such a way as to restore the conditions of some lost Eden, or to anticipate a future realm from which the old mortality and imperfections will have been effaced. Romance, therefore, does not involve the substitution of some more ideal realm for ordinary reality . . . but rather a process of *transforming* ordinary reality."[51] The adventures and resolutions of romance in the Western tradition then, most obviously in the Old Testament quest romance of the Promised Land, as in the coming of the Messiah, the grail quest of the Middle Ages, or even the search for buried treasure "from the Siegfried cycle to *Nostromo*,"[52] all signify for Frye various permutations of an internal or moral struggle between forces projected onto the world. Romance heros are thus like the characters of myth, physical embodiments of the ethical priorities that organize and define a given social structure, but their autonomy is much more limited by the environment through which they pass. The resistance of nature pulls at their daring exploits, constraining the pure mutability of myth and forcing it to conform in greater degree to actual circumstances.

In this sense, romance is a more modern form of storytelling than myth, since it is put in a world that looks almost real. It resembles myth in its representation of a prehistorical, decentered world of forces clashing in irrational, often magical, ways; but unlike myth it projects these forces onto determinate circumstances that begin to look something like history. Indeed, as Jameson reminds us, the early romances in the European tradition bear an "intimate relationship to those historical periods sometimes designated 'the time of troubles,' in which central authority disappears and marauding bands of robbers and brigands range . . . with impunity."[53] In such instances, the narrative structure of romance takes shape to facilitate the identification and differentiation of centralized communities from barbarian outsiders, validating "the good" in contradistinction to ethical practices that are "not ours." When, however, the immediate threat of outside aggression has passed and the community begins to solidify into something like a class, romance finds itself with a new contradiction to resolve: Now "beyond good and evil," it must learn to renegotiate its discriminating tendencies within the very group solidarity it has helped to produce. Thus, Jameson asserts, "The seme of evil can no longer be permanently assigned or attached to this or that human agent, [and] it must find itself expelled from the realm of interpersonal or inner-worldly relations."[54] At this point the ethical investment is relocated into the magical world of fairy-tale sorcery and fantastic landscapes, those imaginary topoi of an enchanted world that themselves seem to play out the tensions of ethical decision even more fully than the "naive and bewildered" characters who pass through them. In this way, the enchanted world of romance can be seen as the physical embodiment of the history that the group has just endured; its ethics are concretized "in nature," in a frozen and simulated version of the story that has brought it to this point. The romance world itself is the perfect invented tradition, as the naturalized world seems to play out the decisions that the group has projected back as the explaining narration of its past.

Bankim's novels take their place by purely formal criteria—along with the adventure plots, authorial interruptions, archaic Sanskrit diction, and other classic markers—within the romance genre. His complex use of this mode shows it thematically straddling the two periods of its European development outlined previously, both sharply defining communities of the good from dangerous others and beginning the internal differentiation of the in-group itself. That he chose to write in the romance form in these novels rather than attempting to imitate the contemporary European fashions available to him in Dickens or Balzac suggests a more developed understanding of genre than those who criticize him for moralizing, didacticism, unreality, or any of the other sins of not being European enough.[55] Bankim's decision to appropriate the romance mode rather than some other genre, such as the scientific pretensions of classic Western realism, was influenced more by the prior "success" of imperial romance than by the availability of countermodels. Romance is attractive to a young patriot because it works. Bankim asserted that nationalist Bengal needed "a single great idea, communicated to the people . . . in their own language, circulated among them in the language which alone *touches their heart,* vivifying and permeating the conceptions of all ranks."[56] To this end, he was willing to simplify and dissemble if necessary, as he bluntly put it in an 1872 letter to Sambhu Chandra Mookherjee on the subject of writing in the vernacular. He endorsed the limited use of the English language to "bring . . . influence to bear upon the Englishman," but he also recognized the long-term importance of mobilizing the population through the native tongue even if that meant a certain rhetorical distortion: "You will find me singing to a different tune on other occasions, on the principle that each side of a question must be put in its strongest light, specially when you have to fight against a popular one."[57]

Romance presents most graphically those pictures of heroic men and women capable of imparting "a single great idea." To some degree, Bankim's appropriation of a European narrative strategy partakes in the "battle for parity" that Ranajit Guha has described in colonial Indian writing, a battle aimed at proving the moral and intellectual equality of rulers and ruled and so, as he phrases it, aimed "to expropriate the expropriators by making the Indian people . . . the subject of their own history."[58] Bankim inverts the narrative technique that itself had been used to "civilize the natives" through English, reversing the exaggerated polarities of ethical forces to depict superior Indian characters triumphant over their corrupt, uncomprehending masters. As Partha Chatterjee has observed in another place, this strategy in Bankim's political writings resulted in a "reverse Orientalism," an impasse by which the "problematic," or manifest content of colonial power was significantly transformed or even inverted, but its latent "thematic" structure remained undisturbed.[59] It would seem that Bankim's romances too fall prey to this type of reduplication, whereby a potentially oppositional political stance is rendered ineffective by its parasitic reliance on the structural logic it sets out to refute. But with a difference, I would argue: The romantic bond desired by nationalist thought is not symmetrical with the dominating intentions of imperial romance. The difference illustrates the movement from a "pure" or binary opposition between hero and villain to the equally stark but much more complicated distinctions between correct action within the communitarian discourse of the nation.

Bankim's representations of women become crucial here. The women in his romance novels who assert an Indian national identity through the study of Sanskrit (Devi Chaudhurani) or traditional Hindu ritual (Shanti) or who possess an intuitive cunning unknown to foreigners (Bimala) approximate the romance heroines of Frye's account: They are "vigorous and young." By capturing the privileged ethical position in the romance hierarchy they take the place of the colonial master, inverting the relationship of dominance. "Indian" practices become associated with the heroic position and are thus extolled as the source of "light"; English attributes are plunged into the "darkness, confusion, sterility, moribund life and old age" associated with the romance villain.[60] This inversion indeed participates in the "reverse Orientalism" cited by Chatterjee, seemingly rewriting every Orientalist "terrible" with a nationalist "fine." But in the colonial context, as we have observed, the stability of gender hierarchy is shaky, not least because of its historical detour through the male-male relationship emphasized in the sentimental education. Bankim's heroines do not simply reverse the roles of colonizer and colonized; by switching places with their colonial masters as the true possessors of ethical superiority, they invert the hierarchy of gender as well. In this move, they go further than mere inversion. These decisively gendered figures cannot be read simply as women, or worse, as symbolic of actually existing Bengali men. Their interpretation must be left open to account for a gendered dynamic within the colonial relationship that is still somewhat fluid and subject to transformation and is not fully comprehended within the strict binary distinctions that tended to order romantic or Victorian patriarchal discourse. Romance is not only the world of ethical wish fulfillment, it is equally the world of magic in which the "good" hero can just as soon disappear and reemerge in another place as he can hold his ground and battle the fire-breathing dragon. The romance world shields its heroes as much as it enables their success, allowing for the contradictory makeup of the hero to triumph in a fashion that retains his ethical priorities, just as those priorities are themselves divided between seemingly inadmissible sides. This is precisely what happens in Bankim's "*kahinis.*" The historically undecidable choice between English and Indian, public and private, modernity and tradition, masculine and feminine, is played out as the *possibility of combination* in which all elements play their part at different times, a magical world of labile transformation and metamorphosis.

The pervasive unreality that characterizes the romance mode is exaggerated by the contradictions within the representation of these triumphant women warriors. They are not only unrealistic as exemplars of some lost traditional Bengali culture; they are also unrealistic—doubly phantasmatic—as inverted images of "worldly" men in the struggle for national mobilization. This representation is contradictory because the novels explicitly stage themselves as nationalist vehicles, each figuring an episode in the breakdown of central authority either precipitated by or taken advantage of by ethnically marked "Bengali" protagonists. If we simply allegorize the female characters as symbolic representatives of the nation, however, as some critics have urged, we lose the transitive force that gender has historically exerted in defining appropriate behavior within the colonial Indian context. As in the later European romance tradition, when group consolidation takes over from the necessary distinction between insider and outsider, the hero becomes an agglomeration of contradictory forces—conquering warrior *and* good householder—rather than a static representative of some clearly delineated ideal. The further presence of the repeated themes of disguise and camouflage, of women leading armies of men, and of their refusal of traditional domestic arrangements in favor of rigorous study and militaristic forms of organization all point to an untangleable complexity of identifications that must occur simultaneously for the scenario to be read with its full force.

A typical passage from Bankim's most famous novel, *Anandamath*, illustrates this point. The Englishman Captain Thomas, searching for rebels in the forest, stumbles upon what appears to be a holy man (*sannyasi*). Bankim's language enacts the failure of recognition and identification so central to the problematic hailing of the imperial romance, and in the process traces out the line of flight taken by the colonial response. I have preserved the dramatic punctuation in attempting to duplicate the peculiar mode of the discourse, somewhere between prose fiction and drama, although the Captain's ludicrous grammar and diction is not easily reproducible for English ears. Italicized words are given in English in the original Bengali text.

> Captain Thomas, knowing a bit of the local language, said "Who are you?"
> The sannyasi said, "I am a sannyasi."
> The Captain said, "You are a *rebel.*"
> Sannyasi: "What's that?"
> Captain: "Him gonna kill all you things."
> Sannyasi: "So kill away."
>
> The captain was a little hesitant then, not knowing whether to kill things or not, when the young sannyasi suddenly fell on him like lightning and snatched his musket. The tiger skin fell from the sannyasi's breasts. The matted locks were torn away; Captain Thomas Sahib saw before him an unbelievably beautiful female figure. Laughing, the beauty said, "Sahib, I am a woman, I don't harm people. I have a question to ask you: Hindus and Muslims are fighting each other; so why are you in the middle of it? Go back to your home *[ghar].*"
>
> Sahib: "Who are you?"
> Shanti: "You're looking at a female sannyasi. I've come to fight along with these people, and I'm also the wife of one of them."
> Sahib: "You will comes live in my tomb?" [mispronunciation of *ghar,* home, room]
> Shanti: "What? Your concubine?"
> Sahib: "You can stay as my wife, but I won't marry you."
> Shanti: "I have another question for you; I had a beautiful monkey at my place, but it just died; his little house is empty. I'll give you a pretty chain to wear around your waist. Will you come live in his cage? We have delicious bananas in our garden these days."
> Sahib: "You are a very *spirited woman,* your *courage* pleases me. Come to my tomb. Your husband will dies in the ware. Then what will I do with you?"
> Shanti: "Then let's agree on this. War will come in the next few days. If you win, and I survive, then I will consent to live with you as your concubine. And if we win, but you survive, will you come and live in our cage as a banana-eating monkey?"
> Sahib: "Eating bananas is my favorite thing. You have some?"
> Shanti: "Here, take back your musket. How can you talk to a savage?"
> Shanti dropped the musket and walked away laughing.[61]

This scenario is typical of Bankim's romance mode: Misrecognition followed by surprise revelation and linguistic misunderstanding prompted by the English ignorance of the vernacular. This misunderstanding leads to a semantic reversal by way of hilarious puns and slippages, and to a parody of legalistic negotiation that in turn lead to the Englishman becoming the dupe of an agreement he cannot understand. Such scenes are replayed multiple times in Bankim's fiction, constituting an imaginary locus of anticolonial subversion within the adopted machinery of the romance novel. That these encounters refuse engagement with English (il)logic points to their potential radicalness; rather than merely inverting the romance paradigm, such scenes attempt to demystify the terms of engagement by offering new modes of action that question and undermine the prerogatives of imperial power so that they need not negotiate with it on the unequal terms it has erected. Bankim's romantic representations of Indian women do not merely simulate the Bengali conquest of an unrealizable European public culture; they skew the terms of English and Indian, public and private, such that any imaginary resolution to the cultural contradictions of the Indian middle class will inevitably be forced to cross the gender divide between the two supposedly autonomous states of existence. The loaded play on the word *ghar* (room or home, the signifier of domesticity or inner life, as in the title of Tagore's *Home and the World*) evokes the charged location of this struggle, which the Englishman cannot properly pronounce or the Bengali "properly" restrict to merely domestic concerns. Unlike the imperial romance, which simulates a normative heterosexuality and its gender hierarchy to legitimate territorial possession and cultural superiority, colonial romance invests gender with critical potential to unseat these relationships by questioning the European presumption of fixed identities.

Bankim's heroic women not only substitute supposedly masculine attributes for the failures of Bengali men to achieve power and freedom in the world, they critique the conformist logic of the colonial relationship by chastising both Bengali and English conceptions of masculinity and its public conventions in the face of the historic defeat of Bengal by a "handful of British troops." Female characters are the true nationalists in Bankim's fiction, but they confront the British with a direct and forceful demand for recognition rather than with constitutional appeals for democratic equality, bypassing the hypocrisy of justice in the inequitable gendering of the public sphere. In doing so they challenge the prerogatives of the *babu* to control public discourse, most obviously when they refuse the rules of parliamentary engagement and fight force with force and, even more successfully, with cunning.

Thus colonial romance is not a mere inversion of the thematic of the imported romance genre. Though it preserves the ethical imperative of the romance mode to narrativize the difference between contiguous groups, it reconstructs this hierarchy on a tentative *identity* between nationalist actors rather than on the difference between rulers and ruled. The principle of order becomes the sameness of all who can read and identify with the linguistic subversion of colonial authority and of whoever is implicated in the unsteady gendering of the colonial subject. Colonial romance acts to demonstrate the parity—or better, interchangeability—of Bengali and English as cultures of reference rather than denigrate either one as racial, sexual, or civilizational other. Significantly, in the process of replacing cultures, the evaluative difference between "races" drops out of the equation, or rather attains a position of parity, while the representation of gender continues to remain unbalanced and problematic. The classical Indian tradition is extolled as a source of power and action, but improbable women warriors form the interface between ancient India and modern England. This symbolic use of women in Bankim's fiction, I would suggest, signifies at least two processes simultaneously: (1) the recognition of the historic feminization of Indian culture by the colonizers, and (2) the psychological pressure to speak back to the colonizers in a language (or genre) that one hopes could be understood but is now exaggerated to the point where such understanding will mark the power differential between speakers as intolerable. Women voice the aspirations of the nation, embodied as figures who could never hope to realize them. But if Indian and European civilizations are culturally equal, why does heroic virtue accrue to woman? Bengali femininity becomes an unquantifiable variable neither idealized as equal to English masculine strength nor realistically described as a practical alternative to the historic feminization of Indian men imposed by colonial rule. The heroines of Bankim's romance novels not only represent the subordinate position of Bengali masculinity within the colonial relationship but figure the very site of negotiation between English and Indian culture, public and private, home and world.

Romancing the Real

I possess nowhere near the cultural capital necessary to authoritatively comment on the gendered ambivalence of Tagore's image in his many incarnations as Vaishnavite devotee, disciple of Bankimchandra, Nobel laureate, Swadeshi radical, gurudev, universal humanist, and so on within the Bengali cultural imaginary. In the Nobel phase of his career, when European fame suddenly struck him at the age of fifty-one, contemporary photographs illustrated the legendary effeminacy of his public persona, which stood in such marked contrast to Bankimchandra's exaggerated masculinity and the inverted macho of his romance heroines. Seated cross-legged on the carpets of William Rothenstein's Hampstead villa, hands folded as if in meditation, Tagore's public persona seemed to Nirad C. Chaudhuri nothing less than the chicanery of a trumped-up holy man in Edwardian drag. While Rothenstein and his friends Sturge Moore, Ezra Pound, and W. B. Yeats were arranging for the publication of the English *Gitanjali,* soon to be followed by the Nobel Prize for literature in 1913, Tagore was increasingly tailoring his physical appearance and personality to approximate a stereotypical Asian passivity: meditative and serene, mysterious and intuitive, supine and feminine. In accordance with Western preconceptions of what constituted Eastern spirituality, Tagore progressively adopted signifiers of beatitude on his trips to London: The flowing robes, hair, and beard; the refusal to carry money; and the monosyllabic commands issued to his attendants all sparked in Sturge Moore a vision of Oriental sublimity: "The poet himself is a sweet creature, beautiful to the eye in a silken turban."[62] To Frances Cornford he appeared "like a saint, and the beauty and dignity of his whole being is wonderful to remember. I can now imagine a powerful and gentle Christ" (*T*, 1031). D. H. Lawrence, that notorious *man,* however, found "this wretched worship-of-Tagore attitude . . . disgusting" (*T,* 1031).

In the eyes of the prewar London literary cabal, Eastern femininity was good business. For Tagore, according to Chaudhuri, the aura of feminized spirituality was assumed as part of a forced retreat from an uncomprehending and hectoring Bengali literary public who neither appreciated his literary gifts nor forgave his upper-class dabbling in the economic realities of the predominantly petit bourgeois literary market. Rabindranath turned to the West at this strategic moment for a literary appreciation he could not find in India, and countered the European spiritual crisis on the eve of World War I with a public persona designed to assuage its sterile materialism. In either case, his exaggerated effeminacy, not unlike Bankimchandra's masculine posture, was consciously adopted as a strategy for dealing with the West. In the world of public discourse, gendered identities serve conflictual pragmatic purposes.

If it is the case, as I have been arguing, that genre indicates a deeper, structural site of negotiation with colonial discourse than does manifest content, it is surely appropriate to draw some tentative connections between Tagore's representations of gender identity and the largely realist mode of his novels. Classic Western realism, as noted earlier, is a heuristic construct useful only as a hypothetical ideal against which actual novelistic practice can be measured. For one of its most persuasive theorists, Colin MacCabe, the elementary distinguishing feature of the realist text is "a hierarchy amongst the discourses which compose the text . . . defined in terms of an empirical notion of truth."[63] The real defined by realism is not, in other words, a matter of the adequacy of written words to reflect or represent a pre-given reality but rather the capacity of the text to produce a dominant version of the real by valorizing certain styles of writing above others. The realist text does this by "hierarchization," elevating its own seemingly neutral style and thus marginalizing "quotations" from competing discourses. By placing these secondary discourses within inverted commas, the realist narrative signifies their subordinate relationship to the central discourse. While providing accurate representations of these secondary, subjective voices, hierarchization in effect relegates these competing discourses to the sidelines, opening the field to a consensual voice, embodied by the narrator, that produces its "reality effect" by seeming to express the common sense of the dominant community. This dominant voice, which MacCabe calls the metalanguage, thus becomes transparent and presents itself as *unwritten* in opposition to the materiality of the quotations, disavowing its constructed status in order to appear natural. The effect generated is a discourse of truth. "Whereas other discourses within the text are considered as material which are open to re-interpretation, the narrative discourse simply allows reality to appear and denies its own status as articulation."[64]

The development of realism in India, as in Europe, is often taken as a sign of civilizational advance rather than the invention of a discursive technique for producing the worldview of a dominant group. That the colonized intelligentsia of Bengal was capable of imitating the realist technology to produce the pleasant illusion of European middle-class "reality" was not very shocking given the educational legacy. What is surprising is that realism of the Tagorean sort could ever have attained the status that it did within India (and that it continues to maintain) given that the conditions for its production were "misplaced" by colonialism within the Indian context.[65] Whereas classic Western realism can be seen to serve as the transparent expression of a world-historical subject—the European bourgeoisie in its moment of global ascendancy, buoyed by the related successes of the Industrial Revolution and its territorial domination of the globe—its very narrative mechanisms cannot but work to marginalize any viable "reality" of the subjective expression of the colonized. A novel like Conrad's *Heart of Darkness* (1902), contemporaneous with Tagore's first major novel, *Choker Bali* (Eyesore, 1903), illustrates this process brilliantly. The "natives" seldom speak in Conrad's text, issuing instead unintelligible grunts, moans, and mumbles or, at best, cryptic fragments ("Mistah Kurtz—he dead") that must then be "interpreted" by the central discourse of Marlow in order to yield accurate expressions of the message—that Africa and Africans are barbarous, primitive, subhuman, ineducable—or to yield whatever other adjectives that describe and legitimate "the conquest of the earth, which mostly means the taking it away from those who have a different complexion or slightly flatter noses than ourselves."[66] As quotations representing the discursive "reality" of Africans, such inarticulate grunts work to reinforce the truth-effect of the realist technique by framing them as marginal. Conrad's novel, to be sure, works to subvert the claims of the realist apparatus through such techniques as the frame tale and the slightly paranoid nature of Marlow's own narration. But the basic procedure is a canny exposition of the realist machinery at work, which exposes and ridicules the ideology of modernization that accompanies it.

Tagore's political novel *Ghare Baire* (*The Home and the World,* 1916), set during the Swadeshi Movement to boycott English goods surrounding the partition of Bengal in 1906, provides another perfect example of realist quotation. *The Home and the World* in fact takes realist quotation as its organizing principle, presenting the subjective narratives of its three main characters—Nikhilesh, a wealthy *zamindar,* his wife, Bimala, and the Swadeshi agitator Sandip—as competing versions of the same event, namely Sandip's visit to Nikhilesh's estate and his fervent nationalist activities there. Whereas *Heart of Darkness* parodically quotes the unintelligible grunts of African bushmen, *The Home and the World* takes realist quotation further, constituting its narrative structure almost exclusively of quotations from the three main characters. The text's reality effect is derived from the seemingly uninterrupted nature of these conflicting accounts. I say "seemingly" because even though all of the novel is composed of such "verbatim" quotations, the hidden hand of the narrator still guides the assembly of the viewpoints as a fourth element that arranges the other three into a narrative ensemble. This ordering is designed to simulate a three-way conversation about the nature of "reality," but it is in fact a monological ordering, as events occurring in the "real" world are never open to dispute. Thus this dialogism (or triologism) is not a true Bakhtinian heteroglossia, which could open the text to social contradiction, but is rather built in as an ordering device carefully controlled by the invisible writing (or metalanguage) of the narrator. Although the characters have differing opinions about how to interpret events, the real is empirically given and is not subject to disagreement. As MacCabe tersely asserts, "The classic realist text . . . cannot deal with the real in its contradictions."[67] *The Home and the World* illustrates this dilemma in its author's flattening of the potentially heterodox perspectives within which the "world" could possibly be represented.

Paradoxically, the increased complexity and ambiguity of point of view in realism results in a hardening of the identities it represents. As opposed to the magical possibilities of combination and change in romance, Tagore's characters become locked into static roles even as they struggle against them. Woman, once again, is the preeminent site of the negotiation over reality. Bimala is the central character of *The Home and the World,* her psychological development (or *Bildung*) forming the dynamic movement indicated by the novel's title. Her passage from the *zenana* to the public sphere of politics, rhetoric, and finally violence, a passage at least partially mediated by English education, traces the imperial myth of civilization: It is the White Man's Burden to stimulate the general movement of Indian society as a whole under the developmental logic of imperial capital. Just as Indian society will "improve" under the tutoring of the English (represented in the text by Bimala's schoolmistress, Mrs. Gilbey), its women will graduate from the seclusion of the "home" and take their place in the "world" of public interaction. Bimala's personal development thus mirrors the development of Indian civilization from immature seclusion to modern worldliness. That the public sphere will remain, nonetheless, an enclave governed by the laws of a semimodern colonial patriarchy is amply ensured in the text's repeated blaming of Bimala for the violence unleashed by nationalist politics. Her increasing psychological worldliness becomes the motor for severe social disruption, resulting in the violation of other Hindu women and finally the critical wounding of her husband. In Tagore's novel, the metaphoric identity of Bimala with colonial modernity is cautionary; the movement toward the modern, signified by the education of women and their flight from the *zenana* results in disruption and death. The plot of her story is meant to illustrate for the reader the complex experience of self-discovery. But we know what to expect in the end by the very form of the narration, whose realist epistemology privileges from the outset the equanimity of the householder Nikhilesh over either the rhetorical excesses of Sandip or the tortuous reality of Bimala's experiments with the masculine world. Ironically, the presentation of this antidevelopmental parable within the predominantly realist mode of Tagore's fiction results in a glaring inauthenticity, for it relies on the most advanced narrative apparatus of contemporary European modernity to make its antimodern point.

Though realism wins in advance, along with its bourgeois norms of domestic heterosexuality, political moderation, the accumulation of wealth, and a certain mild philanthropy, the novel is not entirely free from anxiety over its narrative strategy. In fact, the generic tension between realism and romance is reactivated as Bimala becomes the allegorical ground over which the representational struggle is fought. As in Bankimchandra, the world of politics, debate, and public masculinity is associated with the persuasive rhetoric of romance, the distillation and simplification of ethical forces battling on a public stage. Sandip is the obvious representative of this narrative style, condensing the whole ensemble of "public" elements into a manipulative oratory revealed from the start as inimical to the "real" world of spiritual truth. Sandip flaunts his disingenuous, self-serving charisma in order to accomplish his goals. "Who says 'Truth shall Triumph?' Delusion will win in the end."[68] Bimala suits his purpose perfectly as he searches for a visual icon to represent the abstractions of nationalist identification. "We must make a goddess of her. . . . Illusions are necessary for lesser minds" (*HW,* 159). The exclusiveness of Sandip's concept of the nation echoes the historic "resolution" of the women's question: Bimala is simultaneously deified and devalued as he installs her as goddess of his movement before seducing and finally robbing her.

Nikhilesh, in contrast, condenses the characteristics of the home—spiritual cultivation, truth, retirement, and lyrical gentleness—within a typically realist view, in its European bourgeois sense, that modestly claims to be adequate rather than reformist, rational rather than romantic, conciliating rather than mobilizing. He is appalled by the violent side effects of nationalist organization, such as the attack on Mrs. Gilbey, and rightly criticizes Swadeshi slogans and tactics for their anti-Muslim bias. Sandip derisively comments, "He has such a prejudice in favor of truth—as though there exists such an objective reality!" (*HW,* 160). In Nikhilesh's "objective reality," women can be educated and released from the home just as they are (said to be) in Europe. The European goods that furnish the home, against which the Swadeshi activists "outside" direct their anger, have an empirical rather than a symbolic value to him—they are no more responsible for India's subjection than the "innocent" English schoolmistress. Nikhilesh's equanimity, which has often been identified with the author's, registers the empirical world with a confident neutrality and faith in the essential stability of the real, and asserts that the reformist tendencies of the semimodern colonial domesticity emerging in middle-class and upper-caste Hindu homes can become the model for structuring society in the outside world. The realist attitude, however, promoted as it is in this novel as only one option among three, proves to be an even more diabolic entrapment than the other two. By staging itself as partial, but quietly valorizing that viewpoint as the ultimate in "objective" technique, the realist apparatus could insinuate itself into the political and artistic culture of Indian semimodernity as the real. Once Tagore's international reputation had been sealed by the Nobel Prize, it would be difficult to turn back.

The difficulty of adapting realism to the colonial context lies precisely in its unproblematic relationship to the real. The reality produced by classic Western realism is the Western reality of a globally dominant middle-class patriarchy, not that of a subjugated and semifeudal populace with its own specific structure of class and gender relations. The world generated by classic Western realism is dependent on a Cartesian cogito, inevitably masculine, that predicates its identity on an unproblematic synonymy between being and consciousness: I think therefore I am. The unsutured appearance of the realist metalanguage issues from the desire of this subject to project its seeming autonomy onto the external world, representing things with the apparent ease of its ability to represent itself. This autonomous subject, in fact deeply contingent on the historical and psychological specificity of the rising European bourgeoisie, is manifestly not the class subject of colonial dependency. Nor can it adequately negotiate with the historical gendering of the colonial subject.

As Rita Felski has pointed out in *Beyond Feminist Aesthetics*, the classic realist aesthetic undergoes mutation when it is appropriated as the reality principle of feminist autobiography, resulting in compromises with and subversions of both the empirical reality offered by realist technique and the cogito that registers them.[69] The reality effect of feminist autobiography is often considered to be its assertion of a uniquely feminine subjectivity and authenticity over and against the patriarchal dominance of the symbolic order. Bimala's story can be considered in some sense as feminist autobiography, a form that Tagore observed at first hand in the literary writing of his sister, Swarnakumari Devi, from whom he is said to have borrowed a great deal.[70] However we try to consider Bimala's story as such, it is nonetheless forced to maneuver between the preexisting generic prescriptions of romance and realism in its attempts to steer a middle path through these competing foreign ideologies. Indeed, as Eric Hayot has recently observed, Bimala's character is produced in the novel as a semantic agent through the competing claims of "mistress" and "mother" made upon her by the two major male characters.[71] Similarly, the specificity and truth value of her testimony arises only in juxtaposition to the extremes of romance and realism indulged by the other two protagonists. Her one moment of liberation from the closed plots of both genres occurs when her relations with both men are, however fleetingly, broken off. For a mere moment, when Bimala sees through Sandip's manipulative rhetoric, she glimpses a vision of ecstatic freedom: "Sandip, the wielder of magic spells, is reduced to utter powerlessness, whenever his spell refuses to work. From a king he fell to the level of a boor. Oh, the joy of witnessing his weakness! The harsher he became in his rudeness, the more did this joy well up within me. His snaky coils, with which he used to snare me, are exhausted,—I am free. I am saved, saved. . . . My husband came in at this juncture" (*HW,* 239–240). Just as Bimala's joy announces the possibility of escape, perhaps into another narrative form that would not snare the subject within imported rhetorical spells, the mise-en-scène immediately forecloses it, reinscribing Sandip's defeat not as a victory for Bimala but for her husband. The possibility of an alternative narrative form that could express this sense of potential freedom, whether feminist autobiography or otherwise, is raised but quickly dropped. Any further survey of colonial realism in India would have to account for the rise of women's autobiographies in this period.

In the end, a heterosexist, Hindu reality principle is reasserted over the competing claims of either nationalist mobilization or feminist autobiography, closing off the possibilities of subversion potentially available in those other genres. We learn that the waywardness of Bimala's experiments with truth are directly responsible for the death of her protégé, Amulya, the possibly fatal wounding of her husband, and most disturbingly, the rape of Hindu women at the hands of rioting Muslim hordes. This final transformation leaves Bimala divested of the possible strengths offered by either mother or mistress positions, placing her firmly within the category of ultimate helplessness by the novel's end as a motherless, widowed wife who has betrayed her traditional source of strength, Hindu femininity. The threat of difference proliferating is foreclosed; truth does in fact triumph as the most realistic answer possible to the conundrum of colonial acculturation: There is no answer within the borrowed terms of engagement short of enduring the nightmare of history.

NOTES

I am indebted to Richard Dienst and Sangeeta Ray for their close critical readings of this essay through its many drafts. I have benefitted enormously from the wisdom of Leona Fisher and Patricia O'Connor in their generous attention to some sections. Parvin Huda provided invaluable research assistance. I would also like to thank the audiences who heard parts of it at the University of Wisconsin at Madison annual South Asia Conference, 1993, and the National Association for the Study of Romanticism, 1995, for their reactions.

1. On literary education, see Gauri Viswanathan, "Currying Favor: The Beginnings of English Literary Study in British India, 1813–1858," *Social Text* 19/20 (Fall 1988), and *Masks of Conquest: Literary Study and British Rule in India* (New York: Columbia University Press, 1989). On the practice of literature in colonial Bengal, there are several standard histories: S. K. De, *Bengali Literature in the Nineteenth Century, 1757–1857,* 2 vols. (Calcutta: Firma K.L.M, 1962); J. C. Ghosh, *Bengali Literature* (London: Oxford University Press, 1948); D. C. Sen, *History of the Bengali Language and Literature,* 2nd ed. (Calcutta: University of Calcutta, 1954); Sukumar Sen, *History of Bengali Literature* (Delhi: Sahitya Akademi, 1960); Dusan Zbavitel, *Bengali Literature* (Weisbaden: Otto Harrasowitz, 1976).

On gender and the "women's question" in the nineteenth century see Jashodhara Bagchi, "Representing Nationalism: Ideology of Motherhood in Colonial Bengal,"

Economic and Political Weekly (October 20, 1990), WS pp. 65–71; Meredith Borthwick, *The Changing Role of Women in Bengal, 1849–1905* (Princeton: Princeton University Press, 1984); Ipshita Chanda, "In Search of Sweetness: The Diaspora as a Cultural Idea in the Work of Ama Ata Aidoo," in this volume; Partha Chatterjee, *The Nation and Its Fragments* (Princeton: Princeton University Press, 1993); Malavika Karlekar, *Voices from Within: Early Personal Narratives of Bengali Women* (Delhi: Oxford University Press, 1991); Ghulam Murshid, *Reluctant Debutante: Responses of Bengali Women to Modernization, 1849–1905* (Rajshahi: Sahitya Samsad, 1983); Manisha Roy, *Bengali Women* (Chicago: University of Chicago Press, 1992); Sumit Sarkar, *A Critique of Colonial India* (Calcutta: Papyrus, 1985); Tanika Sarkar, "Nationalist Iconography: Image of Women in 19th Century Bengali Literature," *Economic and Political Weekly* (November 21, 1987), WS pp. 2011–2015.

On the role of women and femininity in Bankimchandra, see Lou Ratté, "A Dangerous Alliance: Anglo-Indian Literary Criticism and Bengali Literary Production," *Genders,* no. 2 (Summer 1988), pp. 42–59; S. N. Mukherjee, "Women's Space and Women's Language in the Novels of Bankim Chandra Chatterjee," *Journal of the Oriental Society of Australia* 17 (1985), pp. 64–94.

2. Partha Chatterjee, "The Nationalist Resolution of the Women's Question," in *Recasting Women: Essays in Indian Colonial History,* ed. Kumkum Sangari and Sudesh Vaid (New Brunswick, NJ: Rutgers University Press, 1990), p. 249.

3. Chatterjee, *The Nation and Its Fragments,* p. 116.

4. Ibid., p. 120.

5. Ibid., p. 117.

6. Ibid., p. 118; Lata Mani, "Contentious Traditions: The Debate on *Sati* in Colonial Indian," in Sangari and Vaid, *Recasting Women,* pp. 88–126.

7. I borrow the term "invented traditions" from the volume *The Invention of Tradition,* eds. Eric Hobsbawm and Terrence Ranger (Cambridge: Cambridge University Press, 1983). See especially Bernard S. Cohn, "Representing Authority in Victorian India," pp. 165–209. Although he does not use the term "semimodern," the basic process is elaborated brilliantly in David Ludden, "Orientalist Empiricism: Transformations of Colonial Knowledge," in *Orientalism and the Postcolonial Predicament,* eds. Carol Breckenridge and Peter Van der Veer (Philadelphia: University of Pennsylvania Press, 1993), pp. 250–278.

8. H. Sharp, ed., *Selections from Educational Records, Part I, 1781–1839* (Calcutta: Superintendent Government Printing, India, 1920), p. 22.

9. Raymond Williams, *Keywords* (London: Fontana, 1974), and *Marxism and Literature* (Oxford: Oxford University Press, 1977), esp. pp. 45–54.

10. Jürgen Habermas, *The Structural Transformation of the Public Sphere,* trans. Thomas Berger (Cambridge: MIT Press, 1989).

11. The phrase "imaginary relations" is taken directly from Louis Althusser, *Lenin and Philosophy,* trans. Ben Brewster (New York: Monthly Review Press, 1971). Michael Sprinker has explicated the relation of the aesthetic to ideology in general in *Imaginary Relations: Aesthetics and Ideology in the Theory of Historical Materialism* (New York and London: Verso, 1987).

12. Terry Eagleton, *Literary Theory: An Introduction* (Minneapolis: University of Minnesota Press, 1980), pp. 17–53.

13. Ibid., p. 21.

14. H. H. Wilson, "Education of the Natives of India," *Asiatic Journal,* n.s. 19, no. 73 (January–April 1836), pp. 1. Further references are given in the text as *ENI.*

15. This is an interpretation of the reformers' intentions as ironically parodied by Wilson in ibid., 1.

16. Thomas Babington Macaulay, "Minute on Indian Education," in *Selected Writings,* ed. John Clare and Thomas Pinney (Chicago: University of Chicago Press, 1972), pp. 237–251. Further references are given in the text with the abbreviation *MIE.*

17. Lord William Bentinck, "Resolution of 7th March, 1835," in *Selections from Educational Records,* p. 130.

18. Wilson, "Education of the Natives of India," p. 1

19. John Stuart Mills, "Recent Changes in Native Education," India Office Records, Home Miscellaneous Series 723; Revenue, Judicial and Legislative Committee—Miscellaneous Papers, 9. Other commentators have mentioned the draft, but without drawing these conclusions. See Percival Spear, "Bentinck and Education," *Cambridge Historical Journal* 6, no. 1 (1938), pp. 78–101; K. A. Ballhatchet, "The Home Government and Bentinck's Educational Policy," *Cambridge Historical Journal* 10, no. 2 (1951), pp. 224–229; Abram L. Harris, "John Stuart Mill: Servant of the East India Company," *Canadian Journal of Economics and Political Science* 30, no. 2 (1964), pp. 185–202; Lynn Zastoupil, *John Stuart Mill and India* (Stanford: Stanford University Press, 1994), pp. 28–50.

20. John Stuart Mill, "Letter to Henry Taylor," no. 18.1 (dated "Monday, 1837"), in *The Later Letters of John Stuart Mill 1849–1873,* ed. Francis E. Mineka and Dwight N. Lindley (Toronto: University of Toronto Press, 1972).

21. John Stuart Mill, *Mill on Bentham and Coleridge,* ed. F. R. Leavis (Cambridge: Cambridge University Press, 1980), pp. 61–62. Subsequent references are given in the text as *BC.*

22. Sprinker, *Imaginary Relations,* p. 11.

23. C. E. Trevelyan, *On the Education of the People of India* (London: Longman, Orme, Brown, Green and Longman, 1838), p. 176.

24. Vishwanathan, "Currying Favor," p. 103.

25. Marion Filipiuk, Michael Lane, and John M. Robson, eds., *Additional Letters of John Stuart Mill* (Toronto: University of Toronto Press, 1991), p. 30.

26. Homi Bhabha, *The Location of Culture* (New York: Routledge, 1994), esp. pp. 66–122.

27. Mill, "Recent Changes in Native Education," p. 77.

28. Ibid., p. 45.

29. Ibid., pp. 99–101.

30. Calla Chand Bose, "English Essay," in *Scholarship Examinations of 1846–47* (Bengal: Council of Education), Appendix C, p. xviii.

31. The composer of the twelfth-century Sanskrit lyric Gitagovinda. Though the poem is written in Sanskrit and Jayadeva is usually considered to have been from Orissa (though associated with the Bengal court of Laksmanasena), it is common in this period to appropriate him into literary history as the great founder of Bengali literature. This is clearly a nationalist gesture intended to push back the ancient origins of the vernacular, and its intimate connection to Sanskrit, as a way of elongating a sense of the national past. Romesh Chandra Dutt repeats this gesture in *The Cultural Heritage of Bengal* (1896) (Calcutta:

Punthi Pustak, 1962), first serialized in the *Calcutta Review* from 1873 to 1877. It has been imitated in many literary histories since. See especially Sen, *History of Bengali Literature,* and Ghosh, *Bengali Literature,* for similar readings.

32. Bankimchandra Chatterjee, *Bankim Rachanabali* vol. 3, ed. J. C. Bagal (Calcutta: Sahitya Samsad, 1969), p. 98, my emphasis.

33. See Chatterjee, *The Nation and Its Fragments,* pp. 76–115.

34. Chatterjee, *Bankim Rachanabali,* p. 99.

35. Ibid., p. 124.

36. Chatterjee, *The Nation and Its Fragments,* p. 117.

37. Nancy Armstrong, *Desire and Domestic Fiction: A Political History of the Novel* (New York: Oxford University Press, 1987), p. 4. Interestingly, the historian Carolyn Steedman has recently stated that despite Williams's neglect of the rich historical record of feminine sensibility in this period, his fundamental insights remain undisturbed. Williams's "words ... occluded a whole history: of women and children in English society. ... But without the history ... Raymond Williams was probably right." "Culture, Cultural Studies, and the Historians," in *Cultural Studies,* ed. Lawrence Grossberg, Cary Nelson, and Paula Treichler (New York: Routledge, 1992), pp. 613–622, quotation on pp. 615–616. A project for further research could be to examine the applicability of this claim for the British Empire.

38. See K. A. Ballhatchet, *Race, Sex and Class Under the Raj: Imperial Attitudes and Policies and Their Critics* (New York: St. Martin's Press, 1980); Sara Suleri, *The Rhetoric of English India* (Chicago: University of Chicago Press, 1992).

39. Chatterjee, *The Nation and Its Fragments,* pp. 121–126; Dipesh Chakrabarty, "Postcoloniality and the Artifice of History: Who Speaks for 'Indian' Pasts?" *Representations* 37 (Winter 1992), pp. 1–26; "The Difference-Deferral of (A) Colonial Modernity: Public Debates on Domesticity in British Bengal," *History Workshop Journal* 36 (Autumn 1993), pp. 1–34, esp. p. 5. Monisha Roy's *Bengali Women* is an excellent source of contemporary apparatuses for the training of femininity, many of which have their roots in the nineteenth century.

40. Charles E. Trevelyan, *On the Education of the People of India* (London: Longman, Orme, Brown, Green and Longman, 1838), p. 176.

41. Homi Bhabha, "Signs Taken for Wonders: Questions of Ambivalence and Authority Under a Tree Outside Delhi, May 1817," in *"Race," Writing, and Difference,* ed. H. L. Gates Jr. (Chicago: University of Chicago Press, 1986), p. 169.

42. Rabindranath Tagore, cited in Mukherjee, "Women's Space," p. 79.

43. See Roy, Bengali Women, pp. 46–58. The *Calcutta Gazette* listed the circulation of *Bangadarshan,* the periodical in which most of Bankimchandra's novels were serialized, at 1,800 per month in 1879.

44. Fredric Jameson, *The Political Unconscious: Narrative as a Socially Symbolic Act* (Ithaca: Cornell University Press, 1980), p. 106.

45. Vincent Leitch, "(De)Coding (Generic) Discourse," *Genre* 24 (Spring 1991), p. 83.

46. It is not possible to document this assertion in this space. It is, however, a widely regarded perception within Bengali literary history since the second half of the nineteenth century. Representative statements can be found in Sen, *History of the Bengali Language and Literature,* p. 766: "Towards the end of the 18th century, the Vaisnavas and Saktas were practically driven out of the field. . . . Europeans and chiefly missionaries . . . trained the Pandits to write Bengali—not as they would have it, but as their European masters wanted

it." De, *Bengali Literature in the Nineteenth Century,* offers a graphic account of the destruction of native literature under company rule. The poet Bishnu Dey, eulogizing what he called "the popular mind," describes the loss of the "representative character" of the language by the mid-nineteenth century: "This quality of mind . . . one finds . . . in all the notable works in our language until we come to our Western period. . . . With Iswar Chandra [Gupta] we come to our last reputable popular poet. . . . And what little strength of the popular idiom, the racy turns and twists of words and phrases, emphatic signs of the genius of the language we find in Madhusudan's plays, we find neither in Bankim nor in Tagore." "Notes on Progressive Writing in Bengal," in *Marxist Cultural Movement in India: Chronicles and Documents (1936–1947),* vol. 1, ed. Sudhi Pradhan (Calcutta: Mrs. Santi Pradhan, 1979), p. 223.

47. See his obituary of Mill in *Sociological Essays: Utilitarianism and Positivism in Bengal,* trans. and ed. by S. N. Mukherjee and Marian Maddern (Calcutta: Riddhi-India, 1986), pp. 203–206.

48. Bankimchandra Chatterjee, "Letter to Mookherjee," in Chatterjee, *Bankim Rachanabali,* p. 170.

49. Mill, *Mill on Bentham and Coleridge,* pp. 61–62.

50. Northrop Frye, *Anatomy of Criticism: Four Essays* (Princeton: Princeton University Press, 1957), pp. 187–188.

51. Jameson, *The Political Unconscious,* p. 110.

52. Frye, *Anatomy of Criticism,* p. 193.

53. Jameson, *The Political Unconscious,* p. 118.

54. Ibid.

55. For a hilarious attack on Bankim's "backwardness," see Ghosh, *Bengali Literature.*

56. Bankimchandra Chatterjee, "A Popular Literature for Bengal," in Chatterjee, *Bankim Rachanabali,* pp. 97–102, my emphasis.

57. Chatterjee, *Bankim Rachanabali,* p. 170.

58. Ranajit Guha, *An Indian Historiography of India: A Nineteenth Century Agenda and Its Implications* (Calcutta: K. P. Bagchi, 1988), p. 61.

59. Partha Chatterjee, *Nationalist Thought and the Colonial World* (London: Zed Books, 1986). See esp. chapter 2.

60. Frye, *Anatomy of Criticism,* pp. 187–188.

61. *Anandamath,* in Chatterjee, *Bankim Rachanabali,* vol. 1, p. 707–708. My translation, with many thanks to Zahed Khan for his insights into the peculiar resonances of late-nineteenth-century vocabulary.

62. Nirad C. Chaudhuri, "Tagore: The True and the False," *Times Literary Supplement* 27 (September 1974), p. 1031. Further references are given in the text as *T.* A significantly expanded version of this article can be found in *Thy Hand, Great Anarch!* (London: Chatto and Windus, 1987).

63. Colin MacCabe, *Tracking the Signifier. Theoretical Essays: Film, Linguistics, Literature* (Minneapolis: University of Minnesota Press, 1985), p. 34.

64. Ibid., p. 36.

65. See Roberto Schwarz, *Misplaced Ideas: Essays on Brazilian Culture,* ed. John Gledson (London: Verso, 1992), esp. chapter 2.

66. Joseph Conrad, *Heart of Darkness and the Secret Sharer* (New York: Bantam, 1981), p. 9.

67. MacCabe, *Tracking the Signifier,* p. 44.

68. Rabindranath Tagore, *The Home and the World,* trans. Surendranath Tagore (London: Macmillan, 1957), p. 165. Further references are given in the text as *HW.*

69. Rita Felski, *Beyond Feminist Aesthetics* (London: Routledge, 1992).

70. See Susie Tharu and K. Lalitha, eds., *Women Writing in India,* vol. 1 (Delhi: Oxford University Press, 1991), pp. 235–238.

71. Eric Hayot, "Bimala's Wound," paper presented at "Nationalism(s), Culture, and the Shape of the World Today Conference," Georgetown University, April 30, 1994.

PART FOUR

THE DYNAMICS OF RECOGNITION

14

In Search of Sweetness: The Diaspora as a Cultural Idea in the Work of Ama Ata Aidoo

IPSHITA CHANDA

AS AN INDIAN WOMAN contributing to a collection of "international" culture studies, I would like to begin with a story that the Ghanaian writer Ama Ata Aidoo tells in her novel *Our Sister Killjoy: Reflections from a Blackeyed Squint.*[1] Her heroine, Sissie, goes to Germany on a trip sponsored by the "post" colonial government of Ghana and meets a German woman, Marija, who befriends her. Marija has little clue as to the location of Ghana, but she has earlier met two Indian students who were on a similar sponsored trip to her country. Says Marija: "I really liked zose Indians. I sink of zem weri much as you speak English" (*OSK*, 28). Sissie thinks:

A common heritage
Dubious bargain that left us
Plundered of
Our gold
Our tongue
Our life—while our
Dead fingers clutch
English—a
Doubtful weapon fashioned
Elsewhere to give might to a
Soul that is already
Fled (OSK, 28)

This passage directly addresses the two primary concerns I have in this chapter. First, I examine the specific nature of the cultures of once-colonized societies that are now being increasingly brought within the purview of mainstream academic consideration through the language of the once dominant Other. Within this process, which appears quite natural to us English-educated academics of Asian, African, or Latin American origin, lies the seed of a spurious humanism that irons out differences and in-built hierarchies in an effort to "internationalize." Second, the currency of a shared language leaves us in India, as it does Sissie in Ghana, with a "common heritage." Dubious though it certainly is, and fraught with our own sense of unbelonging, it still allows us to investigate our common history, take stock of the presents produced by that history, and reach out across them. As Sissie points out, "We are victims of our History and our Present. They place too many obstacles in the Way of Love. And we cannot enjoy even our Differences in peace" (*OSK*, 29).

The similar histories of bondage and resistance that unite us in our common search for difference is the cultural and political project that confronts us, citizens of a "post" colonized world. Ironically, this dialogue is being carried on thanks to a language that once symbolized oppression and still has an uneasy relationship with its "post" colonized speakers. Yet the language once used for our exclusion can now be appropriated by some of us to make space for our dialogue. This seems to be a point of commonality that enables us to reach out across cultural boundaries. A strategy of engagement that this chapter foregrounds is a differential cultural analysis within an interdisciplinary framework. Also, given my own concerns and those that surface in Aidoo's work, the key to this framework is a feminist approach. This approach, in its rudiments, confronts not only capitalist patriarchal hegemony but also a dominant version of feminism that theoretically extends approaches rooted in Western social practices. These theoretical generalizations are now being contested from various quarters, but in the contestations themselves lies a subterranean trace; and this is the other side of the coin, another dubious heritage that the language of the colonizer has left us. Conceptually oriented toward the fundamentals of a language that has little direct relation to life as it was/is generally lived in our society, the oppositional theory produced by English-speaking academics seems rooted in the very epistemological ground that it seeks to refute. The diaspora that we will study in Aidoo's work comprises not only what she calls

> *Gambian ophthalmologist in Glasgow*
> *Phillipino lung specialist in Boston*
> *Brazilian cancer expert in*
> *Brooklyn or*
> *Basle or*
> *Nancy (OSK, 32)*

but also those of us who do not physically leave our own homes but are mentally part of an international market trading in the latest conceptual and theoretical goods to understand our own selves, our own cultural products.

Sissie meets an Indian doctor,
General Dispenser to the
Imaginary ailments of
Suburbia Germania (OSK, 29)

She reacts to him thus:

I had looked at him
And switched on
Memory's images,
Pieced together from other
Travellers' tales of sick people in
Calcutta.
'Why did you remain
Here?' . . .
'Do they need you as a Doctor
Here
As desperately?' (OSK, 29–30)

He replies:

'There are as many Ghanaian doctors
practising here as there are Indians . . .
Going to work in a
State hospital is
Unnecessary
Slavery . . . (OSK, 30)

Sissie's question to my fictitious countryman, and his reply and the rationale that underpins this exchange, inform all our efforts at constructing what we have learned to call a "counterdiscourse." This often ends up becoming a part of the mainstream archives or institutions, for two specific reasons. First, as has already been pointed out, because our efforts are circumscribed within the terms set for us by the mainstream discourse itself, we are often unable to transgress the limits that are demarcated by this hegemonic discourse and so cannot think in any other terms—a true "internationalization" of a particular set of ideas and practices that overdetermine our engagement with our own realities. The other reason our counterdiscourses do not effectively counter much is that the construction of these counters are based on the needs of the other, on the lack in us identified by the other, which must be filled in by the domestication of our oppositional impulses. As Sissie succinctly points out, there may be a "need" for more qualified doctors in Calcutta, but the prestige attached to all things international, be it a theory, a lifestyle, or even an issue to oppose, is too overwhelming to disregard. In fact, the language itself, and the education that it enables a particular class of people to benefit from, is aptly described by Sissie as "leftovers of imperial handouts" (*OSK*, 86). She has a scathing comment to make on the motive force behind much spurious internationalization of culture studies when she says:

> *For a few pennies now*
> *And a*
> *Doctoral degree later,*
> *Tell us about*
> *Your people*
> *Your history*
> *Your mind (OSK, 87)*

All our engagements on the side of difference, when conducted for an international intellectual market, may well fall prey to these problems—the writing of this chapter being no exception. It seems imperative, therefore, to consider this element of a willing mental diaspora that implicates us as critics and members of "post" colonial societies. Culture studies, to retain its cutting edge, must take theorizing beyond the impasse of a romanticized search for roots in one direction and a problematic alignment with Western technology in the other. This is probably one of the contributions that it can make to the understanding of the more invidious forms of hegemony in the current context.

Ideas crucial to a particular culture at a particular conjuncture enter into the historical narratives of those who belong to the same cultural group. Ideas form and shape culture, being in themselves formed and shaped by the complex of other ideas that they interact with in creating matrices of shared meaning. Besides this, mediated by cultural production, such ideas also often becomes part of the global signification system, forming a kind of metonymic shorthand for the culture that they are supposed to "symbolize." These habitual images become, more often than not, stereotypical, covering in their easy currency the context in which they became crucial to the culture and the resonance that they are able to effect in the past, present, and future conditions of people who belong to that cultural group.

In a sense, the diaspora is my point of entry into the culture of the Akan-speaking group to which Aidoo belongs. As an outsider, my concern in this project is twofold. The elements of commonality have already been pointed out—common language as medium and the common condition of "post" coloniality that induces certain activities such as the activity-in-flight that I here name the "willing" diaspora of the young. But there is also the element of difference that is crucial to my reading of Aidoo's texts, a difference that prevents me from maintaining a simple "I-It" relationship with the texts and makes it an engagement that causes me to review the interpretation of my own experiences and the discourses of nationalism and reconstruction in my own society, where too, the themes of duty to nation and duty to mother are used in conjunction. I shall indicate the details further on; at this point I need only to record that on first reading, these themes seemed to occur in conjunction in Aidoo's texts also, and they seemed as unacceptable to me there as they has seemed in the key texts that made up the discourse of Indian, and especially Bengali, nationalism and reconstruction. This, I submit, is the result of the difference in gender ideology that underpins these discourses: The existing gender ideology in the Indian context was vastly different from that prevalent in the society of which Aidoo writes. As a result, the gender ideology introduced by the British colonizers in both these areas had apparently similar but actually divergent effects. Studying this difference and contextualizing it enables me in my reading at Aidoo's texts to modify, strengthen, or change my own perception of certain problems that exist not only on the level of the texts produced by our respective cultures but in the sphere of our daily praxis as women in "post" colonial cultures. This is a personal example of the value of what appears to be a "culture studies" exercise.

Since I have evoked the discourses of nation and motherhood as they are current in my society as a point of contrast, I shall elaborate on this theme before moving on to these discourses as they structure the world of Aidoo's texts. The nineteenth-century Bengali intelligentsia contributed significantly to the discourse of Indian nationalism, most especially to the element of Westernized modernity that formed its reformative impulse. The image of the mother in this discourse has a double orientation. In the realm of the political, or rather the *overtly* political thrust of the nationalist enterprise, the idea of mother was constructed on the lines of a heroic mother goddess who would inspire her sons to vanquish the colonizers and rescue the nation from bondage.[2] The nation also, needless to say, was in the image of a woman ravished by colonial oppression, the most crucial deprivation being the damage done to her honor through the colonial occupation. Thus not only did the nation-as-mother demand the male valor of her sons, she also represented an idol that was worth fighting for. But this is only one part of the story. Besides the ideal of the heroic *Bangamata* type, there was also the sentimental education that women were given such that they would be able to raise children, sons to become brave or at least civilized gentry and daughters to become carbon copies of themselves, that is, the ideal wife and mother.[3] These images were substantiated by men who were leaders of reform movements in the late-nineteenth and early-twentieth centuries. Reformers of all hues and persuasions joined in advocating female education, as Shivaji Bandyopadhyay points out,[4] partly to enter the sweeping current of modernity that was identified with learning lessons from the colonizers but certainly also to retain their control over women's lives and thoughts, to keep them in strict line with the shifting frame of patriarchy that added new modes of control to the already existing ones. Himani Bannerji has pointed out that contemporary women understood this attempt and tried to counter it with their own programs of more education and a reform of social relations.[5] But the question that arises is what form these counteractions actually took. They were doubtless modeled on the liberal individualized ethic of domestic partnership and conjugal harmony that characterized the monogamous family. Bannerji indicates this when she distinguishes between *andar* (inner house) and *griha* (home/hearth)as the two contrasting spaces around which the ideology of gender was organized.[6] The latter privileged the activity of the modern educated mother in the bringing up of children; the former was an archaic concept that symbolized the segregation of men and women within the family itself, construed as the source of women's oppression, illiteracy, and superstition. As a matter of fact, within the *andarmahal,* the relationship between the child and the mother was not so well defined because of the existence of other female relatives and, in the houses that could afford the segregation, servants both male and female. In contrast, the ideal relationship between mother and child was supposed to obtain in the *griha,* which appears to be another name for the archetypal monogamous nuclear household, a norm that the reformist gentry of Bengal seemed eager to borrow from the colonizer. Patriarchy in the Indian, especially in the Bengali context, was thus reorganized along lines advocated by the colonizer. Both parents were exhorted to be careful of the education and upbringing the child received,[7] a far cry from the completely communal effort that child rearing largely was before these Westernized gentlefolk took it upon themselves to intervene. The ideal of motherhood, both as inspiration to the incipient liberators of the land and as model for flesh-and-blood mothers, was therefore directly and indirectly linked to the discourse of the nation. Whether the ideal was mother as the bearer of heroic sons or mother as the rearer of modern, civilized gentry of the future, the image of mother was a powerful one. It was used by reformist women as their argument for the betterment of the condition of their kind and equally used by men who paid it lip service and who relegated the burden of ideology to it.

Marilyn Strathern characterizes Euramerican conjugal relations as voluntarist and altruist and as predicated on an individualized perception of the self as a separate entity establishing relations with either other specific individualized entities or an abstract whole, society.[8] The elements of choice of reproductive technology and the language that underpins the availability of these technologies in the consumer culture prompt these observations. But even apart from these considerations, the idea of marriage as a meeting and fusing of two minds, bodies, and labor powers orchestrated by the choice of two "free" adults hinges on similar considerations in the West, especially among the Euramerican cultures that influenced the colonies and still continue to do so. This form of marriage and its consequent family structure are indeed persuasive in the Indian context. The institutionalizing of such an ideal as "normal" marks the colonial intervention. The woman's only active role in the struggle for independence was the rearing and training of sons. But this role also kept her firmly within the bounds of partriarchal control. Besides, her role was symbolically privileged, though actively undervalued. As Krishnabhabini Das, one of the leading turn-of-the-century reformist women asks rhetorically, "whenever there is talk of righting the wrongs of Hindu women, and establishing their equality with men, many (men) refer to the scriptures and allude to the status (of women) as *devi.* But where do we see any respect for these *devis?*"[9] In this she indicates the truth beyond the symbolism, and that leads us to see how this discourse of nation-as-mother works, entirely burdening the woman with its operation. In capitalist patriarchal state structure, woman-as-mother plays the role of the domesticated other. She is necessary to preserve the acceptability of a discourse that would otherwise be revealed as weighted in favor of the dominant group. In her role as mother, woman is idealized, sanitized of any shred of threatening sexuality, burdened with preserving and reproducing the basic social relation on which capitalist patriarchy is hinged, all in one economical move. Women, despite being the suppressed group, or perhaps because of it, are crucial to the smooth functioning of this structure. They have to be socialized to accept their role, and this is done through the idealization that attaches to woman-as-mother. From this basic relation between mother and child, the relation between nation and national is extended; all the emotional investment that attaches to the biological relation, it is expected, will accrue to the imagined political constitution of a subject. The conflation of nation with mother yokes the intimate with the political through a powerful symbol; the nation's cause then becomes an abstract affective duty, neatly sweeping under the ideological carpet questions of materiality, power and class, and domination. This is precisely what liberal nationalism achieved, whether it wished to or not, and liberal nationalism was the reigning ideology of the groups that led the colonized to independence struggles and then presided over the transfer of power. It was in their hands that the newly independent nations passed when the colonizers departed.

Given the nature of "post" colonial reconstruction and its dependence on the nature of the anticolonial struggle and given the nature of the role played in this process by the nation-as-mother ideal, my initial reaction to the proximity of motherhood and nationhood in Aidoo's texts was that her choice was not in keeping with feminist practices. However, when I read the texts in relation to the gender ideology prevalent in Aidoo's matrifocal society before the colonial intervention, this reaction was modified. It is to this ideology that I now turn in my approach to the texts. Writing in the journal of the Plymouth Brethren, *Echoes of Service,* the missionary Marcia Wright lamented: "In Africa, socialism, polygamy and the law of 'mother right' deprives the father of all authority over his own children. . . . All this makes it difficult to apply New Testament injunctions to 'fathers,' 'mothers,' 'husbands,' 'wives,' 'parents' and 'children' in the family. Until there is some semblance of family life produced as a result of gospel teaching, it is out of the question to rush into the third or the church circle."[10] Writing in 1897, Wright had every reason to be nonplussed. If we take the case of the Akan-speaking peoples of West Africa, the group to which Aidoo belongs, we may guess what Wright was confronted with. Among the Akan, as among many matrifocal societies in Africa, marriage was polygamous and there was strict separation of economic wealth within marriage. The idea of shared worldly goods, either held commonly by the conjugal couple as a unit or by the husband, did not exist. This extended to custody of children, too—they did not belong to both parents but to one, depending upon the focus of social organization within the particular group. In matrifocal societies, lineage was traced from the males on the mother's side. Virilocality was not the norm and neither was marriage a legal or a binding relation; hence there was no concept of the 'illegitimacy' of children. In the polygamous structure, as Wright noticed, the family unit consisted of the mother and her children rather than the conjugal couple and their children. The mother was solely responsible for the upbringing of her offspring, and since the father took little or no financial responsibility, his status in the family was not congruent with that enjoyed by his Western counterpart.[11] Thus, it may be clear what the emotional investment in motherhood connotes for a matrifocal society, added to the economic and social investments. The nature of family relationships as Aidoo views them is therefore different from the relationships that obtain in my society and leads to the difference in gender ideology and in the nationalist discourse underpinned by this ideology.

Yet the colonizers managed to effect a change in a very important sphere, a change that was to prove decisive in divesting the women in these societies of their power and status and imposing upon them what Amilcar Cabral called the "extraordinary dimensions" of a double oppression that resulted from the existing systems of subordination as well as from the new ones imposed by the colonizers.[12] The colonizers had no experience of dual political systems like those prevalent among the Akan or the Yoruba.[13] Neither did they understand the idea of the separation of wealth within marriage. Hence any form of self-government for the colonized firmly excluded the women, though women had had extremely important roles in precolonial local governments. Besides, the fruits of advanced Western agrotechnology were made available only to men, ostensibly because men grew cash crops and women, subsistence crops, but actually because the colonial policymakers could not conceive of the fact that even when they were "married," men and women could keep their incomes separate. The cultivation of profitable cash crops became the sole preserve of the males, and they could control the economic surplus.[14]

These economic and political changes were brought about by specific colonial policies, served to rearticulate gender ideology along Western lines, and marked the firm entrenchment of patriarchal hegemony in societies where hitherto women had enjoyed important roles in and out of what the Western theorists conceive of as the family circle. There was male primacy and male domination in these societies before the colonial intervention, but women also possessed their own structures of control and were strongly bonded together to resist oppression because the family ideology was so different from that of Western societies.[15] Though childbearing is considered important because the future of the group depends on it, the abstract idealization of the maternal role that is possible in patriarchal societies is not possible among the matrifocal Akan. Hence, one cannot read the texts of the new diaspora as an allegory of the abandonment of the idealized nation-mother. By underlining the constructed nature of this ideal, Aidoo attempts to expose the affective burden of symbols that woman have to bear in patriarchy in a twisted form of assent to their own subjection. She calls this "the mother thing," used as much by those who wish to remain overseas as those who wish to invoke the image of the deprived mother to call them back. Those perennial students whose degrees are never earned, who keep adding to their qualifications just to spend some more time abroad, use mother as an excuse: "Everybody claimed that he wanted to make sure that he did something for 'MY MOTHER.' Send money home to her to build a house while they were still abroad, or the first thing they did when they got back. 'Because,' they would add, 'My mother has suffered'"(*OSK,* 133). Although Sissie accepts the truth of this suffering, her squint-eyed vision is clear enough for her to realize that mother is being used as a shield for shirking the duty to the nation. Her rhetorical retort is sharp enough: "But isn't there a danger that we might think we are solving a very old corporate problem by applying individual piecemeal measures? So all of us who have been overseas build houses for our mothers. Then what next? (*OSK,* 133).

It is because Aidoo refuses to conflate the trials of the "post" colonial nation with the reality of the suffering of the mothers that a story such as "Other Versions" is so poignant.[16] Here, the hero, Kofi, is put through school by his mother's toil. Eventually, he wins a scholarship to go abroad. When he begins to tell us his story, he is well ensconced there. He has been meaning to put by "money for mother," but of course, his own needs keep increasing and the money he wants to send to her keeps being spent. As the story progresses, it is clear that Kofi feels guilty at not being able to do what seems to him a gesture of appreciation for his mother's labor and sacrifice. Then one day when he is returning home by the subway, there is an aged, tired black woman in the same car with him. Unable to contain his guilt any longer, he blurts out: "Eh . . . eh . . . I come from Africa and you remind me of my mother. Please would you take this from me?"[17] And he hands her some money. Kofi's desperate attempt to assuage his guilt is a poignant comment on the nature of the mother image that members of the willing diaspora concoct to deal with the reality of their escape from the milieu their mothers have to struggle in. Aidoo does not fail to highlight the tawdry and inadequate nature of their attempts at compensation.

Aidoo's comments on the willing diaspora thus attempt to go beyond the accepted images of duty and responsibility and reveal the sense of waste that is involved in young skilled professionals not finding the courage to return and face the challenge of reconstructing the society that the colonizers have left behind. If mother as an excuse to stay away is unacceptable, so is mother as a reason to come back. Aidoo does not offer ideals to those whom she invites to return. As she says in an aside during an argument with a brilliant Ghanaian surgeon who insists on staying on abroad, "I was groping for a way to tell him what was in my mind. Of life being relevantly lived. Of intangible realities. Such stuff. Yet I didn't want to get caught up in a lot of metaphysical crap. When an atmosphere is as inert as Africa today the worst thing you can do to anybody is to sell him your dreams" (*OSK*, 122–123).

Neither dreams nor images are the reason for which Aidoo invites the young prodigal to return. When the people she is trying to persuade add to the "horror stories from home" canon, she cannot but agree that the newly independent nations have none of the infrastructural facilities that they take as a matter of course in the West. It is rather an austere commitment, a dedication, that she holds forth. For her, it is presence and activity, rather than theory in absentia that is the first step to solving the "corporate problem" left behind by the willing departures of the young. The woman who speaks in the story "Everything Counts" thinks, after she returns home from overseas, of "her brothers, lovers and husbands. But nearly all of them were still abroad. . . . They used to tell her that they found the thought of returning home frightening. They would be frustrated. . . . Others were still studying for one or two more degrees. . . . That was the other thing about the revolution."[18] To these dissemblers, Sissie has only one thing to say: "Instead of forever gathering together and virtuously spouting such beautiful radical analyses of the situation at home, we should simply hurry back" (*OSK*, 121). This is the core of Sissie's comment on the main task that members of the willing diaspora keep putting off. In a sense, it is also her way of putting the problem in perspective, divesting it of symbolic or idealistic trappings. Barbara Christian has pointed out that motherhood is a uniquely female experience interpreted for women by male agencies of control.[19] Aidoo's intervention in the discourse of national/"post" colonial reconstruction is at once an important position in countering the patriarchal nature of these discourses. In Aidoo's texts, mothers are flesh-and-blood people who form the basis of the family unit with their children. They feel a sense of loss when their children leave home and defer their returns. But they are in no way allowed by Aidoo to take the place of the nation and entreat their children to return. Instead, she exposes all attempts to "use" mother as an argument for going away or staying away, insisting on the mother's experience as one that must be seen in human rather than in symbolical terms.

Taken as a whole, Aidoo's work is organized around the experience of womanhood in her society, and she is careful to delineate the changes that colonial policies effected in the organization and ideology of gender among her people. In fact, in her play *Anowa* she parallels the condition of slaves, members of the first diaspora, with the condition of women in her society after the colonial intervention disrupted the existing social structures.[20] In a society where a bond of kinship forms the basis of social organization, a slave is an outcaste not because of his lack of wealth or status but because "he has no home, no family, no village, no stool of his own; has no feastdays, no holidays, no state, no territory" (*Anowa*, 37).

In African societies, where slaves were owned before colonial traffic in human cargo, the slave was defined by her kinless state. In a corporate social structure, she had no one with whom to form a community, hence no support system or social roots. Aidoo links this alienated state of the slave to the changed position of women, which she shows as resulting from the institutionalization of slave labor and its commercialization after the arrival of the colonial traders. Anowa marries Kofi Ako, and together they start a business. Repudiating the norms that govern marriage in her society, Anowa becomes Kofi's trading partner. They form a conjugal unit with shared economic resources, Anowa giving her labor free to Kofi because of the relation between them. When Kofi begins to make a profit, he wants to buy slaves as a symbol of his newly acquired status and he no longer wants Anowa to work alongside him. Not only does he not consult her anymore, he wants to relegate her to the position of "my glorious wife, the contented mother of my children" (*Anowa,* 38–39). Kofi's trading success is partly owed to Anowa, yet he has taken her labor for granted as part of his right as a husband. She, however, has wanted to establish a conjugal relationship that is different from the norm in their society. In fact, they dream of being the "new husband" and the "new wife," models that their society has not seen so far. In this they are quite successful: Seeing Anowa selflessly struggling alongside her husband and helping him in his business, people mistake her for his sister because wives in their society do not generally allow their husbands to have their labor and if they do, it is rarely given free (*Anowa,* 29). Anowa has willingly sacrificed her separate identity and her economic independence for the sake of a "new," or modern, conjugal relationship between them. Now Kofi clearly tells her that she need not bother with work and refuses to take her advice when she cautions him against buying slaves by succinctly reminding her that she is "*a* woman" while he is "*the* man." She points out: "I had as much a mouth in beginning the trade as you had. And as much a head" (*Anowa,* 29). But by then, Kofi has already internalized the role of *the* man, and Anowa is left without the support of the other women because she has left home and tried, by her own organization of conjugal relations, to change gender ideology within marriage. She feels for the slaves because their state is like her own. As a woman trying to take on a new gender role, she feels that "one can belong to oneself without belonging to a place. What is the difference between any of your men and me? Except that they are men and I am a woman? Neither of us belongs" (*Anowa,* 36). This is true indeed for the woman-as-wife in a monogamous marriage within patriarchy. Like a slave, she is cut off from kith and kin and from sorority with other women, and her labor is used without payment: Her body is owned by the husband-as-master. So because Anowa decides to sever her roots and blaze new trails, she ends up dispossessed like the members of the first diaspora. But what leads to this condition? If we follow her father's analysis of her condition, it will remind us of the members of the second willing diaspora. He says: "But don't other women leave their homes to go and marry? Do they stay away for ever? Do they not return to the old homestead to attend funerals, pay death debts, return for the feeding of their family stools? And if they did not do that what would homes-and-homes do? Would not the clans break up for lack of people at home? The children of women like Anowa and their children-after-them never find their way back. They get lost. For often they do not know the names of the founders of their houses" (*Anowa,* 31–32).

Restless within the confines of their own societies, young people like Anowa wish to chart their own course. Yet their explorations are always partial, what Sissie has told us are personal solutions to corporate problems. They rarely take the whole picture into account. Aidoo links the two diasporas of the African people in *Anowa.* The rise of the slave-based monetized economy ties in with the dispossession of women. And here, monetization and the economy of surplus begin with the colonized era, as does the insistence on the monogamous, mobile family norm. Maria Rosa Cutrufelli points out: "The modern nuclear family does not stem from the evolution of pre-existing structures from the forced integration of traditional societies into a capitalist economy. It arises along with the need for a geographical mobility of the labour forces of individuals."[21] This is exactly what Aidoo shows us in *Anowa.* And she goes further in linking the problem of a crumbling social fabric with the directionless state in which the young find themselves, a state from which no positive agendas for replacing the chaos left by the colonizers can emerge.

The diaspora in Aidoo's work is thus linked to the position of women in patriarchal "post" colonial societies that were once matrifocal. In that sense, it is, as a literary allegory, a mode of reporting on the condition of these societies with special reference to the prevalent gender ideology in "post" colonial times. The importance of the diaspora is threefold. First, forced transportation marks a traumatic break with the ground in which the individual's psyche is based. The sense of unbelonging that characterizes the slave and Anowa as a woman may be ascribed to this severance. Aidoo explores the economic and affective bases for this severance with respect to the alienation of the slave and the woman at the historical conjuncture when global capitalism implicates the peripheries within its system. She avoids the easy parallel between deracination and the distancing of the child from the mother, choosing instead to analytically focus on the problem through representation of changing gender organization. The growth of the slave-based economy and the dispossession of women are materially connected through this analysis; this is the second factor to which the idea of the diaspora introduces us in her work. Finally, the diaspora is not limited to those who were transferred by force; it includes also those who choose a new path without proper respect for the one that exists.

Aijaz Ahmed refuses to give this second movement the same name, for he argues that to connect the experience of pain and devastation that characterized the first with the willful desire for self-aggrandizement that characterizes the second would be an insult to the former.[22] But Aidoo opens up another dimension of this second diaspora, not from the point of view of those who leave but from the point of view of those who stay. Here lies the third aspect of the idea of the diaspora in Aidoo's work. She shows the linkage between the loss suffered by those who await the return of the eternal students from overseas and the loss suffered by their new nations, which need the skills that they have gained there. And once more, she does this without using the allegory of nation-as-mother; rather she focuses on the various reasons the members of the second diaspora manage to forward for their continued absence and deconstructs each one of them. The responsibilities shirked, the jobs left undone both at home and in the public field, are held up again and again to counter any argument that these young people may present in their own favor. And in Aidoo's counterarguments we read the rudiments of a discourse of reconstruction of "post" colonial societies. So instead of outright rejection, Aidoo's stance on the willing diaspora is one of engagement and of dialogue. She senses the need that the newly independent nations have, the intensity of their desire for the presence and labor of the skilled professionals who insist on staying away. Perhaps it is her emotional investment in the relationships between those who stay and those who refuse to return that prompts her to write so poignantly and perceptively of this problem—her own sense of dispossession, of rootlessness as both "post" colonial woman in a patriarchal society and as "post" colonial intellectual struggling to find a direction to reconstruct this society.

Yet it is not only the departures, forced and willing, that Aidoo talks about. To me, as an academic educated and writing in English, she addresses another concern. And this seems to me to be the most important point she makes in the context of the study of "post" colonial cultures carried out in an international language and aimed at an international market. In her meetings with members of the "willing" diaspora, Sissie argues with them, trying to induce them to return. Among them is the young medical practitioner whom we have already met. He retorts that by reaching the top of his profession, he has "made (his) people proud" (*OSK*, 127). Sissie counters: "If we are not careful, we would burn out our brawn and brains and a whole lot more trying to prove what you describe as 'our worth.' . . . And anyway who are they? So please come home, My Brother. Come to our people. They are the only ones who need to know how much we are worth" (*OSK*, 129–130).

Sissie underlines the importance and utility of skills and knowledge acquired from overseas as a strategic device to deal with problems at home. Besides, she also addresses the question of the moral direction that underpins this acquisition, a morality intimately connected to political choice. The spurious allurements of universal humanism fudge over the intentions of a floundering institution at the center that thrives on cosmetic accretions from the periphery. Identifying centers and peripheries of course depends on one's own position—and this is the slip that characterizes our deployment of technology designed at the "center" to read texts produced at or about the "periphery." Given our access to the language in which these texts are written, not only linguistically but conceptually, we tend to use them in ways that reinforce the in-built hierarchies that they put into circulation. Our commitment to our own cultural products can then be compared to that of the medical man whom Sissie is trying to convince. He announces indignantly that he certainly has not lost connection with what is so popularly called "roots," that he does go home once a year because "it is necessary for one's perspective. So refreshing. Keeps one in touch with reality. And not only that. It is proving very useful. . . . You know that area so often discussed, so much speculated upon? The marriage of African medical insights with western clinical expertise? It's an explosion" (*OSK*, 129).

This marriage will probably be one of the pitfalls of a cultural studies project that is not careful of its foundational principles. As someone who erratically forays into the field, I see this as a warning that the diaspora is not really physical anymore—it is epistemological and has to do with our roles as willing or unwilling informers and interpreters.

One may turn, then, to cultural studies to lead to profitable encounters. It is in this context that Gayatri Spivak's critique of the cultural studies "trafficline" becomes valid.[23] Spivak points out that this consists of ways of studying cultures, especially "third" or "fourth" world cultures, that conceal "a complicity between the bourgeoisie of the Third World and the migrants in the First."[24] I hope to have rerouted this traffic flow somewhat in the exercise undertaken previously. But Spivak's own agenda for a project of a kind of "culture praxis" if one may so name it, also creates some discomfort for academics placed as I am in the interstice of indigenous cultural practices that make up the stuff of my daily life and imported theoretical inputs with which to think them through. Spivak talks of ethics as "the experience of the impossible" and maintains, "This understanding only sharpens the sense of the crucial and continuing need for collective political struggle. For a collective struggle *supplemented* by the impossibility of full ethical engagement,—not in the rationalist sense of 'doing the right thing,' but in this more familiar sense of the impossibility of 'love' in the one-on-one way for each human being—the future is always around the corner, there is no victory, but only victories that are also warnings."[25]

There cannot be any disagreement with either the impossibility or the necessity outlined by Spivak; what she states is self-evident anyway. If in the mists of humanitarian essentialism, the delusion of all-conquering love did exist, then its obverse, as evidenced by irreversible impossibility, was bound to surface in the era of poststructuralisms. The question that remains is one of motive; Spivak is acute in discerning "the migrant academic's desire to museumize a culture left behind,"[26] but what of those who remain behind and have to engage with these cultures at various levels on a daily basis? For us, hemmed in by theories of alternatives grounded in alien conceptual systems, it is imperative to reach a position of "love" before its impossibility can be accepted. Our positions, in fact, as Spivak herself diagnoses, are predicated and heavily informed by the constraints of this impossibility, influences that show in the nature and process of our collective struggles.[27] This is a fact that strikes me as contrasting with Aidoo's *Anowa*—"love" (impossible perhaps even in a situation of equality that Spivak indicates as a marker of possibility) needs a full presence, however difficult it may seem for us to imagine it thus when its *difference,* absence, is rooted in our conceptual processes. The various shades and layers that constitute any one level of a cultural spectrum proffer different investment possibilities to different people. For one variety of migrant academic, love is as Spivak and Aidoo describe, an ore to be used; for some others, such as Spivak herself, it is the sign of an impossibility that is nevertheless an imperative and at the same time an illumination of a chosen discourse of Eurocentric theory, it's vindication and qualification. For yet others, such as Aidoo, it is a way of life; it is to be lived. And for those who are placed like I am, it must be a matter of choice, of deciding when and how to march or speak, how to learn what academia has omitted to teach: In effect, learn how to struggle and how to love, for the moments of struggle serve to obliterate the moments of the impossibility of "love." Marilyn Strathern points out, "Western investment in the metaphor of language as a carrier of culture, and of culture texted like a language, projects a counterworld of concrete individuals and natural bodies and of stubborn, non-linguistic forms. Westerners forever try to access that counterworld through composing and decomposing language itself—to trick it into revealing the unintended, to bring speech to the unspoken."[28]

"Literacy" as a cultural medium has gained currency in African societies like Aidoo's as a result of the colonial intervention. The obsession with the written word is a result of the colonial intervention; and its primacy over all other forms of cultural communication, indeed its complete domination over any other form, is perhaps a gift of those who learned the colonizers' language and, with it, the colonizers' habits of thought. This has happened in most "post" colonized societies in varying degrees, depending on whether the precolonized culture of that society was an oral or a script culture. At the end of all this analysis, it appears that reading Aidoo's texts has given me this insight because her society was "visited" by the written word at the entry of the colonizer, whereas mine had it for centuries before this. Given the class background from which I write, where education and literacy are values in themselves, the other forms of cultural communication are less visible and immediate, both mentally and physically, for me than they are for Aidoo. This also ties in with the extent and nature of resistance to colonial cultural hegemony with respect to our two societies. The agenda of cultural studies in the context of "post" colonial societies would therefore seem to be, from personal experience, an attempt to define (not *re*define) our own conceptual apparatus. This is not a return-to-the-roots call, for the colonial "encounter," as it is politely called, has left its residue in the framing of our selves and societies, and present exigencies themselves will direct and influence us as much as we attempt to direct and influence them. It is with all these concerns in mind that we need to engage with our contexts. Beginning from a perception of difference and similarity, from an understanding of broader narratives of different cultures that we need to engage with if we do not shut ourselves off from the worlds that we live in, cultural studies projects can help us in tangible ways—if we remember, with Sissie, "that whatever is sweet has some bitterness in it. . . . We have to determine the amount of bitterness we take from the sweetness of the present" (*OSK*, 115).

NOTES

1. Ama Ata Aidoo, *Our Sister Killjoy: Reflections from a Blackeyed Squint* (London: Longman, 1980). Further references to this edition are cited in the text as *OSK*.

2. Jasodhara Bagchi, "Representing Nationalism: Ideology of Motherhood in Colonial Bengal" *Economic and Political Weekly*, October 20–27, 1990, WS 65–71.

3. Madhusudan Mukhopadhyay, *Sushilar Upakhyan*, reprinted in *College Street*, (Calcutta: Saradiya, 1393 B.S.).

4. Shivaji Bandyopadhyay, *Gopal-Rakhal Dwanda Samas: Upanibesbad O Bangla Shishu Sahitya* (Calcutta: Papyrus, 1398 B.S.), 192–241.

5. Himani Bannerji, "Fashioning a Self: Educational Proposals for and by Women in Popular Magazines in Colonial Bengal," *Economic and Political Weekly*, October 26, 1991, WS 52–53.

6. Ibid., 53.

7. Satischandra Chakravarty, *Sataner Charitragathan* (Calcutta, 1396 B.S.), 74–75.

8. Marilyn Strathern, *Reproducing the Future: Anthropology, Kinship and the New Reproductive Technologies* (Manchester: Manchester University Press, 1992), 118–132.

9. Krishnabhabini Das, "Amader Hobe Ki," *Sahitya* (Kartik-Chaitra, 1890).

10. Marcia Wright in *Echoes of Service*, quoted in R. Robertson, "Post-Proclamation Slavery in Accra," in *Women and Slavery in Africa*, ed. P. Robertson and M. Klein (Madison: University of Wisconsin Press, 1983), 249.

11. For discussions of gender organization in West Africa see C. Oppong, ed., *Female and Male in West Aftica* (London: Allen and Unwin, 1983). For a study of conjugal relations among Aidoo's people, see K. Abu, "The Separateness of Spouses: Conjugal Resources in an Ashanti Town," in Oppong, *Female and Male*, 156–168. See also C. Obbo, *African Women: Their Struggle for Economic Independence* (London: Zed, 1981).

12. Amilcar Cabral, quoted in Maria Rosa Cutrufelli, *African Women: Roots of Oppression*, trans. N. Romano (London: Zed, 1983), 175.

13. For the dual political systems among the Yoruba, see Simi Afenje, "Women, Power and Authority in Traditional Yoruba Society," in *Women, Power and Visibility*, ed. E. Leacock, L. Dube, and S. Ardener (New Delhi: Oxford University Press, 1986), 136–156. For the dual political system among the Akan, see Barbara Callaway, "Women in Ghana," in *Women in the World*, ed. L. Iglitsin and R. Ross (Santa Barbara, Calif.: Clio, 1976), 189–199.

14. For an analysis of economic changes in the position of women as a result of colonial policy, see Ester Boserup, *Women's Role in Economic Development* (London: Allen and Unwin, 1970). See also Obbo, *African Women*, and Cutrufelli, *African Women*.

15. For accounts of the change in the position of women in the social and political spheres as a result of colonial policy and "post" colonial legislation, see Jane L. Parpart, "Women and the State in Africa," in *The Precarious Balance: State and Society in Africa*, ed.

N. Chazan and R. Rothchild (Boulder: Westview Press, 1989), 218. See also Haleh Afshar, ed., *Women, Ideology and the State* (Bassingstoke, Hamp.: Macmillan, 1987). For studies on changes in laws governing marriage in Ghana, see Sefwi Wiaoso, "The State and the Regulation of Marriage (Ghana, 1900–1940)," in Afshar, *Women, Ideology and the State,* 48–69; and D. Lee Vallenga, "Attempts to Change the Marriage Laws in Ghana and the Ivory Coast," in *Ghana and the Ivory Coast: Perspectives on Modernization,* ed. P. Foster and A. R. Zolberg (Chicago: University of Chicago Press, 1971), 125–150.

16. Ama Ata Aidoo, "Other Versions," in *No Sweetness Here* (New York: Doubleday, 1971).

17. Ibid., 86.

18. Ama Ata Aidoo, "Everything Counts," in *No Sweetness Here,* 8.

19. Barbara T. Christian, *Black Feminist Criticism: Perspectives on Black Women Writers* (New York: Pergamon Press, 1985).

20. Ama Ata Aidoo, *Anowa* (London: Longman, 1980). Text references are to this edition.

21. Cutrufelli, *African Women,* 41.

22. Aijaz Ahmad, *In Theory* (London: Verso, 1992), 85.

23. Gayatri C. Spivak, *Imaginary Maps,* (Calcutta: Thema, 1994), p. 201.

24. Ibid., xviii.

25. Ibid., xx.

26. Ibid., xviii.

27. Spivak cites as an example Gita Sahgal's documentary on the *sati* of Rup Kanwar, noting, "None of the urban feminist radicals in the film was able to acknowledge that quite apart from the obvious male coercion, brutality and exploitation, Rup might indeed have seen the *sati* as an ethical choice." Ibid., xxv ff.

28. Strathern, *Reproducing the Future,* 85.

15

Where Do You Come From? Posing and the Culture of Roots

ALICIA BORINSKY

Back to Motherhood?

A pregnant woman in the depths of Africa and a French explorer meet, exchange gazes, are portrayed in magazines. She is the smallest woman in the whole world. He has found a subject of study, but the separation between explorer and woman in unstable. We are told that she loves him. The protagonists of Clarice Lispector's "The Smallest Woman in the World"[1] could not be more different from one another, she loves him precisely because of that difference. His boots, his ring, his not being black in Africa, are the sources of her sentiment. She does not look for a being distinct from possessions because, we are told, "in the humidity of the jungle, there do not exist these cruel refinements; love is not to be devoured, love is to find boots pretty, love is to like the strange color of a man who is not black, love is to smile out of love at a ring that shines"(95). For "Little Flower"—the woman—love is grounded in the material details offered to her gaze; a language soon develops between her and the explorer. We do not know what the explorer feels, but it is made explicit that the note-taking during conversations is a mask for his shyness.

An unlikely romance indeed between someone who is an object of curiosity and a researcher. Beyond the class or cultural differences evoked in the many versions of *Pygmalion,* the story suggests that the very definition of love is at stake here. Whereas in *Pygmalion* the romance works, the interest there is in overcoming difference: One of the partners, frequently the woman, is elevated by the better one to a higher realm of culture and consumption. The "Blue Angel" type romances stress the negative possibilities of the blurring of differences by presenting the older male as going ineluctably toward damnation through his blind misunderstanding of the gap that separates him from the woman, suggesting perhaps that men ought to engage more reluctantly the denial of who they are than women, who have more chance of "improving" themselves through love.[2]

Lispector's story is a rejection of the conventional presentation of cultural clashes and love. "Little Flower's" love is nothing short of interested; we are told that she loves to possess. The explorer cannot utter what he feels. And yet the story closes with the commentary of an anonymous old woman who, upon looking at the news about "Little Flower" in the newspaper, folds it saying: "It just goes to show. I'll say one thing though—God knows what He's about" (95). What has the old woman understood?[3] The cliché "God knows" accompanied by "what He's about," one of Lispector's dark jokes about fate, also points to a secret shared by the comfortably homogeneous community of which the woman is a part.

The readers of the story, consumers of difference, rejoice in their sameness as they consider the enigma of explorer and minute woman. "Little Flower" is a native par excellence: naive and yet materialistic, taken in by the details of appearance. Her being pregnant emphasizes the threat of change posed by "natives": They will multiply; the future may be theirs if the others do not watch out. But Lispector states in the story that "Little Flower" is bound by love. Her size is such that her nativeness may be confused with the cuteness of folkloric ornaments. Thus, the consumption of foreign goods, exoticism, and fear of the unknown are blended in the representation of "Little Flower."

There is something almost brutal in the acknowledgment that it is love she experiences, because the unsentimental treatment of the situation makes us aware of love as a fact we are barely able to qualify. Love is used as a shorthand for something that the readers are supposed to know but do not recognize in this situation. As in the story entitled "The Chicken"—in which a bird singled out for dinner lays an egg, causing the children of the house to interpret it as a sign that it loves them—there is a certain bewilderment in the use of the term "love" in "The Smallest Woman in the World."

Singled out for a newspaper story, the couple poses as a representation of love as difference.[4] Less blatant than the chicken, this other mother—"Little Flower"—offers her sentiment in the language of the reader as something capable of redeeming her difference from them. She is pregnant and she is capable of love. What is the explorer to do? The story does not tell us whether they stayed together or parted, whether his notes were valuable, or what, if anything, in her caused him to leave or stay. We suspect that neither of them changed, that the encounter was brief, and that the scientific mixed with real human experience was resolved without resort to melodrama.

The final appeal to God's mysterious ways restates a silent pact between the pair. Like the bond between children and bird in "The Chicken" that allows the kids to drift away after having obtained a pardon for the chicken, this couple is already fading into the background. The intensity of their encounter is as fleeting as the domestic drama in "The Chicken." "Mummy! Mummy! Don't kill the chicken, she's laid an egg! The chicken loves us!" (51). The mother is not about to be swept away by the enthusiasm of her children or the sentimentalism of her husband, who feels guilty for having made the chicken run, not knowing that she was pregnant. We are told that "the mother, feeling weary, shrugged her shoulders" (51). Not unlike the old woman in "The Smallest Woman in the World," she knows that life may be mysterious but there is nothing to be excited about when an egg is laid. The chicken itself, or rather *herself* (as the story says), is not granted permanent human traits because "In flight or in repose, when she gave birth or while pecking grain, hers was a chicken's head, identical to that drawn at the beginning of time. Until one day they killed her and ate her" (52).

What are these stories telling us about motherhood? With unblinking humor, Lispector rejects commonplaces of the treatment of the subject time and again. Chicken and "Little Flower" are two extreme representations of mothers as a distinct species. But in her view, their differences are not to be enshrined. The chicken's reprieve from death is not very long, "Little Flower" gains no depth for being pregnant, and the children's mother in "The Chicken" in her weariness seems to have done away with the need to respond at all to any recognition of mothers as deserving a special status.

The chicken was a beneficiary of the husband's and the children's pity; the mother remained indifferent, as though the feast of sentiment, the excess involved in sympathy, was not part of her nature. Happier, "Little Flower" is in love, factually in love in a celebration of her capacity of not being subsumed by her feelings. Lispector's gaze depicts pregnancy and motherhood devoid of an ideology of sacralization of the female. An entry in Witold Gombrowicz's *Diary*[5] tells us of his impression as he observes a female friend reacting to the painful agony of a dog: "She suddenly changed into a female—she took refuge in her sex . . . what a sudden eruption of gender into the realm of pain; as if gender could cope somehow with the pain. . . . She became a female, that is love, that is pity. She bent over the dog with a mother's tenderness. Is it possible that as a female she could do no more than as a human being? Or, did she retreat into her sex in order to escape her own humanity?" Gombrowicz thinks that the specificity of gender debases what is universally human and is thus inclined to disregard what he considers to be the most feminine of reactions: love and pity. In the particular situation at stake, the woman's pity has the particularly cruel result of prolonging the dog's agony. Misplaced, female sympathy is both destructive of the ones that seem to be its beneficiaries and the one bestowing it, since she becomes a mere exponent of her own gender. Lispector's carefully drawn apathetic female characters (in marked contrast to the protagonists of the stories she authored under a self-defined erotic rubric[6]) try to avoid the softness of femininity and find, that way, their own humanity as a question mark. Bird and woman in "The Chicken" share their separation from the family; the chicken, we are told, is just that, and the woman, recognizing it, does not place any particular value on her motherhood.

But children need motherhood; they need to know that their emergence into the world is crucial. They need to protect the chicken and then forget her; they would like to think that "Little Flower," instead of loving the boots and ring of the strange explorer, is totally engrossed by her future delivery. If that is not the case, a most important bond will have been severed; there will be no return possible to a home, an origin, a point of departure. The dizziness and aimlessness of the female characters in Lispector's *Family Ties* suggest that being born and giving birth are part of a neutral continuum to be portrayed in a measured, unmoving way.

I Know You, Come Back Home

Max Barabander in Isaac Bashevis Singer's *Scum*[7] has a problem he hopes to solve by going back to his place of birth. A Polish Jew who emigrated to Argentina at the end of the last century, he becomes impotent after the death of his only son. His wife loses her interest in life and sex. The money they made in Argentina allows them to travel extensively, so Max's return to Poland is just one more trip, although its importance is compounded by the fact that it is designed to serve two purposes: mark his success as a businessman and take him back to a source of energy that might rejuvenate him and restore his sexual potency. Max is drawn with great detail, with a propensity to signal his psychological capacity to do just about anything—to lie, betray, and take advantage of others.

Max's impotence is soon overcome once he becomes entangled with women in Poland, but his sexuality, rather than a celebration of regained youth, is an occasion to show his lack of focus and unreliability. A member of the cast of characters that readers of Roberto Arlt recognize as having been marked by the kind of humiliation and moral skepticism of Buenos Aires and tango in the early twentieth century, Max toys with the different possibilities opened up for him in Poland.[8] When he gets, as he wanted, to Krochmalna Street, he goes into a tavern, eats, and talks. Familiar smells, foods, expressions, greet him; a bemused comment in response to his having come back to the place where he once lived dismantles any sense of having entered a truly different domain: "When people come here they say it feels like home. Once a man from London showed up and drove over to Falenicz with us. In London, he said, there's no clean air—it's all smoke and the sun doesn't shine. Every day there's a fog and it rains, too. There money is weighed by the pound or the Devil knows what. But one thing is the same everywhere—you have to hand out bribes constantly" (21). Max's trip is, thus, to a certain extent just a geographic displacement. The same system of bribery is to be found in London, Poland, Argentina. The food may smell and taste different, things are certainly less modern, more provincial, but the lack of reliability approximates all places. Max's voyage was not undertaken for the sake of finding purity; he wanted to recover what made him desire and perform with women. Once he accomplishes this task he is seemingly ready to go back. Where would he go, though?

Buenos Aires begins to take on the allure of home. After all, his wife is there; he has real estate holdings and his mission is completed. Tourism of origins is not the subject of the narrative. As we read on, we realize that this will not be a round-trip affair. Max's search is widened. Among his experiences are spiritualist seances, from which he emerges feeling alternatively duped and inspired, as well as a transaction in which he considers the possibility of becoming a pimp in Buenos Aires by importing unsuspecting young women from Poland.[9] If being part of the white slave trade excites him into new depths of awareness of his capacity for sleaze, his courtship of the Rabbi's daughter, Tsirele, gives him access to an atmosphere of holiness.

The observant Jewish home is described with the fascination of exoticism in the novel: The family members have a different air; they are more austere than others, more direct; money does not interest them; they look wise. They are one possible version of Jewish roots in Poland; their world is complete but not insulated from what goes on outside. Max is afraid of being discovered by them and having all the different, unconnected layers of his behavior thrown into the open: "The rebettzin mumbled something with her thin lips and made a sign that she could not speak. The sun reflected on her wig and lit up silken hairs of many hues. Max suddenly felt afraid of this woman. He sensed that even though she was observant and lived in a religious world, she thoroughly understood all his underhanded ways" (72). Nevertheless, he is able to manipulate them into letting him come into the house and visit with Tsirele. Tsirele's seduction is easy; the attraction he feels for her is compounded by his curiosity about her world. The Jewish roots represented by Tsirele are not a given for Max. He is a different kind of Jew. He falters, experiments, and thinks of religion with great intensity but ultimately as a lifestyle one could drop into and out of, Max convinces the rabbi that he would be willing to grow a beard and wear the clothes characteristic of observant Jews. He will pose as an observant Jew, then, with such conviction that he will become one. The rabbi and his family are part of a Polish fresco, a set scene into which Max bids entrance and in which he promises to wear the right costume. In his logic, this costume will be both a disguise and a partial truth.

But how essential is Tsirele's own relationship to this apparently constant world? Tsirele is not Shosha.[10] Shosha stands for a wisdom that may be confused with childishness and has a relationship to Jewish observance that is at the same time engimatic and unquestioned; Tsirele is a grown, smart woman. In very much the same way as Max, she thinks of changing her appearance, to his surprise. At first, Tsirele is portrayed "pale as if after a sickness, dressed up in a white blouse and in a light green skirt" (100) and Max, in a fling of religiosity thinks that he could "kiss her like a mezuzah" (101). A few pages later, Tsirele visits him in his hotel, markedly changed: "He looked at her, stunned. She was wearing a light-colored suit and the straw hat he had bought her. He had never seen her look so elegant. Nobody would have taken her to be the daughter of a rabbi; she could just as well be a countess. Max was suffused with joy and shame. Is it over her that I'm agonizing? I'd give my last groschen to be with her! he thought" (107).

Max's sentiment is echoed in the lyrics of many a tango: The man, hopelessly in love with a woman he deems innocent, leaves everything he has or changes his ways only to see her later and realize that she has become unworthy. In this case, what devalues Tsirele in Max's eyes is the fact that she has changed in his direction. Max's return home should have been, in his view, such that he would become enveloped by the coherence of a scene and change himself into one of the participants. Whether pimp or observant Jew, Max needs to shape himself as a character by including himself in one of the narratives already in progress. Changes in other characters conspire against the stillness of the poses he wants to affect. For Max, this is not the result of apathy, as is the case of the mother in Lispector's "The Chicken." On the contrary, it is a free-floating energy for drama.

A voyage to a place of birth is thus portrayed as the most hollow of pursuits. There is no density of experience for Max, and what is worse, Tsirele's way of dressing suggests that there had not been enough of it in her own. The timelessness of religious ritual and looks has been cracked by a costume; Max's influence triumphed over her upbringing. Standing in front of Max, Tsirele is testimony to the inexistence of his trip, to the vanishing of the distance between skeptical Buenos Aires and Poland. And yet, Max reacts with passion to her visit and feels that his virility has been restored.

The account of Max's trip ends with him going to prison because of having fired a shot as he was about to have sex with Reyzl, an unscrupulous woman who stands in opposition to whatever was represented by Tsirele: "They all stared at him in silence. Everything had been ordained from the beginning. Max was seized with a kind of piety mixed with fear. He, Max, had come to Warsaw to perpetrate all this craziness for only one purpose, to realize his dream" (218). Finally, Max has been *recognized.* The case he has come to visit, imitate, identify with, has measured him and defined him. Yes, he does belong among them, in Warsaw. In prison. Thus, a voyage to roots approaches perfection. Hollowness and frantic role playing come to an end. With relief, Max assumes the name that the title of the novel proposes: Shoym, Scum.

His place of birth is now devoid of the indifference to origins in Lispector's "The Chicken" and "The Smallest Woman in the World." He has been discovered and defined by his motherland. Max has arrived home at last. These are his roots and here he will meet his punishment. What makes the ending of Max's search so compelling is the coherence with which his life may be gauged. A truly Borgesian turn in the story has made it possible to reread a seemingly ambiguous trip as an ethical imperative.[11]

Lispector and Bashevis Singer, in this joint reading, have woven uncanniness into the issue of origins: Centrality has been taken away from motherhood, and both religious and cultural identity have been revealed as mere elements in Max's diverse poses. Through these disquieting narratives, essentialist views of collective and individual definitions by genealogy are challenged without celebrating each person's capacity to represent a hypothetical universal humanity.

Cultures, Ignorance, a North-American Campus

The mistrust of excess evident from the texture of Lispector's work and in the definition of Max as a character in Bashevis Singer's *Scum* is one of the elements that relates a poetics of sparseness to the suspicion of the kind of folklorism frequently present in the formulation of a problematic of roots. In *Pnin* by Vladimir Nabokov we find a ruthlessly humorous look at efforts of crosscultural transmission.[12]

Pnin, a professor of Russian in the United States, flees "Leninized Russia" and ends up teaching at a North-American university. His efforts at taking up a new identity are immediately visible in his appearance:

> Prior to the nineteen-forties, during the staid European era of his life, he had always worn long underwear, its terminals tucked into the tops of neat silk socks, which were clocked, soberly colored, and held up on his cotton-clad calves by garters. In those days, to reveal a glimpse of that white underwear by pulling up a trouser leg too high would have seemed to Pnin as indecent as showing himself to ladies minus collar and tie. . . . Nowadays, at fifty-two, he was crazy about sunbathing, wore sport-shirts and slacks, and when crossing his legs would carefully, deliberately, brazenly display a tremendous stretch of bare skin. Thus he might have appeared to a fellow passenger; but except for a soldier asleep at one end and two women absorbed in a baby at the other, Pnin had the coach to himself. (8)

Pnin has changed to fit his idea of his surroundings. But as he takes the wrong train to deliver a lecture, he does not have witnesses for his newly acquired looks. His style goes unnoticed. Bound nowhere and missing his appointment, Pnin is introduced to us as a character who is out place in spite of his efforts. He is a learned man and a bemused observer of the United States. The Russia he left is no longer, and the new persona he tries to build is a composite of his insights about the United States and his sense of faithfulness to something intermittently resembling an intellectual pursuit.

Life at Waindell College creates for him the special isolation frequently found in foreign language departments. At a certain point he has only one student, "plump and earnest Betty Bliss in the Transitional Group" (9) and less than a handful in the other levels. His teaching of the Russian language bears no relationship to that of

> those stupendous Russian ladies, scattered all over America, who, without having had any formal training at all, manage by dint of intuition, loquacity, and a kind of maternal bounce, to infuse a magic knowledge of their difficult and beautiful tongue into a group of innocent-eyed students in an atmosphere of Mother Volga songs, red caviar and tea; nor did Pnin as a teacher, ever presume to approach the lofty halls of modern scientific linguistics, that ascetic fraternity of phonemes, that temple wherein earnest young people are taught not the language itself but the method of teaching others to teach that method; which method like a waterfall splashing rock to rock, ceases to be a medium of rational navigation but perhaps in some fabulous future may become instrumental in evolving esoteric dialects. (10)

Pnin speaks English idiosyncratically: He has an accent and speaks in frequently mistaken constructions that clearly point out the fact that he is thinking in Russian. Like his spoken English, Pnin's appearance is the result of an effort at translation. He tries to convey his own person in this different context to his classes by telling them anecdotes of how he was admitted to the United States. Students give him mixed reviews. Some enjoy him; others complain about his bootlegging poetry into classes in which they were expecting to learn only the Russian language. Neither an abstract-minded linguist nor an intuitive transmitter of the customs of Russian, Pnin does not quite fit into Waindell College.

Pnin's awkward presence on the American campus contrasts sharply with that of the well-adapted natives: students who seem to Pnin too wholesome and inclined to the rural life to have any meaningful relationship to culture, and a series of amusing faculty members that includes a language department chairman whose lack of knowledge enables him to be all the more competitive as a chairman, since he will not be distracted from his administrative duties by an undue interest in academic subjects.

Nabokov's *Pnin* suggests that the teaching of a foreign culture even by those who are supposed to know it best leads inevitably to ridicule. The ignorance of students and administrators, on the one hand, and the misplaced earnestness of the few students who strive to excel, on the other, are part of a continuum in which true knowledge is lost. The circuit of lectures and foreign culture discussions are a smorgasbord that trivializes subjects and participants. Beyond a parody of life on an American campus, *Pnin* is an intense portrayal of the irreversible nature of exile. The Russia that Pnin left will never return, and the United States he has encountered is perceived by him only partially. In the States he is a character, a caricature of the open opportunity for travel and intellectual survival. And yet *Pnin* is very much a novel about local color. Its narrative takes us ineluctably to a humorous view of national idiosyncracies; its articulation emphasizes the dictatorship of material details and invites us to join in: Let's look at how you wear your underwear in the States versus in Russia; let's appreciate the differences in food, sunbathing, weight, reading. Reading *Pnin's* mockery of exoticism as consumerism of the picturesque, we cannot but realize that the novel proposes that a humble but decisive form of knowledge about humanity emerges from the arbitrariness with which individuals are tossed in different directions by history. Struggling through the ignorance of his students, a faintly ridiculous Americanized Pnin is learning, like them, the lessons of displacement.

Through my joint reading of Lispector, Bashevis Singer, and Nabokov I have proposed a nonessentialist view of cultural origins. "Little Flower" and the French explorer stare at each other in a fixed pose; although connected by love and objects, they remain simultaneously separate from their roots and strange to each other. The relationship among chicken, egg, and love that children and husband so intensely but fleetingly defend in "The Chicken" provokes a mere shrug of the shoulders in the mother, who really knows what this is all about but keeps it to herself. Max's voyage to his roots in *Scum* is not a return but an encounter with the ethical definition that he had been due since the beginning; thus, rather than a change of place and language, he meets with what is universal and unchanged.

As Professor Pnin plays with language and culture in his difficult attempts at communication, the double effect of the novel's humor reinscribes him. The works of Lispector and Bashevis Singer imply that the collective world of clichés and clear-cut cultural origins favors posing over substance. Nevertheless, for any versions of the self to emerge even awkwardly, that domain of misencounters, capricious pronunciations, and false attributions is of utmost necessity. Crosscultural transmission, condemned by definition to error and misdirection, celebrates its new meanings as it leaves behind an illusion of univocal roots and origins to acknowledge its own uncanniness through images, snatches of conversation, translations, exotic menus, partially understood books, and music.

NOTES

1. Clarice Lispector, *Family Ties* (Austin: Texas University Press, 1972). Further references to this work are cited in the text.

2. Manuel Puig's *The Kiss of the Spider Woman* offers a most important treatment of the political implications of such changes. The two protagonists of the novel are in a jail cell in a relationship precipitated by the police to make one (a leftist guerrilla) give out secret information to the other (a homosexual accused of corruption of minors). In the course of their incarceration the retelling of movie plots becomes a source of intimacy for them. The tendentious separation between love and politics permeates the most explicit layer of the novel, suggesting that radical change in one member of the couple signals unconditional love for the other, whereas the ending of the novel restores and emphasizes the prevalence of the political domain. I have written about this at length elsewhere. See my *Theoretical Fables* (Philadelphia: University of Pennsylvania Press, 1993).

3. Clarice Lispector is particularly eloquent about women and old age. Throughout her fiction she treats the subject with austerity, emphasizing the idea that older women possess a special kind of intuition. Her treatment of this subject is in marked contrast to that by other Latin American authors of this century who, while stressing the intuition of older women, attribute to them the negative traits with which witches are portrayed in Hispanic letters. See, for example, José Donoso's *The Obscene Bird of Night* and Carlos Fuentes's *Aura.*

4. In Lispector's treatment, this is not infrequent. As in María Luisa Bombal's fiction, we encounter the idea that men and women speak different languages. Thus, "Little Flower" is a hyperbole of what we find elsewhere in Lispector's oeuvre.

5. See Witold Gombrowicz, *Diary* (Evanston: Northwestern University Press, 1989), vol. 2. Page numbers in the text are for this edition. The entry quoted belongs to the period that Gombrowicz spent in Argentina.

6. In a last interview before her death in Rio de Janeiro, Brazil, in 1977 Lispector talked about what she saw as two extremes of her own personality—she was shy and daring at the same time—and related them to her work. See "O testamento de Clarice Lispector," *Shalom* no. 296, pp. 62–65.

7. Isaac Bashevis Singer, *Scum* (New York: Farrar Straus Giroux, 1992). Page numbers in text refer to this edition.

8. Max's intensely amoral behavior, intertwined with sexual inadequacy and a will to self-humiliation, recalls Roberto Arlt's Erdosain in *Los siete locos* and *Los lanzallamas,* as well as Balder in *El amor brujo.*

9. Roberto Arlt, as well as other writers of the earlier part of the century, noted the trade in women from Poland for prostitution. Polish and French women, seduced by Argentines who promised them marriage, would be brought to the country and then forced to prostitute themselves, having lost hope of returning to their countries because of the great cost of the trip. Their fate is recorded in novels, films, and tango.

10. In his novel *Shosha,* Bashevis Singer presents us with a female character whose growth seems to have been stunted and, because of that, is able to conjure up for the reader the enigma of her wisdom as a special form of intuition only open to those who have preserved the innocence of youth.

11. In Borges's work, death is frequently seen as completion. He motivates the reader to reread the story or poem as though everything had led to the particular end that took place; in his stories the dying are shown the shape of their lives.

12. See Vladimir Nabokov, *Pnin* (New York: Random House, 1989). All text citations are to this edition.

16

About Face: The Talker Turns

DORIS SOMMER

THE FIRST SENTENCE of *El hablador* gives a start, a shock, a double take, as the narrator misses a step to gasp with surprise. Facing him is precisely the thing he had escaped. "I came to Firenze to forget Peru and the Peruvians for a while, and behold, the damned country forced itself upon me this morning in the most unexpected way" (3; 7).[1] The first move of the story is not a departure but an about-face, a shocking recognition that Peru will not be left behind. Long before the narrator identifies himself as a writer named Mario Vargas Llosa, even before the text spells out any identity or attributes or any subjectivity, background, or future for the speaker, he responds to Peru in this syncopated moment of choosing to leave and being taken aback. His double take is an involuntary reflex that will trigger reflection. He is hailed by an authority that can stop him short and call him home, and that call begins to constitute Vargas Llosa as a character.

Halt

Louis Althusser understood the subject of an ideology as one who responds to authority when, for example, a policeman yells "Hey you" to someone running. The runner can respond by accepting the interpellation of the law and stopping dead.[2] And, more to the point here, the narrator's halt is like the commanding moment in Emmanuel Lévinas's ethics when the subject is born from the labor of facing an unknowable but inescapable Other who demands recognition. Transfixed and helpless in their derivative identity and in their humbling mortality, Lévinas's subject and Vargas Llosa's character practically shudder at the awe-ful impact of a human face that issues divine demands. The novel that follows is about the face, which is inscrutable on ethical, not on epistemological, grounds. After the stunning first sentence stops the narrator in his escapist tracks, the paragraph continues, fixed on photos from Peru:

> I had visited Dante's restored house, the little Church of San Martino del Véscovo, and the lane where, so legend has it, he first saw Beatrice, when, in the little Via Santa Margherita, a window display *stopped me short (me paró en seco):* bows, arrows, a carved oar, a pot with a geometric design, a mannequin bundled into a wild cotton cushma. But it was three or four photographs that *suddenly (de golpe)* brought back to me the flavor of the Peruvian jungle. The wide rivers, the enormous trees, the fragile canoes, the frail huts raised up on pilings, and the knots of men and women, naked to the waist and daubed with paint, *looking at me unblinkingly (contemplándome fijamente)* from the glossy prints.
>
> Naturally, I went in. With a strange shiver and the presentiment that I was doing something foolish, that I was *putting myself at risk (arriesgándome)* out of mere curiosity. (3–4; 7; my emphasis)

The commanding images draw Vargas Llosa, turn him toward Peru, and threaten nothing less than his freedom to be far away, a subject-centered freedom that Lévinas would have recognized as ethically suspect.[3] Curiously, though, the riveting presence of Peru exists only as a trace here, not as the flesh and blood that would command a face-to-face Lévinasian engagement.[4] The glare of pictures comes from already absent faces, flattened into two photographic dimensions to show already evacuated Indians, as well as the modern technologies of evacuation. The contradiction between the passivity of pictures and their active subject-effect on the narrator—"staring at me"—is not just a symptom of what Lacan might have called paranoia about things that know more than people.[5] We will see that the contradiction is also a symptom of the novel's general indecision about Indians in a country where they are either its deepest soul or its most stubborn obstacle to development.

Besides providing a double start for this story, the scene of impossible flight may also be an evocation of a Peruvian writer who had stopped in Italy years before and had been just as dramatically pulled homeward. Perhaps himself a sign for so many New World subjects digging for European roots, he turned up more contrasts than confirmations and confirmed instead his Americanist calling. In any case, the reflexive traveler seems, by now, an unlikely secret sharer for a narrator named after the increasingly conservative Mario Vargas Llosa.[6] That other errant American in Italy was José Carlos Mariátegui, chief ideologue in the 1920s for the indigenized Marxism that has, until now, marked left-wing Peruvian politics.[7]

> In Italy I felt the fragility of the lie that makes us a spiritual annex of Rome [Mariátegui mused]. I understood how alien we Spanish-Americans were at that banquet. I perceived simply and precisely how artificial and arbitrary was the flimsy myth of our kinship with Rome. . . . Like him [Waldo Frank], I didn't feel American except in Europe; on the streets of Europe I encountered that American country which I had left and where I had lived almost in absence, as a stranger. Europe revealed how much I belonged to a primitive and chaotic world, and at the same time it imposed on me the responsibility for an American project.[8]

Visions of a primitive world would compel Vargas Llosa's narrator too, but more theatrically than in Mariátegui's nonfictional memoirs. The novel practically makes the pictures into protagonists who hail the speaker and dictate his mission. Whereas Mariátegui turns inward on his own American self during the famous disencounter with Italy, Vargas Llosa stages a sharp turn around toward the American Other. The jolt of recognition is dramatic, probably to capture the disaffected narrator and perhaps to capture readers who may have imagined themselves equally free from home. If Mariátegui had located an internally divided Peruvian self, between modernized occidental and traditional "oriental," Vargas Llosa doesn't presume to contain the contradictory sides.

Either this reluctance to contain Peru is a facile admission of limits based on rigid notions of difference between Indian tradition and modern projects, or the lack of presumption can be an ethical caution against containment and control of the incommensurate cultures in a multifarious nation. On the one hand, Vargas Llosa could be absolving himself from the moral obligation of inclusiveness and tolerance, likely given his impatient prescriptions for neutralizing and nationalizing specifically Indian cultures. But on the other hand, more promisingly, the refusal could be read against his politics as a defense of difference. *El hablador* may not be an argument for the survival of parallel and simultaneous story lines; but the novel *is* a sustained performance of simultaneity. Primitive Peru is, admittedly, outside of the narrator named Vargas Llosa. But it holds him, along with us, hostage in its gaze.

The promise of recognition is gripping, and it announces the recursive shape of the entire novel, circling around the same sticking point of Peru's claim on our attention and returning obsessively to the confrontation in Florence. To repeat the danger and to predict calamities inside the novel as well as out, we should note that the grip may be paralyzing and nonnegotiable in ways that portend unethical responses to entrapment.[9] The dilemma underlines a certain peril in the Lévinasian moment of ethical engagement, a peril that comes into focus once the moment of confrontation drags into the messiness of narrative development. The problem is that unstinting attention to the Other cannot remain static and unblinking; the following move is either an identification with otherness so complete that it denies one's self or a self-preserving dismissal of the agonist. Absolute alterity, it seems, can make one kind of aggression or another practically inevitable. It leaves no room, philosopher Enrique Dussel worries, for the social dynamism that Latin America desperately needs.[10]

Vargas Llosa would experiment with both ways out of the Lévinasian hold. Through a selfless storyteller, he wrote that any interference with the Other is murder: "'These cultures must be respected,' he said. . . . 'And the only way to respect them is not to go near them. Not touch them'" (98–99; 96–97). But more consistently, he has argued as a sorry but single-minded spokesperson for necessary interference and incorporations: "It is tragic to destroy what is still living, still a driving cultural possibility, but I am afraid we shall have to make a choice. . . .

[W]here there is such an economic and social gap, modernization is possible only with the sacrifice of the Indian cultures."[11] Nevertheless, *El hablador,* at least, keeps the alternatives in tension and fixes the dilemma into static, unnerving irresolution. The rhythm of this novel is almost lyrical in its reluctance to move beyond the gripping moment into the unethical disorder of historical time.

Turn

The visions that rush at the halting narrator would soon conjure up memories of talk as if to move him from confrontation to engagement[12] or perhaps simply to move into a medium that might privilege narrative. The memories bring back a Jewish friend who had studied anthropology in Lima and become fascinated with the fragile existence of the Amazonian Machiguengas. That was before the misfit friend called Mascarita, for the birthmark that covered half his face disappeared from the capital, maybe to settle in Israel. His non-Jewish mother and his refugee father had produced the divided or doubled identity of their son, grotesquely masked by the two-tone face, so that Saúl fit nowhere in Peru. (The splintered life and the line of escape are apparently modeled after the novelist Isaac Goldemberg. Like Mascarita, Goldemberg moved from his mother's province to his father's Jewish community in Lima. Then he went to Israel and to New York, where he told the story "The Fragmented Life of Don Jacobo Lerner" (1979).[13]

Saúl Zuratas had abandoned anthropology early on because, he said, among other murderous incursions of modernity, ethnography itself was killing Indians. His professor seems incredulous:

> Saúl's starting to have doubts about research and fieldwork. Ethical doubts. . . . [H]e's taken it into his head, can you believe it, that the work we're doing is immoral. . . . He's convinced that we're attacking them, doing violence to their culture. . . . That with our tape recorders and ball-point pens we're the worm that works its way into the fruit and rots it." Saúl Zuratas had flabbergasted everyone, proclaiming that the consequences of the ethnologists' work were similar to those of the activities of the rubber tappers, the timber cutters, the army recruiters, and other mestizos and whites who were decimating the tribes. "He maintained that we've taken up where the colonial missionaries left off. That we, in the name of science, like them in the name of evangelization, are the spearhead of the effort to wipe out the Indians. (32–33; 33–34)

In a novel structure redeployed from Vargas Llosa's *Aunt Julia and the Script Writer* (1977),[14] where chapters from young Mario's autobiographical romance alternated with suggestively similar scenes in radio soap operas, *El hablador* switches back and forth from one kind of narration to another, from a history of the Hispanic intelligentsia in Lima to an evocation of repetitive Amazonian lore. The style of the evocation, it should be said, is a cause for concern in a novel that seems to respect culturally specific languages, because the indigenous sounds are familiar from Quechua-inflected Spanish with its trailing gerunds (*diciendo, hablando*) at the end of sentences, for example.[15] The Andean sounds are so improbable in the jungle that the effect is to suggest the writer's in-difference to Indians.

One structural disparity between *El hablador* and *Aunt Julia* is that the story lines of the ethnographic novel don't implode into the hilarious jumble of the radio-style romance, where real life takes leads from fiction and high art aspires to the charm of kitsch. Instead, the slips from one side to the other in *El hablador* feel like raids or contaminations. One story line overtakes the other, tragically. The overlaps are aggressions, not ironies; and differences vanish because they are overridden, not because they are misprised. Alternating chapters move from the narrator's memories of Saúl amid activities in Lima's mass media to chapters in the *hablador's* voice, recitations of creation myths, and the cultural history of a people described as the dispersed and precarious Machiguengas. The tribe barely holds together through the act of ritual telling. That is why the North American missionaries are so monstrous in the end with their translated vernacular Bibles that evacuate lore from language. By the time Bible fragments filter into the jungle stories (adapted from the translations of Padre Joaquín Barriales), they sound like a prelude to doom.

The narrative slips might have suggested flexibility, the creative indefinition of frontiers that animates *Aunt Julia.* If one culture is not entirely immune to another, it may not be allergic either. Millennial traditions can be adaptive, as activists for cultural survival argue.[16] But here, the Machiguenga names that the narrator drops in his own story (e.g., 173, 181–182; 168, 176) amount to decoration rather than to a dynamic cultural disturbance. And on the other side, the unbidden biblicized tales of Tasurinchi-jehová—his triple form, an expulsion and a future annihilating wind (215–221; 207–212)—profoundly disturb listeners for whom time itself should work differently. "For the Machiguengas," the narrator explains unambiguously as if to forestall any more interpretation, "history marches neither forward nor backward: it goes around and around in circles, repeats itself" (240; 229). So their response is to leave, to further disperse in an ever more precarious jungle (240; 230). A small number of the tribe had survived natural disasters (thanks to their modest expectations of nature and to inflexible standards for themselves), and some had escaped forced labor under lumber and rubber barons (by moving ever deeper into hardly habitable jungle), but the remnant is finally overpowered by translators. "Those apostolic linguists of yours [Saúl protests to Mario] are the worst of all. They work their way into the tribes to destroy them from within. . . . The others steal their vital space and exploit them or push them farther into the interior. At worst, they kill them physically. Your linguists are more refined. They want to kill them in another way. Translating the Bible into Machiguenga! How about that!" (95–96; 93–94, see also 162–163; 157).

The accusation, and by extension the whole novel as a debate-driven drama about the future of Indians in the Americas, may remind some readers of the revolutionary climate that the jungle would incubate after Mario and his friend disputed the country's future beween 1953 and 1956 (34; 36). In 1963, when Saúl was reported in Israel (news that makes Mario intone a prayer to Tasurinchi for his friend's safety from border conflicts [108; 106]), student rebellions were flaring in Peru (242; 232). During the same year, long before the Sendero Luminoso launched its guerrilla campaign in 1980,[17] some Cuba-inspired intellectuals were trying to trigger rebellions in focal points throughout the countryside. One early *foco* was the jungle town of Puerto Maldonado, where an unlikely combatant and victim was a personal friend of Mario's. It was Javier Heraud, the well-known poet who was hardly more than a boy and who had recently been in Paris, making the rounds of cafés and bookstores with Vargas Llosa. Heraud is still stunned and grieving; his eulogy is an indictment of a desperate country. "That Javier Heraud should decide to take up arms and become a guerrilla only indicates that Peru has arrived at a breaking point. No one was further from violence than he, by temperament and conviction."[18] The memory returns in the novel when the narrator mentions his frustrating 1981 trip to Puerto Maldonado. The entire production team of his television series *The Tower of Babel* went there to recreate the battle and to commemorate Heraud, although its dysfunctional equipment "screwed up" the effort (149–150; 144–145). The martyred poet is the subject of another novel contemporaneous with *El hablador:* Aida Balta's 1987 *El legado de Caín,* which names Heraud among the country's irrecuperable losses to violence.

Heraud's move from the capital to the tribal interior may find a tribute in Vargas Llosa's portrayal of Saúl's desertion of the academy for the people it studies. But the fictional friend is a different kind of rebel. Saúl's specific rage is about cultural imperialism. Beyond the armed struggle at Puerto Maldonado, there was a distinctively anthropological battle being waged by nationalist ethnographers. One stimulus was the self-reflexive and engaged ethnology of José María Arguedas (1911–1969), whose Andean boyhood and cultural ties were giving social science a local cast. His enormous contributions to ethnology are sometimes overshadowed by Arguedas the novelist, according to Angel Rama in a eulogy for the tormented bicultural man who had committed suicide.[19] It was that novelist with his flair for ethnology who surely inspired Vargas Llosa as he doubled himself, irreconcilably, in the homonymic narrator of personal histories and in the nameless *hablador.*[20] Arguedas is the only Peruvian writer about whom Vargas Llosa repeatedly writes and teaches.[21]

During the 1960s and 1970s, local ethnologists were taking positions for and against interference from foreigners, including North American anthropologists who tended to idealize "native" cultures.[22] The standard line of thought, and of government programs from the 1930s to the 1960s, favored a dynamic *mestizaje* that amounted to progress toward national integration and objected to pristine indigenous cultures.[23] But progressive anthropologists in Vargas Llosa's generation, according to Enrique Mayer, read the North Americans' respect for Andean continuity as welcome relief from the establishment's renewed denigration of Indians. It was conservative Peruvians such as Vargas Llosa, and his conservationist alter ego, Zuratas, who used anthropological romanticism to defend static and extreme distinctions between tradition and modernity; they were counterpoising "deep Peru" (doomed as backward and Indian) to "official Peru" (the modern and whitened future) and getting the country into deep trouble, Mayer says.

Critics are right to say that Zuratas is driven by the same abstract language of cultural incommensurability that defines Vargas Llosa's dichotomous and inflexible politics. But the novel's indigenist hero is not simply a sentimental double for its writer. Saúl is also the novel's vehicle for lingering in "deep Peru" during as many pages as are devoted to the official country. Whatever rush toward modernity may be moving the plot and pushing Vargas Llosa's political pronouncements, whatever evacuation confronts us from the first page of picture-book Indians, the novel *performs* a parity of attention span between tradition and modernity. It detains the rush for as long as we read. In fact, the "deep" and "official" lines will cross in the crossover hero himself and in narrative threads that weave from one context to another. The borrowings bring back the Peruvian tradition of dialectical anthropology even though the novel will frame the dynamism as contamination rather than adaptability. However Zuratas is framed, whether as the conservative's alter ego or as a self-defeating dreamer, his indigenous world holds us throughout the novel. Through Saúl, Vargas Llosa seems reluctant to let go, not just guilty.

Debates about "American" anthropology simmered during the 1960s, but another American interest in Peru was more explosive. The Summer Institute of Linguistics (SIL) outraged traditionalists who, like Saúl, railed against the "apostolic linguists." SIL had been founded in the early 1950s by North American evangelical Protestants known as the Wycliffe Bible Translators (named for the fourteenth-century English translator), who shared McCarthy's anticommunist mission. From the beginning, SIL counted on support from USAID and the CIA to establish bases throughout the underdeveloped world.[24] Its declared purpose was to study indigenous languages; in fact SIL also established bilingual schools and vaccination campaigns and otherwise introduced isolated peoples into an expanding market economy and state institutions, all of which pleased local governments. But SIL's most devout purpose, as everyone knew, was conversion. Indigenous languages mattered because they were potential vehicles for the Bible. The enterprise elicited conspiracy theories left and right. Between them, David Stoll balances some complicated details:

> Wycliffe has fielded linguistic missionaries in more than 300 languages, supported by air and radio networks and sponsored by governments. Although it has started [in 1982] to lose government contracts . . . in the mid-1970s Wycliffe was an official arm of the governments of Mexico, Guatemala, Honduras, Panama, Surinam, Colombia,

> Ecuador, Peru, Bolivia and Brazil. Unless all the mission orders of the Roman Catholic Church were counted as one, no other transnational organization surpassed Wycliffe's influence among Indians. None matched its command of Indian languages and loyalties, its logistical system and official connections. Nor did any collide so spectacularly with Indian civil rights organizing and Latin American nationalism. The ties binding together this interior empire, to native people and to governments, started to snap.[25]

Local pressure strained SIL's delicate legitimacy, as the missionaries of God's truth kept telling strategic lies about their linguistic interests. "Then governments started to decide that SIL might be a useful sacrifice." They warned Washington that SIL's influence had limits as a way of conceding to Indian and indigenist oppositions while maintaining control. In Peru, SIL's days were numbered until 1976; Brazil issued an embargo against SIL in 1977, and Colombia threatened expulsion. And Mexico revoked its contract in 1979, followed by Panama in 1981, when Ecuador ordered it to leave within the year. "Each government faced the same, disquieting phenomenon: increasingly visible, militant Indian organizing. Indigenous nationalism was on the ascent, a trend to which, like a number of other brokers, SIL had contributed in largely unintended ways. Promotion of literacy, the trade language and inter-group contacts helped members of scattered local communities identify themselves as ethnic wholes."[26] Accused of everything from fronting for U.S. imperialism and misleading potentially Catholic souls to fomenting communist conspiracies, the relentless linguists are the main concern of chapter 4 in *El hablador.*[27] It is not that Catholic evangelizers (so visible in *La casa verde* [1965]) were more benign, explains Saúl, but that they had fortunately become too isolated and impoverished to do much harm. By contrast, the Bible-belt evangelists had the resources to conquer peoples who had resisted everyone else, from the Incas to the colonizers and the capitalists (96–97; 94–95).

Vargas Llosa personalizes the history of the Summer Institute with mentions of his own visits (beginning in 1958) to an Amazonian camp, mentions condensed from his memoir about writing *La casa verde.*[28] Despite warnings from the Hispanophile historian Raúl Porras Barrenechea about the nefarious influence of the meddling gringos, the narrator accompanied anthropologist José Matos Mar on an expedition organized for Juan Comas, a Mexican colleague. In his fictional persona, Matos is the mentor of an increasingly unwilling Saúl Zuratas, whose reluctance prefigures the generally "third world" skepticism about ethnography's interests and interferences, as Eduard Said describes it.[29] Today's self-critical anthropology is one response, although sometimes care can lead to even more self-interestedness, precisely by focusing on the investigating self instead of "objective" data. Conversely, some missionaries respond to the moral dilemmas of conversion—to saving souls by denigrating native religious identities—with tolerance (or at least forbearance) of "specific, limited, cultures." Their mission can be preventive rather than acquisitive; it can be the obligation to bear witness in order to obstruct authoritarian power. "Not being able to speak for others, however, does not mean we have no obligation toward them."[30]

Other observers take liberties to speak. And one who spoke up for the Summer Institute's meddling was Mario Vargas Llosa. In 1976, seven years after the Soviet invasion of Czechoslovakia showed that Cuba was in dutiful step with the aggression, Vargas Llosa had long since abandoned socialist ideals. As he moved to ever more conservative positions, he found SIL in need of support. The novelist was grateful to the translators; their literal agility had helped him to write *La casa verde.* They were adept not only at moving from one language to another but also at getting from one place to another inside the apparently impassable greenery. Vargas Llosa did his research among the "primitives" with the help of the polyglots' airplanes.[31] Other outsiders had benefited too, he recalls, echoing Saúl's (and David Stoll's) list of ethically suspect allies: ethnologists, missionaries, teachers, and soldiers (72; 71). But the suspicions didn't complicate Vargas Llosa's political support. In a public letter of April 25, 1976, he urged the Peruvian government to renew SIL's contract with the country. The linguists should be liberated from the suspicious indigenists, he declared. The government evidently agreed because if SIL were to leave, the institutions it had initiated could be overtaken by more dangerous groups such as communists and Indian organizers. The letter was published in the major papers of Lima and cosigned by sixty-five notable citizens, later seconded by sixty-six others. None of these was a linguist, Stoll reports; and the few participating education officials, indigenists, and anti-Marxist academics hardly offset the number of retired military leaders.[32]

But a dozen years later, and despite the echo of thanks to the linguists on the back page of the acknowledgments in *El hablador,* despite his alleged support for scientific investigation beyond "nativism,"[33] the dilemma about the rights of translation had apparently revisited the troubled novelist. The return of the repressed is written into every aggressive photo that accosts his narrator in Florence. During the interim between *La casa verde* and *El hablador,* the world had turned, and anxieties once directed at the jungle were now fixed on the Andes. From 1985 to 1987, while Vargas Llosa was writing *El hablador,* Peru's splitting political seams were unraveling more dangerously along the Andean mountain range than inside the Amazonian basin. And the Indians who now seemed most at risk, and risky, were no longer the tribesmen of the lowlands but the perhaps dangerous peasants of the Altiplano. Once the Sendero Luminoso loosed confusion on the Andes, outside observers had trouble distinguishing "revolutionary" terrorism from "official" military abuses. Nor was it clear where the doubly imperiled indigenous communities stood politically. Once the Indians had been displaced to the jungle, the worries over them were minimized.

Displacement is a mechanism that Freud named when he noticed that problems so grave as to threaten the subject with annihilating abjection were routinely replaced by peripheral signs. When an experience is too painful to remember and too intense to forget, memory replaces that event with a related but inoffensive element. The process is metonymic, a sliding from the essential part of that experience to "something in the neighborhood."[34] And in the general neighborhood of the country, the most urgent problem was no longer in Amazonia. Vargas Llosa's soul-searching and sympathy during the 1980s might well have been displaced from the tangles of the highlands onto the forgotten front in the jungle. How sobering, and sad, it is to notice that a defensive mechanism like displacement finds no safe terrain in Peru but only more or less urgently troubled territory. Self-conscious novel that this is (or self-interpretive in ways that preempt criticism), the text glosses or rationalizes the difference. Saúl argues that Andean culture has been contaminated since the conquest, and the faster it can be fully absorbed into the Peruvian nation the better for the already marginalized Indians; but Amazonia is still unconquered and independent. Absorption there, Saúl says, would bring only cultural death and ecological disaster (100; 98).

In the quiescent jungle, the novel's peace-loving Machiguengas are at first reticent to change, but then they become institutionalized in translation camps (161–162; 155–156). They had raised little resistance to the culturally annihilating goodwill of the foreign linguists, little resistance except for the hostile vagrancy of the storyteller. It is his aggressive anxiety that most distinguished him from the others, and it becomes the last piece of the novel's puzzle over the *hablador's* identity (181; 175). During Mario's second visit to the missionaries' camp, where he is preparing a television special, rumors about a skittish and obscure ritual talker are far more fascinating to him than the "athletic" and well-scrubbed hosts who are translating the Machiguengas into transparency. Readers, of course, have been hearing the *hablador's* ritualized narrative for several chapters and don't doubt his existence. What is more, his identity had, for a long while, been coming into focus as the red-headed, blotchy-faced, mixed-breed Jew, a millennial martyr to Christianity's forced conversions. He used to be Saúl Zuratas.

Is it Saúl whom Mario anxiously anticipates as he looks through the fifty photos in Florence? After fixing on scenes of scarce, scattered natives bent over their recent and meager crops, crouched among brilliant plumes for weaving crowns, and poised behind bow and arrow near a jungle river, Mario spots him "at first glance" (*a primer golpe de vista*): a silhouette standing in profile and talking animatedly inside a circle of cross-legged "hypnotically concentrated" Indians. What doubt can there be now? Mario has seen the real thing: "Un hablador" (9; 10). The first chapter ends with this two-word gasp of recognition, after the clerk at the gallery has unglued the speculator from the photo and ushered him out. The very next words, in evident apposition on a second reading, are from Saúl Zuratas. They begin chapter 2 as well as the novel's pendular rhythm between the city and the *selva*.

Turn Around

For a while, though, the rhythm is detained. The narrative delays its exploration of exotic folklore, and it stays the flights of political reflection. It invites, or commands, readers to withstand, for a bit longer, the Amazonian gaze that accosts and commands the narrator and his readers, perhaps to his peril and to ours. It will take an effort of submission to another's will to stay here because an unwillingness to stop may be the most flagrant symptom of our spiritually diminished modernity, as Stanley Cavell puts it. He calls attention to this dehumanizing loss of attention span in a classic essay on *King Lear,* "The Avoidance of Love." Relentless movement toward problems to be solved, toward anticipated developments, and an uncompromising need for conclusions—all this dynamism rushes beyond presentness and its insoluble mysteries, rushes to impoverish modern art forms of music, theater, and narrative.[35] Vargas Llosa's missionaries of monotheism and modernity are named Schneil, by the way, and mentioned by name in Saúl's diatribe (34; 36). The name obviously seems a corruption of the German "quick" in a heavy-handed, redundant image of modernizing assimilation and acceleration. In fact, Snell was the name of the real missionaries who translated and then published manageable condensations of Machiguenga lore.[36] Vargas Llosa took an orthographic liberty with the name, but history is already uncanny. Being quick and efficient in translating, moving one thing toward another, they have little capacity for the presentness that myth makes palpable in the recursive recitation of lore. Without that capacity, the most binding human relationships come undone, Cavell complains. Even love can be avoided.

Vargas Llosa's first pages call a temporary halt to the ravages of modernity, a pause in the acquisitive and problem-solving movement through time. They stop to stare hypnotically into the mystery of lost presence. And the following pages, until the very last one, keep up the recursive rhythm that holds Florence in focus. Everything there, from the picture gallery to the mosquitos, returns the reader to Peru (33, 73–74, 78, 90, 94, 236–246; 35, 72, 77, 88, 92, 225–235). Arrested from the first page by photographs, in his exercise of a modern prerogative called escape, the narrator doubles back with surprise at seeing an object he had escaped transformed into the subject before him. Vargas Llosa had left Peru behind only to find the country confronting him, defiantly, across the distance. To take a lead from the ironic "behold" in the opening line, it is almost like God confronting Jonah after the reluctant prophet tried to take a different route. Or to follow up on the feeling of double take, Peru may be more like that unrelenting cat in classic cartoons who is poised, ready to pounce, in the very room to which a desperate mouse has just escaped.

Face-to-face with the cat's demanding ubiquity, in response to its hunger and to the time-space-bending enigma of its always being there before one arrives, a mouse is compelled to respond. And the responses to danger, to unsatisfiable demands, to the incommensurable differences between the cat and himself, constitute the mouse as a subject (like the vulnerable narrator who becomes a persona by stopping at Peru's call). Without the confrontation, what would either character be in the cartoon? A deconstructive reading could point to the constitutive overlaps between the agonists: the same turf, the understanding of conflict, the same desire for victory and survival. Without sharing so much there could be no cat-and-mouse conflict. On another, psychological, reading, the mutual imbrication of antagonists might have a developmental dimension, since the mouse has become what he is through a series of near catastrophes. And because there is no escaping what he is, the catastrophic fantasies accompany the mouse as a structural necessity of his character; a cat appears because the mouse practically conjures him in order to feel normally neurotic.

On one reading, and on the other, I should note that the constructions and imbrications are mutual. They are reflexive in the sense that reciprocal verbs are reflexive; we see one another, for example. Whether the subjects of the story are called antagonists or, more benignly, interlocutors, an assumption of both deconstruction and of a particular psychological reading is a fundamental parity between the partners. Some years ago, deconstruction's ironizing project promised to level, to decenter and democratize, the polarized terms that structuralism had deployed almost inevitably in hierarchical relationships. It was liberating to see beyond the confining oppositions between male and female, black and white, self and other, to see both into the mire of mutually dependent constructions and into the corollary of destabilizing traces constitutive of meaning itself. This fundamental skepticism about the possibility of true meaning had a profound philosophical and even moral appeal. By denouncing the arrogance of knowing anything absolutely, it made an appeal to carefulness and circumspection.

The problem, of course, for any democratic use of these insights is that political difference is at risk if difference seems universally constitutive of any terms and if all tensions relax into partnerships. Self can appreciate its collusion with the Other in ways that mitigate antagonism; male can presume to ally with female, and black becomes an enlightened, recuperable category for right-thinking whites. If troubling barriers seem less important than the fissures that make barriers collapse, from what position does one make demands? The sticking point of an argument can get stuck in the rubble of collapsed categories. A more politically creative style of deconstruction might move from the cracks in one "language game" into another game, through political confrontation, to legal *adjustment.* Acknowledging difference then, would not be the final word but a first step toward enabling ethical negotiations.

. . . and Around

Dynamic and meritorious, maybe even feasible, this unstuck (Wittgensteinian?) twist on deconstruction may be a promising lead for pursuing some readings and some politics.[37] But it has almost nothing to do with the opening lines of *El hablador.* There, relationship is not reflexive in the reciprocal sense of mutually affective verbs and character constructions. Instead one character is reflective in both senses of the word: The narrator thinks hard about the Other he would have preferred to ignore, and he is made visible in the Other's light. Instead of partnership between the narrator and Peru, there is astonishment before an already existing, ubiquitously demanding agonist.

Rather than reciprocity, the opening lines offer an initiating asymmetry; what is staged is not a deconstructive tangle of hand-to-hand struggles for meaning or a complicitous version of hand-in-hand conspiracies to make meaning stable but something close to a Lévinasian face-to-face. It is a confrontation with an inscrutable face whose godlike stare frames the yet formless "hostage" in a demand for recognition. The very fact that the Other (country, cat, God) is there before us, the fact of time, locks us into responsibility: "Diachrony is the refusal of conjunction, the non-totalizable, and in this sense, infinite. But . . . this commands me and ordains me to the other, to the first one on the scene, and makes me approach him, makes me his neighbor. . . . It provokes this responsiblity against my will, that is, by substituting me for the other as a hostage. . . . It is the very fact of finding oneself while losing oneself."[38] Hostage first, and persona as a consequence; the Other first, as a precondition for the response that constitutes a subject. The self as a by-product; persona as response-able. With this dramatic reversal of subject-centered ontologies, Emmanuel Lévinas wants to trap traditional philosophy in its ethical shortcomings. He focuses on the unmanageable Other, who can face off against philosophy and stop short its rapacious march against difference. In a stance similar to Vargas Llosa's tarrying with Amazonian images, Lévinas's style detains readers in front of a difference that doesn't go away. Since Socrates, he says, fundamentally developmentalist and aggressive Western ontology has made difference disappear: It has welcomed difference as a challenge to be overcome and incorporated into the self. Difference has been an opportunity to quest for greater and deeper dimensions of one's own humanity.

> This primacy of the same was Socrates's teaching: to receive nothing of the Other but what is in me, as though from all eternity I was in possession of what comes to me from the outside—to receive nothing, or to be free. Freedom does not resemble the capricious spontaneity of free will; its ultimate meaning lies in this permanence in the same, which is reason. Cognition is the deployment of this identity; it is freedom. That reason in the last analysis would be the manifestation of a freedom, neutralizing the other and encompassing him, can come as no surprise once it was laid down that sovereign reason knows only itself, that nothing other limits it. The neutralization of the other who becomes a theme or an object—appearing, that is, taking its place in the light—is precisely his reduction to the same.[39]

"Philosophy is egology."[40] This is a lapidary charge that Lévinas hurls against voracious reason. The uncharacteristic staccato rhythm is surely meant to shock us with lucid simplicity. Sentences like these are stop signs along otherwise rambling and repetitive, passionate and almost excessive, passages. My observation is certainly not made to dismiss the page-filling patience of his arguments with philosophy as he veers away from its totalizing projects of cognitive control toward an openness onto infinity and vulnerability. I do not presume to judge how much detail a philosophical argument requires, though I call attention to Lévinas's exorbitant performance. Some of his sentences frankly hover about an issue rather than press a point. The issues related to respect for Otherness and responsiveness as initiating behavior are glaringly simple. Anyone who cares to get the point will do so in the first few pages of his two long books and his many essays. But readers who are driven to follow more intellectually complicated and therefore self-flattering routes manage to avoid the obvious, as Stanley Cavell and Stanley Fish can remind us.[41] Readers do not necessarily stop at the signs of difference that command respect, so Lévinas engages us there, for a long time, to circle the barricades and to underscore the threshold he is pointing to. Like Vargas Llosa's circular novel, like the mythic time that preserves the Machiguengas, a dizzy reader can imagine that Lévinas's text "marches neither forward nor backward: it goes around and around, repeats itself" (240; 229). He insists doggedly and keeps us occupied with the unflagging energy of almost encantatory reiteration, riveted by the bulletlike condensations, possibly humbled and probably too overwhelmed to muster objections.

With this thrust and parry Lévinas manages to detain philosophers who are circumspect enough to listen. Perhaps he will detain them long enough to impart a different kind of sensibility. From the drive toward closed, controlling, philosophical totality, the alternative sensibility would divert them toward a capacity for wonder at infinity. It might spoil the imperializing appetite for philosophical knowledge ("To know amounts to grasping *being* out of nothing or reducing it to nothing, removing from it its alterity"[42]) and leave room for an infinite, unsatisfiable desire for the Other. Then social science would cede to sociability and instrumentality, to love. Saúl Zuratas made that move when he turned from anthropology to the people it presumes to study. "Surely more emotional than rational," the narrator knows that Saúl's fascination with the Machiguengas is "an act of love rather than intellectual curiosity or the taste for adventure that seemed to lurk in the choice of career made by so many of his fellow students in the Department of Ethnology" (16; 19). This possibility of disinterested identification is the liberating commitment that Enrique Dussel holds out for Latin America as a step beyond Lévinasian awe of the absolutely Other.[43]

The "being" whose difference Lévinas is loathe to reduce, dissents profoundly from its Heideggerian homonym, which was written with a capital letter and pointed beyond people to a general, almost other-worldly, horizon between life and death. No less awe-inspiring for Lévinas but more exacting of response is the "being" that resides in a particular human face, which is the ultimate horizon of our devotion and obligation. His transcendent ethics is rigorously grounded in worldly relationships; nothing is more holy or more commanding than a human being.

Turning Away

There is one disturbing reason to remember the silhouette standing inside the enraptured circle of the Peruvian picture: It is the man's posture that is disturbing, vis-à-vis (but not face-to-face with) the camera. The photographer catches him sideways, looking at his listeners or at the jungle, in an obviously stolen shot. Probably warned by the traducing missionaries that the *hablador* would refuse to cooperate, as so many South American Indians do, turning away from camera-toting tourists, the professional resorts to sharpshooting. And he produces gorgeous pictures worthy of his best work on fashion models and furnishings for magazines like *Vogue* and *Uomo.* It is surely not the quality of the photos that earns him the novel's name of Malfatti. The pictures are far from badly done. But malfeasance has produced them. Evidence of stealth is, as I said, one disturbing feature of the photo. ("How did that Malfatti get them to allow him to . . . How did he manage to . . . ?" [6; 10]). Another worry is the very fact that the subject refuses to show his face.

The talker turns away from the host of modernizing Malfattis and missionaries. He makes no demand on the camera's eye and none on the viewer from the Florentine gallery. The man who denies his face thereby refuses to interpellate either viewer or reader as a subject. He won't talk to outsiders because talking, he knows better than anyone else, works the social magic of acknowledging and legitimating one's interlocutors. The *hablador* is practically an allegorical figure for what Lévinas calls the Saying. Saying is a sonorous appeal to the Other, more gripping than dynamic and as different from the data that are Said as sociality is from science. The talker knows he can preserve an entire vulnerable society by continuing to talk. That is what makes us human, after all, as Wittgenstein would remind philosophers who were losing their way in technical languages and forgetting the commonality of words and their social contexts. The translatable "content" of what the talker says is not the main point of his performance.

The point is to appreciate the enabling enchantment of address. That is why the title character of the novel is the "talker," in Mrs. Schneil's tentative term (91; 89), or "*speaker*" in Edwin Schneil's variation (173; 168).[44] The word is something of a neologism that seems neutralized by the common "storyteller" of the English translation. Nevertheless, it may be wonderfully apt as a reminder of an obsolescent tradition, a premodern narrative practice that Walter Benjamin embraced in an essay called "The Storyteller." It is a tradition of sparse and suggestive tales told to communities in contrast to modern novels that are written, pounced upon, and devoured in private.[45] The distinction between storyteller and narrator is by now hard to maintain in English and even harder to hear in the existing Spanish words *narrador* or *cuentero* or *cuentista.* So Vargas Llosa forced a new use for *hablador.* He evidently borrowed it from a colloquial register of Spanish that gives a name to unusual loquacity; but here, out of context and conjured to capture a role of anonymous, ceremonial locutor, *hablador* calls attention to its foreignness in European uses. "*Escuchadores*" is the equally uncommon, even clumsy, counterpart for those who hear the talk. *Oyente* would have been the standard Spanish word; it is as unremarkable as the English translation "listener" (209; 201). What is lost in this neutralization of strangeness into easily assimilable terms, I want to argue, is the use-value of the denaturalized words. Vargas Llosa's slightly strained semantics had fixed attention on the socializing activity of talking and listening. He had emphasized the contact as opposed to the content, the process rather than what was being processed.

Given the arresting first sentence of the novel, where Peru itself came out to confront the narrator, the cold shoulder from its most fascinating talker feels like an indictment. Startled into book-length reflections on the tragic heroism of indigenous cultures (reflections exhaustively interpreted and thematized in a novel that seems to make criticism superfluous), the narrator knows that he was the first to turn his back. Vargas Llosa, after all, is a runaway who had forfeited his chance for subjecthood (even in the Hegelian, pre-Lévinasian, sense of being recognized by the Other) when he averted his eyes from the Amazon that his fellow student was bringing home. The narrator stared a bit then; but only later as the jungle pursued him did he stare uncomfortably, unable to look away.

Toward Jerusalem

Some years earlier, the novelist Mario Vargas Llosa publicly reminisced about another shock brought on by photographs, and about his helplessness in the face of unanswerable demands. The occasion was his acceptance speech of the Human Rights Award from the Congreso Judío Latinoamericano in 1977. At a time when dictatorship was the norm for the continent, the long address in Lima was more concerned with abuses elsewhere. It featured a roster of totalitarian menaces, mostly from misguided socialism abroad and, by extension, from misguided supporters at home. His theme of culturally and technologically advanced civilization that can develop devastating policies of homogenization and control begins, as one may imagine for this occasion, with the national socialism of Germany. Specifically, it begins with a personal memory. Two years before the speech, Vargas Llosa was in Jerusalem, where he was enjoying the rose-colored light and the distance from Peru. He was there not to think about persecution or even to feel connected with the millennial culture that surrounded him but to relax and to write *Aunt Julia and the Scriptwriter.* This is the novel that develops the alternating structure used later in *El hablador.* During the mornings that autumn, he would write in an apartment that looked out on the Tower of David, the Jaffa Gate, and toward hills on the horizon just beyond the Dead Sea.

The vision was beautiful beyond reality, and it contributed every morning "to accenting my sensation of being apart from the world. The story which I was trying to write had as its theme precisely the shifting of reality into unreality by means of melodrama. Since the story took place in Lima, thousands of miles from where I was, it required a real effort to disconnect from my immediate surroundings. In that state of somnambulism, my friend found me, the friend who came every afternoon to show me around the city."[46] That particular afternoon, the escort didn't take Vargas Llosa to the markets or to streets that seemed like stage sets for the *Arabian Nights:* He drove past temple excavations, the orthodox quarters of Meah Shearim (the Hundred Gates), and the rest of the magical city. That afternoon, the writer remembers, "*the return to reality was brutal.* My friend took me to Yad Vashem, the memorial consecrated to the Holocaust, which rises on one of the pine-covered hills that circle Jerusalem."[47]

What was it, exactly, about the memorial that startled the touring somnambulist back to reality? What is it, in fact, that foreign diplomats may have seen when standard Israeli protocol, until very recently, required them to visit the shrine? It certainly was not the modern building or the isolated setting or even the knowledge that 6 million Jews were exterminated by the Nazis in a high-tech eugenic cleanup campaign. Everybody knew that. The otherwise inert historical data about mass graves, advanced biological experiments on practically dead meat, artifacts hewn from human skin, teeth, and bones, these came into brutal focus through the pictures on the wall. "There, in front of the photos," Vargas Llosa was also facing Nazi horror and the world's complicity. The pictures frame the 1977 human rights speech[48] from the initiating shock to a final image of an absolutely lucid demand on the viewer.

> There is in Yad Vashem a photograph which, I am sure, everyone has seen at one time or another. . . . It was taken after the destruction of the Warsaw Ghetto. The picture is of a little Jewish boy, only a few years old, stuffed into a cap too big for him and a coat that looks old, with his hands in the air. A German soldier, wearing a helmet and boots, is aiming at the boy with a short-barrelled rifle, and looking toward the photographer with that blank look they call martial. The soldier looks neither proud nor ashamed of his trophy. His face shows only tranquil indifference to the scene he is acting. In the boy's expression, on the other hand—in the sadness of his eyes, the constriction of his face distorted by fear, and the squeezed shoulders of a body that wants to disappear—there is a dizzying clarity about what that moment means.[49]

One scene of confronting photos and another cannot be a fortuitous parallel. The liberating distance from home that he hoped to enjoy in Jerusalem and in Florence, the haunting history memorialized in Yad Vashem and the picture gallery, and the structurally sibling novels about narrative and historical contamination between modern reality and lines of escape seem beyond coincidence. This cluster of coincidence suggests a corollary cluster of observations.

Through Diaspora

One cluster of observations is that Jewish Saúl becomes a figure for the Machiguengas for reasons beyond a general affinity between one marginalized group and another. He is more than a metaphor for the minority culture condemned to extinction by majoritarian redemption campaigns. For one thing, both nomadic tribes cling to and are sustained by ritually repeated narratives that amount to the Law. Diasporic Jews know, in a folk refrain, that "Torah is the best Skhorah [merchandise]" because learning is one thing that cannot be confiscated. And the oral—post-biblical—Torah is traditionally as important as Scripture itself. For another thing, the Jew as *hablador* is the kind of metaphor that earns some of its evocative power through a shared history. Had it kept the memory of horrible connections, the figure would have been a metonymy. The world that had stood by in disingenuous disbelief while extermination camps reduced Jews to smoke is the same world that stands by again while Amazonian Indians are translated and traduced and jungle is processed into slum.

To recover the metonymy turned metaphor is not to minimize the differences of fate and possible futures between one remnant of a people and another. But we might note that just as Peru's Indians have been demoted and displaced since the Spanish conquest, Jews were pushed out of Spain in the internal warm-up wars of the reconquest. And like the Machiguenga misfits who are being squeezed deeper into the Amazon, perhaps to be squeezed out of conservative Peru, European Jews were at a loss to find a place almost anywhere in the Americas. "It is likely that many of them, faced with the upheavals of the last few years, will have opted for the traditional response ensuring their survival: diaspora" (240; 230). During World War II, ships full of refugees were refused at American ports and sent back to German authorities. Even after the war, the Americas kept immigration quotas for survivers so inhospitably low that some waited for years in displaced-persons camps. Others managed to buy visas from the corrupt bureaucracies of Bolivia and Paraguay, and Ecuador and the Dominican Republic were officially hospitable to small numbers of refugees. Brazil took in larger numbers, but only later after having barred "semites" before and throughout the war of extermination.[50] Sometimes without ever reaching their official destinations, the cosmopolites wandered to centers of Westernized economy and culture or they remained conveniently stuck on the active coastlands.

Mario banters about the last Peruvian indigenist being his friend the Jew. But Saúl knows that he is a natural:

> "Well, a Jew is better prepared than most people to defend the rights of minority cultures," he retorted. "And, after all, as my old man says, the problem of the Boras, of the Shapras, of the Piros, has been our problem for three thousand years."
>
> Is that what he said? Could one at least infer something of the sort from what he was saying? I'm not sure. Perhaps this is pure invention on my part after the event. Saúl didn't practice his religion, or even believe in it. I often heard him say that the only reason he went to the synagogue was so as not to disappoint Don Salomón. On the other hand, some such association, whether superficial or profound, must have existed. Wasn't Saúl's stubborn defense of the life led by those Stone Age Peruvians explained, at least in part, by the stories he'd heard at home, at school, in the syna-

> gogue, through his inevitable contacts with other members of the community, stories of persecution and of dispersion, of attempts by more powerful cultures to stamp out Jewish faith, language, customs, which, at the cost of great sacrifice, the Jewish people had resisted, preserving their identity?" (99; 97)[51]

Before I had read or even known about the Jewish Congress speech, before I could guess at any autobiographical link between photographs at Yad Vashem and Vargas Llosa's haunting book about Peru, I might have imagined that the novel was picking up a narrative design where Julio Cortázar had left off, a design in which pictures of reality put a stop to artistic escape. In "Apocalypse in Solentiname," the last scene shows Cortázar back in Paris after a trip to Nicaragua. The slides he developed refused to repeat the fanciful primitive paintings by Nicaraguan peasants that had filled his camera frame; instead, the pictures played back the horrors of military repression that he had refused to see. Likewise, photos would force Vargas Llosa to look at an endangered people. The possibility of literary borrowing exists, no doubt. But when I had the opportunity to talk to Vargas Llosa about his novel, the question seemed uninviting. Instead, I asked what had motivated his pairing of the mosaic cult with the Machiguenga. Almost an idle query, it was meant to go elsewhere, perhaps into the pairing structure of the novel as an experiment in politically tolerant imaginings. If parallel narrative lines were legible and preserved a relative autonomy one from the other, perhaps a country could imagine itself along those lines despite the narrator's postsocialist skepticism about a future mosaic of Peruvian cultures (78; 76).

As far as the question about Jews and Indians goes, the very leitmotifs of the novel insist on obvious answers: the parallel marginalizations of Jews and Indians, the annihilating dangers of assimilation, and their survival against all odds thanks to a collective narrative, although the novel does not play this up. The point would, of course, have helped Vargas Llosa to explain why he seems as taken with "the people of the Book" as with the Machiguengas. For both premodern cultures, his vocation as narrator would have amounted to the ultimate political career. "I believe that his identification with this small, marginal, nomadic community had—as his father conjectured—something to do with the fact that he was Jewish, a member of another community which had also been a wandering, marginal one throughout its history, a pariah among the world's societies, like the Machiguengas in Peru, grafted onto them, yet not assimilated and never entirely accepted" (243; 233). But the answer I got from Vargas Llosa was neither about obvious parallels nor about overlaps. It was, instead, the polar extremes of their difference, he said, that attracted him. They revive the kinds of social and geographic differences whose coordination was the heroic project of nineteenth-century national consolidation, a project inherited from colonial times.[52] Together, Indians and Jews represented Peru at its limits, like the geohistorical limits of dusty Piura in the north and the steamy jungle on the south side of the Andes that *La casa verde* barely braces together.[53] Primitive and poor Amazonian

Indians and generally rich cosmopolitan Jews were at opposite ends of the country's population, he explained. And the novel was an effort to talk about Peru in the most inclusive and capacious way possible, from a focus on its demographic extremities.[54] I was surprised by what I took to be an about-face from the intimacy of the vulnerable bedfellows I found in the book, and perhaps personally reluctant to pursue a line that cast Jews, once again, as extraneous to national constructions, so the conversation hobbled onto other issues. Only now do I begin to appreciate Vargas Llosa's narrative reach. It went purposefully beyond mainstream Peru, toward an idealized nation, either to argue for continuing the homogenizing conquest that pursued Indians after it had finished with the Jews or to show the country as too narrowly focused on consolidation and as obliged to open into a capacious embrace.

Talk Christian

Vargas Llosa, the political persona, evidently holds on to the culturally coherent focus. The hold is notorious in a 1983 document commissioned by Peru's president, Balaúnde Terry. Appointed to lead an investigation of eight reporters and photographers who were murdered in the Andean town of Uchuraccay, Vargas Llosa wrote up the collective report. His authoritative voice there gives the tone as well to an equally notorious journalistic version of the report called "Inquest in the Andes" (*New York Times,* July 31, 1983) and "Historia de una matanza" in its Spanish form. The possibly profitable *Times* article, among other damaging details of Vargas Llosa's comportment, was an issue in a subsequent investigation. A skeptical provincial judge, Hermenegildo Ventura Huayhua, appointed to the case in November 1984, grilled the urbane defendent about allegations of an official cover-up for military malfeasance and governmental complicity.[55]

In the *Times* article, Vargas Llosa recalled early speculations that blamed the Sendero Luminoso for yet another act of terrorism against Indians, police, tourists, and now reporters, speculations that the newspapers were dying to develop. But the evidence that the commission gathered, of ritual mutilations and the victims' distinctive burial positions, indicted the "innocent" Indians themselves. Skeptics wondered because, although the residents of Uchuraccay were known to take reprisals against terrorism and were therefore capable of collective violence, their action had always been a response to evident abuse. Moreover, the peasants were clearly outgunned on both sides, by the military and by the guerrillas. And since the signs of violence against the newspapermen differed from the Sendero's typical traces, suspicion fell on the notoriously aggressive and insecure armed forces. The army was new to the area, had been stationed there in order to replace the openly abusive police, and it was just as new to the rigors of legitimate authority. Suspicious too was the fact that each of the Indians who testified in the case turned up dead soon after the commission had absolved the authorities. Later reports, and the incriminating photographs that Vargas Llosa managed not to face, confirmed that neither the killings nor the burials showed any signs of Andean ritual. Instead, bodies were found in pairs, wrapped in plastic, and buried in lowlands to promote decomposition, the way North American soldiers buried the Viet Cong.[56]

The commission's report had speculated about various motives and scenarios. Oddly, it affirmed them all: Maybe the residents had decided to keep all white men safely away from their community, imagining that Senderista encroachments were no different in kind from others; maybe they were especially incensed or terrified by the photographers, who didn't bother to hide from their subjects (much harder to do on the Altiplano than in Amazonia for Malfatti). Vargas Llosa even takes seriously a careless quip by General Roberto Clemente Noel, military commander of counterinsurgency, who said that the Indians probably couldn't tell a camera from a gun.[57] In any case, the Indians' alleged failures to distinguish between professionals and delinquents, and no less the Spanish speakers' failure to fully understand their Quechua informants (rushing over the fact that two of the victims spoke Quechua), bring Vargas Llosa to the conclusion that incomprehension is deadly, and dead-ended. The Indians will simply have to become real Peruvians, to "talk Christian" in Spain's enduring jargon of the reconquest, because the difference is paid too dearly in white, and mestizo, blood. Indians will finally have to assimilate into a modern state derived from Western principles of democratic responsibility.

The conjectures about ritual murders would later take on more fabulous proportions in the 1993 novel *Lituma en los Andes,* where the benighted but lovable army lieutenant takes almost 400 pages to figure out why his host village has been safe from the Sendero.[58] The implicit absolution of the army is one measure of the distance between this novel and *El hablador,* where memories of "civilized" savagery by militiamen and mercenaries against Indian leaders revived the horrors detailed in *La casa verde.*[59] On his way out of the mining town, now a ghost town without metal or men, Lituma can hardly control his nausea. He has finally solved the mystery of missing bodies, sacrifices to a decaying culture of drunken homosexuality and ritualized cannibalism that appeases pre-Incan gods.[60] In the novel, homosexuality is a figure for cannibalism, as if one invasion of the flesh opens irreversibly onto the other. Vargas Llosa's willful version of Andean practices is no doubt a metaphor to capture a country turned against itself, but he takes dangerous liberties with poetic license that recall his commission report, both its allegations of Indian barbarism and its vindication of the army.[61]

Homosexuality evidently disturbs Vargas Llosa the novelist.[62] It disturbs the journalist too, as when he fretted about the Rainbow Crusade in a piece that chronicles the gay rights march on Washington, D.C., April 25, 1993. He notes that the democratizing effects of gay activism are now irreversible in the United States, where sexual politics has practically eclipsed other concerns. But the price of legitimacy for the "perverse" population of apparently normal citizens who thronged to the capital and represented far greater numbers could be, he warned, the desexualization of sex. Without some secrecy, without the titillation of almost unspeakable urges or the discreet dangers that whet desire, sex threatens to stop being fun, at least for Vargas Llosa. "Gays and lesbians might come to discover at the end of their efforts to be recognized and considered 'normal' that, once the transgressive character of their sexual choice has disappeared, it has lost, if not all, then a good part of its reason for being. Totally 'normalized' sex ceases to be sex."[63]

Similar objections to banalized homosexuality in the United States had been raised by Reinaldo Arenas in the book that he finished before ending his own AIDS-ridden life.[64] But why should Vargas Llosa be ruffled, and even defensive, about the democratizing "perversities" that the Rainbow Crusade chose to flaunt? In the article, he stays carefully uncontaminated by Arenas's sympathies. So cautious to write himself into the company of his wife during the march and during the conversations with activists, Vargas Llosa seems to safeguard against any possible implication of self-interest in the homoerotic debates between ludicism and legitimacy. Hardly at stake here are the violent intimacies that Vargas Llosa's fictional men visit on their women in one novel after another, including *Lituma.* In the heterosexual love story of its subplot, the heroine is "saved" from a scene of mock abuse when her naive hero shoots the client who was paying the prostitute to plead for her life between desperate screams. Hardly in danger at the march, I am saying, are Vargas Llosa's titillating representations of remunerated abuse or the almost ritualized rape we get in *The War of the End of the World* or the range of heterosexual tussles that evidently excite his fiction and fantasy. Vargas Llosa's discomfort at the gay rights march, therefore, seems unfounded on the alleged grounds that it secularizes sex if heterosexuality remains, as Foucault said of the Victorians, discreetly underrepresented in political arenas. (More obviously threatening is the notorious incident of Lorena Gallo, who castrated an abusive husband.)[65] The uneasiness, perhaps, hovers around homoeroticism itself, not around a loss of intimacy but around a loss of shame.

The shameful sexual perversity in *Lituma* is, as I said, an irreversible step toward the ultimate perversion as physical contact translates into a more perverse "communion": the baneful banquet of blood and flesh from sacrificial bodies. "'Everyone had communion and, although it disgusted me, I did too,' said the worker, stumbling over himself, 'That's what's screwing me up. The mouthfuls I swallowed.'"[66] The cult's bar-tending and prostituting priests are Dionisio and Adriana, declensions of their Greek namesakes, as the town named Naccos is a corruption of Naxos,[67] and perhaps a hint of Soccos, site of a massacre by the police in 1983.[68] The explicit analogies between one primitive cult and another call to mind Garcilaso's comparison between the heathen prehistories of both Europe and Peru. We should not be surprised, he says, by the spottiness or by the fabulous quality of founding Incan fictions. Are not the first murmurs of Old World civilization equally faint, and their fables just as laughable?[69] In both the Greek and the pre-Incan cases, barbarous practices of cannibalism and promiscuity were what civilization had wisely conquered. The problem for *Lituma* is that heathen remnants remain. The detective story ends with the frustration of having learned too much, enough to know that horror outstrips any hope of overcoming it. "I regret having been so stubborn about finding out what happened to them. Better to have stayed suspicious."[70] Knowing, it should be noted here, is dangerous for the detective himself in Lituma's epistemological trap. His is a tale of self-preservation. How different this is from the epistemological problem that plagues *El hablador.* There, knowledge was threatening to neutralize difference, to cannibalize the "primitive" Other into the insatiable sameness of modernity. The danger was ethical in nature, worrying about the ravages we modernizers wreak on others; for Lituma, in stark contrast, worry is self-centered in a world too imperfectly modernized.

The unhappy hero descends toward the coast and hopes not to remain haunted. The novel groans at a political impasse, but the greater effect is a sigh of fatigue. Peru's predicament is inherited, perhaps insoluble. It is not merely that the Europeans never finished the job of consolidating the country. It is also that the Incas failed in their preparatory work. Barbarism stubbornly persisted in "many regions never conquered by the Incas, and is still today found in many places conquered by the Spaniards," grumbled Garcilaso.[71] In gory detail, he quotes the mestizo Jesuit Blas Valera, who locates cannibalism mostly in the unconquered jungle, far away from Incan practices; but his care to distance the taste for human blood from Peru removes it suspiciously as far as Mexico, where it was a staple of urban life and possibly an influence on other urbane Indians. "They performed these sacrifices of men and women, lads and children by opening their breasts while they were still alive and plucking out their hearts and lungs. The idol that had bidden the sacrifice was then sprinkled with still-warm blood."[72] By the time Lituma abandons the terror-breeding mountains that gobble up men in avalanches, mud slides, and demonic lusts (by the time Vargas Llosa himself leaves Peru), the authorities have to admit that they cannot gauge or even stomach the degree of unfinished business.

Guilty Choices

The self-conscious narrator of *El hablador* felt far less victimized than does Lituma. The Vargas Llosa who doubled back from Florence to Peru suggested lingering complicities with an ethnic disappearing act. His country's campaigns to "reduce Indians" to civilization, in Garcilaso's language, through a history that runs from Manco Cápac's Incan foundations to Lituma's farce pause and lose their way amid the jungle talk. Here, Vargas Llosa's writing takes a step back from the journalistic problem-solving of "Inquest in the Andes," where it was requiring that misfits be made to fit, and takes another step down from the Andes to the Amazon. From there, if we stretch our view to the limits of Peru's peripheral vision, the probing fiction of *El hablador* deliberately stages a coincidence between the country's polar opposites as if they mattered most as indices of the country's humanity. But the solidary response in this fantasy about Jews and Indians is also a sure index of their shared danger inside paralyzed civilizations, the danger of complicity between oppressors and bystanders. Theirs (his, ours) is the guilt of passive association, of unresponsiveness, and of nonacknowledgment, in Cavell's term. In the speech framed by Yad Vashem, Vargas Llosa says that Jerusalem's holocaust memorial tells the story of "good, educated, gentle citizens of an ancient country who one day turned into wild animals, lunging at defenseless victims, or letting others do the dirty work for them, while the surprised and stupid world stared complicitously. And that is Yad Vashem's terrible accusation; it is directed against not one, but all, countries."[73] Vargas Llosa's novel of a decade later would writhe in the guilt-ridden hyperconsciousness of collusion. Novels can make these admissions with impunity, cynics may be saying. Fiction's reckless lucidity and breast-beating histrionics can act out a self-criticism that doesn't demand redress. If the novel turns out to have a tragic shape, it may make us suffer; but it lets us off in the end, exhausted with grief and relieved to have finished.

The essay is a different form, at least in the case of Vargas Llosa's essays about the Indian question, from the "Inquest" to his 1990 presidential campaign and afterward. His essays take sides. The status of Indians in Peru has been perhaps *the* most burning question since independence, since the Spanish conquest, in fact. It began when Quechua chroniclers contested Spanish authorities, and it continued with the rash of seventeenth- and eighteenth-century uprisings that delayed cautious Creoles in proclaiming independence. From the nineteenth century on, liberal programs in law and literature have striven to incorporate Indians. These programs produced novels such as Narciso Aréstegui's *El Padre Horán* (1848), Clorinda Matto de Turner's *Aves sin nido* (1889), and José María Arguedas's classic *Los ríos profundos* (1957) and culminated ideologically in the indigenized Marxism of Mariátegui's slogan *Peruanicemos al Perú,* the title of a posthumous collection.[74] Like the 1983 report "Inquest in the Andes," Vargas Llosa's postelection essay "Questions of Conquest: What Columbus Wrought, and What He Did Not" takes sides to affirm the value of a coherent country.[75] The essay would reappear as chapter 2 of *A Writer's Reality*[76] without the first page that had marked it as an occasional piece.

The occasion was his response to a press conference held in Madrid by "a shadowy group calling itself the Association of Indian Cultures" that was preparing acts of sabotage in Spain and throughout Latin America to protest the planned celebrations of Columbus's quincentennial conquest. The threats, for Vargas Llosa, seemed fixed on the past, misguided as "means of achieving justice, or self-determination."[77] To him they were obviously inspired by the same kind of fanaticism that was making Peruvian terrorists blow up their country along a "shining path." In fact, the media blitz from Madrid continued, consisting mostly of footage on demonstrations and spectacular "sabotages" of celebrations. Nevertheless, and despite what he considers to be self-defeating efforts at self-determination, Vargas Llosa impugns his own Hispanicized culture for fomenting the misguided protests when he asks, "Why have the postcolonial republics of the Americas—republics that might have been expected to have deeper and broader notions of liberty, equality, and fraternity—failed so miserably to improve the lives of their Indian citizens? Even as I write, not only the Amazonian rain forests but the small tribes who have managed for so long to survive there are being barbarously exterminated in the name of progress."[78] He gives no answers that could lead to reversals of the failure or to relief from guilt. "We, the westernized Latin Americans, have persevered in the worst habits of our forebears," he continues. "We must remember that in countries like Chile and Argentina, it was during the Republic, not during the colony, that the native cultures were systematically exterminated."[79] But it is useless, concludes Vargas Llosa, to speculate about whether the conquest was a good thing or bad.[80] What is significant is simply that the conquest happened, which is to say, in the narrative logic of things past, that it was historically necessary.

What are we to do now? This is a different kind of question from the one about redress of past sins, a question presumably suspended because it led nowhere. Pointing nowhere, in Vargas Llosa's essay, is a gesture that erases the politics of indigenous rights, including efforts to achieve autonomy, a politics that would fissure Vargas Llosa's imagined community of Peru. This putative "nowhere" in fact marks a dynamic somewhere in which non-Western strains of culture and politics have a distinguished national history from the indigenous chroniclers of conquest through to the Indian organizations spurred by SIL's meddling. So the question of amends is silenced along with the possibility of lessons to be learned from historical blunders. The argument skips, with no apparent textual motivation, to present programs. There is nothing to be done, Vargas Llosa concludes, but sorrowfully to choose modernization, as if Indian tradition were incapable of adaptation. Referring to the anguish scripted into *El hablador,* he admits, "It is tragic to destroy what is still living, still a driving cultural possibility, even if it is archaic; but I am afraid we shall have to make a choice."[81] That is, to sacrifice the Indian cultures, since they interfere with modernity's fight against hunger and need. The line of argument has now made two skips: first by eliding any consequence to the question about the West's failures regarding Indians and then by moving from choices that Indians face to choosing for them. Of course, Vargas Llosa had already noted that leaders of Latin American republics inherited reprehensible traits from their forebears.

Choice is the pivotal concept on which his essay turns. It is the apparently nonideological axis on which the individual can turn. But in Peru, the words choice, individuality, and freedom are part of an abstract and inflexibly "ideological" vocabulary that paralyzes political debate because the abstraction doesn't acknowledge dissent, as critics of Vargas Llosa have complained.[82] It preempts dialogue, just as the self-interpretive passages that I occasionally note in *El hablador* want to preclude more interpretation. In both genres, Vargas Llosa tries to fix the delicate anthropological balance between observer and participant into the noncontested collusion between witness and judge, a move that had raised suspicions about his Uchuraccay report. The collapse of ethics into pragmatics confuses authoritarian means with allegedly liberal (free market) ends, according to William Rowe.[83] What gets lost in the crush, Mirko Lauer points out, is liberalism as a form of politics that defends individual freedom.[84] Vargas Llosa exercises his own freedom by making authoritative, enlightened, and despotic choices for others. He tends to speak for them in general. Even in the commision's report, witnesses in Uchuraccay lose their voices to mediating "experts" who truncate sentences and translate the peasants away.[85]

Indian words won't fit into the "official" nation, Vargas Llosa laments. "Perhaps there is no realistic way to integrate our societies other than by asking the Indians to pay that price."[86] Personal freedom is at the heart of Western culture, and it was the magic charm that allowed a handful of willful Spaniards to topple Amerindian empires, according to Vargas Llosa. Hosts of overly disciplined and suicidally obedient soldiers were at a loss for what to do after the Inca was taken hostage. Overlooking the forty years of sustained resistance under four successive Incas,[87] Vargas Llosa alleges that rather than run or fight or decide on any move at all, the Indians allowed themselves to be slaughtered. Personal initiative, voluntary and self-determining capacities in the face of the unexpected, these characterize Western, or modern, subjects.[88] Freedom is not only a liberating slogan from the French Revolution on; it is also the voluntarism of the conquest's most crass and criminal agents.[89] Still, Vargas Llosa celebrates it as the West's greatest contribution to static and hierarchical cultures. "The first culture to interrogate and question itself, the first to break up the masses into individual beings who with time gradually gained the right to think and act for themselves, was to become, thanks to that unknown exercise, *freedom*, the most powerful civilization in our world."[90]

Could the skips in his argument be symptoms of bad faith? Do they recall his unacknowledged nervousness about homoeroticism? The doubt follows in the wake of inexplicable contradictions. On the one hand, if Western voluntarism was so devastating to Indians both because they were unaccustomed to making choices and because the Spaniards insisted on choosing for them, what justifies making more sorrowful choices for others? And on the other hand, if the essay's point is to show the enabling virtues of freedom and self-determination, why do Indian initiatives seem so pointless when they write history or take over bilingual schools and establish autonomous institutions? In the absence of answers, Vargas Llosa sees no dearth of solutions.

The contradiction here is not just personal or Peruvian. It is practically constitutive of modern cultures. In the language of political philosophy, it is the disparity between (Lockean) liberty and (Rousseauian) rights to free access. To a great degree, the difference between them is what motivates modern history, its conflicts and negotiations. Emmanuel Lévinas refuses to get caught up in the action. He would agree that freedom is at the core of Western culture; that is why he targets it for attack in his argument about philosophy having bulldozed alterity into sameness. Freedom, for Lévinas, is not simply *available* for abuses, not merely given to skipping from negotiation to conquest; it is the very *vehicle* of abuse and recklessness. The same caution that focuses the dilemma in Vargas Llosa's novel now haunts the discussion of his essay. "Freedom has its ultimate meaning in this permanence in the same, which is reason. . . . That reason in the last analysis would be the manifestation of a freedom, neutralizing the other and encompassing him, can come as no surprise once it was laid down that sovereign reason knows only itself, that nothing other limits it."[91] The ravages of subject-centered freedom, the raids on difference led by a tautological reason that presumes, potentially, to comprehend, literally to contain, everything—these are the dangers that *El hablador* exposes in Peru's drive toward modernity. Vargas Llosa's programmatic pronouncements would take sides, as I said; but the unconnected dots in "Questions of Conquest" link to show the scars of an ethical wound that had worried the narrator of his novel. Vargas Llosa's critics don't hesitate to connect those dots.[92]

Halting and Haunted

The most trenchant critic of them all, however, may be the Vargas Llosa who narrates *El hablador;* more precisely, he is the writer who doubled himself through the novel: as the troubled tourist in Italy and as the traditional talker of the alternating chapters. Saúl asked Mario why thinking about the *habladores* gave him goose bumps. "'They're a tangible proof that storytelling can be something more than mere entertainment,' it occurred to me to say to him. 'Something primordial, something that the very existence of a people may depend on'" (94; 92). Both narrators turned their backs on Peru: one with weariness, the other with purpose. Both know the power of narrative even if the essayist Vargas Llosa makes bitter jokes about the connection between literature and political life after the 1990 election defeat. Is this why a possibly self-serving novelist sometimes holds back from the modernity that loosens the social grip of stories, whereas the essayist rushes forward to modernize? The Latin American habit of mixing fiction and reality, he banters, is one reason "we are so impractical and inept in political matters."[93] And both storytellers could be fictional figures for the philosopher Lévinas, who draws a line between the sociality of Saying and the crippling control of fixing on the Said. They know that presuming to understand the Other willfully ignores the mystery of his Saying; it razes difference and replaces it with the same. "Learn the aboriginal languages! What a swindle! What for? To make the Amazonian Indians into good Westerners, good modern men, good capitalists, good Christians of the Reformed Church? Not even that. Just to wipe out their culture, their gods, their institutions off the map and corrupt even their dreams" (96–97; 95).

Vargas Llosa's novel displays the flair for self-criticism that the essays credit with dignifying Western culture. Bartolomé de Las Casas is his best example of "those nonconformists" who turned their backs on adventure in order to face Indians.[94] We know, although Vargas Llosa doesn't say, that blind spots obstructed Las Casas's view; they were deadly blind spots for the Africans who, Las Casas briefly suggested, could replace the disappearing Indian laborers and deadly too for many Indians whom he persuaded to deal peaceably with the Spaniards. Even the successful evangelizations and the liberalizing laws that he championed were, in the spirit of *El hablador's* radical indictment of encroachment, travesties against the Indians. His most laudable work was probably not programmatic or problem-solving; it was the published stories of devastation, so devastating for Spanish readers that many simply dismiss Las Casas as a madman or a liar. No doubt he exaggerated some things and misremembered others. But the glaring truth is that only one generation after the "discovery," so few Indians were left in the Caribbean that, to save the remnant, a man like Las Casas would promote African slavery only to rue it later.[95] His "fiction" confronts the facts of conquest even though his policies negotiated with conquerors. Las Casas was one inspiration for Andrés Bello when this dean of nineteenth-century education advised young historians to train themselves on the personal narratives and fictionalized accounts of Latin America's past. They were truer in spirit than the professional histories.[96]

The spirit of Las Casas's stories implicates his readers. No wonder some Spaniards tried to discredit him. Their entire country would become his ideal targeted reader in this question of conquest. It almost doesn't matter if Las Casas himself is vindicated or condemned along with the company he kept because the text survives as an indictment of general complicity. Instead of judging his text, readers are invited to judge themselves. Vargas Llosa's novel survives his essays in the way that Las Casas's history survives pedantry. *El hablador* can bring some critics to decry the author's fatalism about Amazonian cultures, so apparently doomed from the first page of the novel.[97] And some can call him cynical, alleging that the novel repeates his patronizing lament over cultures that refuse to be redeemed from primitivism and poverty, that it dismisses Indians' "utopian" efforts to plot a self-determined future.[98] One could say of Mario Vargas Llosa the novelist something like Angel Rama's comment about José María Arguedas the ethnologist: He has sometimes been overshadowed by Mario Vargas Llosa the politician. Whether unsympathetic critics complain about fatalism or about aggressive dismissal, they read the novel like formalists, from its tragic ending backward toward a general meaning.[99] Bakhtin, of course, cautioned against reading novels reductively and retrospectively because the "genre" defies fixed forms; to fix on a novel's closure is to lose sight of its experimental risks and specificity. In literary criticism, to jump to the conclusion of novels is to fall into the interpretive trap that *El hablador* talks endlessly about. It reduces wonder to legible signs; it translates alterity into a language that we already know, and it flattens difference into sameness.

The attendant danger to interpreting the novel away as so much predictable disaster or necessary pain is that the reduction allows us to turn away from the book, like the disingenuous readers of Las Casas who prefer to quibble about numbers of Indians massacred and dates of devastations than to get the glaring point. And the point of Vargas Llosa's Amazonian novel, for readers who want to face it, is our general complicity with the cultural extermination campaigns. Our uncontainable modernity expands in concentric circles, turning peripheries into reflections of the center. *El hablador* doesn't simply dissolve into a tragedy that can be a mere diversion from activity, the way that classical tragedy managed to divert revolutionary rumblings into paralyzing horror and cathartic tears. Detained for many pages and fixed on visions that refuse to evaporate, readers rehearse the narrator's turn toward Peru once the country takes him hostage and refuses to let go. At the end of the novel, Mario knows that the country occupies him. Through the friend who defends particular traditions against homogenizing modernity, a vision of Peru grips Mario more powerfully than any feelings of fear or love: "It opens my heart more forcefully than fear or love has ever done" (245; 234). The very last words admit that all lines of escape would be futile. The voice of the Other is ubiquitous: "But tonight I know that wherever I might wander—on the ocher stone bridges over the Arno, . . . I will still hear, close by, unceasing, crackling, immemorial, that Machiguenga storyteller" (245–246; 235).

We have heard that voice too, and perhaps sullied by a sense that we cannot or will not respond to demands for respect because cultural *convivencia* was never really an option for the modern West,[100] readers remain caught inside the doubled narrative of Spanish exploits and Machiguenga tradition. Unresolvable as the book is, it is in the same measure uncontainable by a tragic frame, by Shakespeare's frame for *Lear,* for example, which displays the impossibility of love. That play dramatizes the corrosive effect of dynamic modernity on the mystery of presence as each of the main characters turns away from the Other's love-demanding gaze. Vargas Llosa's "Questions of Conquest" also sighs for refusals to look and to love: Peru, he says, is "an artificial gathering of men from different languages, customs, and traditions whose only common denominator was having been condemned by history to live together without knowing or loving each other."[101] The complaint repeats after Abimael Guzmán is captured in September 1992: Unlike other Latin American countries, where *mestizaje* and middle-class mobility helped to heal historical wounds, Peru stays schizophrenic.[102]

El hablador performs the doubling act without diagnosing it as schizophrenia. The duality, as I said at the beginning of this chapter, is a source of both concern and of hope. It can lead to dismissing indigenous otherness as inassimilable and inessential to the Peruvian body politic, a dismissal that countrymen read in Vargas Llosa's consistent carelessness about Indian cultures and lives. Instead of two souls in one body, his novel shows two faces as one confronts the Other in an endless but intimate standoff. This literarily sustained confrontation also holds out a hope. It is the possibility of recognition—on a reading from this geographic remove—even if the promise is betrayed by the man called Vargas Llosa.

The fact is that the confrontation he stages generates an unresolved tale that stops to look, learns to listen, and dares to love. It loves selflessly, through a narrator whose face is the color of an open wound. The novel stares, uncomprehendingly perhaps, but respectfully, at the Other. A voyeur like Malfatti ends badly here; mediated by his camera and motivated by self-interest, he is literally a victim of jungle fever. Along with him, all of us selfish visitors are contaminated by the contact. But after the reading ends, the novel may survive, hauntingly, like the talker who will accost Vargas Llosa beyond the very last line: ". . . I will still hear, close by, unceasing, crackling, immemorial, that Machiguenga storyteller" (246; 235). Or, like the little Jewish boy—lost in his cap and very present in his lucidity—pictures and sounds from the novel may survive to haunt a range of readers.

What do we do with a hostage imagination? This is the question that Dussel demands of Lévinas. Perhaps we will plan our escape to magical cities. And maybe we'll stop there, at museums erected to the boy's memory. It may even be possible that we will pause for a while in our translations of living areas like Amazonia into empty, available space for more of the same modernity. Can we also imagine some creative responses to jungle talk? They would go beyond the paralyzing awe that grips Vargas Llosa the narrator, and they would break out of the brittle redundancy that dooms the Other talker. Real responses would also stop short of the cultural conquest demanded by Vargas Llosa the politician. Creativity can come after the speechlessness of first confrontations and before the murderous monolingualism of final solutions. It can come inside experiments like *El hablador,* where the novelist Vargas Llosa has been engaging us, patiently, in the slippery space that moves back and forth from one permeable language to another.

NOTES

I am profoundly grateful to Julio Ortega, José Mazzotti, and David Maybury-Lewis for their expert advice, for their erudition and generosity. I am also indebted to Francisco Ortega and José Ayalamacedo for their unstinting bibliographical support and to Rael Meyerowitz, Judith Elkin, and Harvey Mendelsohn for lucid readings.

1. Mario Vargas Llosa, *The Storyteller,* trans. Helen Lane (Boston: Faber and Faber, 1989); originally published as *El hablador* (Barcelona: Seix Barral, 1987). Subsequent references to this work are cited parenthetically with English translation page numbers, followed by a semicolon, and original Spanish-edition page numbers. Lane's translations are occasionally altered here; all other translations are mine.

2. Louis Althusser, "Ideology and Ideological State Apparatuses (Notes Towards an Investigation)," in *Lenin and Philosophy and Other Essays* (New York: Monthly Review Press, 1971), 162.

3. Emmanuel Lévinas, *Totality and Infinity: An Essay on Exteriority,* trans. Alphonso Lingis (Pittsburgh: Duquesne University Press, 1969), 43.

4. Francisco Ortega made this intelligent observation to me.

5. Jacques Lacan, "Aggressivity in Psychoanalysis," in *Écrits: A Selection,* trans. Alan Sheridan (New York: Norton, 1977), 8–29.

6. For an excellent summary of Vargas Llosa's ideological trajectory, from socialist sympathies in the early 1960s to increasingly authoritarian postures, see William Rowe, "Liberalism and Authority: The Case of Mario Vargas Llosa" in *On Edge: The Crisis of Contemporary Latin American Culture,* ed. George Yúdice, Jean Franco and Juan Flores (Minneapolis: University of Minnesota Press, 1992), 45–64. For a recent example of Vargas Llosa's conservative animus, see his editorial "Jouer avec le feu" *Le Monde,* Thursday, May 18, 1995, 17, where he offers his opinion that the recent confessions of the Argentine military leaders during the Dirty War makes them no more culpable than the revolutionaries who incited the army to terror.

7. The parallel with the author of the notoriously deployed slogan "Sendero Luminoso" may be surprising. Nevertheless, Mariátegui was a model for the youthful Vargas Llosa and was remembered in *The Storyteller* (78; 76).

8. José Carlos Mariátegui, *El Alma matinal y otras estaciones del hombre de hoy* (Lima: Amauta, 1972), 146–147, (article of 1925); and 192–193 (article of 1929). Quoted in José Guillermo Nugent, *Conflicto de las sensibilidades: Propuesta para una interpretación y crítica del siglo XX peruano* (Rimac: Instituto Bartolomé de las Casas-Rimac, 1991), 55–57.

9. See James Dunkerley's review, "Mario Vargas Llosa: Parables and Deceits," *New Left Review* 162 (March–April 1987): 112–23, 118–119.

10. Enrique Dussel, Daniel E. Guillot, *Liberación Latinoamericana y Emmanuel Lévinas* (Buenos Aires: Editorial Bonum, 1975), 9.

11. Mario Vargas Llosa, *A Writer's Reality* (Boston: Houghton Mifflin, 1991), 37.

12. Dussel and Guillot, *Liberación Latinoamericana,* 25. "*Persona* is what makes a sound, and what makes a sound is the voice and the eruption of the Other in us; it does not erupt as 'the seen,' but as 'the heard.' We should no longer privilege the seen, but the heard."

13. Ilán Stavans, ed., *Tropical Synagogues: Short Stories by Jewish–Latin American Writers* (New York: Holmes & Meier, 1994), 31.

14. The structure repeats as well in Vargas Llosa's *Historia de Mayta* and *Elogio de la madrastra,* as Mary Berg and José Mazzotti remind me.

15. José Mazzotti confirmed this impression, in a letter of April 5, 1995. The Quechua-flavored Spanish appears—importantly too—in José María Arguedas's Andean stories, which Professor Vargas Llosa assigns to students. "El Wamani está ya sobre el corazón!-exclamó 'Atok' sayku,' mirando. . . . Ahistá en tu cabeza el blanco de su espalda como el sol del mediodía en el nevado, brillando." See José María Arguedas, "La agonía de Rasu-Ñiti," in *Relatos Completos* (Alianza: Madrid, 1983), 140–141.

16. I am grateful for conversations with David Maybury-Lewis on these issues, and for his leadership in Cultural Survival, Inc.

17. Sendero Luminoso, or the Communist Party of Peru, had been organizing and slowly building bases during the 1960s and throughout the 1970s from its regional headquarters at the public University of Huamanga, near Ayacucho, but it launched its military campaign against the state in 1980. See David Scott Palmer, ed. *Shining Path* (New York: St. Martin's Press, 1992).

18. Mario Vargas Llosa, "Homenaje a Javier Heraud, Paris, 19 mayo 1963," in *Contra viento y marea (1962–1982)* (Barcelona: Seix Barral, 1983), 36–37.

19. Angel Rama, "Introducción," José María Arguedas, *Formación de una cultura nacional indoamericana,* selección y prólogo de Angel Rama (Mexico: Siglo XXI, 1975), ix.

20. The same speculation, though more elaborate and convincing, is in Enrique Mayer, "Peru in Deep Trouble: Mario Vargas Llosa's 'Inquest in the Andes' Reexamined" *Cultural Anthropology* 6, no. 4 (November 1991), 466–504. The article was reprinted in *Rereading Cultural Anthropology,* ed. George E. Marcus. (Durham: Duke University Press, 1992), 181–219 (see especially 196). Subsequent references are from the latter publication. His vehicle is the caricature of Arguedas published in the Senderista newspaper *El Diario* (Cited in Carlos Iván Degregori, "Intre los fuegos de sendery en el ejército: Regreso de los pishtacos," in *Pishtacos: De verdugos a sacaojos,* ed. Juan Ansión [Lima: Ediciones Taréa, 1989], 109–114): "Internationlism has to fight against magical-whining nationalism, whose fossilized remains we have had and continue to have in a chauvinist nationalism, whose promoter was none other than that writer who rejoiced in declaring himself 'purely apolitical,' but who, during World War II, was proud of his little Hitler moustache. His name: Jose María Arguedas, affable disciple and animator in Peru of North American anthropology. . . . Such is *indiofilia zorra.*" Mayer glosses this skewed picture of anthropological intransigence with "The image of Zuratas again!"

21. See Rafael Humberto Moreno Durán, included in *Semana de Autor: Mario Vargas Llosa* (Madrid: Ediciones Cultura Hispánica, Instituto de Cooperación Iberoamericana, 1985), 82; and Mario Vargas Llosa, *José María Arguedas: Entre sapos y halcones* (Madrid: Ediciónes Cultura Hispánica, 1978). He continues to engage Arguedas even if it is to disengage the writer from the ideologue. For example, the entire undergraduate course he taught at Harvard University in fall 1992 was dedicated to Arguedas.

22. For criticism of American anthropology in Peru, see Orin Starn, "Missing the Revolution: Anthropologists and the War in Peru" *Cultural Anthropology* 6, no. 1 (1991), 63–91; reprinted in Marcus, *Rereading Cultural Anthropology,* 153–180.

23. Mayer, "Peru in Deep Trouble," 190–191. The line goes from the 1930s with men like Julio Tello through Luis Valcárcel (both ministers of education), Arguedas himself (head of the National Institute of Culture), and Mario Vázquez (designer of agrarian reform in the 1960s).

24. David Stoll, *Fishers of Men or Founders of Empire? The Wycliffe Bible Translators in Latin America* (London: Zed Press, Cambridge, Mass.: Cultural Survival Inc., 1982), 7.

25. Ibid., 2.

26. Ibid., 201.

27. "The Schneils, like all the other linguists, had degrees from the University of Oklahoma, but they and their colleagues were motivated above all by a spiritual goal: spreading the Glad Tidings of the Bible. I don't know what their precise religious affiliation was, since there were members of a number of different churches among the linguists of the Institute. The ultimate purpose that had led them to study primitive cultures was religious: translating the Bible into the tribes' own languages so that those peoples could hear God's word in the rhythms and inflections of their own tongue. This was the aim that had led Dr. Peter Townsend to found the Institute. He was an interesting person, half evangelist and half pioneer, a friend of the Mexican president Lázaro Cárdenas and the author of a book about him. The goal set by Dr. Townsend still motivates the linguists to continue the patient labor they have undertaken" (86–87; 85).

28. Mario Vargas Llosa, *Historia secreta de una novela* (Barcelona, Tusquets, 1968).

29. Edward Said, "Representing the Colonized: Anthropology's Interlocutors," *Critical Inquiry* 15 (Winter 1989), 215.

30. Kristin Herzog, *Finding Their Voice: Peruvian Women's Testimonies of War* (Valley Forge, Pa.: Trinity Press International, 1993), 145, 156.

31. Vargas Llosa's unacknowledged debt to Catholic missionaries is the subject of an angry editorial by Domiciano García Benito, Superintendent of Catholic Schools in the Diocese of Caguas, Puerto Rico. "Truenan contra Vargas Llosa," *El Nuevo Día* (Puerto Rico), February 22, 1995.

32. Stoll, *Fishers of Men,* 205.

33. Nevertheless, anthropologist Luis Millones expresses dismay at the novelist's careless and prejudiced portrayals of Andean culture. See Luis Millones, "Vargas Llosa y la mirada de Occidente: *Lituma en los Andes,*" *El Peruano* (Lima), "Opinión" January 12, 1994.

34. Sigmund Freud, "Notes Upon a Case of Obsessional Neurosis (1909)," in *Collected Papers,* trans. Alix Strachey and James Strachey (New York: Basic Books, 1959), vol. 3, 376. See also "Screen Memories (1899)," in *Collected Papers,* vol. 5, 52–53.

35. Stanley Cavell, "The Avoidance of Love: A Reading of *King Lear,*" in *Must We Mean What We Say: A Book of Essays* (Cambridge: Cambridge University Press, 1969), 267–353. Rael Meyerowitz reminds me that this is a sweeping simplification of Cavell's position. He also approves of American "onwardness," what Emerson calls "abandonment." For an excellent reading of Cavell's subtle and humane balancing acts, see Rael Meyerowitz, "Welcome Back to the Republic: Stanley Cavell and the Acknowledgment of Literature" *Lit: Literature Interpretation Theory* 4 (1993), 329–352.

36. Betty Elkins de Snell, *Cuentos folklóricos de los machiguenga* (Yarinacocha: Instituto Linguístico de Verano, 1979).

37. Two recent and provocative explorations are Paul Ricouer's *Oneself as Another* (Chicago: University of Chicago Press, 1992); and Julia Kristeva's *Strangers to Ourselves,* trans. Leon S. Roudiez (New York: Columbia University Press, 1991).

38. Emmanuel Lévinas, *Otherwise Than Being, or Beyond Essence,* trans. Alphonso Lingis (Boston: Kluwer Academic, 1991), 11.

39. Lévinas, *Totality and Infinity,* 43.

40. Ibid., 44.

41. Stanley Fish, *Surprised by Sin: The Reader in "Paradise Lost"* (Berkeley: University of California Press, 1971; originally published by Macmillan, 1967). See for example 208, where he quotes C. S. Lewis on the "blind alleys" pursued by readers of *Paradise Lost.* "How are we to account for the fact that great modern scholars have missed what is so dazzlingly simple?" (from Lewis's *A Preface to Paradise Lost* [London: Oxford University Press, 1942], 69–70). See also Cavell, "The Avoidance of Love," whose very title announces a brilliant development of the theme.

42. Lévinas, *Totality and Infinity,* 44; my emphasis.

43. Dussel and Guillot, *Liberación Latinoamericana,* 29.

44. Reflecting later on his obsession with that role, the narrator remembers how he hounded Irish friends to introduce him to an equally untranslatable "*Seanchaí:* 'teller of ancient stories,' 'the one who knows things,' as someone in a Dublin bar had off-handedly translated the word into English" (165; 159).

45. Walter Benjamin, "The Storyteller," in *Illuminations,* ed. and introduction by Hannah Arendt, trans. Harry Zohn (New York: Schocken, 1969), 83–109.

46. Mario Vargas Llosa, "En torno a los derechos humanos." Lima, dated at the end of the essay September 19, 1978. First published in *Premio Derechos Humanos, 1977* (Lima: Una edición de la Asociación Judía del Peru, por encargo especial del Congreso Judío Latinoamericano, Junio 1979), 5; my translation. The speech was reprinted as "Ganar batallas, no la guerra," in *Contra viento y marea (1962–1982)*, 309–323.

47. Vargas Llosa, "En torno," 6; my emphasis.

48. Ibid., 17.

49. Ibid.

50. I am grateful to Judith Laikin Elkin for this information on immigration and for her lucid suggestions in general.

51. When Vargas Llosa first ventures that Mascarita's deformity is felt in exclusions and allies him to the excluded tribes of the jungle, his friend answers: "Still laughing, he told me that Don Salomón Zuratas, being sharper than I was, had suggested a Jewish interpretation. 'That I'm identifying the Amazonian Indians with the Jewish people, always a minority and always persecuted for their religion and their mores that are different from those of the rest of society . . . Okay . . . Suddenly being half Jewish and half monster has made me more sensitive to the fate of the jungle tribes than someone as appallingly normal as you," (28–29; 30).

52. I thank José Mazzotti for this clear formulation.

53. Vargas Llosa, *Historia secreta de una novel*, 8–9.

54. I am grateful to Mario Vargas Llosa for his personal generosity and attention during that conversation of October 23, 1993, during his teaching semester as John F. Kennedy Professor of Latin American Studies at Harvard University.

55. Mayer, "Peru in Deep Trouble," 202–203. Ventura Huayhua was later removed, for "mistrial," but not before he garnered immense popular support.

56. See ibid. for documentation of the gory details, remembered too by Julio Ortega and José Mazzotti, and for facts that don't fit the commission's report.

57. Ibid., 187. See also Mario Vargas Llosa, *Informe de la comisión investigadora de los sucesos de Uchuraccay* (Lima: Editora Peru, 1983), 23.

58. Mario Vargas Llosa, *Lituma en los Andes* (Barcelona: Planeta, 1993).

59. The story of repression against Jum, a chief of the Aguaruna, is a continuous thread, from his refusal to be robbed by a local rubber boss to an Indian resistance against a soldier and a general vengeance by the whites and mestizos. See Mario Vargas Llosa, *The Green House,* trans. Gregory Rabassa (New York: Avon, 1968), 49–50, 119–120, 156, 172, 231, 252–253, 271, 281–284, 324, 339–341.

In *Fishers of Men or Founders of Empire?* David Stoll refers to Vargas Llosa's version of these events (see 117). *El hablador* summarizes: "But in Urakusa, besides the copper-colored bodies, the dangling tits, the children with parasite-swollen bellies and skins striped red or black, a sight awaited us that I have never forgotten: that of a man recently tortured. It was the headman of the locality, whose name was Jum. . . . The ostensible reason for this savagery was a minor incident that had taken place in Urakusa between the Aguarunas and a detachment of soldiers passing through (74–75; 72–73).

60. For a responsible history in English, see Sabine MacCormack, *Religion in the Andes: Vision and Imagination in Early Colonial Peru* (Princeton: Princeton University Press, 1991).

61. One of the anthropologists who collaborated in Vargas Llosa's commission to investigate Uchuracay writes that the novelist should know better. See Luis Millones, "Vargas

Llosa y la mirada de Occidente: *Lituma en los Andes,*" *El Peruano* (Lima), "Opinión" January 12, 1994.

62. To Vargas Llosa's arguments about Mayta's inability to fit into society, a Brazilian interviewer repeatedly asks, "Mas por que tambén homosexual?" Ricardo A. Setti, *Conversas com Vargas Llosa* (Sao Paolo: Editora Brasiliense, 1986), 59.

63. Mario Vargas Llosa, "Cruzados del Arcoiris," in *Desafíos a la libertad* (Madrid: El País/Aguilar S.A. 1994), 234.

64. Reinaldo Arenas, *Antes que anochezca (Autobiografía)* (Barcelona: Tusquets Editores, 1992), translated as *Before Night Falls: A Memoir,* trans. Dolores M. Koch (New York: Penguin Books, 1993), 106.

65. Mario Vargas Llosa, "El pene o la vida" in *Desafíos a la libertad,* 301–306.

66. Vargas Llosa, *Lituma en los Andes,* 311.

67. I thank Mary Berg for her reading of the parallels.

68. Herzog, *Finding Their Voice,* 83.

69. From pt. 1 *Los comentarios reales* (1609). English translations come from Garcilaso de la Vega, El Inca, *Royal Commentaries of the Incas and General History of Peru,* translated by Harold V. Livermore, foreword by Arnold J. Toynbee (Austin: University of Texas Press, 1966), bk. 1, chap. 18.

70. Vargas Llosa, *Lituma en los Andes,* 312.

71. Vega Garcilaso, *Royal Commentaries,* bk. 1, chaps. 11, 13.

72. Ibid., chap. 11.

73. Vargas Llosa, "En torno," 16.

74. See Efraín Kristal, *The Andes Viewed from the City: Literary and Political Discourse on the Indian in Peru, 1848–1930* (New York: P. Lang, 1987).

75. Mario Vargas Llosa, "Questions of Conquest: What Columbus Wrought, and What He Did Not," *Harper's,* December 1990, 45.

76. See Mario Vargas Llosa, "Novels Disguised as History: The Chronicles of the Birth of Peru," in *A Writer's Reality,* 21–38.

77. Vargas Llosa, *A Writer's Reality,* 46.

78. Ibid.

79. Ibid., 35.

80. Ibid., 34.

81. Ibid., 37.

82. See Rowe, "Liberalism and Authority," who cites and agrees with Mirko Lauer, Julio Ortega, James Dunkerley, Julio Cotler, Gerald Martin (who comes to the defense as well), and Elizabeth Farnsworth. Rowe himself points out that "along with the globalizing attitude that flattens out historical differences, the language tends to solidify into imperviousness, losing referential accuracy and analytical precision (49).

83. Ibid.

84. Mirko Lauer, "Vargas Llosa: Los límites de la imaginación no liberal," *La República* (Lima) April 15, 1984, 30.

85. Mayer, "Peru in Deep Trouble," 207.

86. Vargas Llosa, *A Writer's Reality,* 36.

87. In a letter to me, José Mazzotti names them: Manco Inca, Sayri Túpac, Titu Cusi Yupanqui, and Túpac Amarul, who fought in Vilcabamba until 1572.

88. Vargas Llosa, *A Writer's Reality,* 29.

89. Ibid., 32.

90. Ibid., 33–34; my emphasis.

91. Lévinas, *Totality and Infinity,* 43.

92. One simplified version of the impatience Vargas Llosa's novel, along with his fiction in general, elicits among educated Peruvian readers, is presented by Mirko Lauer in *El sitio de la literatura: Escritores y política en el Perú del siglo XX* (Lima: Mosca Azul Editores, 1989) 10, 97–119. His fundamental objection, it seems, is that the novelist fails to maintain an ethical and coherent position. I prefer to think of this demand for ethics in Julio Ortega's terms of holding a position that is open to doubt rather than dogmatic and orthodox. See Julio Ortega's review of *El pez en el agua,* "El pez en la sartén," *La Jornada* (Mexico), June 9, 1993.

93. Vargas Llosa, *A Writer's Reality,* 25.

94. Ibid., 33.

95. See Helen Rand Parish on the polemical Las Casas, who wrote, in addition to the *Brevísima relación de la destrucción de las Indias,* the less well known *Brevísima relación de la destrucción de Africa.*

96. Andrés Bello, "Autonomía cultural de América" (1848), in *Conciencia intelectual de América,* ed. Carlos Ripoll (New York: Eliseo Torres, 1966), 48–49. An editor's note informs that the present title "has been used in various Anthologies to present this piece."

97. See Mayer's essay "Peru in Deep Trouble," especially the section "Anthropological Authority," 190–200.

98. Rowe's Liberalism and Authority" represents this tendency (61).

99. Stanley Fish, *Is There a Text in This Class? The Authority of Interpretive Communities* (Cambridge: Harvard University Press, 1980), 3.

100. See Marc Shell, *Children of the Earth: Literature, Politics, and Nationhood* (New York: Oxford Universtiy Press, 1993).

101. Vargas Llosa, *A Writer's Reality,* 35.

102. Mario Vargas Llosa, "El Preso 1.509," *Desafíos a la libertad,* 153. José Mazzotti points out that it is Aníbal Quijano who coined the term "dualismo medular" to describe Peruvian society as irreconcilably diverse, so that some pieces have to be sacrified.

About the Book and Editors

This collection extends the boundaries of cultural studies beyond its current Euro-American emphasis. It takes readers on a wide-ranging journey from the stock market to Islamic law, from the African household to the Soviet apartment, from the nuances of nationalism to the rude noises of capitalistic rhetoric, introducing readers to the social and historical forces that shape textual practice. The essays are richly imaginative and empirically detailed, ingeniously connecting regional debates and local dynamics to universal global issues. Finally, *Reading the Shape of the World* reconfigures cultural studies theories and methodologies, resulting in a fresh and empowering approach to this dynamic field of inquiry. At the heart of this study is the optimistic belief that reading still matters, that the world can be shaped by reading, and that critical practices of reading can transform the contours of social life.

Henry Schwarz is assistant professor of English at Georgetown University. He is author of *Writing Cultural History in Colonial and Postcolonial Bengal* (forthcoming) and has published on British orientalism, literary theory, and cultural studies. **Richard Dienst** is associate professor of English and teaches in the English and Philosophy Program at Purdue University. He is author of *Still Life in Real Time: Theory After Television* (1994) and is currently writing a book on the imaginary constitution of the global economy.

About the Book and Author

About the Contributors

Samir Amin is currently director of Forum Tiers Monde in Dakar, Senegal. He is the author of numerous books, including (in English) *Unequal Development* (1976), *Eurocentrism* (1989), and most recently *Re-Reading the Postwar Period* (1994).

Alicia Borinsky is a literary scholar, fiction writer, and poet. She has published extensively in Spanish and in English in the United States, Latin America, and Europe. Her most recent books are *Mean Woman* (novel, 1993); *Timorous Women* (poetry, 1992); and *Theoretical Fables: The Pedagogical Dream in Contemporary Latin-American Fiction* (literary criticism, 1993). She is professor of Latin American and comparative literature at Boston University.

Svetlana Boym is John L. Loeb Associate Professor of Humanities at Harvard University and a film editor of the *Slavic Review*. She is the author of *Death in Quotation Marks: Cultural Myths of the Modern Poet* (1991) and *Common Places: Mythologies of Everyday Life in Russia* (1994), and of the play and film, "The Woman Who Shot Lenin."

Ipshita Chanda teaches in the Department of Comparative Literature at Jadavpur University, Calcutta. She has authored many articles on Bengali literature from the classical, folk, and popular traditions, has edited a volume on paraliterature, and is currently at work on a study of African literature and its social contexts.

Grant Farred is assistant professor of comparative literature and English at the University of Michigan in Ann Arbor. He is editor of *Rethinking C.L.R. James* (forthcoming) and author of articles in such journals as *Social Text, Architecture New York,* and *New Politics.*

Neil Larsen is professor of modern languages and Latin American studies at Northeastern University in Boston. He is the author of *Modernism and Hegemony* (Minnesota, 1990) and *Reading North by South: On Latin American Literature, Culture, and Politics* (Minnesota, 1995) and publishes frequently in the areas of Latin American literature and literary and postcolonial theory. He recently taught as a visiting professor at the University of São Paulo in Brazil.

Supriya Nair teaches at Tulane Universtiy. Her first book is *Caliban's Curse: George Lamming's Revisioning of History* (1996). She is currently working on a project on colonial education in Africa and the Caribbean.

Sangeeta Ray teaches at the University of Maryland at College Park. She is working on a book entitled *Engendering a Nation: Feminism and Imperialism in Colonial and Postcolonial*

British and Indian Narrative. Her essays have appeared in *Hypatia, Modern Fiction Studies, Genders, Ariel,* and elsewhere.

Joel Reed is assistant professor of English at Syracuse University and coedits *The Eighteenth Century: Theory and Interpretation.* His essays have appeared in *Studies in Eighteenth Century Culture, MLQ,* and *Genre,* and he is editing a collection to be called *The Cultures of Early English Nationalism.* He is completing a book called *Academic Discourse: Instituting Nationalism in Seventeenth and Eighteenth Century England.*

Azade Seyhan is associate professor of German and comparative literature and adjunct professor in philosophy at Bryn Mawr College. She has published articles on literary history and theory, German romanticism, modernity, and cultural criticism. She is the author of *Representation and Its Discontents: The Critical Legacy of German Romanticism* (1992) and has completed a book entitled *Geographies of Memory: Women's Narratives on the Modern Diaspora.*

Doris Sommer is the author of *Foundational Fictions: The National Romances of Latin America* (1989) as well as many essays on literary theory and Latin American fiction. Her forthcoming book is entitled *Proceed with Caution: A Rhetoric of Particularism.*

Michael Sprinker is the author of *Imaginary Relations: Aesthetics and Ideology in the Theory of Historical Materialism* (1987), *History and Ideology in Proust* (1994), and many articles on Marxist science and aesthetics, Indian cultural politics, and European literature. He teaches at the State University of New York, Stony Brook.

George Yúdice teaches Latin American literature at Hunter College and cultural studies at the City University of New York Graduate Center. He is coeditor, with Jean Franco and Juan Flores, of *On Edge: The Crisis of Contemporary Latin American Culture* (1992) and author of *We Are (Not) the World: Identity and Representation in an Age of Global Restructuring* (forthcoming). He is a member of the *Social Text* editorial board and the director of the Inter-American Cultural Studies Network.

Index